HENRI FAYOL, THE MANAGER

Studies in Business History

Titles in this Series

1 The Modern American Wine Industry: Market Formation and Growth in North Carolina
Ian M. Taplin

2 Multinationals, Subsidiaries and National Business Systems: The Nickel Industry and Falconbridge Nikkelverk
Pål Thonstad Sandvik

3 Entrepreneurial Families: Business, Marriage and Life in the Early Nineteenth Century
Andrew Popp

4 Rockefeller Philanthropy and Modern Social Science
David L. Seim

5 The Optical Munitions Industry in Great Britain, 1888–1923
Stephen C. Sambrook

HENRI FAYOL, THE MANAGER

BY

Jean-Louis Peaucelle and Cameron Guthrie

Routledge
Taylor & Francis Group
LONDON AND NEW YORK

First published 2015 by Pickering & Chatto (Publishers) Limited

2 Park Square, Milton Park, Abingdon, Oxfordshire OX14 4RN
52 Vanderbilt Avenue, New York, NY 10017

Routledge is an imprint of the Taylor & Francis Group, an informa business

First issued in paperback 2020

BRITISH LIBRARY CATALOGUING IN PUBLICATION DATA

Guthrie, Cameron, author.
Henri Fayol, the manager. – (Studies in business history)
1. Fayol, Henri, 1841–1925 2. Mineral industries – Management – History – 20th century. 3. Compagnie de Commentry-Fourchambault-Decazeville.
I. Title II. Series III. Peaucelle, Jean Louis, author.
658'.0092-dc23

ISBN-13: 978-1-84893-419-1 (hbk)
ISBN-13: 978-0-367-66892-1 (pbk)

Typset by Pickering & Chatto (Publishers) Limited

CONTENTS

FOREWORD

Jean-Louis Peaucelle and Cameron Guthrie's *Henri Fayol, the Manager* provides readers with a comprehensive, in-depth study of Henri Fayol's approach to the job of the manager and how he developed his theory from his managerial experiences and actions taken. This is the first full-length, fully documented book about Fayol's life, work and contribution to management knowledge available to English readers. The authors rely on French archival sources and publications in French to meticulously examine corporate records, correspondence, minutes of meetings of boards of directors and firm and industry data to portray Fayol's lengthy and successful career as managing director of Commentry-Fourchambault and Decazeville. This research reveals new and additional insights into the pioneering work of Fayol whose writings provide much of our modern understanding of the activities of managerial work.

The authors use the archival records to bring a new focus on specifics of Fayol's theory and avoid generalizations that result in less understanding and applicability. Readers of Fayol have noted how he often generalizes, offering aphorisms to managers, without explaining how and why such advice would be useful. An example is Fayol's presentation of fourteen principles of management offered 'as flexible and capable of adaptation to every need' and when necessary 'to make allowance for different and changing circumstances'. The list of fourteen, he notes, is not exhaustive but ones he found useful in his experience. The authors do not focus on each principle but provide correspondence and records that allow an understanding of how principles such as 'equity' or 'order' or 'remuneration' could be ideas growing from Fayol's work as a manager and suggesting to him these ideas were important in becoming successful.

Fayol's principles have been called 'proverbs of administration' by critics because of this vague, ungrounded offering of advice without adding the experiences that led to his thinking about management that would be improved by better practices. Guthrie and Peaucelle's analysis, based on the records, enlighten us about what is not just good advice but *why* it is good advice.

The authors' findings for Fayol's elements of administration form the substance of how experiences led to theory. Planning, organizing, commanding, coordinating and verifying form a larger part of the archival records and provide substance to how each element of managerial work was applied and could be generalized to broader applications. Planning emphasizes how the future was anticipated, forecasts made and the contingency nature of plans when unexpected circumstances arose. The other elements are supported with examples of decisions that support a more fundamental understanding of organizing, commanding, coordinating and verifying. Fayol's accounting department, for example, gives the reader an illustration of how this information-gathering served business practice and all elements of administration. His study of accounting at the National School of Mines at Saint-Etienne enabled an understanding of the function of an information system for Commentry-Fourchambault. Data flowed into the department from sales, purchases, expenses, etc. and, when necessary, flowed outward as reports for managers, stockholders and others who needed information for decision-making. Accounting information became a connection between the elements of administration and the functions of the firm to be found in Commentry-Fourchambault.

Readers who are new or who are refreshing their memory of the place of Henri Fayol in the history of management thought will find his career beginning in the late nineteenth century, and his active writing years in the early twentieth century, in France. Management, as we are familiar with this word, was not a formal subject of study in academics and no body of knowledge or writings on how to manage existed beyond anecdotal advice for those wishing to become managers. It was considered an innate ability, one being born to manage or lead, or an ability to be acquired through experience on the job, preferably under the tutelage of an older, experienced practitioner. The Wharton School of Finance and Economy at the University of Pennsylvania, USA., was founded in 1881 to teach business subjects, but management was not one of them.

During a period roughly parallel to Fayol's years as managing director of Commentry-Fourchambault, the American industrial engineer, Frederick Winslow Taylor, was formulating ideas about improving production performance in workshops and factories. Setting performance standards through the study of work to reduce waste, improving worker selection, providing wage incentives, planning workflows, establishing accounting standards and other ideas were offered as means to systematize and improve performance. Taylor's *Shop Management* (1903) proposed methods for increasing efficiency in the production activity of a firm. Numerous followers promoted Taylor's ideas and his *Principles of Scientific Management* (1911) became a classic and the prevailing view of management in France and other countries.

Fayol was familiar with Taylor's ideas but noted this approach to shop-level management did not fit his experiences. For example, Taylor advocated a planning department for scheduling the flow of work, dispatching orders and following work through the shop to its successful completion. Fayol's experiences found all managers planned to various degrees, devoting a portion of their time to planning in their particular activity within the firm – sales, production, accounting, finance or security. Planning, in this case, becoming a portion of each manager's time and effort and not relegated to a separate department. As managing director, Fayol was responsible for the entire task of planning for the firm in order for Commentry-Fourchambault and Decazeville to fulfill its objectives.

Taylor's ideas then, and now, were applicable when improving shop-level performance and today can be readily found largely in industrial engineering education. Fayol's ideas, however, were more appropriate when the economics of the firm called for planning efforts, guiding the enterprise toward its goals, coordinating the efforts of the different functions of the firm, and verifying how well the firm performed. If it is not too trite to summarize – Fayol viewed management from the top, Taylor from the shop. Fayol's view of the job of the manager did not achieve the early recognition of Taylor's but times change. Over a period of years, these giants of our management literature, Frederick Taylor and Henri Fayol, would find their respective places in furthering our study and practice of management.

It is unusual to discover a practising executive writing about the practice of management, even more remote to find one gathering and putting forth ideas that become the standard framework for the teaching and research about the job of the manager. Henri Fayol was both of the above, plus a successful managing director of a firm that was in financial difficulty when he came to office. Commentry-Fourchambault recovered and competed successfully over decades, paid substantial dividends and, not incidentally, had an outstanding record of mine safety for its workers. Further, Fayol achieved recognition for his scientific findings, was prominent in professional associations, was reimbursed well for his consulting on methods to extinguish mine fires and was rewarded with the top salary of his firm. His peer respect was so great a Center for Administrative Studies was founded in his honour.

Why, then, at age seventy-five did he not rest on his laurels, but prepare the *magnum opus* that Peaucelle and Guthrie analyze and use to explain how he built his management doctrine from his experiences? Readers are entitled to form an opinion about this and each may be arguably defensible. My reading, based on what is developed in the text plus years of study of Fayol, is that he had the curiosity of a scientist whose inquisitive mind led to the pursuit of knowledge, demonstrating for others how to inquire, examine and improve for the sake of knowing how to do something better – in this case, manage. Fayol's scientific abilities are well known – extinguishing mine fires, the formation of coal deltas, spontaneous combustion of coal and so forth. He applied his curiosity and scientific abilities into the study of how to manage and, for modern readers, how to manage better.

The book is organized logically to present the reader with the industrial context for Fayol's managerial career, corporate governance for the firm, the elements of his administrative function and the functions found in Commentry-Fourchambault. The industrial setting is a longitudinal case study and supports a conclusion of Fayol as a manager over a long term of technological and industrial change. He was not a quick-fix director but took actions to build and sustain the firm into prosperous years. In discussing Fayol's work with the directors and shareholders of the firm, the authors illustrate corporate governance in action over a substantial period of years. The importance of finance, with some corporate politics included, is described as critical to Commentry-Fourchambault remaining competitive during a lengthy period, in which they replaced depleting iron and coal resources, adopted new steel-making technology and developed specialty steel products to compete with substantially larger firms. These give the reader a richer understanding of the challenges and confrontations Fayol endured.

The elements of Fayol's administrative function follow and become his enduring legacy for management. *Planning* for the short and the long term, remaining flexible by building contingency plans; *organizing* by structuring relations with managers and workers; *coordinating* the efforts to achieve a wholeness for the firm; *commanding* as instructions for actions to be taken; and *verifying* to determine whether or not plans had been achieved and deciding what corrective action may be needed. The authors provide a useful translation of what Fayol intended as follow-on action for comparing plans with results, by substituting 'verify' for the long-accepted use of 'control' in English. The French verb *contrôle* does not translate well into English, as it carries connotations of unilateral, top-down management and may encourage resistance to positive decision-making. 'Verify' as a part of the manager's job improves our understanding of Fayol's thinking, and should become an addition to a more positive view of monitoring plans and performance to gauge a firm's progress toward achieving its goals.

Separating the elements of administration from the functions of the firm enabled Fayol to make his long-lasting contribution to the study of management. The functions of the firm – commercial, technical, etc.– would be different depending on the type of business or activity of a particular organization. The elements of administration, in contrast, were found in all firms, varying in degrees by a person's location in the managerial hierarchy, and could be separated for study and teaching. Fayol built these elements from his experiences as a manager: planning, organizing, commanding, coordinating and verifying.

Henri Fayol, the Manager makes a lasting contribution to management history and theory by replacing aphorisms with details about how Fayol's experiences became his management doctrine. With examples from practice his ideas become less abstract and yield a more firmly embedded flow of ideas about managerial work. Management theory is more firmly grounded in practice and, as a consequence, will ask us to extend these ideas as we seek further understanding. Fayol thought his theory was correct because Commentry-Fourchambault and Decazeville succeeded. This is partially correct – Fayol's theory is sound because of its longevity in teaching and practice and our continuing unfolding evidence about its foundation.

Daniel A. Wren, David Ross Boyd Professor Emeritus,
University of Oklahoma, USA

LIST OF FIGURES AND TABLES

INTRODUCTION

In 1916 Henri Fayol (1841–1925) published his book on the theory of business management, *Administration Industrielle et Générale*. The work was translated into English in 1930 by J. A. Coubrough, and then by J. Storrs in 1949 with the title *General and Industrial Management*. It has since been regularly re-edited, lastly by Wren and Sasaki in 2004.[1] Fayol writes of the principles of good management yet these principles cannot be understood if we forget that their author was the managing director of the Commentry-Fourchambault et Decazeville Company – a large mining and steel firm for 30 years. Fayol drew his theory from his everyday practice of management, with a concern for theorizing such as that of the scientist who knows that a theory, if it is true, corresponds to a large number of practical cases. The more general the theory, the wider its application. Yet the degree of abstraction used by Fayol has no doubt often hampered our comprehension of his thought. His theory becomes clearer when it is confronted by the facts and it gains depth and flexibility when we consider how Henri Fayol himself acted as a manager. For example, Fayol's theory of 'planning' appears rigid, yet his practice shows that he continually adapted his plans as his vision of the future changed. This management-tool was flexible by necessity.

We examine Henri Fayol's concrete management actions such as the management of workers, sales, strikes and the coordination of operations between geographically dispersed sites. His day-to-day management is similar to what can be observed in companies today, and while they are a century apart the many similarities with yesterday's practices help better appreciate how managers work today.

Fayol describes a 'managerial function' that anticipates actions (planning), structures the company (organizing), transmits orders (commanding), ensures the coherence of actions (coordinating) and verifies the results (verifying).

To make each of these five 'elements of management' more concrete, Fayol proposed the concept of 'management tools',[2] each matched to an element of management. In doing so, he anticipated a large number of today's management practices. Management tools help managers anticipate and avoid common mistakes. For example, the objective of cost pricing is to ensure that sales prices are not fixed too low. Meetings of department heads allow leaders to ensure that orders given to subordinates are feasible. He presented the management tools as a way of compensating for a manager's eventual lack of skill. Fayol believed, as did others at the time, that while a manager must have a large number of qualities, in practice this is rarely the case. He himself, for example, personally lacked knowledge in steel metallurgy. Fayol also argued that leaders should make up for their weaknesses by forming a 'staff' of advisers who help them in areas where their skills are lacking. His ideas were original at the time and are no doubt still relevant today. We will examine how Henri Fayol personally used and deployed management tools during his thirty-year tenure as managing director at the Commentry-Fourchambault et Decazeville Company.

This book follows and builds on the work of others that have studied the Commentry-Fourchambault et Decazeville Company. Tsuneo Sasaki was the first to write about the company in 1984[3] and Donald Reid wrote a historiography of the Decazeville coal miners in the nineteenth and twentieth centuries in which he studied the points of view of the miners and their unions as well as the role played by corporate management, including Henri Fayol.[4] Alain Boscus studied industry in the Aveyron department at the beginning of the twentieth century,[5] widening our understanding of the workings of the Decazeville factory. Alain Auclair has published several works on companies in the Allier department during the nineteenth century, including the Commentry-Fourchambault Company. He notably analysed the company's technical and financial evolution in detail.[6] These are all excellent works and are often cited here.

This book takes a wider perspective by considering all establishments irrespective of their locality. The period it covers is more restrained, limited to the twenty-six years between Henri Fayol's nomination as managing director in 1888 and the outbreak of World War I in 1914. We have chosen to ignore the war years as French companies at the time were strictly controlled by the Ministry of War, thus limiting the freedom of action of managers.

The main difference from previous works is the accent this book places on the relationship between Henri Fayol's theory and the actions he took as a manager. The objective is to describe Fayol's actions and compare them with his doctrinal thought. We will see both his scientific method at work in the way his experiments helped build his theory, and examples that clearly illustrate the main aspects of his management doctrine.

It is useful to recall some key characteristics of industry at the time. The first chapter describes the economic, industrial and legal context that French steel and mining companies operated in at the end of the nineteenth century, far from today's globalized economy. These industries were expanding rapidly. Coal was still the main source of energy, and iron was indispensable for all constructions and in particular for building railways, which were the main means of land transport and communication. Henri Fayol's business was of a modest size, and included several mines and steel foundries spread through France's Massif Central region. Surrounded by agricultural lands, this region had been industrialized since the start of the nineteenth century, but was less well placed in the following century compared to the mines and the factories located in the north and the east of France with their rich deposits of iron ore and coal. The company remained profitable, while other similar companies had disappeared well before 1900.

After describing the historical industrial context, the book explores the five 'elements of management' identified by Fayol (plan, organize, coordinate, command and verify) and the six functions of the company (accounting, commercial, financial, technical, security and administration). They are developed in the following chapters: the financial function, planning, the organization of managers, the organization of workers, command, coordination, verification and the accounting function, the sales function, the technical function and the security function. These ten major aspects of Fayol's theory structure this work and are briefly outlined below.

The financial function was the responsibility of shareholders and the Board of Directors of the Commentry-Fourchambault company. The board named Henri Fayol in 1888 after a long selection process during which he benefited from internal disagreements. He strengthened his authority by perceiving the unspoken wishes of the majority and gained their trust by generating unexpected profits. He prudently reinvested funds to ensure growth and then argued for capital increases to finance larger and more ambitious projects.

Planning and forecasting were widely practised at Commentry-Fourchambault et Decazeville. Several ten-year plans were presented to the board of directors that were used to evaluate investment plans. Each year, site managers submitted their forecasts for the coming year. Such anticipation characterized all levels of management at Commentry-Fourchambault et Decazeville.

Organizing involved structuring the company through organizational charts and job descriptions. A study of the facts allows us to answer questions that the theory ignored: are real organizational charts the same as the examples given in *Industrial and General Management (IGM)*? Was the theory of 'span of control' really followed? How did organizational charts evolve in practice? How were people promoted? What influence did the personal desires of employees have on the drawing of charts? Did people leave when their wishes were not met? Organizing concerned the management of engineers, recruitment, career management and the retirement of incompetent individuals.

The workers in the factories and in the mines made up the majority of the workforce and determined production levels in these labour-intensive industries. The setting of wages was Fayol's seventh 'principle of management' and the eleventh principle advanced the notion of equity that directly applies to workers who Fayol argues should never feel they are victims of discrimination. In practice, Fayol used wages to recruit, retain and manage workers. He also paid careful attention to strikes that were costly if they lasted too long and described two very different strikes in the third part of *IGM*. We compare his account as managing director to other sources including press reports and the recollections of unionists.

Coordinating, commanding and verifying are examined in a chapter that also studies the role of the accounting function. We have grouped these elements together as the management tools used to practice them are often the same. Meetings of department heads for example were often used to command by transmitting orders, to coordinate by informing everyone present of each other's tasks and to verify through oral reporting in advance of written reports.

The commercial function is vital for any company. Henri Fayol had understood its essential character and he directly negotiated with his biggest customers. He also built a sales network to limit their influence and sell at the most favourable price. Fayol believed, however, that agreements between producers were more effective than competition. His company was vertically integrated as the mines sold coal to the steel foundries, although these internal sales only represented a small share of sales.

The technical function was essential for his company. Henri Fayol was a skilled mining engineer and he surrounded himself with specialists for steel metallurgy. He simultaneously invested in new technologies to lower operating costs and to develop special steels in the company's Imphy factory that were adapted for new demands.

The security function is the last function identified by Henri Fayol in *IGM* and it was similar to today's 'risk management'. Managers must deal with accidents, breakdowns, theft and other incidents in the everyday running of a company, and the security function involves leveraging this experience to reduce the occurrence of these events.

Henri Fayol had already confronted his practice with theory in the third part of *IGM*. When he published his work in 1916, he announced four parts but only ever published two of them. He provided titles for the other two parts: 'Personal observations and experiments'[7] and 'Lessons of the war', and said 'I shall have occasion to cite some examples in the third part of these studies ... I shall show how I have amassed, in the course of a long industrial career, the material for this work'.[8] Henri Fayol even sketched out the ideas that would be found in this third chapter in 1908.[9] In 1995 Wren demonstrated that Henri Fayol's theory came from his industrial experience.[10] The text of the third chapter was archived at the Fondation des Sciences Politiques in Paris.[11] It has already been consulted by other scholars, including Donald Reid[12] but was not previously identified as a part of *IGM*. It is translated and included here as an appendix.

The third part of *IGM* is a professional autobiography that follows the course of Henri Fayol's career, first as an engineer and then as director of the Commentry collieries. He developed what he would later call 'management tools', such as weekly meetings with colleagues, plans, monthly and annual reports, recruitment and training of personnel. He believed that his nomination to managing director and the deployment of management tools were experiments equivalent to scientific experiments in a laboratory. As the company recovered after changing only its management, he concluded that management was central to industrial success. He argued his case in much the same way a clinician would present the case of a patient who recovered by following a new treatment.

Henri Fayol collected data from a selection of events he encountered during his professional experience. The way he chose and interpreted them helps us better understand his intellectual approach. For example, he mentions strikes and explains that a good manager should know how to avoid them. He describes two strikes, one long and one short, in two different sets of circumstances, but where in both cases he took an inflexible position and did not waver. At the same time he chose not to describe other strikes, including one that cost the company dearly. The third part of *IGM* is incomplete with a number of sections left empty. We do not know if he lacked the time or the words to describe what may have been more complex or less flattering cases.

The second text reproduced in the annex is Henri Fayol's last publication that was published in a social Christian publication. It is an interview published in 1925 just before his death, in which the old master dialogues openly with Louis Marie du Crouzet, who was in reality Louis de Mijolla, a young disciple he had recruited as an engineer and who would succeed him at the head of the company seventeen years later. He talks at length of 'management tools' before giving his opinion about the 'social question', that of worker poverty, that so revolted the social Christians that Louis de Mijolla belonged to, and about governance and shareholder-control of a director's actions. The interview then moves on to more familiar themes including his work at reforming public bodies such as the postal service and the tobacco monopoly. The interview concludes with a discussion of the League of Nations, whose role, according to Fayol, was to help nations improve their industry or administration by promoting organizational studies. It is interesting to note that such studies were undertaken in the 1920s in French mines, after 1945 in industries across Europe and in the 1980s in the civil service under the aegis of the Organization for Economic Co-operation and Development.

Studying Henri Fayol's professional activities shows just how concrete his theory really is. Far from being outmoded, his thought underlies much of today's management thinking and practice. The way he named a concept, or the translation difficulties Fayol's words have sometimes encountered in other languages, are no longer important when we can compare the facts and events to the solutions he used to manage them. The situations he found himself in still exist in business today. The temporal continuity we can see in organizations is what favours their scientific study, and still make Fayol's thinking of a century ago relevant today.

1 THE INDUSTRIAL CONTEXT: THE COAL AND STEEL INDUSTRIES IN NINETEENTH-CENTURY FRANCE

Henri Fayol was the managing director of a mining and steel-making company from 1888 to 1918. The coal and steel industries were important motors of industrial development, and production increased over this period. It was a time of great technological advances, obliging industrialists to reinvest regularly. On a global scale, France was a modestly ranked producer.

The situation in France was characterized by a number of laws governing mining, and a strict state oversight of industrial activities both to levy taxes and ensure that security measures were taken to avoid disasters. Wages were freely set but remained low, although they doubled during the nineteenth century. As wages were higher in industry than in agriculture, labour was attracted to factories and mines and this was the main driving force behind peasant migration.

To better understand Henri Fayol's actions, we present his company in 1898 after he had been managing director for ten years. It was a large company employing some 10,000 workers, but it remained of a modest size compared to others in the same industry. Schneider et Cie, for example, employed 10,000 workers on one site in the town of Le Creusot, and just as many at its other sites. It made comfortable profits in its four coal mines and four steel factories.

The Coal and Steel Industries in the Nineteenth Century

Man has known how to make iron for more than 3,000 years with iron ore deposits and mines spread throughout the world. Production increased significantly with the invention of the charcoal-fuelled blast furnace to produce pig iron that was used by the Chinese for around 2,500 years before it was introduced across Europe in the sixteenth century.

The English invented the modern steel-making process when they began heating blast furnaces with charcoal in the eighteenth century. The pig iron extracted from the blast furnace was transformed into iron by slow carbon oxidation which involved stirring the molten iron in a reverberatory furnace. This puddling technique was invented in 1784 by the Englishmen Peter Onions and Henry Cort, and was significantly improved by Joseph Hall in 1839.

In the early nineteenth century, the English industry was ahead of its time. French factories began using the English charcoal-based process in 1820, and they replaced charcoal with coke in 1840.

Two inventions then allowed steel to be produced in high volumes. In 1856 Henry Bessemer (1813–98) invented the Bessemer process that could rapidly process large quantities of metal. The process was adapted for phosphoric iron in 1877 by Sydney Gilchrist-Thomas (1850–85) and his cousin Percy Carlyle Gilchrist (1851–1935) using a basic refractory lining (Thomas-Gilchrist process). This allowed impure iron ores to be used, notably those from the Lorraine region in France.

Five years later, Carl Wilhelm Siemens (1823–83), a German-born British engineer, patented the regenerative furnace in 1861. The waste heat in the fumes from the furnace was fed back through a chamber containing bricks, heating it to a high temperature and then using the same path to introduce air into the furnace – the preheated air significantly increased the flame temperature.

In 1863 this preheating system was used by the Frenchman Pierre Emile Martin (1824–1915) in a furnace that slowly transformed iron into steel using iron ore and scrap iron. This open hearth process (known as the Siemens-Martin process) became widely used for special steels of precise composition. In 1867 Carl Wilhelm Siemens built a similar furnace, and in 1879 an engineer working with Henri Fayol by the name of Alexandre Pourcel adapted the furnace for phosphoric irons.

Pig iron: Molten iron between 2.1% and 6.67% carbon, melting point between 1135°c and 1350°c.

Wrought iron: Less than 0.05% carbon, melting point at 1538°c.

Steel: Between 0.05% and 2.1% carbon, melting point between 1400°c and 1500°c.

Figure 1.1: Technical definitions for pig iron, wrought iron and steel.

These successive inventions allowed for the production of greater quantities of iron and steel at lower prices. The steel industry became the main market for coal producers, followed by heating and gas lighting. Coal was the main source of energy prior to the use of petrol. By the end of the nineteenth century steel had essentially replaced iron, and iron works had to constantly invest to increase their capacity and modernize their tooling.

Growth over the period was dampened by several economic downturns. For example, during the Long Depression from 1873 to 1896 growth slowed and production dropped. Iron production in 1886 was 25 per cent lower than in 1883. The production cycles for the coal and steel industries were not, however, synchronized with the rest of the French economy. Economic fluctuations led mining and steel companies to accumulate large cash reserves, distribute dividends prudently and favour self-funded projects rather than opening their capital to new shareholders.

In 1830 30 million tons of coal was mined in Great Britain, representing 80 per cent of global production. The United States of America overtook the United Kingdom as the world's main coal producer in 1900, and accounted for 500 out of the 1,216 million tons mined globally in 1913. Over this eighty-three-year period world production grew by 4.3 per cent per year, with 3 per cent growth in the UK and 8 per cent in the USA.[1]

The growth in iron production was similar to that of coal. In 1913 the USA produced approximately 30 million tons, which was three times that produced in the UK. With an annual average growth rate of 6.5 per cent, by 1890 the USA were producing more iron than the UK, where growth was only 3.5 per cent.

Steel was produced in large quantities starting in 1870. Production grew annually at a rate of 8 per cent in the UK and 15 per cent in the USA. By 1913 the USA was producing 30 million tons of steel, compared with 8 million tons in the UK. In 1900 the USA was the main producer of coal, iron and steel.

Germany also experienced a strong 6 per cent annual growth in coal and iron production from 1830 onwards, and a 12 per cent growth in steel from 1870. By 1913 German coal production was two thirds that of the UK, but the country produced 60 per cent more iron and twice as much steel. It was the world's second producer of iron and steel.

France remained the fourth global producer of coal and iron. It accounted for 5 per cent of global coal production in 1830, and only 3 per cent in 1913, despite average annual growth of nearly 4 per cent. It was in a similar position for its iron and steel production which, despite increasing by 10 per cent from 1870 levels, was surpassed by Russia whose steel industry grew at the same 15 per cent per year rate as that of the USA.

The French coal, iron and steel industries were relatively small on a global scale. Activity around the Massif Central area (in central France) during the 1850s accounted for 57 per cent of total national production. The discovery of coalfields in the Nord and the Pas de Calais departments towards the end of the nineteenth century shifted the industry to the north-west of France, where it would later be exposed to World War I. By the 1890s, the Centre region only accounted for 32 per cent of national production.

The number of workers in the collieries grew as production levels increased. In 1888 105,000 workers were employed by the mines, of which two thirds worked underground. The numbers rose to 150,000 in 1898, and 200,000 in 1913.

Productivity in the French minefields was low due to difficulties in mining the relatively thin coal deposits. By comparison, in 1913 the 450,000-strong

German mining workforce extracted 190 million tons, representing an output of 422 tons per worker per year, while in the same year 200,000 French workers only mined 41 million tons, representing an output of 205 tons per worker per year, at half of German productivity levels.

French production remained relatively low and always beneath its own needs. Coal was imported to meet 30 per cent of national consumption. Steel and iron products slightly exceeded local demand allowing some produce to be exported. France was a main importer of UK coal, accounting for 17 per cent of the United Kingdom's coal exports between 1870 and 1904. Shipping costs were relatively low, in particular between Cardiff and Bordeaux, making up 40 per cent of sales price. Import duties increased prices by a further 5 per cent. British coal that arrived into the ports of Normandy, Brittany, the Atlantic and Channel coasts and even Marseilles was still 40 per cent cheaper than French coal, and also of superior quality. The British mines made healthy profits on their coal exports to France.[2]

French Mining Legislation

During the nineteenth century all industrializing countries adhered to the doctrine of economic liberalism. While companies could freely invest and sell their produce, laws and regulations differed between countries. France had mining laws that provided for oversight by a controlling body, the state Mines Service,[3] which regularly visited each mine. Towards the end of the century, French mining legislation was used as a model for legislation in other industries.

Mining in France was governed by the Law of 21 April 1810 that distinguishes the ownership of the land on the surface by private owners from resources lying underground that belong to the state. Operating a mine involved obtaining the authorization of the state in the form of a concession and then paying annual royalties, which were calculated based on the surface area of the mine plus 5 per cent of profits. Mining companies had to negotiate with private owners either to acquire the land on the surface, or to pay for any damages to the land caused by mining activities.

This law was completed by a decree on 3 January 1813 that required the reporting of accidents, the monitoring of arriving and departing miners and the interdiction for children under ten years of age to work underground. These measures reflect the growing social preoccupations and pressures at the time. Mining laws were also progressively updated to limit the working day of young and female workers. When Henri Fayol became managing director, the law stated that women and children less than 12 years old could not work underground,[4] the minimum working age was 8 years and the maximum working day was eight hours for children below 12, and twelve hours for those below the age of 16.[5]

The Law of 25 May 1864 authorized strikes, but still allowed employers to dismiss workers, in particular the ringleaders. The required notice for a strike was usually fifteen days. After the Law of 21 March 1884 authorized the formation of unions, their influence progressively increased. Mining unions adhered to the Confédération Générale du Travail (CGT) founded in 1895. It had 130,000 members in 1902, 200,000 in 1906, 300,000 in 1908, 400,000 in 1910 and 600,000 in 1914.

The Mines Service, made up of graduates from the Ecole des Mines de Paris, monitored French mines and quarries for the state. It made a regular visit to all mines once a year and whenever there was an accident or a fire. It audited the accounts of each mine and calculated the annual royalties. Exhaustive statistics were published on the mining industry in the journal *Statistiques de l'Industrie Minérale* based on the detailed accounting information collected from each mine. The Mines Service processed requests for mining concessions and generally tried to avoid attributing an entire field to one operator which meant that ownership of mines in France was quite fragmented. Whenever a mine owner wanted to sell a concession, he was required to obtain authorization from the state who took advice from the Mines Service. State intervention in the mining sector was exceptionally pronounced in France.

Wages in Nineteenth-Century France

In the nineteenth century salaries were very low in France but grew at an average annual rate of 1 per cent, doubling from 1840 to 1900. Over the same period prices remained relatively stable, notably for wheat, which was the main staple food at the time with bread representing 33 per cent of a worker's food budget.[6] Wage growth can be attributed to productivity improvements in agriculture, where the majority of the work force worked at the time.

Wages in nineteenth-century France depended on one's trade, qualification, gender, age, region and the season and were generally higher in the cities. For example, in 1892 a farm worker earned 2.04 francs per day[7] in winter and 2.94F/day in summer. Women earned 1.35F/day in winter and 1.78F/day in summer.[8] Wages in winter were two thirds of those in summer as farmers offered higher wages to attract labour for the July-August harvest. As Donald Reid notes, 'many of Decazeville's miners retained strong ties to the land. Cabrol referred to the harvest season as "the annual tribute which we are obliged to pay to agriculture"'.[9] It was common throughout France at the time for workers from the cities and the factories to leave work to help with the harvest.

Workers laboured six days a week without holidays, working a theoretical total of 312 days a year, although in practice only 288 days were worked on average during the year.[10]Absence for festivals, sickness and seasonal farm work accounted for the twenty-four available days that were not worked.

Industrial companies offered higher wages to attract labour. For example, in 1895 collieries paid double the farm wage at an average of 4.10F/day.[11] Wages grew strongly at the start of the twentieth century, averaging an annual rate of 2 per cent per year over the ten years preceding the World War I, but also fell during economic downturns.

Wage levels varied according to the worker's trade and were generally calculated based on a worker's output.

> In the coal mines, extraction workers work on tasks in teams. Work conditions, difficulties supervising impose this mode of wage calculation ... Task rates are agreed upon at the work site itself for a period of fifteen days, a month or even several months, depending on the regularity of the deposit.[12]

A rate was fixed for each cart of coal or each meter of excavated gallery. In addition, timbering and backfill were also remunerated.

> On pay day, accounts are settled, labourers, if there are any, are paid their days work, and the surplus is shared amongst the other workers following agreed upon percentages.[13]
>
> For the miners, vein miners or rock miners, piece work wages are set in a quite particular fashion. These workers work in small groups (of three, four or five), 'teams' or 'work sites' (each of these groups is made up of several miners and one or two aids, young workers or labourers); on pay day each team receives and shares on pay day a sum that is proportional to the number of carts or trolleys (around half a ton) of coal that it mined, or the number of meters gained in the gallery at the coal face; but the unit rate per ton extracted or per meter gained strongly varies within the same mine.[14]

Wages were formally calculated based on the team's output and shared amongst its members. It was a means of motivating workers to maximize their work efforts. However this system was entirely dependent on the way rates were set. Engineers and foremen set rates based on the technical conditions of each site as well as an individual target wage. 'It is the daily earnings, much more than the earnings by unit of work, that serves as the basis of wage determination'.[15]

> In all concessions, writes the reporter of a parliamentary enquiry (in 1896), a general remark is to be made: piecework tends to be increasingly transformed into a uniform and regular wage. What is particular in this tendency towards a fixed wage is that it appears to be the work of both the labourer and the company. For the company ... the preoccupation [of engineers] is to assure the worker a fixed average wage: the rate per piece is calculated with this objective. The wage has a fixed base: the day rate, according to a consulting engineer from a large mine in 1884; if a worker in one mine who produces 3000 kilogram per day earns 4.50F, another worker in another mine who only produces 1800 kilogram earns the same rate. Likewise, on several occasions, in their answers to the latest parliamentary enquiry, companies indicate that labour rates are fixed in such a way as to ensure the worker average daily earnings. Workers have the same idea ... : 'Most often workers do not always earn their day', says a mining union delegate; 'tariffs are almost always set in such a manner that the worker does

not earn his day', says another. The expression 'earn (or not earn) his day' clearly shows for those who use it, that the idea of daily earnings is the norm for workers earnings, it is the notion that estimations refer to and that are used as a basis ... The notion of daily wage has a recognized strength. In reality the desire by workers to fix wages to a set unit of effort does not seek for the daily wage to cease being the norm for workers earnings, but rather that the strength of this notion not be used to obtain a greater effort for the same wage; it does not look to change the basis for calculating earnings, but to fix, aside the basis of earnings, the relationship between gain and effort ... The daily wage is the essential notion concerning workers earnings.[16]

Economists have known for some time that a daily remuneration was targeted when fixing the piece rate, 'Experience quite quickly informs the entrepreneur of the quantity of work that a worker can execute in a day, he knows what daily salary each of his workers can earn with piecework; and it is as to the amount of this day that master and worker debate over the rate'.[17] Daily wages were familiar to both workers and employers, and were not the result of counting daily outputs as might have been expected.

Employers however did not wish to pay daily wages so as to maintain the pressure on production and also discretely manipulate remunerations. 'Remuneration for piecework has the main advantage of facilitating the incessant compression of labour costs'.[18] Claims for a minimum daily wage were rejected by employers. 'The attitudes of workers and employers with regard to the minimum wage are both exactly based on their own interests. A minimum wage is desired by workers, and it is energetically rejected by employers'.[19]

Henri Fayol wrote at length about this central subject of wage setting in *IGM*. We examine his own practices as a manager in chapter 5.

Commentry-Fourchambault et Decazeville

Henri Fayol managed a company that occupied a modest place in French industry. In 1913 it was ranked sixteenth by the number of miners employed and accounted for only 2.5 per cent of national coal production and 1.2 per cent of France's iron and steel output.[20] The history of the Commentry-Fourchambault et Decazeville Company is told by Henri Fayol in the third part of *IGM*.[21] We now complete this description with a presentation of the situation of the company after ten years under Henri Fayol's management from 1888 to 1898.

The financial year began on 1 September and finished on 31 August. The 1897–8 year was profitable. Sales were 24.8 million francs[22] for an annual production of 1 million tons[23] of coal and 57,000 tons of iron and steel products.[24] Gross profit was 4MF. All sites were profitable with the exception of Brassac (see table 1), and the Commentry mine was still the company's 'cash cow' accounting for the majority of profits due to the quality of its coal and its low production costs. The Decazeville mine employed twice as many workers but produced only

30 per cent more coal of a mediocre quality. It was decided at the annual general meeting (AGM) on 25 March 1899 to include the Decazeville site in the company's name alongside the two historical establishments of Commentry and Fourchambault.

Table 1.1: The sites of Commentry-Fourchambault et Decazeville during the 1897–8 financial year.[25]

Site	Profit ('000 F)	Production	Quantity produced ('000 tonnes)	Number of workers	Managers and employees	Investment ('000 F)
Commentry	2223	Coal	353	1443	150	0
Montvicq	367	Coal	187	911		0
Brassac	-15	Coal	97	764	Unknown	255
Decazeville mine	377	Coal	444	2873	166	1600
Decazeville factory	408	Iron and steel	21	854		260
Imphy	414	Steel	7	769	49	421
Fourchambault	121	Steel	15	454	28	23
Montluçon	51	Pig iron	17.7	454	20	115
Headquarters			0	0	50	
Total	3946			8522	147	2674

Mines and factories were partially integrated: the Commentry and Montvicq mines sold coal to the Montluçon and Fourchambault factories; the Decazeville mine supplied the neighbouring factory; the Montluçon factory sent pig iron to Fourchambault and to Imphy. All of these products could also be sold to third parties at market conditions.

The company's factories and mines were located around the Massif Central. This mountainous zone had been covered by tropical forests some 300 million years ago. Cyclones had blown wood into lakes that accumulated there, and would later be transformed into coal. Numerous collieries were spread throughout the area.

The Commentry mine was a historic site for the company. Its deposit of quality coal had been mined there since 1820, first on the surface and later using underground mining techniques. The mine was very profitable but by 1898 the fields were almost exhausted and it was planned for the mine to cease activity in 1904, although it still continued to produce significant quantities of coal up until 1911. In 1898 a small share of the mine's production (15 per cent) was consumed by the factories.

The neighbouring Montvicq mine was less profitable, producing a lower quality coal at a higher cost. A quarter of its production was reserved for the company's factories. The coalfields were also close to exhaustion and expected to close in 1907, but the mine remained operational up until 1914.

The Fourchambault forge was the other historic corporate site. It used pig iron from Montluçon and coal from Commentry to produce wires, rails and sheet metal. The forge enjoyed easy access to the Paris market for iron and steel products via the Loire River and the Briare canal. Investments were regularly made to save the sporadically profitable forge from closure.

The Imphy forge was close to Fourchambault and its Martin-Siemens furnaces used pig iron from Montluçon. Henri Fayol specialized the forge in the production of nickel steels and it made comfortable profits that nonetheless fluctuated depending on the specific orders that were mainly received from the military.

The Montluçon factory used a blast furnace, fuelled by iron ore from Berry and coke made in the Commentry coal mine, to make cast iron parts, pipes and moulded objects and sell its pig iron to the Fourchambault and Imphy factories.

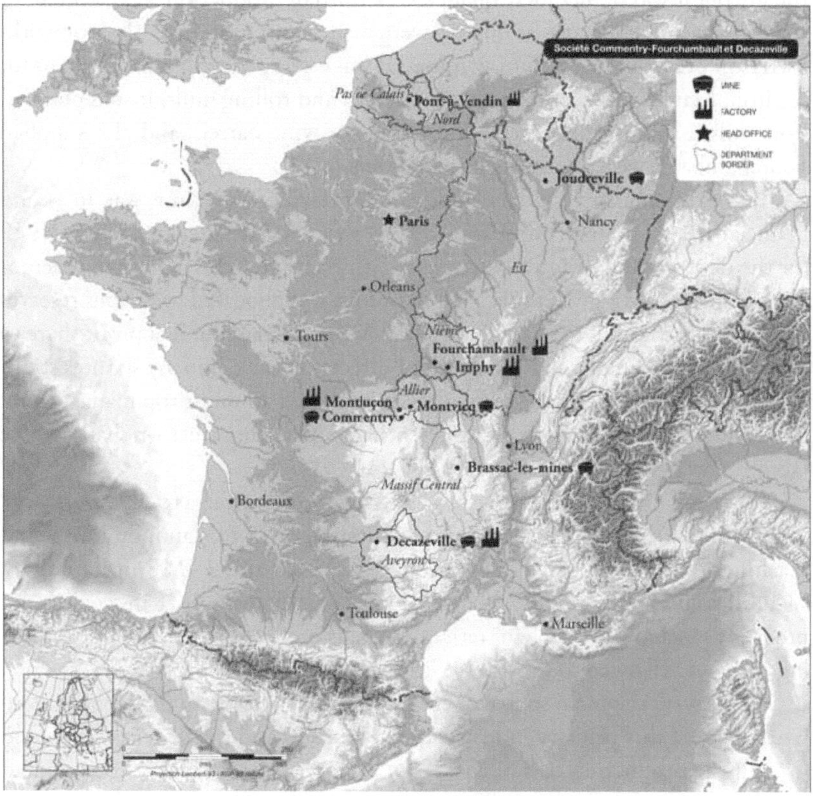

Figure 1.2: The sites of the Commentry-Fourchambault et Decazeville Company between 1888 and 1914

All of these sites were connected with one another; a private railway linked the Commentry mine to the Montvicq and Montluçon factories; the Berry canal allowed barges to carry coal and pig iron to the Fourchambault and Imphy factories. The competitive advantage the company enjoyed with the interconnection of sites disappeared as the railway network expanded towards the end of the nineteenth century.

The Brassac mine was difficult to operate as its coalfields lay beneath the bed of the Allier River. Large quantities of water had to be pumped in order to mine the coal, and large investments were required before the mine became profitable. A large quantity of coal dust was mined, agglomerated into briquettes and then sold on the market. The mine was eventually sold in 1891 to Schneider et Cie, who operated a factory in Le Creusot.

The Decazeville site with its coal mine and ironworks was merged with Commentry-Fourchambault and completely renovated in 1892. Coal was plentiful at the site but it was of mediocre quality. One third of production was reserved for the factory, and coke and briquettes were made from coal dust. The ironworks used iron ore from neighbouring mines. It was equipped with blast furnaces for pig iron, Martin furnaces for steel production and rolling mills. It sold puddled iron, rails, I-beams, sheet metal and hoops for wine barrels, and also supplied Fourchambault with a little pig iron and steel ingots.

The Commentry-Fourchambault et Decazeville Company was in sound financial health. Its net profit for 1897–8 was 2.5 MF after deducting 1 MF for the depreciation of infrastructure investments and 0.5 MF in loan redemptions from its 4 MF gross profit. The net profit was allocated to various reserves (1.2 MF), distributed to shareholders (1.1 MF) and paid out as a profit share to executive management and the board of directors. The company statutes stipulated that 14 per cent of all profits should be shared amongst top management. The dividend was 35F per share, representing a 7 per cent return on shares whose face value was 500F.

The company's balance sheet on 31 August 1898 showed a total of 25.4MF.[26] Assets included 8.3MF in mining concessions, 4.6MF for land, buildings and machinery,[27] 5MF of stock, 4.1MF in unpaid bills and 3.4MF in liquidities. Liabilities and owner's equity included 11.6MF in shares, 6.4MF in reserves and provisions including 3.9MF for retirement pension funds, 3MF in employee savings and 4.4MF owed to various creditors.

Wages were the main source of cost at the collieries due to the labour-intensive nature of this primary industry. Between 1880 and 1920 wages accounted for half the production cost of coal.[28] For example, personnel costs represented 47 per cent of total costs at the Commentry mine in 1892.[29]

In the iron and steel industry, wages only represented a quarter of the value of annual sales. For example, the Decazeville factory paid 1.4MF in wages to workers for a turnover of 5.9MF in 1904–5.[30] The main production cost was the consumption a large quantity of raw materials, such as iron ore and coal. The cost price of pig iron was made up of the cost of iron ore for 47 per cent and the cost of coke for 41 per cent.[31]

Dividends were paid by Commentry-Fourchambault et Decazeville from 1889 until the end of Henri Fayol's tenure as managing director, and he argued that the restoration and growth in dividends under his management was proof that his theory worked.[32] He could also have mentioned the tripling of the company's stock price across this same period. When Henri Fayol became managing director in 1889, the stock price was below its face value of 500F following a 50 per cent capital reduction, and ten years later the stock was priced at 1000F. It slightly fell during the depression at the beginning of the century but began rising in 1907 to be worth around 1500F on the eve of World War I in 1914.[33] Fluctuations in stock prices mirrored those of dividends and net profits.

Gross profits fluctuated during Henri Fayol's tenure as managing director and were used to fund investments and build reserves, which were both useful in times of economic downturn. Fayol brought profits back to 1MF in 1889 and maintained them at 2MF over the following years. There were four good years between 1897 and 1901 with gross profits averaging 4MF and rising as high as 6MF in 1900. Profits fell to 2MF during the ensuing recession and the economic recovery of 1907 brought profits back to between 3MF and 4MF and later to a high of 7MF in 1912.[34]

According to traditional performance indicators Henri Fayol's tenure was very successful, especially considering that he took over a company that he was mandated to liquidate. He had reason to be proud of his achievements. His success makes his management theory all the more interesting. The company did not benefit from any extraordinary technological innovation, or from a protected market position, or a controlled source of raw materials. The Commentry-Fourchambault et Decazeville Company was of a modest size and was exposed to competition from all other mining, iron and steel concerns of the time.

Conclusion

When the board of directors named Henri Fayol managing director it gave him the mandate to liquidate the company. After four years of losses the company's future was bleak, but ten years later in 1898 the company was prospering and this was probably due to Fayol's actions as a manager.[35] The company had four mines and four factories with a total workforce of 8,500 workers– a modest size compared with other French companies in the same industry at the time. At a time when other companies were going bankrupt, the Commentry-Fourchambault et Decazeville Company benefited from no particular privileges or protections that could explain its turnaround. The quality of the company's management practices would appear a reasonable explanation for its survival, just as Henri Fayol himself believed.

The functioning of the French economy was quite liberal at the time and the close state monitoring by the Mines Service and the restrictive social laws voted towards the end of the twentieth century did little to influence the market mechanisms at work. While Henri Fayol was opposed to the new social laws, he applied them punctiliously irrespective of their impact on profitability.

Overall growth throughout the period was tempered by periods of economic recession. Growth was slowed considerably during the Long Depression from 1873 to 1896 and some production volumes even decreased. Pig iron production fell by 25 per cent from 1883 to 1886, but coal and steel production followed other cycles that were different to those of the French economy. Market fluctuations led companies to build large reserves, restrain dividend payouts and prefer to self-finance their projects rather than open their capital to new shareholders.

Management theories today highlight the importance of a firm's financial policy and its governance structure. The financial and governance practices of the Commentry-Fourchambault et Decazeville Company can be found in the archived minutes of board meetings. The next chapter examines the essential role of the 'financial function' under Henri Fayol's management as well as his relationship with different corporate stakeholders, including the board of directors and shareholders.

2 THE FINANCIAL FUNCTION AND CORPORATE GOVERNANCE

Modern theories of management stress the importance of the finance function. Henri Fayol said as much in *Industrial and General Management*:

> Nothing is done without this function entering into it. Capital is required for personnel, plant, tools, raw materials, dividends, development, reserves, etc. Shrewd financial management is necessary to obtain capital, to make optimum use of available funds, to avoid foolhardy commitments ... An essential condition of success is to keep constant watch over the financial position of the business.[1]

Fayol argued that this function was essentially the domain of the shareholders and the members of the board of directors. The financial abilities of shareholders are 80 per cent while those of the board of directors are 15 per cent.[2] These abilities give the shareholders and the board the main roles in the finance function.

As managing director, Henri Fayol regularly reported on the financial state of the company and prepared decisions concerning dividends, reserves, investments, loans and capital increases. He explained in *IGM* that 'the board has wide statutory powers which are collective and a large part of which it normally delegates to general management appointed by it. The board must be in a position to assess the proposals of the general management and exercise control in a general way'.[3] Henri Fayol always operated on the authority of the board of directors and only took action once his propositions had been validated.

The organization chart[4] gives a company a pyramidal structure with the head at its peak. In a similar way, shareholders form the base of a second pyramid that elects the board of directors that in turn elects a chairman. The company head is once again at the summit (see Appendix 1).

The activity of the board of directors is related in the minutes of its meetings. Henri Fayol largely drew on them when he wrote the third part of *IGM*, and in particular the pages concerning his own nomination as managing director and the board's description of the 1901 Montluçon casters' strike.[5] Other meeting minutes reveal further details of Henri Fayol's management practices. We begin by presenting the composition of the board of directors, which was mainly made up of the founders' descendants, and then examine how Henri Fayol was chosen by the board to be managing director and how his relationship with the board evolved over time. We then consider the board of directors' role in the company's relationship with public authorities and the chapter concludes with an outline of the company's financial policy.

The Composition of the Board of Directors

In 1888 the members of the board of directors were also the company's main shareholders. They belonged to the French upper middle class and aristocracy, and received a specific share of corporate profits. The number of shareholders tended to increase with each divided estate and capital increase. Over time members of the board were more frequently chosen for their expertise rather than the number of shares that they held.

The Boigues-Rambourg limited partnership was incorporated as the Commentry-Fourchambault Company in 1874 with 25,000,000F[6] in capital. The Boigues contributed the Fourchambault factory that was built in 1822 (8.4MF, representing 33.6 per cent of total capital), the Rambourgs mainly contributed the Commentry mine that opened in 1821 (10.4MF, 41.6 per cent of total capital) and a number of other shareholders contributed a number of other sites to complete the capital (6.2MF, 24.8 per cent). As Tsuneo Sasaki noted, the descendants of the two founding families always occupied an important place on the board even though their proportionate stake in the company eroded over time with successive inheritances and capital increases.[7] Sons and son-in-laws often succeeded their fathers, and the major stockholders protected their patrimony by ensuring that their children married into other wealthy families.[8] As a result, each family's holding was spread amongst relatives and remained protected. None of the shareholders appears to have suffered during the four years when the company did not pay a dividend.

The board of directors had around ten members, and over a period of thirty years twenty-four different people sat on the board for an average tenure of eight years. An exception was Anatole Le Brun de Sessevalle (1821–1902), Henri Fayol's predecessor, who sat on the board for forty-three years. Members of the board were often elderly and fifteen passed away during their tenure.

Although their families were often from the provinces, board members typically belonged to the Parisian upper class, owned a château in the surrounding countryside and led an idle life. For example, Albert Moreau du Breuil de Saint-Germain owned a Renaissance château in the village of Pailly near the city of Langres, the baron Charles Moreau de la Rochette (1820–89) owned the Château de la Rochette near the city of Melun, and Paul Rambourg had a château rebuilt at Néris les Bains, near Commentry.

Each board member held at least 100 shares, while the president held at least 1,000. They were expected to attend monthly board meetings, visit the factories and the mines once a year and write management reports to other members of the board in their capacity as 'members of the audit committee'.

They were remunerated with a 5 per cent profit allotment,[9] one third of which was equally shared amongst board members and two thirds was distributed according to their attendance record. In 1898, the nine members of the board shared 125,000F of profits.

After the Decazeville merger, four new shareholders from the absorbed entity joined the board of directors: Paul Hély d'Oissel, Arthur Joly de Bammerville, Henri Rémaury and Louis Savoye. From that time on, the board's nomination process became more selective. Candidates were chosen by the chairman of the board based on their expertise, most probably with the help of Henri Fayol, and elected by shareholders at the annual general meeting. For example, Baron Amédée Girod de l'Ain (1852–1939), director of the Paris Lyon Mediterranean railways, and Baron Jules Le Loup de Sancy de Rolland (1846–1922), a retired army general, were elected to the board in 1898; and Paul Bourlon de Sarty, a banker, and Maurice Sabatier, a barrister to the Council of State and the Court of Cassation, were elected in 1910. Sabatier resigned a year later, however, in 1911, as he found the workload too great: 'Based on what you have told me, I note that the direction of the Commentry Fourchambault Company carries more work than I thought. For lack of time, I am regrettably obliged to submit my resignation'.[10] The members of the board of directors took an active role in the company that required a non-negligible quantity of work. For example, in early 1897 the frequency of meetings was doubled to two per month as monthly meetings from December to June were deemed insufficient.[11]

The role of the chairman of the board was to unify the opinion of board members and to prepare decisions. Baron Charles Moreau de la Rochette was chairman when the board recruited Henri Fayol in 1888. When he died the following year, Joseph Aubert was elected chairman for a period of two years to appease the tensions within the board following Fayol's nomination. He was replaced in 1891 by Albert Moreau du Breuil de Saint Germain, who would become an invaluable ally of Henri Fayol, as would Louis de Mieulle who succeeded him in 1901. In 1894, it was decided that the chairman should personally receive a yearly remuneration of 8,000F.[12]

Henri Fayol's influence over the board grew as the company's financial situation improved, and his salary also progressively increased. In 1888 he was appointed for a four-year mandate with a salary based on a 6 per cent profit share with a minimum guaranteed wage of 28,000F and a maximum fixed annual salary of 48,000F. In 1889 he earned the maximal amount and four years later his salary was increased to include a fixed base of 36,000F per year, plus 5,000F living allowance and a 3 per cent share in profits, with no ceiling, which amounted to a salary of 75,000F in 1898.[13] On 5 April 1900, twelve years after he had been appointed managing director Henri Fayol was elected to the board of directors. It was testimony to the success of his management, although he no doubt felt it was a little overdue.

While Henri Fayol had no direct contact with the annual general meeting of shareholders, he wrote them a succinct activity report. In *IGM* he explained that the role of shareholders 'is very restricted and consists chiefly in a) Appointing members of the board of directors and auditors, b) Considering the board's recommendations. They meet at least once a year and their most important and most difficult task is the appointment of the members of the board'.[14] The role of shareholders at the AGM was considered a formal one as the biggest shareholders were already represented by the members of the board who, together with their families, held a majority stake in the company.

Ownership was diluted from 1892 onwards mainly due to capital increases. Forty-one shareholders attended the 1888 AGM representing 50 per cent of shares held, sixty-one attended in 1905 representing 63 per cent of shares held, and eighty-seven attended the AGM in 1911 representing 57 per cent of company stock.

The Choice of Managing Director in 1888

After reading his work, it is difficult to imagine Henri Fayol as anything but a managing director. His appointment, however, was far from a certainty, and he could have continued his career as a mine director as he was chosen only after the preferred candidate made a strategic error.

Executive managers were habitually chosen from amongst board members, but they generally found the managing director's responsibilities and workload too exhausting. For example, when Sessevalle became the company's first solo managing director after previously sharing the role with Eugène Glachant and Stéphane Mony, he complained that he was 'very fatigued by the constant work and the intense preoccupations'.[15] Furthermore, in 1888 Commentry-Fourchambault was in an exceptionally difficult situation with losses at the ironworks absorbing the profits from the collieries at a time when the coalfields were reaching exhaustion. As the company's liquidation seemed inevitable, the managing director, Anatole de Sessevalle, resigned.

Henri Fayol's nomination did not have unanimous support, as he explained: 'I was told that a worried and malcontent shareholder said at the time, not without reason: "A metallurgist was needed, it was a miner that was chosen!" ... a managing director skilled both in mines, metallurgy and mechanical construction was necessary as the company was operating at the same time in these three industries'.[16] At the time of Fayol's nomination there was a member of the board who was experienced in these three industries: Ivan Flachat (1830–1918). He had been recruited by Stéphane Mony (1800–84), who had groomed his as his successor.

Stéphane Mony had been appointed director of the Commentry mine by one of its owners, Paul Rambourg (1799–1873), in 1840. He was the architect of the 1854 merger with the ironworks at Fourchambault and Montluçon. Over time, his management role grew and he became one of the three managing directors of the incorporated entity in 1874, together with Glachant in Fourchambault and de Sessevalle who remained in Paris to deal with financial matters.

Stéphane Mony would have liked his son, Adolphe Mony (1831–1909), to succeed him. He made him enrol in his alma mater, the Ecole des Mines de Paris,[17] but after graduating as an engineer in 1852, Adolphe chose to become a doctor and passed his doctorate in 1860.[18]

Mony had a nephew of the same age as his son, Ivan Flachat.[19] Ivan Flachat graduated as an engineer from the Ecole Centrale des Arts et Manufactures[20] (hereafter ECP) in Paris in 1850. He began working for the railways, joining Paris-Saint-Germain in 1850, the Compagnie du Midi in 1853 and the Compagnie de l'Ouest in 1856. Mony recruited him to head the Paris design office for construction works where one of his projects was the Solferino Bridge built from Fourchambault wrought iron in 1859.[21] He later supervised the testing of the Bessemer converter at Imphy in 1868 and the trials of ferro manganese at Montluçon. He presented his global vision of the company's operations at the World Fair in 1878.[22] and was elected to the board of directors four years later. As Alain Auclair notes, 'we can consider that Mony, who had wished that his son succeed him, placed his hopes on Ivan Flachat'.[23]

Ivan Flachat was a good candidate to take over the management of the Commentry-Fourchambault Company: he was a member of the board, he was knowledgeable in iron and steel making and he understood the workings of the company as a whole. However, he disqualified himself by fuelling a conflict within the board itself.

The board was averse to internal conflicts after a major disagreement between board members before Flachat joined the company. A first disagreement arose in 1856 when Paul Benoist d'Azy, a member of the board and an ally of the Boigues family, insisted that the business acquire the Alès foundry and a second disagreement occurred in 1860 over the high transfer price of coal paid by the factories. Benoist d'Azy eventually resigned after an altercation with Mony[24] which, while it momentarily resolved the conflict, left a number of traces.

A similar conflict arose in 1887 when Fourchambault was experiencing financial difficulties. Ivan Flachat promptly argued for the closure of the factory[25] in opposition to the line held by the managing director and after several confrontations on the issue, Anatole Le Brun de Sessevalle resigned on 12 August 1887.[26] He stayed on only at the request of the chairman of the board until a new managing director could be appointed. On 29 December 1887 there was a new altercation between the two men[27] and Flachat requested that his opposition to the continuance of operations at Fourchambault be noted in the minutes.[28]

The tension that Ivan Flachat fuelled within the board may have been justified from an economic point of view, but it stopped his career advancement at Commentry-Fourchambault. Not only did the board not want to relive the conflicts of 1860, but it was also difficult for the board to accept Flachat's rational solution when four of its members were related to the Boigues who had founded the Fourchambault factory. The chairman, Moreau de La Rochette was married to Louise Elisabeth Boigues, daughter of Bertrand Boigues who had built the factory; the cousins Louis de Mieulle (1839–1921) et Maurice de Mieulle (1842–92) were the great-grandsons of Bertrand Boigues' sister, Gabrielle Boigues (1788–1855); and Charles Paignon was the son of the former director of Fourchambault. These four members were favourable to saving Fourchambault, as was Sessevalle, who was irritated by Flachat's criticisms.

The search for a new managing director that began in August 1887 was a difficult one, as no board member wanted to take on the responsibility. The board had a choice between recruiting an external manager or promoting a talented manager from within the company. The first option was unsuccessful, no doubt complicated by the company's poor business prospects that made it an unattractive proposition for an executive manager. Internal promotion was the only solution. On 21 February 1888 the board summoned two directors and an engineer: Henri Fayol, the director of the Commentry mine; Pierredon de Férron, the director of the Fourchambault forge; and an engineer by the name of Goetsch.[29] The board and the candidates debated the continuance of the unprofitable operations at the Fourchambault factory as well as its costly closure. The two iron and steel workers lacked credibility considering the difficulties the company faced in its ironworks, and Fayol appeared the most trustworthy of the three candidates. He was summoned by the chairman of the board Charles Moreau de la Rochette on 3 March 1888 who, in agreement with Sessevalle, offered him the position of managing director. Three board members, Paul Benoist d'Azy, Albert Moreau du Breuil de Saint Germain (1838–1919) and Etienne Trubert (1845–1909) did not attend the board meeting of 8 March 1888 when Henri Fayol was appointed managing director but supported his appointment. Another member, Joseph Aubert aligned himself to the majority decision. Seven board members voted in favour of Henri Fayol, and Flachat abstained.[30] Ivan Flachat continued to oppose any projects concerning Fourchambault and to criticize Henri Fayol's management.[31]

Henri Fayol obtained the board's support more by default than as an acknowledgement of his qualities. Little about him was known apart from his excellent management of the Commentry mine and his opposition to Mony in 1875 when he announced that deposits were reaching exhaustion.[32] He was appointed as a transitional managing director who was tasked with liquidating the company and nothing more.

He remained dependent on the majority of the board that was favourable to Fourchambault, yet despite formal instructions from the board to close the factory, he hesitated for thirteen years, most probably in response to oral requests to do all he could to save it. One month after his nomination he already spoke of his efforts to find the most appropriate solution: 'In conformance with instructions that he received from the board, [he] is examining a plan for liquidation that is as rapid and as inexpensive as possible, and at the same time he is looking if it would be possible to maintain the forge operating without significant losses'.[33] He defended his approach by arguing that despite its losses, the factory contributed to financing overhead costs at head office and it allowed the mines to make a profit by buying their coal and coke.

The decision to close the Fourchambault factory was taken thirteen years later, on 25 July 1901 after losses of 545,000F in the 1899–1900 financial year. The chairman of the board, Louis de Mieulle was particularly emotional: 'I cannot forget that on this board I am one of the representatives of the Boigues family that founded the Fourchambault factories'.[34] In 1901 the Mieulle cousins were the only two Boigues descendants that were still members of the board and together with Du Breuil de Saint Germain and Etienne Trubert they could not change the opinion of the eight other board members that were in favour of closure. Fayol ordered reports from four metallurgists including two external experts who confirmed that liquidation was inevitable and that it would result in a loss of 400,000F. All orders could be satisfied within four or five months and the remaining iron ore could be converted to ingots.[35] A pension scale was adopted for workers who would find themselves without employment.

Ivan Flachat remained on the board until his death in 1918. He was a candidate for the chairmanship on 16 April 1891 but lost by three to four votes (out of a total of ten members) in favour of Louis de Mieulle. De Mieulle desisted when faced with a resurgence of previous tensions within the board and new elections were organized on 21 May. Albert Moreau du Breuil de Saint Germain was elected unanimously.[36] He best represented unity amongst various shareholders as he had remained discreet during Henri Fayol's nomination. In 1901, Louis de Mieulle was again elected chairman of the board receiving the votes of all members with the exception of Flachat, who cast a blank vote.

Henri Fayol gradually gained the trust of the board once he had restored the company to profitability. In 1893 he announced the appointment of a deputy director at Decazeville, thus applying the principle that he had previously noted in January 1888: 'Authority having always to be represented in case the head is absent or delayed, his deputy, his delegate, must be designated in advance'.[37] He told the board of directors 'that his principle is to designate, everywhere in advance deputies destined to replace heads that are absent or delayed, so that the office is always ensured'.[38] The chairman of the board replied that it was an excellent idea and proposed to elect a vice-chairman of the board. This is the first trace of one of Fayol's management principles and of its concrete application by someone other than Fayol himself.

Relations with the Board of Directors

Henri Fayol sometimes disagreed with the board of directors. One such case concerned the development of the Imphy factory, when after a visit to Imphy in July 1899, the board noted that 'the chairman fears that the importance of the new factory at Imphy is exaggerated'. While the new building appeared too big to the board, Henri Fayol considered it to be a strategic investment and of the required size to conduct research into new steels. He replied that,

> we could no doubt slightly reduce both the surface and the cost price of the Imphy laboratory, but the saving we could make would not be a sufficient compensation for the loss of work facilities that we must find in a large and well-equipped laboratory.[39]

Henri Fayol stood by his investment in the new facility which would later allow Imphy to become a successful specialist producer of new steels.

The most significant disagreements between Henri Fayol and the board of directors concerned the latter's refusals to support projects that Fayol proposed in 1889, 1898 and 1902.

In 1889 the Drôme department made a call for tenders for the construction and operation of a narrow gauge railway. This would represent an exclusive market for Fourchambault's rails, bridges and wagons. The board refused to support the project and Henri Fayol eventually changed his mind, finding that the advantages were insufficient.[40]

In 1898, Fernand Schmatzer, an Austrian businessman based in Brussels with business dealings in Russia, was looking to invest in the Russian iron and steel industry in Neviansk in the Oural region and sought out Commmentry-Fourchambault's technical assistance. Henri Fayol presented the opportunity in a favourable light but the board rejected the project: 'Such an affair is necessarily very uncertain, and we do not know the promoter well enough to commit ourselves with confidence and a failure would have a regrettable effect on the company's reputation'. It also opposed the additional workload such a project would impose on executive management, including a trip to Russia of at least four to six weeks. 'The board would not view without concern at this time a prolonged absence of the managing director and his principle collaborators in far off countries'.[41] Schmatzer's business dealings did fail, even before the events of 1917 in Russia.[42]

A new opportunity for international business arose in 1902 when the Milan foundries asked Commentry-Fourchambault et Decazeville for technical assistance in installing a Martin furnace and a spring factory. 'The managing director could not ignore the company's reluctance in committing to foreign business dealings'.[43] Henri Fayol did nonetheless submit the question to the board to confirm its opposition to international collaborations.

While the board generally supported Henri Fayol's initiatives to ensure the company's survival, it refused every attempt he made at international expansion. He gained the board's trust after the company was restored to profitability, but the board's overly prudent financial decisions bridled the company's growth.

Relations with Public Authorities

During the twentieth century, while the actions of successive French governments favoured economic liberalism, ministers took decisions that favoured particular companies or markets by deciding who would benefit from mining concessions for example or by modifying customs' duties in order to protect internal markets. Corporations also exerted political influence in so far as their owners could be elected to Parliament. Henri Fayol understood this reciprocal relationship between business and politics and his opinion towards it changed over time. He first adopted a line of 'electoral abstention'[44] before later lobbying the government through a pressure group made up of several industrialists called the Comité Central des Houillères de France (CCHF)[45] at the beginning of the twentieth century. Fayol believed that his lobbying was an act of liberalism and his principled stance led him to support the enemies of his enemies, including the Decazeville Member of Parliament from the centre-left, who was later awarded a ministerial portfolio. Commentry-Fourchambault et Decazeville benefited from the Minister's favours in at least two situations and while these opportunities were no doubt unintended, they were profitable for the company.

The owners of Commentry-Fourchambault et Decazeville were from French nobility, and notables were often Members of Parliament. Suffrages were census-based at the start of the nineteenth century in France, and only those who paid enough taxes were allowed to vote. When financial conditions were abolished and universal suffrage was introduced in 1848, Emperor Napoléon the Third nominated official candidates that had every chance of being elected. As a result, members of Parliament were often rich local land owners and a position in Parliament was considered a sign of local power. Most circumscriptions were rural with the exception of several large cities, which meant that peasants, who were generally conservative, always had a great influence.

Over time, ten board members had also been members of Parliament: Paul Rambourg (1799–1873) was a Member of Parliament from 1857 to 1863 and was named Mayor of Commentry by the Prefect from 1830 to 1848; Stéphane Mony (1800–84) was a Member of Parliament from 1868 to 1870 and was named Mayor of Commentry from 1865 to 1870. Both played an important role in the development of the town and it was considered normal at the time that these major property owners hold office and support the government. The company directors at Decazeville had also been mayors, and sometimes members of Parliament. The last director was Jules Gastambide (1846–1944) who held a 3 per cent share of the company.[46] He was elected mayor in 1888 but lost elections to the Parliament in 1889 and to the mayor's office in 1892. He was a vocal opponent of the Decazeville merger with Commentry-Fourchambault and took legal action to have it annulled.

Henri Fayol theorized that a company should not be involved in elections[47] when Mony's defeat in the 1877 elections eroded his authority within the mine itself. In practice, it was difficult for Fayol to exercise his policy of neutrality in municipal elections. For example, he was asked by the Prefect for the company to intervene against Gastambide in the 1892 campaign. Henri Fayol first replied that he did not wish to field any candidates:

> The rule of the Commentry Fourchambault Company is to not exert any electoral pressures on its personnel ... The plan was not to do politics; to keep us as far as possible out of electoral fights, even municipal, in spite of the great interest we have featuring in the municipalities where our industry is the main source of wealth'. In the case of Gastambide the company 'yielded not without having resisted.[48]

He accepted that eight company employees, apart from the director and his deputies, participate in the elections and Gastambide was beaten. It was difficult for the company not to be present on the city council as Decazeville was completely dependent on the mine and the factory. In a town of 9,000 inhabitants and around 2,500 households, the company employed more than 3,000 workers.

The same ambiguous attitude was adopted in the 1893 parliamentary elections. The outgoing Member of Parliament Émile Maruéjouls (1835–1908) had beaten Gastambide in 1889, and even though he belonged to the 'radical' wing and opposed the 'conservative' wing, Henri Fayol decided to discretely support him. 'Under the circumstances, the company's sympathies are not questionable. It strongly wishes for the success of Mr Maruéjouls, who never hesitated to render services'.[49] He seems to have ignored that Maruéjouls owned 0.5 per cent of the Decazeville company. 'If, to keep to its official neutral line of conduct it does not intervene in favour of Mr Maruéjouls, it will not allow any opposition against Mr Maruéjouls to take place on its work sites'.[50] Maruéjouls was elected and when he requested financial support the following year to start a journal, Henri Fayol personally paid him 20,000F so that the company would not appear to be supporting a Member of Parliament from the left.[51]

While the goal of such discrete political support was to stymie the local election of an adversary, the company was rewarded in two national affairs. Maruéjouls was appointed minister in charge of industry, and therefore mines, from 28 June to 1 November 1898 and was most likely instrumental in the Mines Service requesting that Commentry-Fourchambault et Decazeville prospect for iron ore in the Lorraine region, north of Nancy. On 21 July 1898 the board of directors accepted Fayol's proposition to explore the Joudreville iron ore deposits at a cost of 50,000F. Prospecting activities were successful and the Council of State awarded the Joudreville concession to Commentry-Fourchambault et Decazeville in February 1900[52] and while Maruéjouls was no longer minister, the Higher Council for Mines validated the initial decision. Commentry-Fourchambault et Decazeville paid 250,000F to the state to obtain the concession after spending 100,000F in prospecting costs, and by 1905 it was worth 2.5MF, seven times the total outlaid expenses.[53] This affair turned out to be a generous gift from the minister.

Maruéjouls was again minister in charge of industry from 7 June 1902 to 24 January 1905 in Emile Combes' left-wing government. He again helped Henri Fayol with an affair in Bouxhors after strikes had led to losses and the closure of the Bouxhors (Brassac) mine. Fayol wanted to sell the concession to a neighbouring mine but the request to conjoin the concessions was refused by the Council of State in 1889. The miners proposed to take over operations at the mine themselves with the support of local politicians who were opposed to any concentration of mines that would give more power to employers. It would appear that Maruéjouls, in league with Henri Fayol, played a game of posturing. Senior public servants summoned Henri Fayol in December 1902 to establish whether he would sell the mine to his workers. He agreed to at a price of 300,000F that he later lowered to 250,000F with the offer first open until February 1903, and then until 5 March 1903. The minister himself announced that the miners had not secured the necessary funding[54] in time and Henri Fayol immediately ceased the maintenance work that had been ongoing despite the stoppage of the mine. Fayol was then free to find another buyer and first began negotiating with a local banker who later desisted. He then contacted the owner of the neighbouring concession, the Société Anonyme des Houillères de la Haute Loire, who had previously in 1889 expressed an interest, and in August 1903 the sale was agreed at a price of 225,000F, some 25,000F below that proposed to the unions. The company's application to adjoin the concessions was strongly supported by the minister despite local political resistance,[55] the Council of State accepted the request in July 1905 and the sale was signed in December that same year.[56] Commentry-Fourchambault et Decazeville managed to divest of this loss-making mine despite opposition from local politicians. Two years later, mining operations at Bouxhors were restarted through the shaft of the neighbouring mine.

Henri Fayol's acceptance to sell the mine to the workers can be interpreted as a manoeuvre so that he would be allowed to sell to another company. Employers were not as a whole favourable to workers' cooperatives and Henri Fayol fixed a high price and a short deadline. For any other buyer he would no doubt have agreed to a lower price and a deferred payment plan as he had previously done at Fourchambault and at La Pique. The offer was designed to show the Minister the impossibility of a workers' cooperative at Bouxhors and to obtain his support both for a sale to a neighbouring mine and for the unification of the concessions, despite the hostility of the local population. The local section of the *Ligue des Droits de l'Homme et du Citoyen* in September 1905[57] was unable to influence the minister, even though the League supported his political party.

By 1898, most governments were run by left-wing parties that were less inclined to follow the line of employers and sought to influence their decisions. For example, in 1902 the head of government, Pierre Waldeck-Rousseau, personally called Henri Fayol to support a low offer for the Fourchambault factory. Fayol refused to lower his price and the potential buyer withdrew his offer.[58]

In the same year, Waldeck-Rousseau's successor, Emile Combes, took an interest in the striking Decazeville mine. He offered to mediate but, in the meantime, workers had returned to work.[59] Henri Fayol took pleasure writing to him that his offer was no longer necessary. Emile Combes's private secretary later offered to mediate the La Combelle (Brassac) strike in November 1902 and while the company refused his offer, Henri Fayol was summoned together with a neighbouring striking mine by the Minister of Industry to sign a document that would satisfy the miners' claims.[60]

Henri Fayol did not appreciate these interventions and said that 'the company head has to deal with another difficulty, the intervention of the state'.[61] It led him to actively participate in collective lobbying of the government on all mining subjects through the Comité Central des Houillères de France that grouped together the heads of all French coal mines.

When the ironworks employers' federation, the Comité de Forges de France announced that it would launch a publication in 1893 to influence public opinion, the CCHF believed that the same objective could be reached through existing publications,[62] before copying the approach in 1920. Employers' organizations owned numerous newspapers including 'Le Temps', which was the most influential daily newspaper at the time.[63]

Henri Fayol was pragmatic and entertained courteous relations with local administrations and municipalities. For example, he visited the Prefect of the Aveyron department at the time of the Decazeville acquisition; he donated a 3,100 square metre parcel of land to build the Decazeville police station in 1892, which would benefit both the commune and the company in times of social unrest; in May 1914 the company authorized the Red Cross to use the mine's hospital in the event of war;[64] and the company also participated in locally run official ceremonies such as when the French president, Félix Faure made a half-hour visit to the Fourchambault factory whilst visiting the Centre region in 1895. He was received by four members of the board of directors[65] and he decorated elderly workers with a medal of honour. In a valley town such as Decazeville where land is rare and the extension of the ironworks had often been obstructed by the presence of roads, goods relations with the municipality were invaluable. In 1893, the municipality supported and agreed to the company's extension plans.[66] In 1906, when other roads needed to be moved by the municipality to build a new steel mill for a cost to the company of 600,000F, Henri Fayol offered to pay a quarter of the municipality's asking price and an agreement was reached in 1907 for 240,000F.[67]

Commentry-Fourchambault et Decazeville also had good relations with the Catholic Church. For example in May 1895, the new Decazeville forge was inaugurated with the blessing of his Eminence Cardinal Bourret, Bishop of Rodez in the presence of a delegation of directors composed of Louis and Maurice de Mieulle and Joly de Bammerville, the latter of Protestant confession.[68] Every year the company also made a donation to each parish where it had a site and it contributed to creating and financing local Catholic schools.

The company continued to support religious schools when the church and state were separated in 1905 and 30,000 priests and nuns, including a large number of teachers, emigrated and many schools closed. The company paid indemnities to emigrating nuns and continued to support schools whose teachers had been secularized. For example, Commentry-Fourchambault et Decazeville paid 400F each to the sisters at the Commentry school who were expelled in 1904, 300F to the four sisters working at the Decazeville hospital, who were forced to leave their order in 1905,[69] and another 300F to nurses in 1909. Many teachers also left their order to continue teaching and the company continued to support the non-state schools that replaced the religious schools. Such was the case in Decazeville and surrounding areas where private secular schools were founded and their operations were financed as before by the company. In 1907, the Decazeville site paid 2,000F to priests, 4,200F to their charities, 2,200F to sporting and artistic associations and 7,400F to non-state schools for the children of workers, be they boys or girls.[70] When the Brothers of the Christian Schools were secularized in Commentry in 1908 they also received a grant based on the number of workers' children they cared for.[71]

Commentry-Fourchambault et Decazeville was always concerned that its social works would continue. Louis Rambourg created the Saint Louis hospice in Commentry and bequeathed to it his fortune upon his death in 1894;[72] the buildings of the Fourchambault religious school were given to a private citizen in 1902 so that the activity would continue.[73] In 1902 the company transferred the asylum founded by Jules Hochet in La Pique to the Société Magnard et Cie, the new owner of the buildings stating that: 'It is a moral duty for the company to leave intact the religious works created by the founders of the Fourchambault factory'.[74]The company owned the Imphy girls' school and when it was closed it decided nevertheless to conserve the buildings.[75]

Despite the company's institutional ties to the Catholic Church, Henri Fayol remained an atheist. He wrote in one of his non-dated thoughts that 'God is the ensemble of forces and laws which the world subdues'. He criticized the Catholic Church, noting that 'the Catholic peoples are in decline, the Protestant peoples are prospering'. His thinking was as follows: 'Consider briefly if the absence of will, of initiative, that we suffer from is not mainly caused by the way in which the Catholic priests have undertaken their mission'.[76]

Another major public authority that Commentry-Fourchambault et Decazeville was in contact with was the tate Mines Service. Established by the Law of 1810 as the controlling body for French mines, the Mines Service collected royalties and processed requests for concessions. Every mine had to submit their accounts for the calculation of royalties that were fixed at 5 per cent of net mining profits. Up until 1880 the Commentry mine refused to submit its accounts to the Mines Service and was charged a standard fee.[77] After Mony's death the information provided by the mine conformed more and more to that requested by the administration. Two years later a conflict arose with the Mines Service over the private railway that linked the Commentry mine to Montluçon. As the railway's operating cost was below the transfer price set at 0.12F per ton per kilometre by ministerial decision on September 29 1882, the Mines Service included this profit in the calculation of the mine's royalties. Henri Fayol argued that the railway was not part of the mine and the administrative tribunal ordered that the excess payment be reimbursed in 1888 and 1889.[78] The sum of 250,000F improved the company's accounts at a difficult time. In 1893 the Mines Service allowed Henri Fayol to unify the Decazeville concessions.[79] When the company acquired other mines in the area it was also authorized to unify them in exchange for relinquishing the unused Armoi concession near Brassac.[80] The intervention of the state administration was a constraint but it also provided profitable opportunities. The relation was much more complex than liberal theories presuppose.

Finance Policy

Commentry-Fourchambault was listed on the Lyon Stock Exchange and later the Paris Stock Exchange in 1899. The company did not pay dividends between 1884 and 1888 and the share price fell from 500F in 1883 to a low of 145F in January 1889.[81] A small dividend of 20F was paid in 1890 for the 1888–89 financial year and the stock price moved up to 240F in April 1890.

In December 1889 the board of directors voted for a 50 per cent capital reduction where two old shares with a nominal value of 500F would be exchanged for one new 500F share. The number of shares was reduced from 50,000 to 25,000,[82] and when the exchange took place in April 1890 the price of the new stock settled at around 500F. This operation allowed the company to reduce the value of its fixed capital as its machinery and equipment had not been depreciated for a number of years and raw materials were overvalued. For example, the Montluçon factory held a stock of iron ore equivalent to five years' consumption that was valued at its extraction cost which was largely above the market price. Its value was subsequently reduced. The capital reduction also mathematically reduced the interest charges that each site had to pay on their fixed assets.

As dividends increased, so too did the share price. After being listed on the Paris Stock Exchange in 1899 at 500F, the share price rose to 1,000F in 1900 for a dividend of 50F. The dividend was cut to 40F in 1902 and the stock price fell to a little over 800F. In 1908 dividends were fixed at 60F and stock prices rose to 1,200F and 1,500F by 1912. The share value was multiplied by five between 1888 and 1912, representing an average annual growth of 7 per cent, even though there was no inflation over this period.

The company statutes stipulated that Commentry-Fourchambault had to reduce the number of outstanding shares as the mines became exhausted. In 1880 an annual sum of 150,000F was fixed for share repurchases that was unconnected to the fall in the book value of the mines, and shares were repurchased according to established rules: when the share price was below par, the company bought back 3,000 shares on the market;[83] when the market value reached the share's face value, the reimbursement procedure involved selecting shareholders randomly by drawing lots and then paying out 500F per share, and a bonus share that gave the holder a right to a dividend that was 25F less than that paid on an ordinary share. For example, a dividend of 40F was paid per ordinary share and 15F per bonus share in 1905, and 60F and 35F in 1911.

In 1899 new corporate statutes made this practice less rigid, and article 22 of the statutes allowed the board of directors to fix the amount of shares to be repurchased annually. The previous year Henri Fayol had opposed this financial mechanism arguing that 'concerning the repurchase of shares, the managing director points out that there is less interest than before in hastening the reimbursement of shares. By continuing this reimbursement using only the resources provided by dividends we would increase the amount of reserves that could be more gainfully employed in undertaking the major planned works.'[84] The board did not agree and the share capital of 31,500 shares at 500F for a total of 15,750,000F fell to 9,452,500F (18,905 shares) in 1904. The 12,595 of repurchased shares represented 40 per cent of total share capital.[85] In 1914, 15,833 shares were bought back for 7,916,500F, representing 36 per cent of capital.

These repurchases were slightly below the 18,500 shares first issued to finance the company's industrial development.

Henri Fayol had to arrange financing for five major projects during his tenure as managing director. The first project was the acquisition of the Brassac mine for a cost of 1.4MF that was voted on 31 July and 18 September 1890.[86] The board readily agreed to the project as the exhaustion of the Commentry mine hung over the future of the company and the required capital was taken out of the company's reserves.

The second major project was the merger with the owners of the Decazeville site. The decision was taken in nine meetings between 10 July 1891 and 27 February 1892. The factory and the mine were valued at 3.25MF[87] and the investments necessary to modernize the site were first estimated at 3MF and later 4.6MF. The board unanimously supported the project that it saw as a means to resolve the recurring difficulties in the company's ageing factories. 6,500 shares were issued to the Decazeville shareholders.

In 1892 the Decazeville mine was reorganized and the factory was completely rebuilt. Over the nine years from 1892 to 1901 the Commentry-Fourchambault et Decazeville Company invested 5.3MF in its mines and 4.3MF in its factories.[88] The company's gross profits over this period were 30MF and its net profits were 13MF. The 17MF difference was used to fund its reserves and investments including 9.6MF in Decazeville. As the profits made at the Decazeville site could not alone finance these investments, those of Commentry were also used, as self-financing was the favoured means of funding and allowed it to avoid bank loans.[89] As a precautionary measure the company built numerous reserves and held large quantities of liquid assets often including railway bonds.[90]

The third major project was the development of the Joudreville iron ore mine. Discussions began on 24 February 1898 and continued for seven meetings over small exploration costs until the concession was acquired on 8 May 1900. The board of directors then discussed the mining of the iron ore over eighteen sessions through until 28 March 1905, eventually deciding to enter a joint venture with another company. Two solutions were considered, the first being the creation of a new entity where Commentry-Fourchambault et Decazeville would hold a minority share and only contribute the concession itself with the advantage that it required no cash flows, and the second defended by Henri Fayol involved retaining a two-third share in the new entity. Fayol explained: 'One should not renounce the possibility of a profit, which is in our hands, to avoid an industrial burden and a financial burden, that are in the nature of our company's business and that are not above its capacities.'[91] A contribution of 2.5MF in fresh liquidities was necessary and the board authorized a loan of 2MF.[92] The investment was less than that of the Decazeville merger, yet the decision was long and difficult and Henri Fayol himself hesitated four years before deciding on an alliance.

The fourth project was the construction of the Thomas steel mill in Decazeville at an estimated cost of 5MF[93] that was debated by the board over eleven sessions from 18 May 1905 to 8 March 1906. The investment required a 3MF capital increase and a 1MF loan.[94] In 1907 the company issued 6,000 new shares with a face value of 500F that were sold at the market rate of 800F per share, bringing the total number of outstanding shares to 37,500. Two iron mines were bought in Muret for 380,000F and in Batère for 1,550,000F to increase the production capacity around the mill.

The fifth major project was the purchase of the factory at Pont-à-Vendin in collaboration with the Lens collieries that was discussed by the board over five sessions between 12 January 1911 and 6 April 1911. A 40 per cent share in the project was expected to cost 12.2MF which would be financed by the issue of 6,000 shares and a 5MF loan.[95] The board voted unanimously in favour of the project despite some hesitations: 'It would have been preferable, from the point of view of our finances that this opportunity presents itself in two of three years' time'.[96] However, as the planned capacity of the factory increased, so too did its cost. In 1912 Commentry-Fourchambault et Decazeville had to find an additional 2.8MF if it wanted to maintain its share and Henri Fayol argued that the company had a moral responsibility to reinvest: 'If our company is free to not participate in the capital increase of the Pont-à-Vendin company, it is nonetheless to a certain extent morally obliged, and for that matter, the financial resources of the company allows us to contribute our share'.[97] The board agreed with Fayol and increased the company's share capital in 1911 to 21,750,000 shares by issuing 6,000 shares with a face value of 500F at a sales price of 1,200F per share and sold 10,000 bonds for 500F each in 1912. Existing shareholders mainly benefited from these share and bond issues.

For each of these five major projects, Henri Fayol had to obtain the board's approval to secure funding by a capital increase, borrowing or self-financing with the latter solution the most readily adopted by the board.

There were other financial operations during Henri Fayol's tenure as managing director, such as the 1908 acquisition of the Campagnac collieries near Decazeville for 2.3MF and the Batère iron ore mines for 1.55MF. In 1912 and 1913 the company also took minority stakes in the Anjou mining and metallurgical company (0.15MF for a 25 per cent share), in the Rouen blast furnaces for access to ferro manganese produced from imported ores (0.8MF for 16 per cent), in the iron mines of Ouenza in eastern Algeria where the iron content of ore was 54 per cent (0.2MF for 2 per cent) and in the Union of Moroccan mines for 0.02MF. By August 1914, all of these investments had created cash flow difficulties and the board used World War I as a pretext to cancel the dividend payments planned for October that year.[98]

The company used its gross profits to fund its reserves, finance investments and pay dividends. Gross profits rose to 5MF in its three best years in 1898, 1899 and 1901, and 27 per cent was distributed as a dividend of 45F and 50F. The larger part of gross profits funded reserves and investments. The following four years were less profitable with annual gross profits falling to around 2MF from 1902 to 1906. Dividends fell to 40F and were funded by 55 per cent of gross profits. The funds transferred to reserves and investments were adjusted to ensure that dividends did not vary too sharply to keep the confidence of the stock market.

The company offered its employees the possibility of opening a remunerated savings account and there was 3MF in employee savings on the books in 1898. The board considered this practice dangerous as there was a risk that all employees withdraw their funds at the same time and so limited the size of these accounts by setting a ceiling on remunerated capital.[99]

Conclusion

The board of directors supervised the managing director's actions and most often approved his decisions. Over time, Henri Fayol gave the board a management role, requesting that members alternately study the reports written by site directors and then report back to the other directors.[100] This procedure was introduced in 1893 and it helped board members understand the details of industrial projects and the difficulties encountered by each site.

Each month the board of directors was informed of the company's finances and it always discussed the year's dividend, investment of liquid assets, funding of reserves, investment levels for each site as well as loans and capital increases. The board's main decisions were then ratified at the AGM.

One of the questions debated by the board was the corporate headquarters' move from the prestigious Place Vendôme in Paris. When the lease expired in 1912, the rent was greatly increased and Henri Fayol began searching for new offices that were large enough for the growing company, and on 23 June 1913 he moved the company to an office building at 84 rue de Lille.[101]

Henri Fayol was appointed managing director by default in 1888 and progressively gained the trust of the board of directors. He built his power by responding to the official instructions from his board but also by satisfying the implicit wishes of a small majority of its members. He had the full confidence of the board's chairman from 1891 onwards and was elected to the board in 1900.[102] While the board accepted more and more of his propositions over time, it continued to judge each and every one according to its capital requirements. During his tenure as managing director, Henri Fayol managed to convince a sometimes reticent board to invest in five major undertakings. As a minority shareholder, he had to gain the support of the company's major shareholders and sometimes of several families at the same time. He tactfully shared his industrial vision by obliging board members to prepare an annual report on each site which required them to examine their accounts in detail, read the reports written by site directors and adopt an industrial perspective even if they were more interested in financial aspects, profits and investments.

Henri Fayol knew how to conceive industrial strategies and explain them to the company's owners. He considered the financial function as subordinate to industrial projects, without any autonomy of its own: either profits were sufficient to invest, or the company's capital should be increased. The board members adopted an industrial perspective and looked for the best means of financing projects. Fayol's plans then explained how industrial projects would generate financial results.

and sometimes of several families at the same time. He certainly shared his indus- trial vision by including board members to promote an actual corporate [illegible]

[illegible]

3 PLANNING

Henri Fayol was the director of the Commentry coal mine from 1865 to 1888. He organized production by planning the extraction of coal at different work sites. 'Fifty years ago I began to use this system of forecasts, when I was engaged in managing a colliery'.[1] In a mine, coal must be extracted in a way that doesn't disturb the layers of coal that are to be extracted later, and that also allows galleries and shafts to be used for as long as possible. Work sites are organized following a plan that takes into account geological constraints, previous extractions and target production volumes. The superficial coal is extracted first before mining deeper layers. Henri Fayol maintained this technical habit of planning when he became managing director of Commentry-Fourchambault et Decazeville.

During his thirty years at the head of Commentry-Fourchambault et Decazeville Henri Fayol produced a large number of plans. In an address to the board of directors he identified three decades of growth under his management, with each providing a higher range of dividends than the last, and each corresponding to a separate ten-year plan: 'From 1888 to 1898, the dividend took a first step when it passed from zero to 35F. It took a second step from 1898 to 1908 passing from 35F to 60F. We have good hope that it will take a third not less important step between 1908 and 1918'. The first plan was loosely drafted, the second plan was formally presented to the board at the start of 1898 and he presented a third ten year plan in early 1908.[2] Events and performances over these three decades were not always as Henri Fayol expected, and plans had to be adapted.

We will first examine the plans for the Fourchambault factory, where the day-to-day decision making meant that these plans changed regularly. Secondly, we will look at the successive plans for the Decazeville site from 1892 onwards for its extension and growth in production, and we will then examine the overall corporate plans for 1898 and 1902 to understand how they were structured.

A study of Henri Fayol's plans helps understand his thought process, his approach to planning, the difficulties he encountered and the way in which he presented his plans to the board of directors. These questions are of interest for management historians, but also for contemporary managers who can see their own difficulties in these historical cases.

Fayol's Plans by Site

The Plans for Fourchambault from 1888 to 1901

For thirteen years, Fayol tried to save the Fourchambault factory by making new investments to improve equipment and balance the accounts. He eventually gave up, and his actions are far from an example of successful planning.

Henri Fayol was named managing director in 1888 in response to a corporate crisis that was in part caused by the loss-making Fourchambault factory that was absorbing the other sites' profits. The factory was founded in 1821 to transform local iron ores with wood from surrounding forests, according to English techniques of the time. When the factory was merged with the Commentry mine in 1854, wood was replaced with coal shipped along the Berry canal.[3] Its highest production output of 71,000 tons was reached in 1877[4] with the labour of around 1,000 workers, but when cheaper iron ores were found in the 1880s, the factory's higher costs led to a fall in production volumes to 21,000 tons with losses of around 1MF and a workforce reduced to 500 in 1886.

Fourchambault's difficulties were caused by the economic depression of 1873–96 and amplified by the poor investment decisions of Henri Fayol's predecessor, Anatole Le Brun de Sessevalle. Sessevalle had had a new factory built on the site in 1884 at an original estimated cost of 1.1MF, but construction costs overran to 1.9MF by 1886 and the managing director was called to order by the board.[5]

The new factory did not operate effectively– it accumulated losses and cost prices were 10 per cent above previsions. Throughout 1887 the board debated how to best make the factory work and the possibility of a closure was regularly discussed. Sessevalle was hesitant: 'Our responsibility towards our shareholders and our workers, demands that all that is possible be tempted before closing our biggest factory and leaving a large dependant population without work'.[6] The older part of the factory was closed in 1887.

When Henri Fayol replaced Sessevalle in March 1888 the situation was disastrous. He was mandated to execute the board's decision to close the factory but as we saw in the previous chapter, he skilfully argued for the site to be maintained. After a visit to the factory in 1888 Fayol declared: 'My investigation is over; it has convinced me not that the forge can immediately operate profitably but that the losses will be inferior to those that all of the company's other sites would burden if the forge was stopped'.[7] An expert undertook a detailed study of the factory and recommended a 5 per cent cost reduction for each product which Fayol then planned to realize by investing 100,000F. He estimated that losses would be limited to 200,000F for the following year and proposed to use monthly reporting by local accountants to monitor progress. The factory's contribution to overhead costs and its consumption of Commentry's coal were used to justify these losses.

Henri Fayol's proposal was a plan: a plan to reduce cost prices accompanied by the timely verification of results. The board approved the plan and work at the factory stopped during summer for it to be reorganized, to take stock and to settle matters outstanding from previous management. Fayol renewed the staff, he recruited new managers in the factory and he reorganized the accounting department to accelerate the calculation of cost prices. He also made changes to the factory's accounts by decreasing the value of assets, the interest rate paid on assets and the value of inventories of iron ore and coal at market prices, thus lowering the different expenses used to calculate cost prices. Fayol also hired a sales manager and four salesmen to work directly for the factory where previously all sales matters had passed through the Paris office.[8]

Six months later the production cost of steel had fallen by 30 per cent and Fayol announced that 'on average cost prices are in accordance with our June previsions ... The experience acquired over the last period gives us hope that the forge will not deviate far from the economic plan that was fixed for it for 1888–9'.[9] The rescue plan was successful and even though the future of the factories was still not assured, the company moved away from bankruptcy. The board particularly appreciated the fact that Fayol's plans were realized, for in the past, realizations were generally disappointing compared to the projections presented at the time of the investment decision.

One year later, Henri Fayol reviewed the situation at the Fourchambault factory and decided to invest heavily in the site and centralize all production there.[10] He presented a plan fifteen days later to the board that included closing the small factory at La Pique, a village close to Fourchambault, specializing Imphy in the manufacture of springs and centralizing the fabrication of other products at Fourchambault.

Henri Fayol would have preferred to merge the factories with a sister company at Châtillon-Commentry, whose products and factories were similar, as rationalizing all of these sites would have significantly reduced expenses. Fayol first mentioned the project to the board on 31 July 1890, and on 23 October 1890 he presented his project as a better alternative to his initial plan for centralization.[11] Châtillon-Commentry refused the partnership one month later as it had recently modernized its Montluçon factory and profitably specialized its production in armour plating for warships, and it did not want to merge it with with Commentry-Fourchambault's older factories.[12] The project to centralize production at Fourchambault went ahead as planned.

While the administrative centralization at Fourchambault was rapid, technical centralization took longer, requiring an investment of 2MF to be undertaken progressively over a period of three or four years starting in 1891 for an annual saving of 0.7MF. All of the rolling plant was to be transferred at the start of 1892 to a new steel mill planned for Fourchambault, but this 1.1MF investment was deferred after the business situation deteriorated in October 1892. It was again suggested that the factory close but Henri Fayol again resisted. 'Public authorities, that we rely on, would take badly to the closure of a workshop employing 600 to 800 workers without having made a serious reorganization attempt'.[13] The La Pique factory with its production of freight wagons was closed as planned in 1893 when Henri Fayol found an interested buyer[14] who benefited from favourable sales terms and an expedited settlement as the company was pressed to sell.

In 1894 Henri Fayol continued to invest in Fourchambault with 0.3MF to repair water heaters and acquire a new rolling mill, but sales fell over the period and the factory made a loss of 0.1MF and another 0.3MF was planned in losses and investments[15] for the following year. Henri Fayol continued to argue that from an accounting point of view Fourchambault contributed to overhead costs, paid interest on its fixed assets and allowed the mines to make a profit of 0.2MF.

Business did not improve and in June 1896 the board decided to stop taking orders for the factory and close it as soon as the current orders were satisfied which allowed the factory to operate until August 1897. Fayol's closure plan involved progressively abandoning production by first lowering output to 10,000 tons per year and worker levels from 750 to 400. Of the 350 dismissed workers, 250 also laboured elsewhere on farms, a pension was planned for senior workers and the remaining workers were transferred to other forges in the region.[16]

Business picked up again in 1897 with several new orders including a large profitable order from the army in August that allowed the factory to make only a small loss of 0.1MF in 1896–7. Henri Fayol decided against closing the factory and in his 1898 plan he even budgeted for an annual profit of 100,000F. However in March 1898 another expert commissioned by Fayol concluded that the factory had no future due to competition from factories in the east of France.

Salesmen continued to canvass customers and signed a large order for rails in August 1898 for a local 50km railway in the Nièvre (from Corbigny to Alligny). Although the company's cost price was generally too high for such products, it benefited in this case from a geographical advantage. To fulfil the order a new 20 ton Martin furnace had to be built at a cost of 140,000F that could be financed from the profits on the order alone. The order was approved by the board in 1898 despite hesitations by one of its members.[17] In the end, it was poor business for the company: deadlines were very tight, the furnace took longer than expected to work and the order finally had to be sold to another company so that the railway would be operational in 1901. Henri Fayol fired the factory director who had made technical errors, yet some believe that Fayol himself erred in accepting the order,[18] although at the time experts concluded that the factory's closure was due to the unpredictable 40 per cent price collapse of 1901. The factory made losses of 0.5MF in 1899–1900 and closure was inevitable after a new expertise in July 1901. When the factory closed on 30 September 1901[19] some of its machines were transferred to the Montluçon, Imphy and Decazeville factories and the remainder of the Fourchambault site was sold.

Henri Fayol spent a great deal of time working on the Fourchambault factory, continuously looking for ways to keep the site operating even as geographical conditions became unfavourable with the exhaustion of local iron ore deposits and competition in the Parisian market from the Lorraine factories. He used his written plans to justify investing in a new plant which allowed the factory to continue operating for another 13 years and the coal mines to progressively adapt to the loss of this major internal customer. Such a chaotic planning practice did not really set a good example for others to follow.

The Plans for Decazeville from 1892 to 1908

Having failed to merge his factories with those of Châtillon-Commentry, Henri Fayol began looking for a partner to supply him with cheaper pig iron than that already produced at Montluçon. He began negotiations with the Société de Montataire, owner of a factory at Frouard to the north of Nancy. The Société de l'Aveyron in Decazeville was also contacted on the advice of Alexandre Pourcel in his role of consultant-engineer. Both negotiations were conducted in parallel and while Montataire did propose a merger, Henri Fayol considered that Aveyron, although in difficulty at the time, would be a better partner. The board approved the merger at the end of 1891, valuing the Société de l'Aveyron at 3.25 MF which was equivalent to one third the value of Commentry-Fourchambault. Fayol planned an additional 3MF in investments.[20]

Officially the companies were not merged until July 1892 after unsuccessful legal action by several shareholders to prevent it. Fayol had already taken control of the Decazeville mines and factories four months earlier in March, replacing directors with engineers from Commentry and Fourchambault and beginning an in-depth study of the situation. The reserves of coal were substantial and were estimated at the equivalent of one hundred years of production. Furthermore, a large part of the deposits could be extracted using strip-mining techniques which could lower the per ton cost price. The ironworks were an essential outlet for Decazeville's coal as local markets were limited, but the production costs of pig iron and steel were both high due to the obsolete or rundown plant and equipment.

Fayol presented his plan for Decazeville towards the end of 1892[21] which involved investing in the site using all of Commentry-Fourchambault's available financial resources in order to lower cost prices by around 10 per cent over five years. After three meetings the board accepted the plan on 15 December 1892 and acknowledged the risk that the company may not be able to completely finance it.[22]

In 1893, after studying a large number of possible strategies, Commentry-Fourchambault had a plan to completely renovate the Decazeville site over a five-year period. The investments were not immediately profitable due to a downturn in the iron and steel industry that lasted until the end of 1895 but sales recovered at all factories in 1896 and vindicated Fayol's plan as the company's new plant and equipment allowed it to profitably fulfil a growing number of orders. The company made a gross profit of 2.5MF in 1891–1892, 3.6MF in 1897–1898, and 5.1MF and 6.6MF in the two following years.[23]

Following his success at Decazeville, Fayol immediately envisaged new investments to double the factory's capacity and he presented his forecasts for the company's different sites at several board meetings from early 1898: it was his second ten-year plan. After a first five-year phase 'metallurgical production will increase from 23,000 to 53,000 tons per year' requiring an additional 100,000 tons of coal before a third phase with a 100,000 ton production target for steel products. The necessary investment of 2.7MF in the factory and 3.2MF in the mine could be self-financed over four years and Decazeville's profits were expected to increase over five years from 0.6MF in 1897–8 to 1.3MF, equally shared between the factory and the mine.[24]

The board was not used to such prospective reasoning and debated the plan over six sessions before accepting it. Henri Fayol explained that 'the incertitude that hangs over the future does not exempt one from planning, having goals, a line of conduct ... The realized will no doubt be considerably distant from these previsions. The plan will need to be modified accordingly'.[25]

Henri Fayol modified his plan the following year and presented new five-year forecasts involving additional investments (1MF) that would increase profits over the five years by 1.7MF.[26] He used the healthy profits on current orders to accelerate the renovation of plant and equipment.

He again modified the plan in early 1900 when he presented a new ten-year plan with an accelerated rate of investment and improved financial results.[27] The 1898 plan budgeted an investment of 1.739MF at the Decazeville mines and 1.6MF in the factories for the three-year period of 1899–1902. In a plan for the same three-year period dated 1 January 1900, investment levels were increased by 40 per cent to 2.9MF and 2.2MF respectively.[28] He planned to increase production capacity at Decazeville over three years to 50,000 tons of iron and steel products and 0.7M tons of coal. Investment levels were high to renovate tooling at 4MF the first year, 3.5 the second and 0.9 the third year and planned investments in the mines were 0.2MF per year. These new investments were readily agreed to by the board as they were financed by 3.6MF in profits.

In late 1900, metallurgical orders, prices and production levels fell before later recovering in 1902, but throughout this difficult period Henri Fayol did not modify his plans. In 1904 he again wanted to invest in the Decazeville site and in January he presented the board with a strategic note explaining that the cost price could be lowered by increasing the factory's capacity to 35,000 tons per year without a major investment: 'The expected increase in production can be achieved without any new major installations and will be prudently pursued taking into account the difficulties for sales and workers'. Production rose as planned to 36,000 tons per year in 1905.[29]

In 1905 a new project to increase production was proposed involving the construction of a Thomas steel plant that was more modern than the Martin furnace and offered a lower cost price but required a minimum production flow of 60,000 tons per year and an investment of 5MF. The board was hesitant as the previous year's profits had not been sufficient to self-finance the project and because the total cost was revised after further studies to 6.5MF. The board debated the project at length from December 1905 to March 1906 and the project was eventually adopted and financed by a 3MF loan and the issue of 6,000 shares, authorized by the annual general meeting on 6 April 1906. Constructors were contacted in May 1906 and orders were passed the following June.[30]

Starting in 1892 in Decazeville, Henri Fayol worked with a planning mindset. He drew up his first plan for the period 1893 to 1898 and then a new five-year plan in 1898 that he modified each year to increase investments and accelerate growth in production. After high initial investments at Decazeville to modernize plant and equipment, Fayol planned increases in production volumes to lower production costs through economies of scale. Henri Fayol's approach to planning involved regularly updating his plans.

The Other Sites

Planning was also used for the other sites but to a lesser extent as Commentry and Montvicq were to cease operations, Brassac required major investments to continue working, Imphy was following a unique path but its future was difficult to foresee and Montluçon continued to disappoint despite showing promise of a turnaround.

Henri Fayol turned his attention to two other sites: the Joudreville iron mine in 1904 and the Pont-à-Vendin steel factory in 1911. Both involved high capital investments that would require the company to seek external funding and a joint venture with other companies.

The 1898 and 1908 Plans

The main plans presented to the board in 1898 and 1908 have been conserved in the archives. The first plan is sixty-four handwritten pages long and the second is 146 typed pages long. Their structure is similar, first presenting the past and then production forecasts by site, profits and the overall financial situation.

The 1898 plan begins with a discussion of how the company planned to maintain future dividend levels, which was a very important subject for shareholders.

A retrospective of the company's activity then accounts for 10 per cent of the document. In 1908, Henri Fayol increased the length of this historical section to account for 30 per cent of the text and he later reused the text in his presentation to the Société de l'Industrie Minérale[31] and in the third part of *IGM*.[32]

The second part of the plan is industrial and outlines the production forecasts and the necessary investments, site by site. In 1898 forecasts were given for the coming five years and accounted for 45 per cent of the document whereas in 1908 ten-year forecasts only occupied 25 per cent of the plan but were more precise than those of 1898, indicating tonnages, investments, cost prices, sales prices and profits. Only the first five years were described in detail however and the second five-year period was only approximately outlined.

The third part of the plan described the global financial situation of the company. In 1898, this section occupied 35 per cent of the document and detailed the investments financed by headquarters, employee savings, contingency funds and capital depreciations. These aspects were more detailed in 1908 and they again took up one third of the total text. Additional items were included in 1908 such as real estate, working capital, bonds, depositor's account, reserves and provisions, profits and dividends. Henri Fayol then highlighted how fixed capital had been halved and production doubled compared to 1856.[33] The expected profit for 1907–1908 was 3.3MF with a dividend of 60F per share and ten years later these numbers were expected to increase to 5.4MF (+63 per cent) and 100F (+67 per cent) respectively for an average growth of 6 per cent per year.

The final section of both the 1898 and the 1908 plans contain tables of key statistics representing 10 per cent of the total number of pages.

Industrial forecasts were central to both of these plans with technology the starting point for the plan at the Decazeville factory, with investments in a new plant and equipment planned to reduce cost prices and allow the factory compete with factories from the east of France. Fayol used the production costs of blast furnaces from the east as target costs for iron at the factory. Investments were expected to lower production costs over the following five years by 19 per cent for pig iron, 25 per cent for commercial irons, 30 per cent for beams and 40 per cent for sheet metal. 'The cost prices were fixed by taking into account likely sales prices of coals and coke as well as the likely cost price of ores'.[34]

In order to reduce cost price, the annual production capacity of iron and steel had to be increased from 36,000 to 70,000 tons in five years and this was to be made possible through the completion of the Thomas steelworks in 1909. Production was budgeted to increase by 15 per cent per year on average and the various investments necessary and their cost were included in the plan for each year they were to be made.[35] These technological forecasts led to two fundamental aspects of the plan; the yearly production cost estimates and the expected investments. These forecasts were made by local management with the support of the Paris steel department and consultant engineers.

Sales price forecasts were then calculated to take into account 'previous contracts signed with both suppliers and customers, probable fluctuations in materials prices, labour prices and all the influences that can intervene'.[36] Sales prices were globally expected to fall by 13 per cent to 17 per cent over three or four years before stabilizing.

Forecast annual profits for each site were calculated based on tonnages, cost prices and sales prices. At the Decazeville collieries for example, production was expected to rise by 2 per cent per year from 480,000 to 600,000 tons over the ten-year planning period by boring new wells at a cost of around 0.4MF per year over four years. Based on forecast sales prices, the mine's profits were expected to fall from 1.4MF to 1MF over two years before increasing to 1.5MF.

Expected profits per site were then consolidated and totalled 4MF in 1908 and 6MF ten years later, representing an annual growth rate of 4 per cent per year despite the planned closure of the Commentry and Montvicq mines in 1911.[37] The profit at the Decazeville factory was expected to double in value over the period, increasing from 30 to 40 per cent of total profits. The Joudreville iron mine was expected to account for 17 per cent of total profits.

The profits of 4MF for the first year of the 1908 plan were to be used for depreciations (0.3MF), dividends (1.8MF), the remuneration of the board and other personnel (0.3MF) and to fund reserves (1.5MF). Ten years later, the profit of 6MF was to be allocated to depreciations (0.8MF), dividends (1.8MF), remunerations (0.3MF) and unspecified allocations (3.1MF). Henri Fayol considered using one third of gross profit for new works, one third for the dividend that could increase from 60F to 100F and one third to buy back shares.[38] As was now customary, Henri Fayol modified this plan at the start of 1911.[39]

The content of these two plans differs from the plan Henri Fayol outlined in *IGM* that had six chapters: 'technical section', 'commercial section', 'financial section', accounting, security and management.[40] He began both the 1898 and the 1908 plans with a short presentation of the company's history before following the order of chapters he outlined in *IGM*, notably a technical section, commercial aspects and then a finance and accounting section that concluded with expected yearly profits. The sections relating to security and management, however, were not included. His practice differed from the theory he outlined a little later in 1916.

Henri Fayol actively used planning during his tenure as managing director of Commentry-Fourchambault et Decazeville. He sought to rationalize activities by centralizing iron and steel production on one site, attempting to merge his factories with those of the neighbouring Châtillon-Commentry Company. When the latter refused, he began centralizing the company's activities and sought out a lower cost pig iron producer. After studying two new merger projects with the aid of external advisors, he chose to merge Commentry-Fourchambault with Decazeville, and despite the high initial investment the merger was profitable. Planning was the mainstay for all of Henri Fayol's business decisions and a number of general features emerge from these diverse plans.

The Features of Henri Fayol's Planning Activity

Henri Fayol took a long-term view of his company and his business. He took planned investments in new technologies as a starting point and then calculated the financial consequences for prices and profits. His main objective was to lower cost prices, as he knew that sales prices were determined by the market and were mainly influenced by his competitors from the east and British imports.

He also took constraints into account. The first was that of the market and the need to find customers for the company's products, the second was the workforce that had to be attracted to the site when it was growing and in need of labour, and the third constraint was financial, with the board preferring to self-finance investments– although Fayol did increasingly use external funding over time.

Despite all the care Henri Fayol took in constructing his plans, reality was of course never exactly as expected. When he was confronted with an unanticipated situation, Henri Fayol investigated the causes of forecasting errors and planned anew for the future. His use of 'rolling plans' meant that his planning did not stop him from seizing opportunities as they arose, including acquisitions and ventures with other companies in the industry. One unexpected development was the strategy of special steels developed at Imphy that was later acknowledged and defended by Henri Fayol. This emergent strategy was not opposed on the grounds that it was not planned for and turned out to be very successful.

Building a Plan from Bottom-Up

Fayol involved the company's engineers, salesmen and managers at different sites in the planning process, all the while verifying their work and motivating them to contribute. For example, on 17 July 1897 the manager in charge of coordinating mines in Paris, Arthur Courtin asked the director of Decazeville to propose a five-year plan. In January 1898 Courtin asked that the plan be modified by changing the transfer prices, a decision that was under the authority of the managing director.[41] Another example was the plan presented in 1905 by the director of the Decazeville factory for the Thomas steel works. He was assisted by the company's steel department and by consultant engineers. By involving managers in the planning process, Fayol ensured that they would carefully study all the technical possibilities of their proposed actions which would then make executing the plan easier.

Sales forecasts were similarly established in consultation with salesmen. For example, when the Thomas steel works was forecast to increase production by 21,000 tons per year the director of the factory estimated sales as follows: 7,000 tons of beams would be sold by the Beam Trading Syndicate; 6,000 tons of half-finished goods would be shipped to Imphy, Marseilles and the Loire; 8,000 tons of commercial iron would be sold in the Midi region. Decazeville could have covered 70 per cent of demand in the three closest administrative departments thanks to lower transport costs, although in practice it only covered 17 per cent of the zone with 8,000 tons sold. Lower production costs allowed the company to lower its sales prices and to sell further afield. It was estimated that a decrease in 5F to 10F per ton could double the planned sales volumes.[42]

Engineers prepared the technical part of the plan and the salesmen prepared the commercial aspects. Executive management only gave the main orientations, such as the investment in the Thomas steel works at Decazeville.

Cost Prices

Henri Fayol built his plans around investments in plant that were made to lower cost prices. This was the main concern in the Fourchambault, Montluçon and Decazeville factories. In the 1908 plan, the planned reduction in cost price was 18 per cent for pig iron, 25 per cent for steels and 41 per cent for sheet metal.[43] These reductions were expected to improve margins, and in turn increase the company's catchment area.

Financing Constraints

The Commentry-Fourchambault et Decazeville shareholders always preferred self-financing. Between 1888 and 1910, 22MF were paid out to shareholders and 37MF were reinvested.[44] Loans and capital increases were only accepted to finance the Thomas converter in 1906 and the Pont-à-Vendin factory in 1912.

The board of directors hesitated before financing the Thomas converter, advancing commercial and operating difficulties to argue for a more progressive approach.

> Faced with such high total outlays ... several members are of the opinion to proceed gradually, if it is possible, either by beginning with the construction of two blast furnaces for example, or by first installing a retort and only proceeding when we are satisfied with what has already done been.

Henri Fayol refused these arrangements: 'The managing director does not believe it would be possible to proceed by a step smaller than that consisting of increasing production from 37,000 to 60,000 tons'.[45]

An Authorization to Invest

While the plan was not officially a multi-year authorization to invest, in reality it did look like one. Each year, planned investments were validated by the board of directors depending on their expected impact on profits. By using five-year and ten-year plans, Henri Fayol made annual investments globally coherent and anticipated the board's annual decisions. 'A member asks if the managing director considers the approval of his plan to be a line of credit', Henri Fayol 'replied that the approval given by the board to his general plan for extraordinary works does not represent for him a line of credit. Before execution definitive studies must be undertaken and the credits requested'.[46]

In practice, Fayol used his plans to influence investment decisions over a period of several years. Once a large project had begun, it was difficult not to follow the plan and to finance any additional unforeseen outlays. When it validated a plan, the board committed the company both to budgeted investments and any variances.

Executing the Plans

Henri Fayol's plans were never executed exactly as written mainly because of new opportunities, changes in the economic context and commercial or technical difficulties. His plans were generally optimistic and his realizations were less favourable, yet he always justified his actions ex post by comparing results to plans. Henri Fayol explained that a plan's usefulness was in 'the attention demanded for executing the plan, the indispensable comparison between predicted and actual facts, the recognition of mistakes made and successes attained, the search for means of repeating the one and avoiding the other'.[47] A plan is a tool for evaluating action.

For example, in 1896 when the board was discussing the situation of the older factories, Henri Fayol demonstrated that the profits and investments of these sites over his seven-year tenure as managing director vindicated his planning. The Fourchambault losses and investments were 125,000F per year on average, below the maximum expected loss of 200,000F and the profits at Imphy covered both losses and outlays meaning that, on the whole, the company did not lose any money.[48] Ex post results justified ex ante plans.

Henri Fayol was not attached to his forecasts and he readily adjusted plans as circumstances changed. In 1897 he admitted to the board that investments at the Decazeville mine would exceed previsions by 400,000F, and decided to fund this overrun by increasing cost prices over the following three years.[49]

The company's greatest planning difficulties were caused by the delays in stalling and operating the Decazeville Thomas converter. While early delays were caused by the supplier, there were a number of later operating incidents that resulted in profits falling by 1MF in 1908–9 and remaining below forecasts by 1.5MF over the two following years.[50] The converter began operating in March 1908, but the necessary technical environment, including trained workers, was lacking. By April 1910 the mixer still did not work satisfactorily and in January 1911 the mill broke and remained idle for two months. These operating delays were caused by workers' lack of experience with the new machines and cost the company dearly in lost production.

Rolling Plans

Henri Fayol regularly modified his own forecasts and the rolling nature of plans appears to have been institutionalized. He remarked that 'Nothing prevents the modification of the plan when the circumstances require it'.[51] Henri Fayol asked mine and factory directors to include forecasts for the coming year with their annual report. These new forecasts were not always in keeping with the decennial plan but they were necessary to authorize investment credits.

For example, in 1900 he revised the plan set in 1898 by inflating investments. At the time, no one objected to the misleading nature of these adjustments, and yet when a plan was modified sunk costs were forgotten and the profitability of new investments was mathematically amplified.

Opportunities

Henri Fayol considered planning as a form of preparation for seizing opportunities. He wrote in *IGM* that 'the plan should be flexible enough to bend before such adjustments, as it is considered well to introduce, whether from pressure of circumstances or from any other reason'.[52] When he presented his plan in 1908, Fayol emphasized the importance of maintaining cash reserves, to be prepared for any opportunity:

> The available funds will increase over the next decade. It is a great strength that we must pay attention to. Our company with its long life ... must encounter from time to time favourable occasions that only those with reserves and available cash flows can enjoy.[53]

The five major projects that were presented in the previous chapter were opportunities that disrupted existing plans and required new planning.

Emergent Strategy at Imphy

The Imphy steel factory was as poorly located as its Fourchambault neighbour, far from quality iron ores, coal and its main industrial markets. Yet instead of failing, the factory was profitable and is still operating at the start of the twenty-first century. Henri Fayol encouraged it to pursue a strategy specializing in springs and pushed the factory to develop its know-how in nickel steels.

In 1892 he acknowledged the specificity of the Imphy factory. 'Several manufacturing successes lend us to believe that this factory can become prosperous again without great outlays in new tooling'. 'Imphy has shown remarkable vitality: new and difficult manufactures have been successful there. We are making serious profits there'. From then on Henri Fayol defended annual investment requests by Imphy's engineers of around 100,000F per year.[54]

The Imphy factory manufactured a variety of products and was very reactive in the way it managed the fluctuations in workloads caused by the irregular flow of orders. Henri Fayol protected the highly skilled factory workers as he understood the factory's niche strategy in special steels. While he was not its architect, he quickly understood the strategy and made all the necessary investments.

Conclusion

Henri Fayol used plans as a means of dialogue to convince the board of directors. He never calculated profitability ratios, and simply provided expected investment and profit levels.

Planning had already been used in a rudimentary manner at Decazeville long before Henri Fayol became managing director. In 1829, a financial forecast was used to justify the construction of the Decazeville factory to its future shareholders, representing an investment of 3.6MF for an annual profit of 0.7MF. The mine would produce 120,000 tons of coal that would be used to make coke for the blast furnaces that would produce 14,000 tons of pig iron, to be transformed into 10,000 tons of iron. Profit was calculated as the difference between the market price and the cost price.[55] However, this plan was wrong as 170,000 tons of coal would have been necessary for these production levels. This analysis is more an industrial profitability analysis intended to inform an investment decision rather than an industrial plan. It does not appear to have been adjusted to take into account actual operating data or other later investments, and the quantitative analysis was not transformed into a temporal plan with deadlines. The inaccuracy of these forecasts can be seen when we compare them to production numbers. In 1832, 30 tons of coal were consumed to produce 1 ton of iron – twice as much as planned, and only 3,500 tons of iron were produced. It was not until 1846 that the original plan was realized and surpassed when iron production levels reached 15,000 tons, generating 1.9MF of profit for double the capital investment at 7.2MF. Henri Fayol's plans were much more precise and closer to actual results.

We can discern a strategy of longevity in these plans. By constantly looking to the future, Henri Fayol promoted the idea of a lasting enterprise, renewing her assets as those on hand eroded. The profits made at the Commentry mine financed investments in the company's future, reinforcing its position in the mining and steel industries that would continue growing for another half century. Commentry-Fourchambault et Decazeville could have chosen another industrial strategy such as that of Schneider at Le Creusot, who invested downstream in the production of canons and locomotives.

Henri Fayol never spoke to his board about strategy and he refused to use this military word that he considered to be a failure. The military doctrine in the early twentieth century was one of movement and was successfully applied by the German army when it penetrated 350 kilometres into France during the month of August 1914. For the remainder of the War the dominant strategy was trench warfare and all military movement and offensives failed. Henri Fayol believed that the military concept of strategy could not be used in business and saw more promise in the transfer of management practices to the conduct of military operations.[56]

The planning process was seen by Henri Fayol to have a number of benefits, such as requiring managers to work together, highlighting management errors and ensuring the continuity of action[57] and yet there was no planning department at Commentry-Fourchambault et Decazeville. Plans were constructed based on industrial investments that determined cost prices, sales analyses to estimate sales prices and then the difference between the two allowed for the calculation of expected profits, and the means available for financing investments. The planning practice at Commentry-Fourchambault et Decazeville was more complex than that described in *IGM*, but was similar in form, built around tables of expected future values for a number of business critical variables and a rich accompanying commentary to justify the choices made. Compared to modern plans, the only part missing was a consideration of alternative hypotheses to take into account events that were outside the company's control.

4 ORGANIZING: THE MANAGEMENT OF MANAGERS

Organizing is the second management principle identified by Henri Fayol. He described it in *IGM* as: 'To organize a business is to provide it with everything useful to its functioning: raw materials, tools, capital, personnel'.[1] In practice he favoured formal structuring and the management of managers: organizational charts, roles for each service, recruitment, training and promotion. He attached great importance to these aspects, and largely developed them. In 1913 he praised the encouraging results of his management approach:

> At a time when I feel that the lessening of my strength will soon no longer permit me to stay at the helm, it's pleasant for me to see and tell you that the personnel from the top to the bottom of the ladder is today much superior to that it has been for a long time. With such personnel the company can confidently look to the future.[2]

Henri Fayol recommended drawing up organizational charts to describe the hierarchy of responsibilities, the chain of command and the functions of aid and advisors to managers that lay outside the hierarchy. He outlined a theory of organizational charts where the number of hierarchical levels determined the number of employees at the base of a company. A foreman can manage fifteen workers and all other heads have four subordinates: with six hierarchical levels, 15,360 workers can be managed.[3] In this hypothetical case that Fayol presented in *IGM*, there are 1,024 foremen, 256 divisional engineers, 64 chief engineers, four site directors and one managing director. In this chapter we will examine how close his theory was to practice in the Commentry-Fourchambault et Decazeville Company's factories and mines, where there were around 10,000 employees.

The management of managers at Commentry-Fourchambault et Decazeville followed classical principles, including a share in profits that doubled fixed salaries, recruitment criteria based on the qualities of a good leader,[4] the promotion of engineers that met expectations and the dismissal of those who poorly carried out their work. During his career, Henri Fayol made some bad recruitment decisions while other recruits remained loyal to him throughout their career and they were rewarded for it.

The Senior Management Hierarchy

Henri Fayol conceived an enterprise as a hierarchy with the scalar chain as the ninth principle of management[5] and with the body corporate[6] represented as a hierarchical structure in organizational charts.[7] He provided three theoretical organizational charts in *IGM*: one for a factory, a second for a colliery and a third for a large industrial undertaking that shows the structure from the shareholders down to the workers. This technique gives a global view of the personnel. Other examples are announced to appear in the third part of *IGM*, but they are missing.[8] In Fayol's theory, the organizational chart does not include everything about the personnel, as other information such as appreciations of the worth of staff, their remit and their deputies should be provided in additional documents.[9] As managing director, Henri Fayol decided on the structure of the company and it was the first of his powers that was vested in him by the board upon his nomination: 'appoint or revoke all employees or agents, determine their remit, fix their wages and bonuses'.[10]

Henri Fayol first presented a chart of the company's management structure that included the directors and main heads of the different sites to the board in 1892.[11] While the organizational chart only concerns senior management, we can reconstruct the complete chart down to the worker level using archives from the Commentry mine. The chart is composed of one simple hierarchical line of authority between foremen and miners for the command of production teams, and a second hierarchical structure of non-productive services that supports and is in constant direct contact with the first, without going through their mutual superior. This second structure is much less clear than the first and inexplicably changed over time. This actual organizational chart is quite different to Fayol's theory of where the span of control was fixed.[12]

Fayol appears twice in the organizational chart, both as managing director and head of the factory department. While he was not a specialist in metallurgy, he was aided by two external consultants, Georges Bresson and Alexandre Pourcel, who do not appear in the table. The Paris headquarters was directly accountable to general management and had no hierarchical authority over the site directors. For Fayol it was his 'staff', while for Frederick Taylor[13]it would have been a functional department. One of the members of the Paris office, Arthur Courtin had a hierarchical relationship with the three collieries and also appeared twice in the organizational chart. There was a false symmetry between the hierarchy of the mines and the factories: the collieries were delegated to a Parisian director whereas the factories were directly overseen by Henri Fayol and a director at Fourchambault.

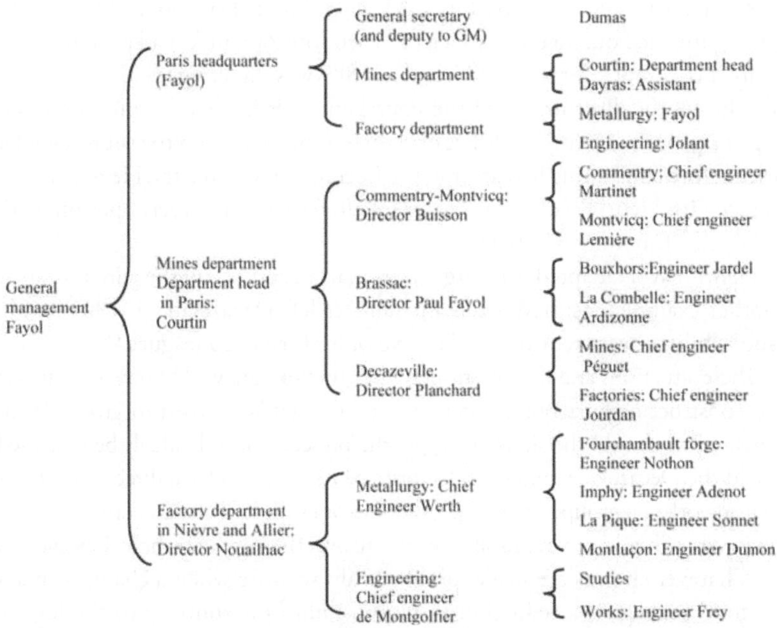

Figure 4.1: The organizational chart of Commentry-Fourchambault in 1892.[14]

The 1892 organizational chart looks like table IX in *IGM*.[15] We note that the Decazeville factory had no line relationship to the factory department. A local director was responsible for the mine and the factory that were both run by chief engineers (Péguet et Jourdan). The director was a miner (Planchard) who received his orders from the mines department in Paris (Courtin) and in 1892 Courtin also had to pass on the orders from the Metallurgy department that came from Fayol himself.

This hierarchical line was not clear and as the financial results of the Decazeville factory were disappointing, Fayol changed it in 1904:

> The managing director was driven to divide up the Decazeville department by the absolute metallurgical incompetency of the previous director and by the difficulty of finding a man possessing the competency, the experience and the strength necessary to head at the same time two industries so different and so complicated.[16]

On 17 November 1904 he appointed Michel Morel director of the Decazeville factory and placed him directly under the authority of the Paris office. Morel had previously replaced Jacques Adenot at the head of the Imphy factory in 1903. Clavelly Péguet, who had previously headed both the Decazeville factory and mine was obviously not pleased with his diminished responsibilities and resigned two months later with a payout of six-months' salary.[17]

A similar problem occurred in 1891 when Henri Fayol looked to recruit a director for the Fourchambault factory. Theodore Zyromski had been recruited to direct the Imphy forge in 1888, and in 1889 was directing the three factories. After losing the directorship of the Fourchambault factory, Zyromski resigned despite a promised pay rise. He left on a three-month mission to visit foreign factories before continuing his career in the Lorraine steel industry. He remained in contact with Henri Fayol and was later solicited to give an expert opinion on the Joudreville iron mine in 1910.[18]

Henri Fayol adapted the organizational structure to the circumstances. Another example occurred when an engineer left Decazeville in 1901 and his responsibilities were redistributed to two of his former colleagues.[19]

These situations and the questioning they provoke are well known to managers who construct organizational charts: what rule should be used to group departments? How should the skills or simply the presence of individuals be best used? Should the Decazeville mines and factories be headed by a local director or should the ironworks be grouped with the other factories under Parisian authority, as the mines were? Should geographical logic prevail over the logic of technical specialities?

Whatever choices are made, problems always arise when a change is made. For good managers, a reduction in responsibilities is contrary to the logic of promotion. Such situations highlight the limits of the hierarchy as a tool for organizing: When the structure is stable, competent individuals can exercise growing responsibilities, but when the structure is modified, this logic of progression may appear to be questioned.

Fayol's hierarchical vision of the firm is also apparent in the ranks he gave to engineers. Junior engineers at the bottom of the ladder performed the same work as engineers, but without formal qualifications. They were promoted to the grade of engineer if their work met expectations. Engineers, who mainly graduated from the Ecole des Mines de Saint Etienne[20] (hereafter ENSMSE), were one rank above junior engineers and were appointed divisional engineers once they had gained sufficient experience, and possibly to chief engineer several years later. Chief engineers could then be promoted to the position of director.

These promotions could cause problems if they concerned some employees and not others. In 1896 Jacques Adenot was named director of the Imphy factory where he was aided by two engineers, Pierre Girin and Louis Dauphin. Girin had a brilliant career, ensuring the interim directorship of Decazeville in 1899, the directorship of the Fourchambault factory in 1901 and the responsibility of the company's factory department in Paris in 1902. When Adenot had to report to his former subordinate he resigned in 1903 at the age of forty-one.[21]

The hierarchical structure renders a manager's career visible. They tend to move towards the summit of the structure, although not all managers are promoted and those who remain immobile while their colleagues rise rapidly may feel resentment and resign. The dynamics of management promotions within a hierarchy is often a source of tension.

The Structure of Mines in 1888

Henri Fayol most probably built his first organizational chart in 1888 for the Commentry and Montvicq collieries that were under his responsibility. He defined a formal structure by writing job descriptions for twenty different functions, from the director down to the concierge. For each function he identified its domain of responsibility, hierarchical subordination, deputation, activities and the requisite field visits and report writing.[22] He did not draw up the organizational chart but we can do so today based on this information. Based on the work of Henry Minzberg,[23] we can assign two thirds of personnel to operational functions and one third to support services that assist operations. The resulting chart is presented in figures 4.2 and 4.3 below.

Operational functions were structured around three levels of engineer: a director, a chief engineer, a divisional engineer and two levels of foremen. The three divisional engineers at Commentry and the two at Montvicq all managed similar organizational structures. Deputation was assured by a subordinate marked with an asterisk on the chart, with the divisional engineers substituting for one another.

The Commentry mine employed three divisional engineers and around 1,500 workers, including 900 working underground and the Montvicq mine employed two engineers and 800 workers, of which 500 worked underground. Engineers were responsible for 250 to 300 miners working underground who reported to a foreman, and two assistants who each were directly responsible for 16 teams of four coal-getters. We will henceforth use the term 'production group' to refer to such groups of miners even though this term was never used in corporate documents. Here is the composition of a production group of around 190 miners, of which 180 are underground: 128 hewers in thirty-two teams of four, twenty-two timberers for the galleries, twelve road-menders, rail-clearers and shovel men, seven carriage valets, two deck men, eight brake men, one groom. There were an additional ten people on the surface: two drivers, two boiler men, two shaft men, one delivery boy and three other people. Transport personnel were accountable to a production team as they could block the extraction of coal from the pit.[24]

When Henri Fayol began his career in 1861, the Commentry mine employed 2,000 workers. Four engineers commanded 400 workers, each through the intermediary of three foremen. Each foreman oversaw a group of around 135 workers.[26] The rest of the personnel worked in auxiliary services, workshops, railways, accounting and so forth. Thirty years later the organization of the mine had changed little, apart from its management structure, as Henri Fayol had reinforced the intermediate hierarchy by providing engineers with six foremen, two chief miners and four deputy chief miners who more closely and continuously supervised workers.

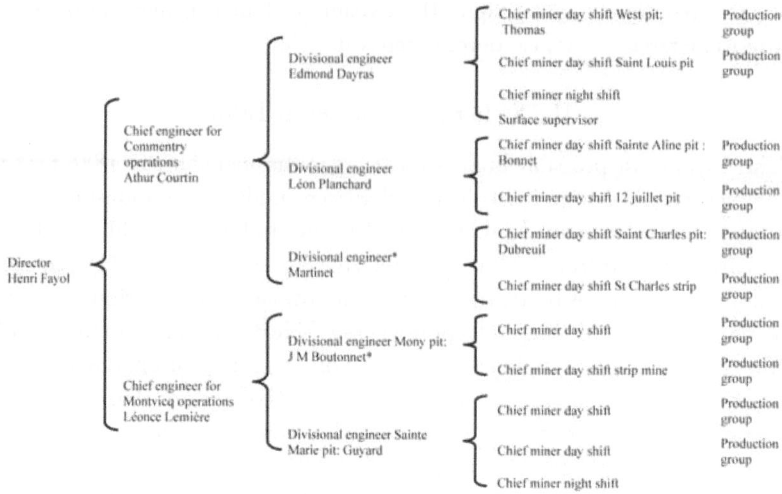

Figure 4.2: The operational structure at Commentry and Montvicq in 1888.[25]

This structure differed from the example published by Henri Fayol in *IGM* in 1916, where a foreman commanded only fifteen workers and could expand his control through four subordinates.[27] The deputy chief miner at Commentry commanded fifty hewers in twelve teams, although he most probably dealt with one of the members of each team that he considered the most responsible even though all the miners were of equal hierarchical rank.

The three engineers at Commentry commanded six production groups including five groups of 180 miners for a total of 900 miners working underground, and one group of 180 strip-miners working on the surface. The company employed around 700 workers on the surface including: 240 in the production teams, 115 working for the private railway, 140 male, female and child labourers that sorted the coal, 105 that carbonized and agglomerated the coke and briquettes, and another 100 that worked in workshops building and maintaining locomotives, wagons and mining machinery.

The Commentry mine also employed a number of other professions, including six engineers, twenty foremen, eight department heads, five salesmen and twenty-five employees of various occupations including bookkeepers. The employees worked in various support departments that aided production. The organizational chart below shows how these employees were organized hierarchically. The director had eight employees directly under his authority, including the heads of two large departments with more than one hundred employees each. The head accountant was responsible for the accounting department but also for sorting, washing and coking, and the railway. The mechanical engineer directed the studies department with three drafts men and two assistants and the workshops that were each specialized in stem boilers, ironwork (forging, boiler making and fitting) and woodwork (joinery, wheelwrighting, carpentry, cart repair, saw milling).

The six other employees including the head surveyor, the station agent, the storehouse, the sales department and the two guards reporting directly to the director. These departments also worked for the Montvicq mine, except for the sorting department and the stables that employed 300 people at the Montvicq site.

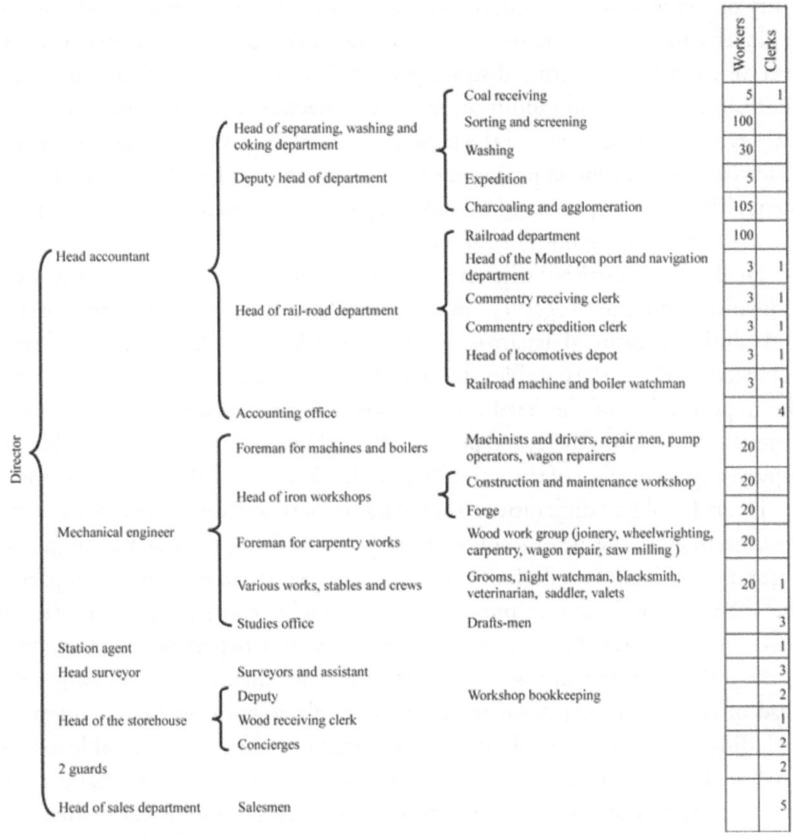

Figure 4.3: The structure of support service at Commentry around 1890.[28]

The 1888 job descriptions indicate that some people were not employed by the mine, including a doctor that visited on call, the two nuns that ran the medical and pharmaceutical service, an external veterinarian that cared for the horses, the port attendant that was employed by the canals but reported to Henri Fayol on boat traffic to Paris, the Lyon association of steam boat owners that worked for several companies including the company once a year, and the bargemen that were contracted for transport along the Berry canal.

The organizational chart would have been difficult to draw up as the hierarchical dependence of all those in contact with material flows was not explicit. For example, the station agent received orders from the sales department and ordered coal from the head of deliveries. Given the difficulty of choosing between these two possible superiors, this person reported directly to the director. Similarly, the saddler reported to the storehouse, but worked for the stables following workshop hours. Such double reporting appears even more explicitly in some cases: 'The machinery foreman, although placed under the responsibility of the workshop engineer, also receives instructions from the divisional engineer and the chief engineer for machine operations' and maintenance. 'As everyone's orders concern a distinct part of their department, there can be no confusion'. Thus for all modifications to the machines, the machine specialists only gave a point of view and the final decision belonged to line management.[29] Likewise, the Montluçon port agent reported to the head of the railway department although he represented the sales department for deliveries from the port. He was answerable to both hierarchies.

Dual authority existed whenever a technical specialist was infrequently used. It involved grouping together specialists to keep them occupied by working with all the operational departments. For example, while the blacksmith farrier belonged to the surface stables division, he also shoed horses in the pit under the responsibility of the head miner of each section. Some supervisory tasks were also undertaken by several people. 'The coking supervisor is responsible for supervising the surface of the Forêt shaft in the same way as the shaft inspector'.[30]

Henri Fayol had difficulties structuring support services as we can see in his decision to make the 'head accountant' responsible for separating, washing, coking and the railway. Fayol's choices varied over time, as can be seen by comparing the 1888 document to that published twenty-eight years later as Table VIII in *IGM*.[31] In this latter chart, the head of the preparation department and the head of the railway department both report to the chief engineer and no longer the head of the accounting department, who is only responsible for accountants, including those in the workshops. The site director is directly responsible for the head of the maintenance and construction workshop, the commercial department manager (sales, procurement, stores), the chief accountant, the cashier and three sundry services (claims, the medical service and the police). The director has fewer direct subordinates but he still manages units of varying sizes.

The difficulty in constructing the 1888 chart was due to support services being grouped by professional speciality and working for operational functions outside their hierarchy. These services were even sometimes common to both the Commentry and Montvicq mines. The overpass[32] concept allows functional services to rapidly communicate and coordinate with each other without passing through their hierarchy.

> So long as [the persons] remain in agreement, and so long as their actions are approved by their immediate superiors, direct contact may be maintained, but from the instant that agreement ceases or there is no approval from the superiors direct contact comes to an end and the scalar chain is straightaway resumed.[33]

In conclusion, the formal structure was very clear for the majority of workers that were in the operational structure. On the other hand, it was difficult to hierarchically structure auxiliary services that by nature worked with a number of operational departments. They reported to them for work performed but remained under the hierarchical authority of their specialization. Henri Fayol hesitated before fixing their place in the organizational structure, initially drawing dual lines of reporting and later modifying his choices. These hesitations did not affect the functioning of these services as they used the overpass– a fundamental mechanism that was no doubt more important to operations than its concise presentation in *IGM*[34] and the third part[35] would lead to believe.

The number of subordinates per manager is not the same in theory and practice. Fayol did not respect his rule of fifteen workers for a foreman and four subordinates for a manager as his organizational chart had to adapt to a number of other considerations, including the cooperation between specialized technical functions and a large number of other units in other hierarchies. The structure published as Table VIII in *IGM* appears more coherent than the one used in Commentry in 1888. There was apparently no graphical representation used in 1888, and the formal written job-by-job description of the structure did not exactly match the reality of operations. A visual representation provides a summary view of the structure and would have helped identify any inconsistencies.

The Management of Managers

As organizing involves providing the enterprise with the necessary resources, it includes the management of managers, their recruitment, career and training. The various nominations, promotions and dismissals at Commentry-Fourchambault et Decazeville illustrate how Henri Fayol managed his managers. We begin with the way he set managers' wages.

Wages

A site director earned 10,000F per year, plus 1,200F in expenses and a share in the profit of his site. The profit share was generally set at 2 per cent with a minimum of around 5,000F, which meant that the variable and fixed component of wages were equal when the site made a profit of 500,000F. Beyond this level, the profit share was reduced to 0.5 per cent.[36] For example, the Decazeville director earned around 20,000F per year in 1904.

Henri Fayol's team in Paris was paid a similar wage of 20,000F per year plus a small profit share and the general secretary earned 25,000F per year. These salaries were similar to Henri Fayol's when he was director of the Commentry and Montvicq mines and earned 20,000F per year, of which half was variable.

The company statutes stipulated that a net profit share of 6 per cent be divided between senior managers and an additional 3 per cent be paid to the managing director.[37] This variable component that represented half of the yearly earnings for site directors was based on consolidated profits and was often paid with a delay of one year. As the accounting period was from 1 September to 31 August, the financial statements were prepared by the start of the following calendar year and approved by the annual general meeting in March or April. For new managers, this payment delay was no doubt compensated by a special bonus.

Henri Fayol's thoughts on profit sharing by managers were mixed. In *IGM* he noted that bonuses based on results are incentive for executive managers:

> The head of the business, in view of his knowledge, ideas, and actions, exerts considerable influence on general results, so it is quite natural to try and provide him with an interest in them. Sometimes it is possible to establish a close connection between his personal activity and its effects.[38]

In some cases, however, he was opposed to profit sharing being a major component of management remuneration:

> There are besides, businesses being built up, wound up, or merely passing through temporary crisis, wherein management depends no less on talent than in the case of prosperous ones, and wherein profit-sharing cannot be a basis for remuneration for the manager.[39]

This was the case at Commentry-Fourchambault et Decazeville from 1885 to 1887 when the company reported low profits while the mine directed by Henri Fayol prospered. According to the company's policy, Fayol should not have been paid a bonus, yet that would not have been fair in 1886. The managing director, Sessevalle, decided to pay a compensatory bonus to colliery directors whose profits had remained stable and stated:

> It may be feared that reduced to their fixed salary several engineers from our mines contemplate leaving the company to our great loss and as for Mr Fayol, the director of our mines, it is certain that an annual salary of 10,000F is quite insufficient considering his personal worth and the services he renders.[40]

Bonuses were paid to the four most senior mine managers: Henri Fayol, the director of the collieries: 10,000F; Arthur Courtin director of Commentry : 4,000F; Lemière, the director of Montvicq: 2,000F; Léon Planchard engineer at Commentry: 1,000F. Fayol's bonus was increased to 12,000F the following year.

These same four managers and the head of the commercial department continued to be paid a bonus until the company returned to profits in 1890.[41] Henri Fayol later based bonuses on the profits of the site for which the director was responsible so as to avoid this situation reoccurring.

Whilst the salaries paid by Henri Fayol would have been similar to those of other companies at the time, better offers were sometimes made by competitors to recruit Commentry-Fourchambault's engineers. In such cases, Fayol raised salaries to keep his personnel. This was the case for example of Michel Morel, the director of the Decazeville forge in 1904 who had initiated the Thomas steelworks project,[42] received a pay rise in 1906 but decided nonetheless to leave in October 1907 for Russia.

Engineers' salaries were largely above those of public servants. Jules Hochet, a member of the Inspection Générale des Finances earned 4,000F per year in 1837 when he was recruited to manage the Fourchambault factory with a salary of 12,000F per year plus a 10 per cent profit share and free accommodation in Paris, and by 1841 he earned 88,000F.[43] Henri Fayol was not so generous with his mine directors. For example, in 1906 at a competing mine in the commune of Courrières in the north of France, the mine director earned 20,000F per year with a dividend share of 0.5 per cent limited at 30,000F. The chief engineers earned 11,500F and the same dividend share, while the company secretary earned 8,000F plus a bonus per ton extracted.[44] These salaries were above those at the much smaller[45] Commentry-Fourchambault et Decazeville. As well as their salaries, accommodation was also paid for by the company. An engineer's house cost the company 20,000F and the director's house cost 35,000F.[46]

Henri Fayol also employed consultant-engineers to counsel him in metallurgical matters such as Alexandre Pourcel, who was paid 4,000F per year for his services.[47]

Recruitment

As Commentry-Fourchambault et Decazeville grew, Henri Fayol had to recruit engineers at all hierarchical levels. Recruitment was more difficult the higher the rank.

> Difficulty in choosing increases with rank; a few days, sometimes a few hours, suffice to assess a workman's usefulness, but weeks or months are needed to know the value of a foreman and sometimes years elapse before there can be any exact assessment of the value of the head of a large concern.[48]

Henri Fayol recruited a number of high level managers during his tenure. In 1906, Claude Muguet (1866–1941) was appointed general secretary and reported directly to the managing director. He had graduated from the Ecole des

Mines de Saint Etienne (hereafter ENSMSE) in 1887 and pursued a career in the mines in the north of France and later at a Hungarian mine. He was the husband of Amélie Marie Fayol, Henri Fayol's niece, although Fayol always claimed that he was not influenced by family relations and he argued that competence was the only determinant when he chose his nephew to succeed him. This was no doubt the case as a similar logic can be seen in his treatment of his brother Paul Fayol who was never promoted after his recruitment to the head of the Brassac mine. Claude Muguet became deputy managing director in 1911 and managing director in 1919 until he retired in 1935.

Henri Fayol also recruited Christophe Buisson in 1892 as head of the Commentry and Montvicq mines and to replace the managers he had transferred to the Decazeville site. He had also graduated from ENSMSE and had worked at other local mines before joining the company. He died in a road accident in 1905, most probably in a horse-drawn carriage.[49]

Jean Charreton, a class of 1891 ENSMSE graduate, was appointed chief engineer at Decazeville in 1905 after working as a mining engineer at Villeboeuf, Saint Etienne and Rochebelle[50] and remained there until 1925. Victor Bousquet (ENSMSE class of 1897), was recruited in 1909 to assist Arthur Courtin in Paris before he retired[51] after working as a mining engineer at Creusot for two years and eight years at Courrières.

Other recruitments were less successful, such as that of a certain Egré in 1901, who was hired to manage the Montluçon site.[52] He resigned in 1909 officially for health reasons[53], but in reality he had great difficulty dealing with the strike that broke out on his arrival and never managed to bring the site back to profit.

The recruitment of Joseph Seigle was another example. After working as an engineer at Neuves Maisons and later in Montluçon at the competing Saint Jacques steelworks, Seigle was recruited by Fayol in 1904 as chief engineer at Imphy where he would later become director.[54] In 1907 he was promoted director of the Decazeville factory to install the Thomas steelworks but resigned in 1910, most probably pressured by Fayol following the planning overruns and early operational difficulties.[55] He later taught metallurgy at the Ecole des Mines de Nancy[56] in 1919.

Others were opportunistic, accepting job offers and then leaving after a few years. Jourjon was named director of the Decazeville factory in 1910 but only stayed a few months.[57] Joseph Mercier (ENSMSE, class of 1887), an engineer from Graissessac was recruited in 1894 to work at Bouxhors (Brassac)[58] and left in 1898. Mignot, who had worked as an engineer at Saint Jacques and at the Aciéries de France, was named chief engineer at the Decazeville factory in 1903[59] and then left the following year.

Henri Fayol mainly recruited young engineering graduates who often remained at Commentry-Fourchambault et Decazeville for their entire careers. For example, Marchoine was hired at the Montvicq site in 1894 upon graduating from the Ecole des Mines de Saint Etienne.[60] Antoine Jardel (ENSMSE, class of 1886) was recruited to Commentry in 1886, and then transferred to Brassac (Bouxhors) in 1892, and Decazeville in 1894 where he became chief engineer in 1898, and mine director in 1907 until 1914. The most outstanding recruitment of a young graduate was no doubt that of Pierre Chevenard (1888–1960) who graduated valedictorian from ENSMSE in 1911. He was hired to manage the Imphy laboratory and was later named the company's scientific director in 1935. He also taught metallurgy at ENSMSE from 1917 to 1935 and later metallography at the Ecole des Mines de Paris, and in 1946 he was elected to the Académie des Sciences.

While the majority of French mining engineers received their training at the ENSMSE, Henri Fayol also recruited engineers trained at the Ecole des Mines de Paris, the Ecole Centrale des Arts et Manufactures and the Ecole des Arts et Métiers.[61] He sought out competence and knowledge wherever it was available at the time.

Promotions

Hierarchical structure allows for the promotion of good managers, as Henri Fayol notes in *IGM*: 'Certain employees ... become fit to assume greater responsibilities'.[62] Fayol offered his engineers good careers, favouring those who had worked with him at the Commentry and Montvicq mines and promoting them to work on his staff in the Paris office or appointing them to positions of responsibility at the Decazeville site. He established a career path for mining engineers that started at the Allier mines and led to Decazeville management, and for metallurgists that began at Imphy, passed through Decazeville and sometimes led to the managing directorship. Here are some examples of engineers who became directors:

- Pierre Girin (1866–1926) graduated valedictorian from ENSMSE in 1887 and began his career at the Pompey steelworks. Henri Fayol hired him in 1891 to manage the laboratory at the Fourchambault factory and two years later he became the deputy director. In 1899 he was named interim director of Decazeville and then returned to Fourchambault two years later as director, spending some of his time at the Paris office. When Fourchambault closed in 1904, he worked permanently in Paris[63] and in 1920 he was appointed assistant managing director of the company and remained in the position until he died in 1926.[64]
- Arthur Courtin (ENSMSE class of 1868) had a similar career that began as a divisional engineer at the Montvicq mine in 1879 and then at Commentry in 1882 where he was later appointed chief engineer in 1886. Henri Fayol knew him well and in 1888 chose him as his successor to manage the Commentry and Montvicq mines. In 1892 Fayol promoted

him to the Paris office to assist him as head of the mines department until he retired in 1910 with an annual pension of 10,000F.[65]

- Léon Planchard (ENSMSE, 1874), was appointed divisional engineer at Commentry in 1881, and was promoted to chief engineer in 1886. Henri Fayol appointed him Decazeville director in 1892 but he fell seriously ill the following year and left the company in 1896 to manage a small local mine.
- Antoine Jardel (ENSMSE, 1886), was recruited on graduation to the Commentry mine and then sent to Brassac in 1892 and Decazeville in 1894. He was appointed chief engineer in 1898 and director in 1905,[66] occupying the function at least until the war.
- Clavelly Péguet (ENSMSE, 1873) began his career at the Graissessac (Hérault) mine before being hired by Henri Fayol to manage the Decazeville mine when Léon Planchard fell ill in 1893. He tended his resignation in 1896, but withdrew it when Henri Fayol offered him the directorship of the Decazeville site that encompassed both the mine and the factory. When Henri Fayol decided to replace him as factory manager in November 1904, he took offence and resigned in February 1905.[67] Henri Fayol paid him termination pay equivalent to one year's salary.
- Louis Lévêque (Ecole Centrale des Arts et Manufactures, 1899) was recruited in 1902 to be chief engineer at the Decazeville factory. He resigned in 1905 to manage the Pauillac blast furnaces but returned to Decazeville in 1909 where he was named interim director when Seigle resigned in September 1910, and again when Jourjon departed soon after his appointment. The head of the factories, Pierre Girin, recommended that Lévêque be permanently appointed director in a written document entitled 'Seeking a Director for Decazeville'[68] and Lévêque was appointed director in December 1910.[69] Yves Cohen sees in Lévêque a prototypical manager according to Fayol's criteria[70] and in fact he is the only manager for whom a document exists that prepares his promotion. Lévêque was promoted director of the Decazeville mine and factory in 1918 and later resigned in 1926.
- René Martinet (ENSMSE, 1884) worked at the Rochebelle (Gard) mines before joining Commentry as an engineer in 1891. He was promoted chief engineer in 1893 and director of the Commentry and Montvicq mines in 1905.
- Louis Dumas (1850–1928) was director of the Châtillon-Commentry forge in Commentry before being recruited by Henri Fayol in 1892 to be his assistant and general secretary. He was given additional responsibilities as head of the metallurgical service in 1893 and the Imphy site in

1896. In 1901 he worked full time at Imphy and managed the laboratory through until 1911.[71]

- Charles Pérard (ENSMSE, 1884) was hired in 1892 as an engineer at the Montluçon factory after having worked at the Fumel blast furnace. He left the company in 1898 to work for a Russian metallurgical company (Droujkova). Upon his return to France in 1907, Henri Fayol recruited him once more to direct the Montluçon site.
- Georges Pielin (ENSMSE, 1879) was recruited in 1900 to manage the Imphy laboratory and was promoted director in 1907.
- Ardizonne (ENSMSE, 1887) worked at the gold mines in La Mane in French Guiana before joining the company as an engineer at Brassac in 1892. In 1906 he was named director of the Joudreville iron mine.

Some engineers were, of course, not promoted and either left the company early in their career or remained in the same position as their level of skills could not justify advancement. This was no doubt the case for Henri Fayol's brother Paul who was named director of the Brassac mine in 1892 and remained there until he retired in 1910 at the age of sixty-five. He received a retirement benefit of 25,000F which was equivalent to his annual salary.[72]

Departures

Henri Fayol was in favour of stability for his managers but he knew that departures were inevitable. He noted in *IGM* that: 'Nevertheless, changes of personnel are inevitable; age, illness, retirement, death, disturb the human make-up of the firm; certain employees are no longer capable of carrying out their duties'.[73] Engineers at Commentry-Fourchambault et Decazeville left the company for natural reasons such as age, sickness or death; sometimes they resigned to pursue their career elsewhere; others were dismissed.

The principal reason for departure was age or health and if a manager worked for a sufficiently long time at Commentry-Fourchambault et Decazeville he was paid a retirement pension or a lump sum payout. For example in 1901, Léon Adhémar, an engineer and secretary of the board of directors retired with a pension of 2,400F per year. The same year, Pelletier a sales manager at the Paris headquarters retired on an annual pension of 2,000F and Michel Dumon, director of the Montluçon foundry retired for health reasons on a pension of 3,000F per year. In 1903, the cashier Charles Belny, received a 2,400F annual pension when he retired at the age of 70, after forty-eight years of service.[74]

Léonce Lemière joined the Commentry and Montvicq mines as an engineer upon graduating from ENSMSE. When he retired at the age of fifty-nine in 1906 after thirty-two years of service, he had never been promoted beyond chief engineer and received an annual pension of 2,400F.[75] In 1919 he began teaching at the Ecole des Mines de Nancy.

In 1891 an engineer by the name of Jourdan received a job offer from the Forges de la Providence, three years after his recruitment by Fourchambault. Henri Fayol managed to convince him to stay, most probably through a pay rise. He was later transferred to Decazeville in 1892 and when he left for health reasons in1896 he received a payout of 20,000F which was equivalent to one year's salary.[76]

As there was no fixed retirement age, employees sometimes died while they were still working for the company and in such cases, Commentry-Fourchambault et Decazeville paid indemnities to the widow. For example, when the secretary to the board, Achille Belny, died in 1893 his widow received an indemnity of 10,000F. In 1905 when Buisson, the director of the Commentry and Montvicq mines, died his widow received a payment of 25,000F. In 1910 when J M Boutonnet died three years after retiring after forty-five years of service at the Montvicq mine and the Commentry railway and workshops, his widow received an indemnity of 5,000F.[77]

There was no fixed policy for indemnities and they could be paid out as a lump sum equivalent to one year's salary, or as an annual pension equivalent to 10 to 15 per cent of annual salary. Nothing was paid if the employee hadn't worked for long at the company. For example in 1893, Charles Boudon, a Decazeville chemical engineer, and Lassus, a Toulouse-based salesman, both died[78] but their widows received no indemnity as they were employees of the former Decazeville owners.

Other engineers resigned and left the company. At the time French engineers were could earn higher salaries in Russia and several of the company's managers accepted offers that Henri Fayol could not match. These engineers were sometimes re-employed by the company upon their return. For example:

- Marquié chief accountant at Commentry-Fourchambault et Decazeville, left to work in Russia in 1901 and died there in 1902.
- Mathon an engineer at Decazeville resigned in 1894 to work for a Russian company.
- Morel left for Russia around 1898, and returned in 1901 to become director of metallurgy at Decazeville before returning to Russia in 1907.
- Richarme, a Decazeville engineer who had worked for the company since 1900, left for Russia in 1905 and returned in 1911 to direct the project at Pont-à-Vendin.
- Verdié, a Decazeville engineer left for Russia in 1899.

Dismissals were another reason for the departure of engineers and managers. Henri Fayol considered them to be an important part of management: 'To keep his unit in good running order the manager must eliminate or suggest elimination of any employee, who for whatsoever reason has become incapable of carrying out his duties'.[79] 'Ambition, nepotism, favouritism or merely ignorance, has multiplied positions without good reason or filled them with incompetent employees'.[80] Henri Fayol performed this duty on several occasions, most notably in 1888 when he was appointed managing director, and in 1892 when he took over Decazeville.

The first concerned was Paul Lauras (1833–96) in May 1888. He had been recruited one year previously as general secretary of the Commentry-Fourchambault Company after working as a prefect from 1871 to 1876. One of his functions included the sale of metallurgical products but he sold at prices below cost price. He received a payout equivalent to six months' salary.[81] When the Fourchambault forge was reorganized in August 1888, the director, three engineers and the chief accountant were dismissed with six months' pay.[82] New engineers were recruited to replace them, the sales department was bolstered and the former director was offered the role of department head, which he refused.[83]

When Henri Fayol took over the Decazeville site in March 1892 he replaced the incumbent management team with his own managers from Commentry-Fourchambault. The previous mine director was ordered to inventory French manganese deposits and he took his mission so seriously that he requested a four-month deadline extension.[84] At the same time, two engineers and a bookkeeper were dismissed and the contracts of two other employees were terminated with an indemnity equal to six months' pay.[85] The entire Decazeville management team was replaced by engineers from the Allier mines and the Imphy factory. Henri Fayol offered positions in sales to some engineers, but most refused.

Henri Fayol also dismissed two inept employees who claimed that the previous management had promised them very high salaries: one reimbursed the equivalent of a year's salary and the other obtained payment of a year's salary in indemnities.[86] The assistant head of hauling at Decazeville was later dismissed in 1894 for stealing coal.[87] Henri Fayol knew that these dismissals set a good example that would avoid any further fraud or theft. Other dismissals concerned managers that Henri Fayol had mistakenly employed or promoted. For example:

- Georgel was head of constructions in 1889 and received a profit share of 3,500F in 1890. He was dismissed in 1891 with an indemnity of 800F.
- Eugène Jolant was in charge of the Fourchambault foundry and later the construction workshop. He received a bonus of 4,000F in 1888 and Henri Fayol promoted him to headquarters in Paris in 1889 to manage all departments. Fayol saw Jolant as his successor and he was given the task of supervising Fourchambault and responsibility for the Paris studies office in late 1892. He was dismissed in March 1894, with six months' salary and a small monthly pension of 200F.[88]
- The recently recruited head of constructions, De Montgolfier was dismissed in 1892.[89]
- Nothon was appointed interim director of Fourchambault in 1896 but was then dismissed in 1901 when the new furnace did not function

correctly. He remained in the region and arranged funding to buy the Fourchambault wireworks from the company the following year. Henri Fayol accepted that he pay 16,900F per year over a ten-year period.[90]

- Fernand Nouailhac, a thirty-six year old graduate from the Ponts et Chaussées engineering school, was recruited by the company to manage the Fourchambault, Montluçon and Imphy factories in April 1892 after working for three years as assistant works director in Panama. He resigned a year later,[91] most probably at Henri Fayol's insistence, as he had failed in his attempt to centralize the factories.
- Denis Sévoz was named head of the commercial department at Fourchambault in early 1889, with an annual salary of 8,000F and a minimum profit share of 4,000F. He was dismissed in 1893 with an indemnity of 8,000F.[92]
- Edmond Dayras (1851–1932) was recruited by Henri Fayol to Commentry in 1891 to become chief engineer and later assistant to Courtin in 1892. He was previously director of the Montigné mines in the Mayenne department in 1887. He was promoted to general secretary in Paris in 1903, and was considered Fayol's likely successor, but left the company in 1906 with a year's salary.[93] His career at the company most probably ended after a disagreement with Fayol, although the men remained on good terms.

Errors were also committed in the recruitment of lower-level managers, such as that of Pinatel, the assistant head of the Brassac drafting office who was dismissed one year after joining the company in 1894.[94]

Training

A final element of Henri Fayol's management of managers was training and he encouraged and aided the acquisition of new skills in several ways. He suggested that managers read technical literature and purchased a number of works and subscriptions to technical journals. For example, he had the Paris headquarters purchase twenty books in 1904[95] and there was also a technical library at the Decazeville site.[96]

Henri Fayol also asked that his engineers join a learned society, and generally favoured the Société de l'Industrie Minérale. He enrolled them in conferences, such as the 1900 conference in Paris[97] and he also encouraged them to write articles on their speciality, and a number of his engineers did publish on their thought and experiences. These publications allowed two of the company's former engineers to join the faculty of the newly formed Ecole des Mines de Nancy in 1919.

Henri Fayol's engineers also regularly visited other factories and mines in France and abroad to enrich their technical knowledge. For example, when the Otto-Hoffman furnace was chosen for coke production at Decazeville, several trips to Silesia were organized to observe a furnace that was successfully operating with coal of an equivalent quality.

The Imphy engineers also improved their metallurgical skills by visiting other factories to learn from the experiences of others. For example, after a failed tender offer they visited a factory using the same technique as the company that had won the contract at a much lower price; they visited a Belgian factory that used a Breuer-Schumacher forge that they planned to acquire;[98] and the electrician that was named to choose the electrical system for Joudreville went on a study tour of Belgium and Germany.[99]

Every manager also was expected to undertake applied research in his field of expertise, as Henri Fayol believed that 'a business which does not go forward is soon behind its competitors, and that consequently progress in every sphere must be pursued unremittingly'.[100]

Conclusion

Henri Fayol spent much time managing his managers, who were most often engineers. He recruited graduates, managers with a little experience, as well as seasoned engineers. He paid them salaries equivalent to that of other firms including a 50 per cent variable component, based on profits. He promoted engineers from the mines and factories through the organizational hierarchy to executive management positions at headquarters in Paris. He also made a number of mistakes with some recruits resigning or pushed to leave, underscoring the difficulties in appreciating the qualities of a manager.

Henri Fayol claimed that selection criteria for managers were 'physical qualities ... mental qualities ... moral qualities ... general education ... special knowledge: that peculiar to the function be it technical, commercial, financial, managerial, etc ... experience: knowledge arising from the work proper'.[101] We don't know how he evaluated these qualities or how he attracted candidates or selected recruits, but he was proud of his approach as he wrote in 1908, after preparing the ten-year plan that:

> I did not have time to complete this note; it is missing an essential chapter: that of personnel. Indeed it is not enough that a large company be well run from a technical standpoint, from a commercial standpoint and from a financial standpoint; it must also – it must above all – be well run from the standpoint of the personnel. Of all the problems it has to resolve, this is assuredly the most important and the most difficult. How was this problem resolved by our company in the past? What is the present situation? What is our business plan? This will be the subject of a future complementary note.[102]

It is not known whether this note was ever written.

The importance that Henri Fayol placed on personnel management in 1908 appears to be linked to his experiences with the Thomas steelworks project in Decazeville at the time. The project was two years behind schedule and the factory director was held responsible and resigned, as did his immediate successor, and the directorship was filled by Louis Lévêque, an engineer who had been working as interim director. At the time there were some weaknesses in the technical skills of a number of managers, and these insufficiencies were disciplined. As Fayol noted in *IGM*: 'Authority is not to be conceived of apart from responsibility, that is apart from sanction – reward or penalty – which goes with the exercise of power'.[103]

The formal structure deployed by Henri Fayol was that of a hierarchy drawn up in organizational charts. In practice, there were a number of difficulties in using this technique, for while it works well with operational divisions, it is more difficult to fit the support services that have fewer staff and are more specialized by trade into the chart. Henri Fayol often made these services report directly to him, but this gave him an excessive management workload and so he sought to resolve this problem by partially delegating this responsibility. The result was sufficiently unwieldy that it created contradictions in the documents he drew up.

In practice he did not respect the theoretical number of workers that should be commanded by each manager that he quantified in *IGM*, as many other factors influence the number of subordinates in any given unit. An interesting extension to Fayol's theory would be to identify the factors that lead to choose one organizational solution or another, and that determine their performance.

The notion of a hierarchy is coherent with a manager's career and remuneration that both progress as he or she nears its summit. Good managers that are not promoted may also become demotivated, if they feel that their efforts have not been rewarded, and leave the company, yet this question was not dealt with by Henri Fayol in his theory on the organizational hierarchy.

If Henri Fayol paid so much attention to his managers, it was because they had a direct influence on workers: 'I have always found French workmen obedient and loyal provided they are ably led'.[104] The following chapter looks at the management of the workers.

5 ORGANIZING: THE MANAGEMENT OF WORKERS

Organizing is installing productive resources, and of these resources labour was essential. Henri Fayol dedicated a large part of *IGM* to the management and remuneration of workers, and three of Fayol's fourteen 'general principles of management', concern the workers: the third principle is discipline, 'obedience, application, energy, behaviour, and outward marks of respect'; the seventh principle is the remuneration of personnel; and the eleventh principle is equity,

> for the personnel to be encouraged to carry out its duties with all the devotion and loyalty of which it is capable it must be treated with kindliness ... Equity excludes neither forcefulness nor sternness ... Desire for equity and equality of treatment are aspirations to be taken into account in dealing with employees.

We could also add the last principle considered to be a main strength, that of the 'esprit de corps' – the corporate culture, the union of personnel. This union also concerns the workers' unions themselves, 'meeting employers on equal terms'.[1]

Who were Henri Fayol's workers? During the twentieth century, the majority of the French were peasants, working on small plots of land as farmers or sharecroppers, and sometimes as owners. Their salaries were low except during the harvest, which was labour-intensive and a time when industry offered more attractive wages to retain workers.[2]

The owners of industrial concerns went to lengths to attract peasants, train them to be workers and retain them so that they would become productive. They also sought to keep labour costs low by making sure that wages remained close to local levels. From coal basin to coal basin, industrialists concerted with one another before increasing salaries and closely observed any nascent social unrest that risked spreading. Throughout Henri Fayol's tenure as managing director, social unrest and union power both grew. In the third part of *IGM*, Fayol described two strikes that he had to deal with and he appears to suggest that the best management approach is to avoid strikes: 'All are grave, some are disastrous'.[3] We will provide some additional details about theses strikes and the situations of social unrest that Fayol had to confront so as to better understand his thought.

Human resource management was an important management preoccupation at the time as companies had to recruit to grow their operations or dismiss workers to close sites. They also had to carefully fix wages as it was the company's main contribution to the quality of its employees' working life, along with other advantages such as retirement pensions, sickness benefits, schools and lodgings. While some of these advantages were made obligatory over time, the company also used them to retain workers. Henry Fayol paid particular attention to these measures and evoked them regularly at board meetings, although he did not take the time to write the 'personnel' section of his 1908 plan as he had promised.[4] Production levels did depend, however, on the number of workers and so there was a clear link between planning and personnel levels.

Adjusting Personnel to Activity Levels

In both the labour-intensive mines and the ironworks, production levels depended on the number of available workers. When the company received large orders, it needed to recruit, and when there was less activity the working week was reduced to five, and sometimes four, days per week instead of the usual six and wages were reduced accordingly.

The Commentry-Fourchambault et Decazeville mines and factories were based in rural areas where workers were recruited from the local peasant population. They were mainly agricultural workers[5] who often owned small plots of land that they cultivated after working at the mine. The turnover of senior workers was low as they remained loyal to the company and there were not many other industrial concerns in the area. A number of workers remained with the company for over thirty years and their children naturally replaced those who grew too old to work. In the older mines such as in Commentry, engineers saw the management of workers in the following way: 'the recruitment of personnel is almost exclusively amongst the sons of workers; they are generally recruited before the age of eighteen years, never after thirty or forty; they begin as sorters aboveground or wagoner'. They then work successively in each of the three categories of hewer, corresponding to a salary difference of 0.25F/day, with a minimum of six months spent in each category. 'A worker becomes a hewer around twenty-five years old and stops being one around forty or fifty years old'; he then becomes a 'timberer, shifter, greaser etc. each categories that required less vigour and are paid less; later he can still be used for work above ground'.[6] This organization only existed under stable economic conditions which were not always the case.

Recruitment

When management decided to increase production at a particular site, new workers had to be recruited. When local labour was in short supply, Fayol either recruited further afield using new means of transport, indirectly helped with the construction of lodgings, or reassigned excess workers from other sites.

Workers generally lived close to the factory or close to the mine, often walking 5 kilometres or more to work each day.[7] At Commentry, Decazeville and Imphy workers living further away commuted by public or private railways. In 1893, workers were allowed to ride the railway that had been built to transport coal between Montvicq, Commentry and Montluçon.[8] This also allowed those who previously worked at Commentry to work 10 km away at Montvicq.

Another narrow gauge railway at Decazeville that had been used exclusively to transport iron ore from the Mondalazac mine 25 kilometres away was modified in 1899 by Henri Fayol so that it could transport workers. 'It is a matter of organizing trains that will bring our workers from afar to work without tiring them'.[9] The required investment was low (18,000F) and operating costs were 7,000F per year. In October 1910, the board of directors took this train when it visited Decazeville.[10]

The railways also allowed the company to expand its recruitment basin. For example, in 1912,

> at Imphy, the worker issue has been markedly improved by the creation by the company PLM of a special train between Cercy la Tour and Nevers for which we promised to guarantee a minimum of 20,000F per year and which allowed Imphy to recruit fifty to sixty workers.[11]

The Imphy factory was situated on the Loire river and it was necessary to go to Nevers some 15 kilometres away to cross the river. In 1904, the mayor of Imphy asked the Commentry-Fourchambault et Decazeville Company to help finance a bridge at a cost of 12,000F,[12] representing 3 per cent of the total cost. The bridge was inaugurated on 6 October 1907 by the minister for Industry and Commerce, Gaston Doumergue who also visited the factory and presented older workers with honorary decorations. The board visited the bridge on 10 July 1909 and noted that 'it enabled the recruitment of several workers from the other side of the Loire'.[13] In Brassac in 1901, the company also paid for half the cost of a suspension bridge across the Allier River to Jumeaux for 60,000F.[14] Bridges and railways widened the company's recruitment basin.

Another way to attract workers was to construct lodgings, but Henri Fayol did not want to pay for them. In 1902 he affirmed that he preferred to 'apply his efforts to improve production conditions, be that tooling, or personnel, or working methods'[15] and suggested leaving the housing market to spontaneously respond to the demand around factories. The recurring lack of housing eventually forced him to react and he subsidized the private construction of workers lodgings in Brassac in 1897,[16] although this was still insufficient and housing shortages continued through 1913 and 1914,[17] and in Imphy in 1906 where he built eight lodgings and subsidized the construction of twenty others in 1910.[18] These investments were low compared to the 1,000 or so workers who lived around the factories at the time.

In Decazeville the previous mine owners had built few lodgings for workers, such that in 1894 the miners rented their lodgings of which only 5 per cent belonged to the company.[19] In 1899 Henri Fayol offered to subsidize workers if they bought their own lodging[20] and he also constructed twelve houses at a cost of 3,000F each to serve as models for private owners that were to have access to cheaper land along the railway line into Decazeville.[21] The board inspected the constructions when it visited Decazeville in 1907 and 1909.[22] In 1912 the mayor of Decazeville planned to build inexpensive housing and asked Commentry-Fourchambault et Decazeville what it could do to support the project, such as guaranteeing rent which Fayol agreed to do.[23]

As the housing problem was never really resolved, there was a permanent labour shortage through until 1914. Henri Fayol no doubt wanted to avoid the problems that a landlord could have with his tenants, such as in 1892 when he evicted retired workers from lodgings that had once been allocated to them in response to the scarcity of housing in Fourchambault. Evicted tenants were compensated with a monthly indemnity of 10F.[24]

Henri Fayol actively sought to recruit farmhands from the region and even paid a foreman to bring in peasants from the nearby Lot department. Industrial wages, however, were no longer as attractive as they once were and in 1909, 'company recruiters found that conditions for agricultural workers had improved greatly; it was harder to persuade them to give industry a try'.[25] This improvement came from the Law of 11 January 1892 (known as the Méline law) which instituted a protectionist customs tax for agriculture. As a result, agricultural prices increased, as did peasants wages.

> At the start of February 1900 the Decazeville management reported that to increase the labour force by 279 men it had been necessary to hire 1,267 individuals. The greatest turnover was in the underground mines: to raise this labour force by three, the mine had to hire 434 workers.[26]

On 1 September 1907, the Decazeville factory employed 1,126 workers but twelve months later 448 workers had left representing 40 per cent of the workforce. The company had to recruit 424 workers so that the workforce at the end of the year had only fallen by 2 per cent.[27] On the eve of the World War I, the mine recruited 1,410 individuals in one year, but 1,296 of them left.[28] Most of these workers had no ties to the region and were very mobile.

The company looked to recruit abroad in order to increase its workforce. For example, in 1907 it unsuccessfully envisaged bringing Italian workers to Decazeville[29] and in 1908, when faced with a shortage of labour Henri Fayol subcontracted the operating of an open cut mine to a company that most probably employed, fed and lodged Spanish workers. Fayol tried to use this same solution himself in 1909 but he had not provided for the necessary infrastructure. 'Several Spanish workers recently brought to Mondalazac by one of their compatriots left the area two days after arriving'. He then decided to build dormitories with canteens for sixty Spanish workers recruited in late 1909.[30] In 1911, there were 469 foreigners in Decazeville for a population of 14,114, representing a proportion of 3 per cent[31] and in 1914 close to 20 per cent of workers in the basin were Spanish.[32] At the end of 1913, 180 Spaniards worked in the factory representing 12 per cent of the 1,200 employees,[33] and 300 worked in the open cut mine where wages were lower, representing 15 per cent of the 2,200 employees. In 1914 there were 800 Spanish workers at the Decazeville mine and factory, representing one quarter of the personnel. They lived eight to ten per room.[34] They were able to make themselves understood as the local dialect, Occitan had some commonalities with Spanish. These workers were often anxious to return home and only one worker in seven stayed for more than one year.[35] Once they had given fifteen days' notice then they could leave with their accrued pay.

The demography of the town of Decazeville was heavily influenced by the recruitment of migrant workers. According to the 1911 census, 40 per cent of workers in the basin were born in Decazeville, another 40 per cent came from within a 50-kilometre radius, 15 per cent of workers came from further away in France and 5 per cent of the population were foreigners,[36] essentially Spaniards coming from a number of poor regions in Spain.

Recruitment was a critical problem in Decazeville and Brassac throughout the start of the twentieth century,[37] making it impossible to stabilize the workforce which restrained development projects. The coal mines in the North and the Pas de Calais departments had an entirely different recruitment policy, building housing to attract vast numbers of workers from Poland and Italy.

Personnel Reductions

When the volume of orders fell, the company sometimes decided to cease work for a few days as a short term regulation of production levels. Henri Fayol chose on several occasions to use unpaid furlough ranging from one day per month to a day per week or more. There were sixty days of inactivity at the Commentry mine in 1885, sixteen in 1886 and despite an increase in activity in that same year, there were seventeen inactive days in 1889.[38] Worker wages fell by 5 per cent to 20 per cent over these three years because of this inactivity. Furlough was taken at Imphy from the end of 1901 through until 1903, and at Decazeville workers were furloughed a day per week in December 1900, in April 1903 and from January to July 1908.[39] When Brassac had difficulty selling its coal at the start of the twentieth century, workers took furlough of between one day and four days per month from August 1904 until 1908.[40]

When production and coal consumption at the Fourchambault factory both fell by 30 per cent in 1894, workers were furloughed for a day per week over an entire year at the Commentry mine starting from August 1894.[41]

One year later the situation had returned to normal after a slight fall in employee levels and the recruitment of new customers. When the Fourchambault factory closed in August 1901, the Commentry and Montvicq mines lost a major customer and they again furloughed workers for one day a week for a year.[42] The Commentry mine used furlough to reduce production up until July 1906[43] all the while reducing personnel levels.

Henri Fayol tried to suppress these inactive days and regulate worker levels. In Commentry for example, 'due to the concentration of washing plants in a central workshop, the number of workers employed at this activity has diminished and, so as not to dismiss them, we employed them to advance the St Charles cutting'.[44] Similarly in 1893, when Henri Fayol began operating the open cut mine in Decazeville, the improved productivity levels meant that the company needed fewer miners. To avoid dismissing workers, Fayol ordered the extraction of 50,000 tons more coal[45] and found the market for them. It was Fayol's concern to maintain work levels for the same number of miners that drove the company's profitable growth.

When there was less work in the factory, the company could compensate by transferring workers to the neighbouring mine. In late 1900 when orders for iron and steel products were low and the company began using short-time work at the factory, Henri Fayol transferred labourers from the factory to the mine. They returned to work at the factory half way through 1901.[46]

When a site closed Henri Fayol looked for a buyer who would continue operations with at least some of the workers and the others received an indemnity or a pension. It was the case in 1893 when Fayol agreed that an engineer by the name of Magnard take over the construction of carriages at Fourchambault and at La Pique.[47]

Another example was when the board decided to reduce production at the Fourchambault factory in 1897 and 350 of the factory's 750 workers were dismissed with fifteen days' notice. The oldest employees were paid pensions, 250 of the dismissed workers already laboured as farmhands and the other workers found work at factories in the area whose activity was buoyant at the time.[48] Similarly, when the Fourchambault factory was definitively closed in September 1901, the fate of the 500 remaining workers was monitored by the company's management based on written reports that they received over a six-month period. The oldest workers (20 per cent) received a pension and the others were paid compensation according to their length of service. While the fate of all the workers is not known, some found work in local factories (15 per cent), most left to seek work elsewhere, sometimes involving a change in trade (30 per cent), and a lowly 2 per cent accepted the company's offer of work at its other sites which was very much below management's expectation of 15 per cent.[49] The population of Fourchambault fell from 6,100 in 1901 to 4,800 in 1906, a loss of 1,300 inhabitants that corresponds to approximately 300 heads of family who left to find work elsewhere.

The company anticipated the planned 1904 closure of the Commentry mine that had been known to be reaching exhaustion since 1875. The company took measures to reduce the workforce, including no longer employing young workers as they returned from military service from 1896 onwards, which meant that the workforce gradually fell by around 5 per cent per year.[50] Wages at Commentry were also frozen to encourage the departure of miners. If they protested they were offered work at Brassac or Decazeville.[51] The main pit was not closed until 3 November 1911 as it took longer for fewer miners to exhaust the deposit and a small unexpected find of coal was also made. The mine employed 600 miners in July, and 250 remained in September to fill the central pit and extract the coal surrounding the shaft, representing a small production volume equivalent to 10 per cent of that mined under normal conditions. Henri Fayol unsuccessfully planned for the transfer of the Commentry miners to the company's other mines. 'We have not managed to steer many workers from Commentry to Brassac and Decazeville; they look to stay in the area or they go elsewhere'[52] although several dozen miners did accept work at the Ruhle mine in Decazeville.[53] Again, two years later when the Montvicq site closed, the workers left the area but not for the company's other sites.[54] Peasant-worker loyalty was an advantage, but loyalty was limited to their site of employment and not to the company itself so that when a mine closed, they sought work nearby. One explanation is that 60 per cent of Commentry workers over thirty years old were home-owners.[55]

Workers came from agriculture and Decazeville was one step in their migration towards the manufacturing industry. They then moved on to other towns or to Paris and sometimes went abroad. In 1902 after a month-long strike, five factory workers requested their due to leave for America[56] and in 1907, sixty miners left for San Francisco and Chile.[57]

The quantitative management of workers should have been subject to a work plan but work planning was constrained by the labour market as any plans to increase production depended on the possibility of recruiting new workers. The closure of Commentry was anticipated and the company successfully adapted its personnel management, but when Fourchambault unexpectedly closed, the site's 500 workers had difficulty finding work locally and most ended up leaving the area.

Wages

Henri Fayol used three distinct modes of worker remuneration: 'time rates ... job rates ... piece rates'.[58] The first method set wages for a fixed length of work; the second method involved setting tasks and wages, and varying the length of work according to the worker's skill or effort; the third mode involved fixing the work length and varying wages according to quantities produced.

Under the piece rate mode,

> payment is related to work done and there is no limit. This system is often used in workshops where a large number of similar articles have to be made, and is found where the product can be measured by weight, length, or cubic capacity, and in general is used wherever possible.[59]

For example, in the mines hewers were paid for the quantity of coal they extracted, a sorter's wages were based on the quantity of stones they sifted and in the factories the professional workers were paid according to the tonnage of metal produced. Other workers, including labourers and young workers were paid for each day worked.

The use of piece rates required that production be measured. Production output was only known for a team such as a workshop in the factory or a production team of four miners. The amount of coal produced by a production team was known as the number of carts it sent to the surface was counted. The production team was paid a wage based on the going rate in francs per cart. Henri Fayol noted that,

> the organization by production teams that were free to constitute themselves as they wished stimulated the workers. There was a continuous process of elimination; the good or strong workers rejected the bad or weak. The latter join together or finish by being discouraged. But the main stimulus is in the worker's certitude that he will be paid proportionally for the work done'.[60]

Years earlier, production teams freely redistributed payment between members and the company had some difficulty learning of individual remunerations. Louis Reybaud recounts that the practice of paying workers collectively on Sundays, when they would divide up their pay at the local café, was stopped a little before 1868. Payments were instead made at the end of the work day and 'from then on co-workers immediately share in front of head miners'.[61] When the 1894 pension law required companies to contribute an amount proportional to each worker's wage, the company necessarily had to know individual remunerations accurately. The amount earned by each team was divided by the number of its members. Any apprentices or labourers that helped the production team received either a fixed sum or a smaller share than the other workers.

Piece work did not motivate workers to exert a maximum effort as the strongest workers had no interest in working harder than their colleagues. Furthermore, if their output led to them earning an above-average wage, the company would reduce the pay rate and consequently the wages of the other workers. Productive efforts were regulated so as to respect the accepted norms for wages at a particular point in time. In practice, this regulation meant that miners modulated their efforts and that production varied day-by-day. As early as 1837, the director at Decazeville had found that locally recruited miners 'generally work more at the end of the month than at the beginning'.[62]

The engineers cooperated in this regulation, as Donald Reid observed:

> At the end of the month the engineer or the master miner often added a bonus to the agreed-upon rate to compensate workers for obstacles they had encountered. The supervisory employee might reduce the rates for advancement in a gallery the following month if he felt that the previous rates had proved too high. Manipulation of the rates was a constant concern of management'.[63]

Henri Fayol was aware of these reciprocal adjustments and remarked in *IGM* that: 'Generally, piece rates give rise to increased earnings which act for some time as a stimulus, then finally a system prevails in which this mode of payment gradually approximates to time rates for a pre-arranged sum'.[64]

Remuneration could also take into account the quality of work. For example, Imphy wages for sheet metal production were raised through quality bonuses: 'This wage increase has in fact been quite advantageous; workers have brought more care and more zeal to their work'.[65]

Despite the piece work mechanism, the main reference was the daily wage. Rates were continually adjusted according to the difficulty of tasks in such a way as to reach a wage that was considered fair by employers and acceptable to workers.

The main problem remained the level of wages. Henri Fayol wrote:

> If wages are low, the workers are not happy. If labour is expensive an employer cannot remain competitive in difficult times and the worker will lose his job. We can pay high remuneration, good wages when results are good. Yes most often, we can reconcile high wages and a good cost price.[66]
>
> Remuneration of personnel is the price of services rendered. It should be fair and, as far as is possible, afford satisfaction both to personnel and firm (employee and employer). The rate of remuneration depends, firstly, on circumstances independent of the employer's will and employee's worth, viz. cost living, abundance or shortage of personnel, general business conditions, the economic position of the business, and after that it depends on the value of the employee and mode of payment adopted.[67]

We will now look at how Henri Fayol set wage levels.

A worker's wage depended on his trade, with foremen paid the most. Some examples of wages paid at Commentry in 1894 were: the head miner earned

275F/month; deputy chief miners earned 200F/month; the hewers earned 4.90F/day; and the other miners in the pit earned between 3F and 4.7F/day. The lowest wages on the surface were those of sorters at 1.93F/day, the labourers earned 3F/day and the other specialists a little more – up to 4.4F/day for engine men for example.[68] These differences were due to the nature of tasks and their difficulty and were less than two to one. On the other hand, women received 2.5 times less than hewers and 30 per cent less than other surface workers. At Decazeville, miners earned 3.84F/day on average in 1899, 3.22F/day on the surface and 4.13F/day in the pit, and hewers earned 4.24F/day. However, 2 per cent of the 3340 labourers earned less than 1.5F/day, mainly women sorters and boys under 16 years old. Wages were higher for 10 per cent of workers, mostly sorters and surface labourers who earned between 1.5 and 2.5F/day more than the average. Most labourers (38 per cent) earned between 2.5F/day and 3.5F/day. Some labourers and hewers (31 per cent) earned between 3.5F/day and 4.5F/day. The 17 per cent of workers who earned between 4.5F/day and 5.5F/day were most likely hewers, and 3 per cent of hewers earned more than 5.5F/day.[69] These statistics show that there was wage differentiation even within the professions themselves.

Wages also differed between pits. In 1898–9 the average wage for hewers was 4.20F/day in the Miramont pit and 4.59F/day in the Raoul pit. On the surface, at the Lassalle strip-mine workers were paid 2.90F/day to extract coal. The average wages for transport workers were respectively 4.04F/day, 4.51F/day and 3.12F/day.[70] The marked differences between miner's wages were no doubt intentional and considered to be normal by workers. Unions demanded a minimum wage, not a uniform wage.[71]

The wage differences were greater still in the factories, sometimes up to five-fold between factory workers. In each workshop, professionals were paid based on workshop output while aids and apprentices were paid a low daily rate. For example, in 1893–4 at Decazeville, the average wages in the factory varied between 3.39 to 4.64F/day with labourers earning the least with a daily wage ranging between 2.52F/day and 2.82F/day.[72] Workers at the blast furnace earned 3.32F/day while founders earned 4.4F/day. The average wage for puddling was 4.62F/day, hammer smiths earned 6.61F/day and rough hewers earned 5.70F/day. The wage differences were even greater in the mills where mill-hands earned between 9.29 and 12.82F/day and drivers[73] between 7.50 and 10.29F/day depending on the site. Alain Boscus found wage differences between workers to be even greater two decades later, at up to eight-fold in 1911, and seven-fold in 1913.[74] Work stations also greatly differed in terms of both the operating skill required and the working conditions, and in particular when working with hot metals, resulting in some factory workers earning more than foremen.

In 1899, there were a larger proportion of both high and low salaries amongst the 1,060 factory workers compared to the mine. 58 per cent of factory workers and 50 per cent of mine workers earned less than 3.5F/day, while 12 per cent of factory workers and 3 per cent of miners earned above 5.5F/day. Wage differences remained more pronounced in the factory.

Henri Fayol raised wages by 0.2F/day at Decazeville in 1899 which represented a significant raise for low salaries, and less so for the better-paid workers. For 2 per cent of the workforce on salaries below 1.5F/day, the raise represented a 13 per cent increase but for workers earning above 6.5F/day, who also accounted for 2 per cent of the workforce, the raise only increased their wage by 3 per cent. For the remaining two thirds of workers earning between 2.5F/day and 4.5F/day, the 0.2F/day increase represented between 5 and 7 per cent of their wage.[75] Such small increases only slightly reduced wage differences.

These wage differences between workers were essential as they allowed workers to envisage wage improvements through professional advancement.

Wage Variations

When a company's profits increase, workers expect their wages to increase accordingly. One way of ensuring this relationship was to base salaries on the market price of coal. This principle underscored the mobile wage scale adopted in Great Britain in the 1880s. A number of different calculations were used and all resulted in salary increases when prices were high without any union intervention.[76]

The mines in the Nord and the Pas de Calais departments signed similar agreements between employers and workers. The Arras conventions of 1891, 1899 and 1900 fixed bonuses to take into account variations in coal market prices.[77] The same arrangement was made in the Loire mines. These agreements led to immediate wage increases as prices were high at the time. When prices fell later, so too did salaries. Henri Fayol wrote that 'this system established a certain fixed relationship between the prosperity of the colliery and the miner's wage. It is criticized on the grounds that it conduces to limitation of production in order to raise selling price'.[78] He opposed these arrangements, arguing that 'whether a business is making a profit or not the worker must have an immediate wage assured him' and should not have to take on the risks associated with profitability. Furthermore, 'the workers' greater or lesser share of activity or ability in the final outcome ... is, moreover, quite insignificant'.[79] His share in profits will always be low compared to his wages.

The regulation of wages using market prices allowed employers to share business risks with workers. In 1888 French mines reported lower profits than the previous year as the fall in coal prices (0.32F per ton)[80] was not compensated by a fall in salaries (0.13F/ton).[81] Wage regulation based on the sales price of coal was also used at the Commentry mine. Between 1860 and 1875, wages paid to hewers increased by 40 per cent and then fell by 30 per cent in 1885 to a level below that of 1860.

It was difficult to maintain salaries at very low levels when the mine was making profits. On 20 February 1890, Henri Fayol discussed Commentry salaries with the board and explained that the average reference wage of hewers was 3.93F in 1872, 4.61F from 1878 to 1887, fell to 3.89 in 1888 and then rose by 4 per cent in September 1889. He believed that is was 'prudent and fair to award this 10 per cent rise for several categories of workers, without waiting for demands'.[82] The estimated cost was 80,000F per year and he justified this adjustment by the general improvement in corporate health and by the fact that coal prices had stopped falling and had risen by 15 per cent from their lowest point. In September 1890 Henri Fayol decided to significantly increase wages at Commentry. This was easy for fixed wages but for wages based on production levels, rates had to be revised for a given level of productivity, yet productivity had fallen as wages had increased. During the 1890–91 financial year output was 900 kilograms per day and per miner, down from 915 kilograms the previous year. This fall made it difficult to exactly reach the target wage increase. Engineers used 1889 production levels when they set the new rates, but as miners now produced less they did not receive the intended wage increase. For example, hewers' pay only increased by 13 per cent over two years instead of the target 15 per cent.[83] When miners began working for higher rates they reduced their efforts as they feared that when management saw their higher wages they would revert back to lower rates. In fact management had never communicated its decision to increase daily pay so as not to alert neighbouring mines.

The wage increase at Commentry was an adjustment for previous wage falls and an insurance against future conflicts. In 1891 hewers' wages at Commentry were 20 per cent above those of neighbouring mines and this helped avoid later social unrest. The state engineer declared in 1890 that 'thanks to this measure the Commentry-Fourchambault company peacefully traversed the period of regional strikes'.[84] Workers in neighbouring mines and at the Châtillon-Commentry factory went on strike to protest low wages and react to the propaganda of the socialist mayor's secretary, Raoul Fréjac. The strikes stopped when Fréjac was arrested.[85]

We can assume that these local strikes sought to obtain the same wage increases as those awarded at Commentry-Fourchambault. As a general rule, employers in the same industrial area met to discuss wage increases before awarding them to avoid any contagion effect. In 1910 for example, Henri Fayol consulted the neighbouring mine before refusing wage increases at Brassac.[86]

Henri Fayol's generous 1890 wage adjustment at Commentry can probably be explained by his opposition to coal market price-based wage adjustments. He refused union demands for a 10 per cent wage increase at the Decazeville mine on 1 May 1906 arguing that there had been no fall in wages in 1902 when coal prices fell, contrary to the mines in the north where wages fell by 10 per cent. He produced a table of wages that showed a 9 per cent increase between 1898 and 1901, a period of stagnation and then a 1 per cent rise in 1906. Even though coal prices were lower in 1906 than in 1899, wages had increased. Fayol pointed out that:

> the company maintained the rise awarded in 1900 and even increased it without waiting for worker's demands ... Coal prices, although on the rise are far from what they were in 1900, while wages are much greater than they were at the same period'.[87]

Although Henri Fayol did not tie wages to coal prices, he was aware of this practice as other employers used it and if he didn't follow suit, his workers may have left the company. In 1898, in spite of rising coal prices he considered that 'there is no reason at this time to decide on a salary increase'[88] but by the end of 1899, as a growing number of companies had increased wages Henri Fayol decided to do so at Decazeville and 'anticipate claims by spontaneously awarding benefits to workers'. After all 'the increase in prices quite rightly attracts the attention of unions'. Henri Fayol offered to finance the 2 per cent wage deduction for the relief fund and he offered to similarly finance pensions at Commentry.[89] These advantages were still low compared to other collieries that had increased wages by 5 per cent and even 10 per cent in the north, and so at the start of 1900 Henri Fayol increased wages by 0.2F/day. As this rise did not prevent workers from leaving Decazeville, Henri Fayol again increased wages by 2.5 per cent in June 1900[90] but this was still not enough, as 'the salaries in the Aveyron are amongst the lowest in France, and those at Decazeville are markedly inferior to those at Aubin and Cransac' the neighbouring mines. As his neighbours were against any wage rise, Henri Fayol decided on a 'gradual rise by group of workers that would better allow salaries to be in harmony with the real value of workers' and above all avoid any talk about disagreements between employers.[91]

He awarded unsolicited wage rises to anticipate social conflicts, arguing in 1907 and 1908 that 'it is in the interest of our company to not wait for worker demands and to spontaneously offer some benefits to our worker population ... It seems opportune to not wait for workers' demands'.[92] He explained that 'it is quite important that all legitimate grievances raised by workers receive satisfaction without waiting for them to make a demand, because there are always drawbacks in letting them make a demand and having to give in to it'.[93] Henri Fayol explained to the board that strong coal prices, rising living costs and benefits awarded by other mines justified awarding a rise of 0.3 to 0.4 F/day at Decazeville in 1908.

While Henri Fayol often increased wages in advance of worker claims, it was not a strict rule. In 1900, when unions at Commentry demanded a 10 per cent pay rise Henri Fayol followed neighbouring mines and agreed to a 5 per cent increase.[94] In August 1912 Henri Fayol did not follow the wage increases awarded at mines in the north but instead waited for union pay claims, however none were forthcoming and he remarked in October that 'the claim for a pay rise that was expected from Decazeville workers did not materialize. It is said that it was because the Confédération Générale du Travail did not consider it to be opportune at this time'.[95] Henri Fayol sometimes adopted a wait-and-see strategy with unions, and never awarded the total wage claim.

The average wage at the Decazeville mines only slightly increased between 1892 and 1899 due to the increasing proportion of lower-paid labourers employed over the period. When the number of labourers reached its peak in 1900, wages were only increasing by 1.7 per cent per year on average.[96] These wage rises were in line with the overall trend for pit miners in France whose wages rose from 4.03F/day in 1888 to 5.96F/day in 1913, representing an increase of 1.6 per cent per year. These wage increases can be attributed both to a general national increase in miners' wages and the growing proportion of miners from the north who earned around 20 per cent more than other miners.

At the Decazeville factory wages were stable until 1897 when they began increasing by an average of 1.9 per cent per year through until 1914.[97] Globally, wages increased more rapidly during the two decades preceding World War I than over the entire nineteenth century.

We can see from these numbers that whenever possible Henri Fayol adopted a wage policy that involved increases that were slightly above average and particularly above those of his local competitors. Wages at the neighbouring Campagnac mine for example were lower than those at Decazeville. Two years after the company acquired the site in 1908, miners claimed a wage adjustment that Henri Fayol promptly awarded both to remain equitable and to stop the movement before it grew.[98]

The Strikes

The French government began tolerating strikes from 1864. Some were spontaneous, with explicit demands from time to time, while others were organized with claims that were clearly stated by workers' unions which were authorized after 1884. Employers tried to counter strikes that always resulted in a fall in production levels and profits. In the third part of *IGM*, Henri Fayol made three remarks concerning strikes: they occurred for various reasons, employers should be firm when faced with demands and that he himself had succeeded in limiting strikes in an industry where they were frequent. Fayol detailed two strikes: the first in Commentary in 1881 which ended in a lockout and the recruitment of new workers, and the second in Montluçon in 1901 where casters remained on strike for five months. He chose not to mention other strikes that are equally interesting and illustrate the diversity of the situations that he faced and that we will present here.

The 1881 Commentry Strike

According to Henri Fayol the 1881 Commentry strike was caused by a fall in sales that obliged the company to reduce production and dismiss 200 workers. When half of the workers were retired and the other half were offered work ten or so kilometres away[99] the miners went on strike to protest. Fayol and his engineers personally saw that non-striking workers could get by the picket lines that had been set up on the road to the mine and the gendarmerie and the army were sent to the site to maintain order. For the following three days work at the mine was completely stopped and the company dismissed all workers through a lock-out and re-employed those who wanted to work, resulting in a 25 per cent fall in the number of pit miners.

Fayol's version is the same as the one Mony presented to the board of directors[100] and it is the same as the prefect's version of events.[101] However, the company's sales figures do not show a fall in coal sales and the fall in production at Commentry was compensated by an increase in production at Montvicq.

Work by a local historian, Georges Rougeron places this strike in its political context. The director of Commentry-Fourchambault, and also former mayor and deputy, Stéphane Mony lost the 1881 municipal elections to the socialists led by Christophe Thivrier (1841–95). All those who spread socialist propaganda were put on file at the time, and 135 of them worked at the mine. They were all dismissed on 4 June 1881 and the workers went on strike.[102] The workers unsuccessfully offered to limit the work week so as to reduce production levels without lay-offs.[103] During the strike another 300 individuals that were considered 'agitators' were put on file and had to pass an interview to be re-employed at the mine. Sixty of these workers were definitively dismissed and sixty-seven were told to return later with certificates of good conduct from their new employers. 'Because of the attitude they took at municipal elections, management dismissed 152 of the "leaders". The others went on strike. It was miserable'.[104] The miners that had been elected to the local council had to leave the area in search of work. 'After the strike the socialist group was dispersed'.[105] Despite this repression, Thivrier became the first French socialist mayor and deputy in 1889.

The purge was orchestrated by Mony who was in Commentry at the time. The strike that was called by workers out of solidarity only increased the repression. Believing that management wanted to reduce production levels, in order to avoid any further dismissals the remaining workers reduced their productivity from 262 tons per worker per year in 1880 to 240 from 1882 onwards. Worker productivity at the mine didn't rise until 1890 when it reached 300 tons per worker per year.

As director of Commentry at the time, Henri Fayol carried out Mony's orders and it was most probably at this time that he wrote his doctrine of electoral abstention that allowed him to avoid further political conflicts and strikes.[106] In his writings he gives no hint of any disagreement on this issue and his description is identical to the official version of the time, yet the 1881 Commentry strike was not simply called out of solidarity, as Fayol said, but was an extension of a local political conflict.

The 1901 Montluçon Strike

The second strike described by Henri Fayol is that of the Montluçon casters in 1901. A caster was a specialist in the process of sand-casting who made individual iron pieces by pouring molten iron into sand moulds. According to Henri Fayol the casters were paid by piece made, and they demanded to be paid a day rate. They went on strike to support their claims and returned to work five months later without the company having conceded to their demands.[107]

Piece work was first used at Montluçon in 1888 to pay labourers and it resulted in productivity improvements.[108] Twenty-five of the 100 casters were paid piece rates and in June 1901 Henri Fayol instructed his newly recruited director to pay all casters this way. The casters went on strike and the remaining 500 factory workers followed their example. The striking workers modified their demands and agreed to accept piece work so long as they were guaranteed a minimum wage.[109] The director of the factory and Pierre Girin, who was in charge of coordinating the factories from Paris headquarters, both offered to mediate but Henri Fayol refused and the strike continued resulting in the company having to give up a large order for the Paris metro. The strikers went back to work in unclear circumstances at the end of December 1901: Henri Fayol claimed that the company had made no concessions, the government claimed the strike ended after mediation by the sub-prefect[110] and the union claimed workers had obtained a guaranteed wage if insufficient production was not the fault of the worker.[111]

This strike cost the company dearly, with a total 55,000F in strike-related expenses appearing in the accounts across the next two financial years[112] and damage to the reputation of the Montluçon factory and that of its cast iron pieces that no doubt contributed to it accumulating losses over the following ten years. The strike was a reaction to Fayol's dogmatic remuneration decision: paying workers per piece was perhaps not the most appropriate mode of remuneration for repetitive work, and the timing for such a decision was also poor as the factory had just received a large order. He appeared less dogmatic in *IGM* when he spoke of piece work: 'Each one of these methods [time rates, job rates, piece rates] has its advantages and drawbacks, and their effectiveness depends on circumstances and the ability of superiors'.[113]

According to Fayol, workers went on strike at Commentry out of solidarity for their dismissed colleagues, while workers at Montluçon went on strike out of principle to protest a method of wage-fixing. His analysis is debatable, as the Commentary strike was most likely a reaction to a political purge orchestrated by the Paris office that increased the number of dismissed workers, and in Montluçon Henri Fayol played the role of an intransigent Parisian director by refusing the compromises suggested by his engineers and this stubbornness seriously threatened the activity of the factory.

Another major strike broke out in Decazeville in 1902, but Henri Fayol never mentioned it.

The 1902 Decazeville Strikes

After the Montluçon strike led to the loss of an equivalent 50,000 days of work in 1901, Decazeville lost almost an equivalent 25,000 days in 1902. There were separate strikes in the factory and in the mine that reinforced one another.

The first strike was caused by differences in wage levels in the mill and it lasted for four days at the end of July 1902.[114] Salaries for milling steel were 30 per cent higher than for milling iron even though the work was the same. This situation was caused by productivity improvements following investments in new technologies and piece rates remaining constant, which together led to an increase in workers' wages. Rates should have been adjusted as soon as technology investments were made but Henri Fayol made late adjustments to wages and this created social unrest. A readjustment was negotiated but the terms were ambiguous and when workers received their August wages they again walked out, blocking work at the new factory for two months. Miners called a two-week strike out of solidarity in September 1902 and they again stopped work when a 'general strike' was called by the miners' union to obtain higher wages from 17 to 24 October. In each of these situations Henri Fayol faced down the unions but at significant expense. The company's poor performance in 1902 could mainly be attributed to social unrest and the financial losses this caused were evaluated at 243,000F.[115]

Strikes were also called by unions to pressure the government, such as the regular strike on the first of May which was tolerated by Henri Fayol.

The May Day Strike

In the nineteenth century, each employer set the length of the working day, and this was sometimes twelve hours or more. In 1817, the Briton Robert Owen invented the slogan 'Eight hours labour, eight hours recreation, eight hours rest' that was adopted by workers unions in a number of countries towards the end of the nineteenth century.

In October 1884, a convention held by the North American Federation of Organized Trades and Labor Unions unanimously set 1 May 1886 as the date to mark the struggle for an eight-hour work day, and US labour unions called for a general strike in support of the eight-hour day that was followed by between 300,000 and 500,000 protesters in the major American cities. On 5 May a Chicago protest was held with more than 40,000 strikers assembling on Haymarket Square and the confrontation that ensued between protesters and the police resulted in ten or so deaths. The American Federation of Labor (AFL) decided in 1888 that 1 May 1890 would be the date on which workers would strike for an eight-hour work day. In 1889 at its Paris meeting, the Second International agreed to this date for a great international demonstration.

The May Day strike for an eight-hour day became a worker tradition in France from 1890 and was particularly followed at the Montvicq, Brassac and Decazeville mines. The striking Decazeville miners were also the most active unionists and on 1 May they demonstrated with other local miners. After the eight-hour day was awarded in 1905, the strike lost its following with only 15 per cent of the workers at the Decazeville mine striking in 1906, for example.[116] Factory workers didn't follow the strike movement that was essentially called for by the unions and the Commentry mine never went on strike on 1 May.

The 1 May strike was tolerated by Henri Fayol but he dismissed those who did not come to work the next day.[117] In 1904 he repeated the 'principle applied in previous years: the work sites would remain open this day as usual, we will occupy those workers that come and those absent will not be punished'.[118]

These national movements were orchestrated by the Paris-based union and targeted the government. A similar strike targeted the government on 16 December 1912 to oppose the war in the Balkans[119] and another in 1914 to oppose retirement legislation passed by Parliament on 25 February 1914. The national miners' union was divided between those who were satisfied with the law, and those who wanted more favourable legislation, and a large social movement ensued that was no doubt timed to coincide with the parliamentary elections of 26 April and 10 May 1914. The Decazeville union representative stated that 'the strike is not directed towards the company, but towards the government'.[120] The miners massively obeyed their union and on Monday 23 February 1914 almost all mines were closed. The Decazeville factory limited operations to the blast furnaces and the steelworks for lack of coal. On 1 March workers were told by national union leaders to return to work and they did so on Tuesday 3 March.

The Other Strikes

Fayol was also confronted with a number of other strikes that sought wage increases. For example, the October 1902 general strike was followed in all French mines to support the union demand for improved wages. In Brassac the strike began at the start of October and lasted for almost one month while in

Montvicq workers went on strike from 13 to 23 October. Fayol systematically refused union demands.

Miners' strikes were generally massive and always coordinated by the unions, whereas unions were weaker in the metallurgical factories and industrial action was limited to workshops. The scenario often observed in factories involved claims being brought by workers in a specific workshop, and if they were serious enough a strike would be called by the union. In such cases management would quickly begin negotiations, inform head office in Paris and propose solutions that partially satisfied demands and workers would then return to work. Management's response could also be quite firm, including the dismissal of striking workers and their replacement by workers from a neighbouring workshop. Henri Fayol always refused to accept either a fixed daily wage or a minimum wage in case production levels were low.

This strike scenario repeated itself on several occasions, and particularly when Henri Fayol adjusted pay rates when he considered wages to be too high. Such a case occurred in early 1897 when investment in the large Fourchambault mill increased its capacity by 20 per cent and output based wages automatically increased leading Henri Fayol to lower the piece rates. The mill's five workers resigned and twenty others refused to be transferred to the large mill. The latter were dismissed and the issue was resolved when a team from the small mill was assigned to the large mill.[121] This situation was caused by the productivity improvements brought by investment in new technologies and as piece rates remained constant, workers' wages increased. Rates should have been adjusted as soon as technology investments were made and Henri Fayol's late adjustments to wages created social unrest.

By presenting two very different strikes, one for the dismissal of workers and another against piece work, Henri Fayol concluded that strikes are called for various reasons and not only for wage increases. His panorama is incomplete however, as strikes were called for a number of other reasons, including calls by national unions, spontaneous strikes started in workshops and of course strikes for better wages. After the 1901 Montluçon strike and the 1902 Decazeville strike both cost the company dearly, Fayol adopted a policy of periodically increasing wages. In fact, he adopted different strategies, with some not as rigid as he would have us believe, such as deftly using his engineers to stymie movements before they spread, awarding small but significant benefits and anticipating claims by setting wages at acceptable levels compared to neighbouring employers.

Henri Fayol was opposed to workers unions. Unions at Commentry-Fourchambault et Decazeville were weak, with only 17 per cent of workers unionized at the Decazeville mine for example.[122] Their role was institutionalized with the first elections for the administration of the relief fund in 1894 and worker delegates for security in 1890 (see chapter 9). 'The agreements of former days fixed by the employer alone are being replaced, in ever increasing measure, by understandings arrived at by discussion between an owner or group of owners and workers' associations'.[123] Over time, heads of business found themselves confronted with associations of growing importance but Henri Fayol refused to negotiate with departmental or national union leaders. When he negotiated locally he relied on his network of informants to learn of the strength and situation of local unions.[124] He prepared counter-arguments with his directors and most often refused any demands.

Non-Wage Benefits

Non-wage benefits were common in French companies in the nineteenth century and they were spontaneously established by employers to improve worker loyalty. They were at the heart of social laws passed towards the end of the century that made old-age pensions, medical care and sick pay compulsory in mines. These benefits cost between 7 and 8 per cent of the total payroll in both mines and factories, although the latter were not legally obliged to offer them.

The Pensions

When old miners grew too weak to work, they were retired from the mine with a pension. Pensions were mainly justified on humanistic grounds, but they also had a business logic as workers could devote their working lives to the company, without concern for their old age, and with no need to save.

In 1890 Henri Fayol decided to constitute a reserve fund for the pensions of mine and factory workers, doted with 4MF in 1898 and 5MF in 1908 and pensions were paid using the interest earned on the funds.[125] The board refused any rules for pension fixing and in 1893 declared that 'anything that could transform the moral costs that weigh on the company due to a very large number of old workers into obligatory costs must be avoided'.[126]

Employees who had worked for the company their entire career were generally paid a pension of around 360F/year compared with a typical wage of 400F. Those who received a lower pension often successfully contested it. The need to establish an official rule to avoid any contestation was gradually recognized.[127]

When the Fourchambault and La Pique wagon building activities were sold to the engineer Magnard in 1893, the workers he chose not to take on received compensation from Henri Fayol in the form of an indemnity for those with only a few years of service and a pension of between 120 and 240F/year for older workers.

In Germany the Law of 22 July 1889 established a pension system that entitled workers over 70 years old to a retirement pension once they had contributed for a minimum of thirty years. Pensions were financed by both employees and employers. The French government was less ambitious, however, and established a pension system exclusively for miners. The pension law passed on 29 June 1894, which came into effect on 1 July 1895, set contributions at 4 per cent of wages to be paid equally by employers and by miners. Contributions were capitalized and paid out at the age of 55, based on mortality statistics under the governance of the National Retirement Fund.

French employers were not happy with the new pension legislation as they found themselves paying both for pensions they had previously set and the obligatory contributions for new pensions. The individual pension books also required a deal of administrative work. Employers would have preferred a pay-as-you-go system with a pension of 10F/year for each year worked. A simulation based on the law estimated that a miner who had begun contributing to the scheme at 16 would receive a pension of 394F/year at age 55, representing around 25 per cent of his last wage[128] which was similar to that paid by Commentry-Fourchambault at the time. As full pensions would only be paid after a career of contributions, and old miners could not expect to be paid a pension when the law came into effect, the government decided in 1900 to pay a special benefit out of the national budget to old miners. In 1894 Commentry-Fourchambault et Decazeville paid 300,000F in pensions under the old system.[129]

The 1894 law had profound consequences as it institutionalized the individual wage and the use of an employee's record book for retirement rights, and a pension became a right and not a largesse. The Commentry-Fourchambault et Decazeville Board of Directors found the new situation to be uncomfortable:

> We have no rules nor well established habits. The company has awarded pensions and relief to a quite large number of workers incapable of working because of their age or their disabilities, but one will not find amongst these liberalities anything that resembles a rule neither for age, nor for length of service nor for the amount of relief; moreover these favours have never been generalized and have only been accorded to the most needy.[130]

When the Fourchambault factory was liquidated in 1901 Henri Fayol suggested the following calculation for metallurgist's pensions: eight days' wages if the length of service was less than two years, fifteen days for up to five years of service, one month for fifteen years of service, one and one half months' wages for up to twenty-five years of service and two months' wages for more than twenty-five years of service. This rule only concerned workers since employees received between three months' and one year's salary. After thirty years of service all retirees received a monthly pension.[131] This system cost 77,000F the first year and 17,000F per year thereafter.

When the central pit at the Commentry mine was closed in 1911, Henri Fayol paid 20,000F in severance pay to 200 young miners and he authorized pensions for 175 old workers and ten employees at a total cost of 36,000F/year to be financed by the provident fund.[132] Workers' pensions were around 194F/year, which they cumulated with the state pension of 170F/year.

As was the case in other mines, Commentry-Fourchambault et Decazeville anticipated pension legislation by awarding pensions before they became obligatory. This largesse was designed to encourage worker loyalty as only those with lengthy company service were paid a pension by the company.

Medical Care

As well as retirement pensions, Commentry-Fourchambault paid compensation to sick or injured workers and to the families of workers killed on the job, as well as any medical expenses. This system was not altruistic, as the director of the Decazeville factory noted:

> With our current fund [for metal workers] we have some control over the worker, in the case of a more or less suspect illness, we can have [the suspect worker] watched by our guards and if we learn that there is a feigned illness ... we warn the worker, [then] we terminate payments.[133]

This view was shared by other employers, as shown by the actions of the director of the neighbouring Aubin mine:

> In 1900 the director of the mines of Aubin reported that all miners who were seriously injured on the job were brought to the company hospital and kept there. 'hospitalization of the injured presents a double advantage: the chance for the doctor to see the patient daily, and the impossibility for the latter to prolong – as is often done by design – the time required to heal the injury'.[134]

Between 1888 and 1893, relief expenditures funded by Commentry management increased from 117F to 140F per miner and were lower at Montvicq, at around 50F per miner in 1891.[135] These expenses included compensation for the injured, the cost of doctors and medicines, pensions including the capital contributions for new pensions, coal given to workers, school subsidies and compensation for several needy workers. These expenses also included the price reduction accorded to miners that was used to discourage miners from stealing coal.

Relief differed markedly between sites with sick pay varying between 0.5F and 5F per day. In 1890 Henri Fayol decided to rule that its calculation be half a normal daily wage although this rule was never formalized and sick pay continued to vary from zero to half wages.[136]

The Law of 29 June 1894 systematized relief by identifying three types of risk, namely old age (retirement pensions), accidents (medical expenses) and illness (sick pay) and by making mutual insurance societies obligatory in every mine to cover these risks. Their funding was the equivalent of 3 per cent of total payroll, of which one third was paid by the company. These societies paid benefits to sick and injured workers and to the families of work accident victims. Existing mutual insurance societies continued operating but were obliged by the law to have an elected board made up for two thirds of workers delegates. These elections took place in October 1894 in Commentry and Montvicq and in November in Decazeville.

After this law came into effect, relief efforts that had previously been at the company's expense, were two-thirds financed by a 2 per cent deduction on workers' pay, and this 2 per cent saving compensated the additional compulsory pension contributions.

For example, in 1897 the Commentry relief fund spent 46,000F including 60 per cent in medical, pharmacy and hospital expenses and 27 per cent in sick pay. Expenses amounted to 26,000F in Montvicq for which 58 per cent was for health care and 30 per cent for sick pay.[137] The company added an additional 44,000F for the two mines of which 46 per cent was for medical expenses, 27 per cent to compensate injured workers and as much again for extraordinary relief. Obligatory pension contributions, participation in the relief fund and additional funding of schools, health expenses and coal amounted to 228,000F at Commentry and 68,000F at Montvicq. These contributions represented respectively 7.7 per cent and 7.4 per cent of total payroll, of which 7 per cent were legally set, 4 per cent being paid by workers and 3 per cent by the company. Commentry-Fourchambault et Decazeville contributed a little more than it was legally obliged to.[138]

In Decazeville there had been a relief fund since 1882 that was financed by a 2.5 per cent wage deduction and a company contribution of 1.25 per cent of payroll. It paid for medicines, doctors and hospital fees (20 per cent of total costs), compensation for injured workers (9 per cent), sick pay (12 per cent) and widows' pensions (42 per cent).[139] The fund was often in surplus and from 1895 its funding fell to 3 per cent of wages. For example, in 1912–13 the Decazeville mine incurred costs 'for the personnel' of 125F per worker, representing 6.7 per cent of wages.[140] The costs incurred by the factory were higher as more factory workers were injured than miners. Around 40 per cent of these costs were company funded pensions, 25 per cent was for free coal provided for workers, 15 per cent was for housing subsidies and 10 per cent was for work accident expenditures.

Female and Child Labour

Mines employed children to work with hewers in the pit so they could learn the trade[141] and on the surface with women to prepare the coal. The Law of 2 September 1892 regulated female and child labour, forbade night work, limited the length of the work day and imposed an obligatory day of rest. Women were no longer authorized to work in the pit and children couldn't work there for more than eight hours at a time. The law set the maximum length of the work day at eleven hours of which one hour was made up of various rest breaks. Consequently, the work day for women working above ground at Decazeville had to be reduced.[142] At Commentry, the inspector from the Mines Service who verified the application of the law declared: 'the Law of 2 September 1892 is well respected'.[143] In 1894 there were forty-three children aged between 13 and 16 years old, seventy-eight children between 16 and 18, and 27 women employed in the coal preparation workshop at Commentry.

The Eight-Hour Day

Six days a week, a worker's daily routine was as follows. He rose, ate breakfast and then walked for up to an hour or more from his village to the mine. In 1891 in Commentry workers went down to the pit at 5am.[144] In general it took them half an hour to reach their work site, they took a quarter-hour break around 8 a.m. and a half-hour rest at 11 a.m., and they went back to the surface at 3 p.m.[145] Workers were present in the mine for around ten hours but they worked at the coal face for less than eight hours. While work hours were similar in other collieries, there were some variations, for example in 1897 in 12 collieries representing around 10 per cent of all miners, the length of the work day was eight hours or less.[146]Workers had previously spent more time in the Commentry mine before the ten-hour limit was established in April 1890, following the example of neighbouring mines. In 1900, the length of the work day at Commentry and Montvicq was again reduced by half an hour.[147]

Following on from the pit miners 1 May demands, the government progressively limited the length of the working day to eight hours (Law of 29 June 1905). It was fully in effect from 1 January 1910.

The Law of 29 June 1905 imposed a progressive reduction over four years in the length of the working day from nine hours on 1 January 1906, to eight and a half hours on 1 January 1908 and finally eight hours on 1 January 1910. As wages were based on a day rate, the reduction in the length of the working day would have no effect on wages. Workers continued to work six days a week.

The first reduction in the length of the working day did not pose a problem. At Commentry the miners were present nine and a half hours from which the meal breaks were simply deducted to arrive at nine worked hours,[148] and from 1908 workers left a quarter of an hour earlier to comply with the second stage without disturbing operations.

The third required reduction to an eight-hour day in 1910 was more difficult. The work time in the pit included the travel time to the work site but excluded meal breaks and the descent time. The Decazeville engineers worked hard to reorganize work[149] but the workers employed in the pit to move the tubs and supervise the loading and unloading in the shaft worked between half an hour and one and a half hours longer than the other miners as they had to cart out the remaining mined coal after the hewers had left, and as these workers were not exempt from the law the company had to employ additional workers for these end of shift tasks.

A second difficulty arose when unions demanded an earlier finish time by reducing meal breaks from one and a quarter hours to twenty minutes. As the other mines had accepted this solution, Henri Fayol felt obliged to follow.[150] The miners would enter the mine at 6 a.m. and leave at 2.20 p.m. reducing the length of the working day to around seven and a half hours depending on the time it took to reach the bottom of the pit.

Management expected to observe a fall in daily yields, although estimations of the extent of the fall varied. In 1908 the director of the Decazeville mine expected that cost prices would increase by 5 per cent and in early 1910 the chief engineer estimated that yields would fall by 10 to 12 per cent.[151] These pessimistic predictions were proved wrong as they did not take into account the fact that by working shorter hours, workers would labour more intensively. As Rousiers pointed out in 1895, 'the worker produces more per hour when one shortens his work day'.[152] Productivity per worker in Montvicq was 170 tons per year in 1906; it fell to 140 in 1908 and increased to 180 in 1910 where it remained the following year before increasing to 185 in 1912, and falling again to 153 in 1913.[153] Yields varied according to factors other than the length of the work day, such as the planned exhaustion of the mine that can explain the drop in 1913 yields. The eight-hour workday actually increased productivity levels.

In Brassac (La Combelle) in 1907 a miner extracted 150 tons of coal per year and his productivity dropped over the following two years to 144 and 131 tons. In 1910 when the eight-hour day was introduced productivity remained at 131 tons and increased to 133 and then 141 tons per worker per year over the following two years. These variations in productivity do not appear related to the length of the work day. Similarly at Decazeville the productivity of hewers increased by 1 per cent between 1905–6 and 1910–11[154] as the fewer hours available were worked more intensively, and thus daily production was not significantly effected.

Between 1900 and 1913, productivity across France was 200 tons per worker per year. It varied by around 1 per cent from one year to the next without any relation to the fall in the length of the work day. The application of the eight-hour work day on 1 January 1910 did not result in a fall in daily production yields but instead hourly production rates increased and compensated the fall in the number of hours worked. The Scottish journalist John Rae (1845–1915) was right when he wrote 'Eight Hours for Work' in 1894 and argued using examples that the reduction in the work week would not lower productivity. The British government voted similar legislation to limit the work week to eight hours for pit miners on 2 December 1908.

Additional Benefits

Commentry-Fourchambault et Decazeville offered its workers a number of non-wage benefits. Each year Saint Thibaut was celebrated at Commentry, Sainte Barbe at Montvicq and at the Decazeville mine, and Saint Eloi at the factories. Large processions were often organized for these celebrations[155] and the company paid the workers for a day that was not worked. These festivals and benefits were cancelled in the 1880s when the company made losses and they were reinstated in 1893 both by the company and in other mines.[156]

Decazeville management also financially helped workers purchase a pig. It was custom for peasants in the south-west of France to raise a pig to be slaughtered, salted and eaten over the following year. The company sometimes helped Decazeville workers buy pigs that they slaughtered and prepared themselves. In 1892–3 such advances amounted to 106,000F, for an average of 20F per worker, but by 1897–8, workers were less needy and these advances had all but disappeared.[157]

A second benefit was the timing of wage payments. Workers were paid monthly although sometimes an advance was paid after a fortnight. One claim by workers was to be paid more often and in 1912 Henri Fayol agreed to pay workers in Brassac fortnightly.[158]

Henri Fayol installed collective showers ('hot rooms') at Commentry in 1891.[159] They were operational in 1894 and the mine engineer remarked: 'Very useful installations are made available for workers so that they can take care of themselves at the beginning and at the end of their work day'.[160] Montvicq workers requested similar installations but the project took some time[161] and they were not installed until 1907, in the same year as they were made obligatory.[162]

Henri Fayol was also concerned with the training of foremen and he organized nighttime classes at Decazeville in May 1901 where physics, chemistry, mechanics, electricity and mine operations were taught by volunteer engineers. The training program included 48 classes that were run throughout the year.[163]

The company also offered workers the possibility of opening an interest-bearing deposit account. In 1898 total savings amounted to 3MF with managers and employees the main beneficiaries, and an interest rate of 3.5 per cent that was above that offered by savings banks at the time. Workers often opened accounts to save for the purchase of a house or a field.

Conclusion

Around 1900 the French working class was not at all homogeneous and within the same enterprise workers toiled at a number of very different trades. All miners followed a similar career path that typically started at 13 years old and evolved depending on their physical strength. They received their maximum wage between the ages of 25 and 35 years old as they were paid based on production yields that diminished as their strength waned and as they were assigned to easier tasks. Differences in salaries at Decazeville were sometimes tenfold, with women and children earning the lowest salaries. Some miners were still peasants who continued to cultivate small parcels of their own land while others came from afar, uprooted to find work and willing to return home or leave for other industrialized areas. Union action was hindered by this heterogeneity while management used it to motivate their workers.

Henri Fayol continued his company's 'social' policy towards workers for retirement, relief for accidents and illness. As the advantages he accorded were progressively made compulsory Henri Fayol complied with laws that replaced the company's previous largesse at a similar cost. He kept watch over wages at other mines and factories to anticipate any claims from his workers as he didn't want his authority eroded during negotiations. He sought to avoid strikes that he knew to be costly yet he still experienced major strikes and in particular those called by the miners' union at a national level.

Non-wage benefits were awarded by the company to retain workers and when relief payments and retirement pensions were set by the government, Henri Fayol scrupulously complied with them. Workers at the Decazeville mine were paid individually on 1 July 1895 as required by the Law of 29 June 1894[164] while other mines complied much later. 'The pay sheet only appeared in the mining basin of the Nord in December 1901'.[165]

Henri Fayol was not 'paternalistic',[166] for unlike other large industrialists at the time, such Schneider at Le Creusot, he built few lodgings for workers, did not manage a store to provide food for workers and didn't found company schools. He preferred to leave these activities to private local actors and lend his support to religious schools that were independent from the state.

Henri Fayol's relationship with his workers changed during his twenty-five-year tenure. It was difficult to begin with, such as during the strikes in Commentry in 1881, in Montluçon in 1901 and in Bouxhors in 1902. He wrote proudly of his firm policy in the third part of *IGM*. Later in his career, Fayol regularly increased wages to remain slightly above those of neighbouring mines and in so doing avoided costly social conflicts. He also argued that workers' grievances should be openly discussed with superiors and he told representatives of the board of inquiry into the mining industry in 1903 that,

> all workers are allowed to expose their claims to their supervisors. They can discuss them with the head miner, the engineers, either during their rounds or in their offices. When they so desire, they also speak to the director who never refuses to meet with them.[167]

We do not know how these principles were applied in practice.

6 COORDINATING, COMMANDING, VERIFYING: INFORMATION SYSTEMS AND THE ACCOUNTING FUNCTION

After 'planning' and 'organizing', Henri Fayol described three other elements of management: 'commanding', 'coordinating' and 'verifying' (controlling).[1] To command is to get activities underway, to coordinate is 'to harmonize all the activities' and to verify involves 'verifying whether everything occurs in conformity with the plan adopted, the instructions issued and principles established'.[2] The five management elements differ by their distance from action, and for three of them the distance is clear: 'planning' is a long-term activity, 'organizing' involves the setting up of productive capacity in the medium term, and 'verifying' occurs after action. Michael Fells underscored this temporal gradation when he compared Fayol's ideas to those of John P. Kotter.[3] 'Commanding' and 'coordinating' on the other hand are short-term activities that seem to overlap.

Fayol explained that 'for every manager the object of command is to get the optimum return from all employees of his unit in the interest of the whole concern'[4] and 'to co-ordinate is to harmonize all the activities of a concern so as to facilitate its working, and its success'.[5] What is the difference between 'the interest of the whole concern' and 'success'? Is it possible to 'get the optimum return from all employees' without 'harmony'? These two management elements are the responsibility of a head with the mission of 'commanding' 'spread over the different heads of the concern'[6] and coordination 'effected by combined action on the part of general management which supervises the whole, plus local managements whose efforts are directed towards the successful working of each particular part'.[7]

We tend to assign common meanings to each of Henri Fayol's elements of management. For example, 'command' is a synonym of 'manage, lead, order, govern, control, supervise'. A narrower usage places the verb in the more immediate term, as a trigger for operations akin to the 'forward, march' command hurled at soldiers to make them advance. There are also commands that are given in advance to be decomposed into elementary actions that can be executed in the immediate term. The command to attack during a battle for example is broken down into orders for each unit that acts at a given time. Commanding takes place in the short term but is more or less close to operations depending on prevailing practice.

What sense did Fayol intend for the word 'command'? What is the difference with his meaning for the word 'coordinate'? To answer these questions we need to look more closely at his writings.

Fayol exhorts managers to 'not become engrossed in detail'[8] when they command which would situate it in the short but not the immediate term. Coordinating requires a manager 'to bear in mind ... the obligations and consequences such action involves for all the functions of the business'[9] and involves keeping all the forces in play 'in equilibrium, and a sudden disturbance threatening the running of the whole occasioned by application of some measure at one point only must be avoided'.[10] 'Each department works in harmony with the rest. Stores knows what has to be supplied and at what time; Production knows its target; Maintenance keeps equipment and tools in good order; Finance procures necessary funds; Security sees to the protection of goods and persons'.[11] Coordination follows on from the commands given to a few and deduces what others must do placing it between commanding and the execution of operations.

An example may help illustrate the difference between the two words. In a mine, a command is given to start a new worksite and assign production teams, whereas coordination involves the daily control of workers' attendance, the screening of coal and deliveries to customers. The first management activity falls under the responsibility of engineers, while the second is performed by lower levels, such as foremen, or it is sorted out between colleagues by using the overpass.

Commanding is a short term activity while coordinating takes place in the immediate term, temporarily closer to operations. Coordination is necessary to ensure that operations that have been commanded are consistent and proceed smoothly. Without coordination, each department would have to wait for the others to become available.

Henri Fayol's 'management elements' exhibit a temporal logic that he did not personally explain. Starting from a plan, the distance to operations falls all the way through to a look back to actions past. There are four preparatory steps before action: 'planning', in the long term, 'organizing', in the medium term, 'command' in the short time and 'coordinating' in the very short time that triggers all operations. 'Verifying' takes place after an operation has occurred to allow for feed back.

Henri Fayol associated management tools to concretely execute each management element.[12] The business plan is the main tool used for planning, the organizational chart makes organizing visible and the meetings of department heads are used for commanding. Henri Fayol noted that,

> In a conference which gathers together his chief direct assistants around him, the manager may explain a programme, garner each one's ideas, make a decision, make sure that his orders are understood, and that each one knows his share in their execution'.[13]

These meetings were also used for coordination that otherwise relied on document flows and use of the overpass. Regular reports were the main means of verification.

This chapter looks at the three final elements of management by examining how Henri Fayol used three main management tools: meetings for commanding, the circulation of documents[14] for coordination and reports for verifying.

Regular Meetings and Inspections

Henri Fayol used regular meetings to animate his management structure, including weekly meetings at sites, monthly meetings at headquarters and annual meetings to evaluate the functioning of the different establishments. The board of directors met every month and senior management most probably also called site directors to meetings on a monthly basis.

On-site meetings were organized on specific weekdays. For example, at Commentry the director met with all engineers and foremen for a progress review meeting on Mondays at 5.30 p.m. and he met with the mechanical engineer and his foremen on Mondays at 4 p.m., and on Fridays at 5 p.m. Every Wednesday at 2.45 p.m. the director met with the station agent who also attended a progress review meeting on Wednesdays at 3 p.m.[15] with the sales department. The Wednesday meeting was still held in Decazeville in 1914 and the subjects discussed included weekly production, stocks, deliveries, work in progress, purchasing, internal quotations, material breakdowns and the order book.[16] All coordinative subjects between factory and mining departments were dealt with at this meeting and work was scheduled in department heads' meetings. Each divisional engineer at the Commentry mine met three times a week with the head miners and together with the deputy head miners at one of these meetings. On Mondays and Fridays the mechanical engineer met with his foremen. Once a month, and prior to pay day the accounts were verified with all the foremen.[17]

These meetings were supplemented by on-site department visits and each manager was expected to regularly visit the departments under his authority. These visits are mentioned in each job description. For example, in Commentry the chief engineer for mining operations visited the pit three times a week; the divisional engineer visited each of his work-sites once a week; the mechanical engineer inspected steam engines once a week in Commentry and once a month in Montvicq; the foreman in charge of machines and boilers inspected the cables and boilers every two days; the forge foreman visited the pits on Saturdays; the chief miner was present at the roll calls at the start and finish of every shift; the deputy head miner made at least four visits during the day and inspected the pit cables once a week; the day foreman examined the fire hoses once a month; the blacksmith inspected the hooves of horses working on the surface twice a day, and once every Saturday for those in the pit; the veterinarian examined the surface horses three times a week, and those working underground once a month; the grooms checked the hooves and the harnesses whenever the horses returned to the stables; and the head of the storehouse verified supplies on delivery. These frequent visits were used to verify and command as they allowed management to follow operations on-site and sometimes give specific orders.

Senior managers from headquarters often went to visit the sites by train. A first-class return ticket cost 140F for Paris to Decazeville, and half that price to travel to Commentry or Montluçon. During the 1904–05 financial year, the head of factories, Pierre Girin spent 2,000F in travel to visit Decazeville and Montluçon a total of nine times; Courtin spent 1,400F to visit Decazeville, Brassac and Commentry five times; and Fayol spent close to 1,000F on travel to visit every site twice. The previous year he had visited six times for a cost of 2,600F. His private secretary spent 1,900F on four trips during the year and 1,000F on two trips the previous year.[18] A manager from headquarters visited each site more than once a month and the local directors also went to Paris at least once a month as did their engineers. The Decazeville factory incurred 12,000F of travel expenses in 1913[19] which included the travel of salesmen. Despite the distances between sites and headquarters, senior management made on-site verifications. As Henri Fayol noted in *IGM*, 'each department supervises its own employees'.[20] Inspections could also be made by an independent department outside the local hierarchy. For example, the accounting department for each site reported to the local director but was audited by the head of accounting who was based in headquarters and outside local reporting lines. In 1913 the head accountant, Edme Moisan, spent 1,100F to visit each site at least twice.[21]

On-site visits were an important part of management, and even the board visited factories and the open cut mines generally once every two years in summer or autumn. They were an opportunity for local management to present their teams and their projects. For example, the Decazeville site welcomed the board of directors a total of eight times between 1892 and 1912. On 25 May 1900 the entire board visited the mines, metallurgy and army sections of the World Fair where the company exposed its products.[22] These visits were completed by regular postal correspondence and coded telegrams in which headquarters requested information, or gave instructions, or the sites made suggestions or reported on actions undertaken. Correspondence and meetings were complementary.[23] As we will see in chapter 8, Henri Fayol installed a telephone system as early as possible to facilitate oral communications.

All such direct contacts served to command, and as Henri Fayol pointed out in *IGM* 'wherever possible, contacts should be verbal; there is a gain in speed, clarity and harmony'.[24] While these contacts also involved a certain amount of verification, written reports were more specifically employed for this purpose.

The Flow of Documents and Operational Information Systems

The mines were required to maintain two registers that could be consulted by the Mines Service if the company chose not to send in a declaration for the calculation of royalties.[25] There was the 'mining register' where the quantities of coal extracted daily were recorded for each pit and there was the 'day register' which recorded the names of the miners who had worked each day. Both of these registers remained on company premises.

The mines also had formal information systems that Henri Fayol referred to as the 'circulation of documents'.[26] The different documents that were created and dispatched are listed in the Commentry job descriptions.[27] The accounting department played a key role, centralizing all the documents and producing the accounts, statistics and pay sheets. Documents were physically circulated by 'messengers', each assigned to a foreman, who delivered the documents to their addressee in the mine, the factory or the offices.[28]

We can discern several formal administrative processes at Commentry-Fourchambault et Decazeville including recruitment, calculation of wages, declaration of accidents, purchasing and customer deliveries.

Recruitment at Decazeville

Prior to being named director of Decazeville in 1892, Planchard wrote up a recruitment procedure where a central admissions office managed a personnel file called the 'matriculation register'.[29] This procedure starts with the foreman, goes to the department head and then the admissions office, before returning back to the foreman via the department head.

A job candidate would go to see the foreman of the department that he wanted to join who would give him (or her) a paper to take to the department head. The head would fill out a slip for the admissions office, the said office would then study the worker's 'travel book'[30] and sometimes send the candidate to the doctor for a check-up. The worker was given a number and then his (or her) name, birth place, marital status, children, dependents, mutual insurance society number, previous employer and assigned workshop were entered into the matriculation register that was kept in chronological order. The information was then recopied out on a form called an 'acceptability form'[31] that was filed in alphabetical order. The worker was handed a mutual insurance society booklet which listed his (or her) rights and obligations and the department head gave him (or her) an admission slip that indicated the department he (or she) belonged to. This slip was then handed to the workshop foreman. Children applying for work had to provide a written authorization from their teacher that had been cosigned by the mayor.

When a worker resigned or was dismissed, the department head calculated his wages due and the admissions office updated the matriculation register and returned the worker's travel book in exchange for his mutual insurance society booklet. The worker was then handed a slip authorizing the cashier to pay out his wages due.

For example, during the 1912–13 financial year at the Decazeville mine there were 1,296 departures and 1,410 arrivals and around 3 per cent of candidates were refused employment due to illness or disability, prior convictions or dismissals.[32]

This procedure ensured the security of operations at the mines as it prohibited unauthorized persons going down to the pit. It also made sure that all time worked would be paid for.

The Calculation of Wages

In order to calculate wages for the large number of workers who were paid piece rates, the output for each team of miners and every factory workshop was recorded at least once a day. To identify and record the workers entering and leaving the mine the Commentry miners had a personal medallion that they left with the caretaker when they entered the mine and retrieved when they departed,[33] the deputy head miners called the roll at the start and the end of each shift, and the attendance sheet was sent to the office every day by the head miner.

Carts of coal were marked to identify the team of hewers and the receiving clerk at the sorting station counted the number of carts per team and each morning sent out a report of the previous evening's numbers per pit so that the miners could check the production numbers and take note of any remarks made concerning the quality of the coal. The miners tasked with boring a shaft or building galleries were paid a salary depending on their progress that was controlled once a week by the head miner and once a month by the surveyor.

The engineers and foremen set the pay scale, and using these rates a team's wage could be calculated based on the quantities produced. The labourers and apprentices were paid a specific wage (fixed or a percentage of the hewers wage) and there was a 0.25F/day difference in hewer's pay depending on their category. The cost of any explosives used by the team was docked from their wages, as was a 2 per cent retirement contribution and a 2 per cent contribution to the relief fund.

All of these details were covered in the monthly verification meeting of deputy head miners where the objective was to avoid all challenges to the calculation of monthly wages. On the day prior to pay day, each worker received an individual pay sheet that detailed wage calculations and that was returned to the company when the employee received his wage.[34] Management told members of parliament that 'this system gave rise to no reclamations'.

This remuneration system was based on the daily collection of information and a monthly payment of wages. Its reliability can be attributed to three mechanisms that helped avoid errors: the daily positing of the previous day's production numbers for each team that allowed workers to check for any errors; the validation by foremen prior to payment to detect discrepancies and treat special cases; and individual pay sheets given to workers a day in advance.

While the same information system existed at the time in all companies that based wages on actual production, mechanisms to avoid complaints were sometimes missing. In Brassac for example, there were no individual pay sheets and miners did not know 'the wage that he was entitled to at the end of the month; for him, a precise basis was not used to establish this wage'[35] which created major discontentment. Team production numbers were not posted at Montvicq until 1909 when miners requested that they be communicated at least once a month. Their request was apparently satisfied.[36]

Production inspections were always a cause of conflict. In Great Britain, the Law of 16 September 1887 instituted the services of a 'checkweigher' to verify the weighing of coal carts. It was an external party, named by workers and remunerated through a wage deduction.

Accidents and Illness

The procedure followed in the case of an accident at Commentry was as follows:

> 1. all workers that are injured while working must inform their superior as soon as possible, whom must determine how the accident occurred; 2. in the case of a serious corporal accident, while one of the workers present goes to notify the supervisor, the other workers must give help to their colleague all the while taking the necessary precautions; 3. the notified supervisor must immediately go to the scene of the accident and take all necessary measures to assist the victim. At the same time he notifies the office by messenger to whom he gives, as far as possible a note explaining what happened. The office immediately notifies the department head or divisional engineer or chief engineer and the director who go to the scene of the accident if their presence is useful; 4. the victim must be transported to hospital, the supervisor sends another messenger to notify the doctor; 5. the supervisor must, as soon as possible bandage the victim following the medical instructions on the first aid kit; 6. the victim is transported inside or on the surface, taking all necessary precautions, and as far as is possible, on a suitably equipped stretcher; 7. when a victim needs to be rescued the engineer remains in the mine to supervise and direct operations following the orders of the chief engineer and the director; 8. accidents that result in the victim being unable to work for more than fifteen days on doctor's orders are brought to the attention of the town mayor and the administration of mines.[37]

The doctor determined the necessary medical treatment and also when the worker should return to work, while the foreman completed an information form to declare the accident to the controlling state services.

Supplies

The mine bought a number of supplies, including wood, to support the galleries, explosives, mechanical parts and machinery, wagons, horses, fodder, lime, cement, bricks, stones, oil, grease, brooms, tools, cables and nails. The iron and steels were provided by the company's factories. All supplies were managed by the store department who directly received the goods and invoices for delivered goods were approved by the head of stores and then the director before being passed on to the cashier for payment. The company often signed annual contracts with suppliers that were chosen by the Paris head office.

Every foreman had a counterfoil book of supplies request forms to order supplies from the store and in some cases an engineer was required to sign a request form. The store then delivered supplies to the various departments at the mine on an allotted day of the week. A consignment note was appended to the delivery. Supply request forms were also used to keep stock of goods in the store.

The store also collected old iron, wood and other unused objects. It also sold retired horses, and old wood for cash on site.

Deliveries

Letters received from customers in Paris or at the sites were recorded, numbered and forwarded to the appropriate addressee, orders were passed on to production departments and requests for quotes were sent to the technical departments, who calculated the cost price that the sales department could then use to calculate the sales price.[38]

At the Commentry mine carts of coal from the main pit were processed by the sorting, screening and washing department, and sorted coal was then transported to the railway station by horse-drawn cart to be sent by train to Montluçon according to instructions given by the head of deliveries. The head of deliveries centralized the coal orders for local cash sales from the Montluçon port and the Commentry and Montvicq stations. Delivery requests were also made by the sales department for major customers. The station agent filled out and dispatched a delivery note with the carts, and also took samples of the coal so that the laboratory could determine the quantity of ash present. A consignment note was written up for the transport between the mine and the station, and the list of deliveries and a monthly running total were sent to the Sales department each day. The delivery system at Commentry-Fourchambault et Decazeville was less formal than those that can be found today mainly because product lines had not been codified.

While this system formed the basis of the sales information system, no trace of it can be found in the company's archives. Invoices would have also been sent and unpaid invoices monitored and, when necessary, followed up as the reports for each annual site specifically mentioned customer litigation.

Regular Reports

The same cycle of reporting repeated itself every year. When the financial year finished on August 31 the accounts were closed and each factory and mine director prepared and sent a report to Paris in November. In January of the following year, the accounts committee, made up of members of the board of directors examined the different reports and accounts. Each member of the committee was in charge of a site and prepared a report on the points he considered most important. The committee also suggested the distribution of profits as dividends and to reserves with the dividend fixed by the board and ratified by shareholders at the annual general meeting in March or April.

There was also a monthly reporting process, with the departments at each site communicating interim results to Paris on the twenty-first of every month.[39] The content of these reports was formalized and often focused on production costs that were mentioned in almost all reports. Henri Fayol also presented the financial situation, and in particular the state of the treasury, at each board meeting

Accounting

Henri Fayol spoke of the 'accounting function',[40] the 'accounting department'[41] and the 'accounting statements'.[42] He noted in *IGM* that the accounting function 'is the visual organ of the business. It must throw up at any given moment, present position and future trend, must afford accurate, clear and precise information about the economic position of the concern'.[43] The accounting department is mainly in charge of this function although managers, foremen and even workers participate by providing and verifying essential information.

We don't know the exact number and roles of accountants. In each of the establishments they were known as 'office',[44] as opposed to workers, foremen and engineers who worked at production sites. When Henri Fayol took over the direction of the Commentry mine he increased the number of these employees and, in 1884, he had a new office building erected close to his own residence. 'In Commentry we built offices for the new director next to his current house'.[45]

Four types of accounting documents can be found in the company's archives: inventories, the general journal, the cash journal and the general ledger.[46] The 1898–9 general ledger is made up of 229 double pages[47] with one account per page. For each entry, the balance is brought forward and the total monthly, annual and previous years movements are recorded. Partial totals shown in red group together several lines and give a summary view of the account. These numbers help gauge the change from one year to the next and are useful for management.

The accounting department produced all of the day to day administrative documents such as pay sheets, financial statements and invoices, as well as the management reports on cost price, production statistics per pit, sales statistics and stocks that were requested by Henri Fayol and included in the annual report.

Accounting played a very special role at Commentry-Fourchambault et Decazeville. Part of the 1889 turnaround can be attributed to new accounting practices when share capital and fixed assets in the factories, including the overvalued stocks of Berry iron ore at Montluçon as well as machines and constructions, were all reduced in value by 50 per cent. Henri Fayol also reduced the 5 per cent levy imposed by head office on the value of fixed assets in each mine and factory to 3.5 per cent which was in line with average returns on capital at the time. These changes resulted in lower levies and lower deficits.

The depreciation of assets, concessions and buildings did not follow a set rule, and depreciation was only charged in years when profits were high. This meant that the poor sales of 1884 to 1888 did not result in losses as there was no depreciation charge over the period. Thus in 1888 capital had to be reduced and fixed assets heavily depreciated since the fall in the value of fixed assets had not been taken into account. The company consequently made a small profit on book values when it sold the Fourchambault plant in 1901.[48] Fayol proudly compared the fixed assets of 1856 with those of 1907; claiming that it shows that 'the company is in a position to produce twice as much than in the beginning with almost half the fixed assets'.[49]

Depending on the situation new works were funded either by a central reserve or by an additional charge to the site's cost price. The use of the reserve meant that works were paid for by the the other sites' profits. Major works, such as the Decazeville investments were funded by the company as a whole, which in practice meant Commentry profits. The second source of funding involved local self-financing and was frequently used for small investments.

Cost Prices

Cost prices (the cost of goods sold) were of particular importance to Henri Fayol. The cost price at the mines was calculated by pit and for the preparation of coal, coking and agglomeration. In the factories cost prices were calculated by product category and by workshop.

For example, at Decazeville in the year 1912–13 there were thirteen workshops (three blast furnaces, a Martin steelworks, a Thomas steelworks, a blooming mill, six rolling mills and a sheet metal workshop) and nine product categories (pig iron, ingots and billets, fabricated steels, special profiled steels, strips, I- and U-shaped beams, rails, sheet and large plate metals, bearings and splice bars). Some of these categories were broken down and cost prices were calculated for a total of thirty-nine product types, although the annual report only described sixteen product types that were grouped into nine categories.[50] The variations between the different product breakdowns can be attributed to the company's efforts to manage closely product categories. In 1913, production at Decazeville was 71 kilotons for a total cost price of 11.6MF, or 162.89F per ton. General expenses (827,000 F including 200,000F for interest on working capital estimated at 6.6MF) were spread across workshops, most probably based on levels of fixed assets.[51] Other expenses of 350,000F that were shared with the mine were also allocated to workshops based on another allocation rate. On average, overhead costs made up 10 per cent of cost price although this proportion varied by product.

The detailed cost prices for each category were made up of between fifteen and thirty components including raw materials, fuel, labour, man power, steam engines, maintenance, improvement works, handling and overhead expenses with the value of by-products deducted from the cost price. These details were used to track changes in cost prices over time as the prior year's cost prices were also provided in every report. For example, cost prices increased in 1912–13 because of coke and iron ore costs and the director was asked to explain these variations.[52] Every month cost prices were calculated and their annual trend was charted.[53] Calculating these cost prices required both technical data, including daily production volumes by workshop, energy and materials used and data relating to the work teams in each workshop and financial data such as the cost of inputs, the quantity and value of stocks, transfer prices, the cost price of electricity, the sales price of by-products and pay conventions for labour that were either fixed or based on production volumes. Maintenance and overhead costs for the Paris headquarters and the site were also included in the calculation of cost price, using the company's accounting records and the cost of fixed assets. Some investments, such as new works, were included in the calculation of cost prices as soon as they were incurred.

The calculation of cost price was quite complicated and required the accounting department that made the calculations to work with great rigor. For example at Decazeville, where cost prices were the most elaborate, thirty-nine products with an average of twenty-five components each were computed monthly. Henri Fayol sometimes imposed his accounting methods by changing those in charge.[54]

Annual Report by Site

The company's sites do not appear to have produced annual reports prior to 1888. All archived reports are posterior to this date. The Decazeville reports were written from 1892 onwards and became more detailed and voluminous year after year. They were written after the closing of accounts on 13 August, and sent to Paris at the end of November although some were not finished until January of the following year.

The longest Decazeville report was for the year 1912–13 and was written at the end of 1913 and in early 1914. The Decazeville mine report is around 450 pages long and divided into five independently bound parts made up of both text and tables for the technical, financial, personal and sales activities. The Decazeville factory report is 200 pages long and is divided into seven parts.[55] We will now outline the content of the factory report to illustrate the nature of annual reports by site.

In the first part of the Decazeville factory report the director discursively gives a thirty-six-page, typed overview and commentary of operations. The habitual concluding previsions for the year in progress are missing.

The second part is devoted to tables with sixty-eight pages numbered in pairs from 1 to 34. The first page presents the profits and losses by product for thirteen products. The following four double pages (numbered 2 to 3) detail these calculations and report the cost price, the sales price and the volumes sold for each product. Three pages (4 to 6) then list the quantities sold by product. Page 7 reports the number of days worked in each of the thirteen workshops, pages 8 and 9 report overhead expenses and pages 10 to 12 present those expenditures on new works that can be amortized by headquarters and those that can be amortized by provisions. Page 13 presents the number of days worked and their cost by workshop for eighteen workshops while pages 14 and 15 give wages and the number of workers per category in each workshop. The three following double pages (numbered 16 to 18) report the stocks of raw materials, supplies and semi-finished goods. The double page numbered 19 provides the volume and value of the stocks of finished goods as well as their yearly variations, and page 20 reports the value of diverse stocks for a total of 3MF at the end of the year. The following 26 pages provide detailed cost prices for each of the thirteen product categories.

The third part of the report is a fifteen-page review written by the chief engineer.

The fourth part entitled 'disputes, hiring, injured' contains twenty-nine pages of information concerning the personnel. The number of employees, including workers, engineers, lower management, salesmen and office workers at the start and end of the year are provided as are the arrivals and departures. The guards and the 'commissioned' and 'non-commissioned' agents are treated separately. Two pages concern injured workers, accidents according to the level of gravity (death or invalidity according to its length and its gravity), indemnities paid to the injured, widows and orphans and litigation brought by injured workers and the corresponding court decisions. A number of issues relating to the management of personnel are then detailed including wage attachment, honorary decorations, the quantity of reduced-price coal, the festival for Saint Eloi, the patron saint of metallurgists, subsidies to schools and religious cults and a summary table of all wage supplements (p. 24). This part concludes with a list of various affairs including expenditure for insurance, telephone, sales litigation, doubtful debts and the management of housing belonging to the company.

The fifth part of the report is entitled 'sales trends' and is eight pages long. It provides a detailed analysis by sales zone (Toulouse, Bordeaux, Decazeville, Lyon-Marseilles, Imphy-Montluçon, Paris, exports to North Africa, and the beam-trading syndicate). The annual changes in tonnage are given for each of the eight areas and the following three pages named the accounts that exhibited the greatest variations. A page entitled 'prices' comments on regional price variations by giving a range of prices in three regions for two products. The following page reports volume and price data for scoria, iron and milling produce and orders and deliveries for the current and prior year are also given. The last two pages mention customer relations issues including bad debts and complaints arising from poor quality goods.

The sixth part is made up of thirty-two pages of tables that report total volumes and values for the main product categories, namely steels (95 per cent of sales), irons and other produce. The figures are then broken down into eighteen product categories with previous years numbers again provided as a benchmark. The same total volumes and values are then broken down according to whether they were commercial sales or internal sales at transfer prices (see chapter 7), by customer location, by sales zone and then by administrative department (four pages). The final twenty-two pages concern sales to major customers that represent around one half of all sales. The customer's name, the start and end dates, the product, the total tonnage, the price, the deliveries made and the price of the previous deal are provided for each of these 250 sales agreements.

The report concludes with a seventh part composed of five pages and eighteen charts showing the monthly change in cost prices compared to forecasts.

Decazeville produced around 650 pages of reports in early 1914, as well as monthly reports. Their structure was fixed by Paris headquarters, they grew in detail and completeness year after year[56] and they required a growing number of accountants and employees to produce them. Reid noted this increase in the proportion of employees that grew from 5 per cent under previous management to 6 per cent with Fayol's organization.[57] These employees included managers, foremen, engineers, accountants and office workers with the latter most probably accounting for most of this increase.

While it is difficult to find accurate comparisons with other companies of the time, a remark made in a report at the time indicates that the number of office workers at Commentry-Fourchambault et Decazeville was seen as excessive. In 1902 the small, loss-making Bouxhors (Brassac) mine was to close (see chapter 2) and the closure was opposed by workers who believed the deficit was caused by an excessive number of clerical staff. At the time it was reported that 'if operations at the Bouxhors mine are making no profits for the Commentry-Fourchambault Company, it is due to its defective mode of operations and it's too great number of office workers. These workers, for the most part unnecessary, took a considerable part of the produce of the said mine'.[58] The mine's defenders considered non-productive services to be costly and the number of office workers at Commentry-Fourchambault et Decazeville appears to have been greater than usual for the time.

Special Reports

Regular reporting was not enough for Henri Fayol and he asked his consulting-engineers and directors to write special reports to prepare all major decisions such as the closure of the Fourchambault factory in 1896 and 1901, the construction of the Thomas converter, the operating of the Joudreville iron ore mine, the geological study of the Decazeville coal basin and possible investments in iron ore deposits, and in the Pont-à-Vendin steelworks in 1911.[59] A large number of technical and financial studies were undertaken even outside normal planning periods. From 1892 onwards Henri Fayol also had a yearly summary drawn up of all quantitative data for both the mine and the factory.[60] The company produced and kept a large quantity of written documents that can be found in the archives today.

Conclusion

A well-staffed accounting department was at the heart of the information system used by Henri Fayol at Commentry-Fourchambault et Decazeville. It centralized all operating data and produced daily documents including pay sheets, accounting statements, cost prices, various management reports and a large number of other documents.

The entire company was involved in collecting data for the company's information systems. For example, the foremen used a personal notebook to record observations made during daily rounds and a register was maintained for all plant and equipment that required regular inspections, such as boilers where all verifications, tests and repairs were noted.

The overpass was no doubt most often used to ensure document flows in the different information systems. The support services and operational functions communicated directly with one another without passing through their management, exchanging production orders for the factory or delivery orders for the mine, production summaries for the office and purchase orders for the store. Communication at Commentry-Fourchambault et Decazeville not only followed the vertical line of authority, but was also horizontal to better deal with day-to-day issues.

As we noted in chapter 4, the overpass was used by the support services, whether they be mutual or specialized, and communication was intense, for Henri Fayol feared that watertight bulkheads would create a 'lack of co-ordination'.[61] With such a degree of horizontal communication, the management hierarchy took on a role of verification, and heads monitored and sanctioned the quality of their subordinates' actions. The goal of Henri Fayol's formal system of verification was more to give feedback than to sanction. As he pointed out in *IGM*, verification 'has for object to point out weaknesses and errors in order to rectify them and prevent recurrence'.[62]

Henri Fayol's company was very modern for the time in so far as it used management tools that later became commonplace in the twentieth century, such as formal procedures, regular meetings and standard documents. Manual information systems were in place and information flowed horizontally using the overpass, and this organization required a large number of office workers both in Paris and at local sites.

7 THE COMMERCIAL FUNCTION: SALES AND PRICING

Sales at Commentry-Fourchambault et Decazeville were 15MF in 1888 and tripled leading up to World War I. Henri Fayol briefly mentions the sales function in *IGM*:

> The prosperity of an industrial concern often depends as much on the commercial as on the technical function. For the product not to sell means ruin ... Commercial ability includes, together with acumen and decision, a thorough knowledge of the market and of the strength of competitors, long-term foresight.[1]

He also details two particular aspects: producer agreements and transfer pricing. Henri Fayol favoured collective sales through agreed-upon production collectives where all producers sold at the same price and he fixed transfer prices between sites, for coal and coke from the mines to the factories, and iron and steel from one factory to another. He also influenced sales by building a sales network and by directly negotiating with major customers.

Commentry-Fourchambault et Decazeville sold coal, iron and steel products. Coal was sorted, washed and measured and coal dust was agglomerated into briquettes or transformed into coke for the blast furnaces. Coal was sold in fifteen or so qualities, and at varying prices, and transport costs meant that each mine sold to a local market where it competed with neighbouring mines and was protected from more distant mines. The sales of iron and steel goods were also local.

Sales Policy

The Sales Network

Mines sold their coal to the iron and steelworks, but also to outside customers. Even before he was named managing director, Henri Fayol put together sales teams and set up a sales network to sell coal to other customers and not just to the company's factories. In 1881, 53 per cent of the coal mined at Commentry was sold commercially, and by 1888 this proportion had increased to

78 per cent, and then 81 per cent by 1889.[2] Coal was sold to outside customers at higher prices, allowing the mines to grow independently of the factories and increasing profits substantially.

Following on from this experience at Commentry, Henri Fayol reinforced sales structures when he was named at the head of the company, assigning salesmen to each site to complete the existing sales department in Paris that dealt with large accounts.

Denis Sévoz, a Saint Etienne engineer who was a little older than Fayol, was recruited in 1889 to sell iron and steel products. He performed poorly and was dismissed in 1893. From late 1888 five sales representatives worked in the Centre and Bordeaux regions to take orders for wire products and also to monitor changes in market prices,[3] a mission that Henri Fayol considered important as he regularly mentioned it at board meetings.

Here are some details about his sales managers:

1. Paris: Pelletier was recruited in 1890[4] and retired in 1901;[5] he was replaced by Carlioz that same year.[6]
2. Commentry: Marlaud was in charge of sales from 1890 onwards.[7]
3. Fourchambault: Pétot was appointed head of sales in 1893.[8] Laffaye, named head of accounting in 1893, was later named head of sales in 1900.[9]
4. Imphy: there were six salesmen in 1896.[10]
5. Brassac: Pellier was recruited in 1900.
6. Montluçon: Bonnel was recruited in 1900.[11]
7. Decazeville: when Lassus turned 70 in 1892 he was assigned to the sales department[12] and died the following year;[13] Blazy was assigned to Toulouse in 1892, but later dismissed in 1896; Augustin Mansion was appointed head of sales and remained there until he retired in 1925.

In the third part of *IGM*, Henri Fayol wrote that his salesmen were attached to the Paris headquarters or a specific site, sometimes residing there, but they always worked for the entire company. When they took orders that their own site could not honour, they directly informed the director of the site that could. It was the overpass concept[14] that combined unity of command and operational efficiency.

In 1890, over one half of all orders (56 per cent), essentially iron and steel products, were taken by headquarters but this proportion was halved by 1912.[15] The company was more present locally and serviced customers through local sales networks. The Decazeville colliery was in charge of three sales regions: Toulouse, Bordeaux and Limoges-Decazeville. The two other regions of Lyon-Marseilles and Imphy-Montluçon were the responsibility of Imphy. In 1912 the Decazeville colliery managed the Toulouse, Bordeaux and Decazeville sales regions and Commentry was in charge of the Orléans, Brassac and the Lyon regions. The Paris office managed the railways, the military and export markets, representing around one tenth of all coal sales.

Local sales departments also contributed to the smooth running of commercial operations. For example, when the Fourchambault factory closed in 1901 the Commentry mine lost a major customer and was forced to reduce the work-week to five days.[16] The situation was restored to normal several months later when the sales department actively sought and found new customers for the mine's coal.

Henri Fayol told his sales staff that loyalty to their company and to their customers was the best guarantee of effective sales operations.[17] Salesmen had to include information on all incidents with customers, returned goods and unpaid bills in the annual report.[18] They were evaluated based on the number of new orders they took and were dismissed for poor performance.

Negotiations with Major Customers

Henri Fayol directly negotiated contracts with major customers such as the Compagnie des Chemins de Fer d'Orléans who purchased large quantities of coal from all of the company's mines. For example, it bought 17,000 tons from Montvicq in 1887, 10,000 in 1888 and 20,000 in 1899. In 1892 Fayol remarked that while the customer paid much less for coal from Decazeville than from Commentry it did acquire one third of the mine's production.[19]

Fayol directly and firmly negotiated contract renewals, naming experts to arbitrate discussions and on technical issue relating to the qualities of coal. In 1893 Fayol agreed to sell 130,000 tons of Decazeville coal dust with 12 per cent ash, at 8.75F/ton and 22,000 tons of Commentry coal containing 14 per cent ash at 14F/ton. This contract was renewed over the following years although the prices of coal from Commentry and Montvicq were lowered. In 1895 prices were again lowered (7.5F/ton for dust) for the Compagnie de Chemin de Fer du Midi in order to compete with English coal.[20] Prices increased slightly from 1896. As leverage in negotiations, quantities were dropped to 70,000 tons in 1897, but the Compagnie d'Orléans needed coal and it made complementary orders for smaller quantities at slightly higher prices through until 1907 when the Decazeville mine could no longer honour the orders for lack of personnel. Quantities fell to 20,000 tons by 1914[21] at a time when the Compagnie du Chemin de Fer d'Orléans was consuming a total of 1.3 million tons of coal[22] per year.

During negotiations with this very big customer Henri Fayol made a global offer covering prices, volumes and delivery. For example, in 1893 he unsuccessfully proposed 100,000 tons per year over ten years at the cost of British coal landed in Bordeaux. He offered to transport his coal from Commentry to Fourchambault by rail, representing additional traffic of 84,000 tons at a cost of 0.02F/

kilometre. Coal between Montluçon and Fourchambault was normally transited by the Berry canal, and this agreement would have cost the company 63,000F. At the time the two companies were negotiating a price of between 8.5F/ton and 9F/ton, and a one-year contract was signed at 8.75F for 130,000 tons.[23]

The railways also purchased products made by the factories, such as springs, axles, bearings and railway ties. For example, in 1891 the Fourchambault construction workshops received an order from the Compagnie des Chemins de Fer d'Orléans worth 1,100,000F.[24]

As these large customers commanded low prices, the mines sought other markets for their coal. In 1897 for example, Brassac sold 11,000 tons per year at a good price to a local glass factory when it replaced a recently closed competing mine.[25]

Sales Promotion

Commentry-Fourchambault participated at world fairs, published product catalogues and advertised in professional magazines to make itself known and develop its reputation.

From 1819 the company participated in all Paris trade fairs and several fairs in provincial cities. The company was awarded a main prize ('grand prix') and six medals in 1878, three gold medals in 1889, a main prize and four medals in 1895 in Bordeaux, a main prize for Henri Fayol and forty or so medals for the company's management, its directors and several workers in Paris in 1900. The company was also awarded a main prize for automobile parts at the 1906 World Fair in Milan[26] and thereafter the Imphy factory became a supplier of Fiat, the Italian automobile manufacturer. The company stopped participating in trade fairs in 1910, most probably to protect trade secrets.[27] The company also participated in the 1897 Brussels World Fair, the car shows in 1904 in Paris and 1906 in Rodez, but not the 1903 car show in Limoges. Commentry-Fourchambault et Decazeville did intend to participate in the cancelled 1914 Lyon fair and it refused to participate in the 1915 San Francisco World Fair.[28] Each participation was expensive, costing the company at least 5,000F, and even ten times that at the Paris World Fair in 1889. In 1900, the company spent 20,000F on the mining fair that took place in the Trocadéro gardens.[29]

Commentry-Fourchambault et Decazeville produced product catalogues and brochures that presented the company and its sites for the 1889, 1895, and 1900 fairs. A brochure for Montluçon was published in 1889, 1897, 1900 and 1905, for the construction workshops in 1890, for Fourchambault in 1894, and for Decazeville in 1896 and 1904.[30] Henri Fayol liked to publicize the company in this way and at a board meeting in 1902 he showed interest in a book published about Schneider at Le Creusot[31] that was written by James Dredge[32] and detailed all of Schneider's product and in particular its cannons and locomotives.

Henri Fayol also worked on building the company's reputation by subsidizing learned societies and inviting them to visit the company's sites. For example, he sponsored the Congrès de la Société de l'Industrie Minérale in Montluçon in 1897 and in Decazeville in 1904, the 1900 International Geological Congress in Paris, the Congrès de la Société de l'Industrie Minérale in Albi in 1904 that included a visit of the Decazeville mine and factory, and the Congrès International des Mines in 1905 in Liège.[33]

Henri Fayol also advertised by publishing small advertisement inserts that presented each factory's products in the annual report of the CCHF and in several professional magazines such as the *Écho des Mines et de la Métallurgie*. The following products were advertised:

- Decazeville: pig iron, steel ingots and billets, beams, rails, bearings and splice bars, sheet, commercial steels, strips, wagon axles, mine cart axles and wheels and metallic constructions.
- Imphy: steels melted in a crucible and electric furnace, Martin steel, steels puddled for tools, crowbars, springs, manganese-silicon steels, steels for carbonizing, gears, nickel steel, Platinite, Invar, cast steel and forged iron, wheels for locomotives, wagons and mine carts, railway axles, railway springs, coachwork and automobile, shovels and spades, foils, cannon parts, shells, armour plates and automobile parts.
- Montluçon: pig iron, cast iron, vertically cast pipes, hydraulic cranes, turntables, rolling carts, loading cranes and rotating 'Comambault' ore grinders.
- Collieries at Commentry, Montvicq, Brassac, Decazeville and Campagnac: bituminous and anthracitic coal, coke, briquettes, ovoid coal balls, by-products of carbonization including ammonium sulphate, benzol, creosote, naphthalene.

Catchment Areas

The mines and factories first serviced nearby areas where competition was weakest because of transport costs. Coal from Commentry and Montvicq were delivered either by a small private railway from the mine to Montluçon and then by the Berry canal to the north, or entirely by commercial railway at a standard transport cost of 0.0275F/ton per km.

The company employed 500 barges including 115 of its own.[34] In 1898 it used the canal to deliver 200,000 tons representing 40 per cent of the production at Commentry and Montvicq.[35] The use of the canal was slow and sometimes hazardous due to a lack of water or freezing in winter. For example, the canal was closed to traffic for sixty-three days during the winter of 1891. A donkey-drawn barge carrying 60 tons of coal only advanced at 3 kilometres per hour, stopped for the night and with the time it took to pass through locks it took five days to navigate the 110 kilometres from Montluçon to Fourchambault. Transport costs at 1.65F/ton were nevertheless some two thirds the cost of the railway.

The railways were privately owned and their prices, although monitored by the government, were often the subject of debate. While the Allier mines lobbied for prices to be reduced, lower prices would extend the catchment area of competitors with lower mining costs, such as the English collieries who sold their coal in French ports and the mines of the Nord who sold to the entire Paris area. In 1894, transport by rail from Commentry to Tours in the Indre et Loire department, a 236-kilometre journey, cost 6.5F/ton. English coal landed at Saint Nazaire was also transported to Tours (256 kilometre) at a cost of 6.5F/ton. This 8 per cent reduction on the per kilometre price meant that Tours was almost entirely supplied with English coal. At the time when the Berry canal operated through to Tours, Commentry coal could be transported there at a cost of 3.5F/ton.[36]

From 1907 to 1913 Decazeville coal sales were around 500,000 tons of which more than half was sold locally (55 per cent) in the Aveyron department and to the factory, and the construction of a new Decazeville steelworks increased this proportion to 60 per cent in 1913. With such strong local demand the mine had few other markets: the faïence manufactures in Limoges some 200 kilometres away were a stable market (5 per cent); sales in the closer Cantal department (65 kilometres) rose from 1 per cent of total sales in 1907 to 10 per cent in 1913 as Decazeville salesmen succeeded in developing a local clientele; commercial actions were also successful in Bordeaux and Angoulême (300 kilometres), where sales increased from 2 per cent to 5 per cent despite competition from English coal; in Brive and Périgueux to the north (150 kilometres) sales rose from 1 per cent to 4 per cent; in Agen and Cahors (150 kilometres) sales increased from 1 per cent to 3 per cent; and in Toulouse to the south (160 kilometres) sales doubled from 2 per cent to 4 per cent; as they did in Montauban and Albi (110 kilometres), increasing from 1 per cent to 2 per cent.[37] The Decazeville sales department successfully expanded its catchment area to a 300-kilometre radius despite direct competition from local mines, imports and mines from other basins.

Sales at the Brassac mine were significantly lower than in Decazeville as the company did not own a factory close to the mine. The majority of production (60 per cent) was sold locally at Clermont-Ferrand (60 kilometres) and between 4 and 6 per cent in the Haute Loire department (75 kilometres). The Allier department (150 kilometres) accounted for a large 12 per cent to 15 per cent of sales, most probably with established customers such as the Montluçon factory that the Commentry mine could no longer supply. Other dispersed markets fell from 30 per cent in 1907 to 22 per cent in 1913 as the Brassac mine refocused its sales activities and mainly sold its coal on local markets where it was more price competitive.

Transport costs were a less important component in the cost of metallurgical product, and the per weight value was ten to twenty times greater than that of coal. The Decazeville factory had no other competitor of its size in the south-west of France after the closure of the neighbouring Aciéries de France at Aubin in 1887, but as the region was lowly industrialized it had to sell further afield. The closest markets were in Toulouse, towns on the Mediterranean coast (200 kilometres) and in Bordeaux (300 kilometres) with each area accounting for 15 per cent of total sales. The Bordeaux wine industry notably ordered large quantities of five centimetre-wide steel strips for barrel-making.[38] The remaining sales were made in a large number of other distant markets, including Marseilles (400km; 5 per cent of sales) and Angers (500km; 1 per cent).

The Paris office took thirty percent of orders for deliveries in the provinces. For example, in 1913 the company recorded a big delivery in the Haute Loire department, most probably for the construction of the Le Puy-Nieigles-Prades railway in the Cévennes.

While the company's customers were almost exclusively French, there were some occasional export opportunities. For example, in 1912–13 a small fraction of sales (0.6 per cent) were made to Northern Africa, iron pipes manufactured in Montluçon were exported to Sicily and Venezuela in 1889–1890,[39] and in 1895 Henri Fayol acquired 1.2 per cent of a company exporting to China.[40]

Internal Sales

Commentry-Fourchambault et Decazeville was a vertically integrated group: the mines sold part of their coal production to the factories as coke, the Montluçon factory sold its iron to Fourchambault and Imphy, Fourchambault sold its steel to Imphy and the iron mines sold iron ore to the factories. Transfer pricing was central to the company's global integration policy.

The board always defended its prerogative to set transfer prices and adopted a doctrine in 1887 stipulating that transfer prices be set close to market values.

> It's important that all elements be removed from cost prices that would prevent an easy appreciation of whether the company should manufacture certain products rather than others, accept or refuse certain markets or certain orders ... the transfer price should be as close as possible to the current average price for similar products.

To simplify calculations, it was decided that the average market price from the previous year be used throughout the entire financial year.[41] The consequence of this policy was that a site would make a loss if it sold commodities for less than their cost price.

Exceptions to this rule were made for limestone and iron ore, which were transferred to factories at cost price. This created a difficult situation for the

Montluçon factory which received large quantities of ore in the 1880s from the Berry region that was costly to mine and priced above market. The factory used this costly ore for ten years and Henri Fayol was obliged to lower its inventoried cost so that the factory could operate in normal business conditions.

The use of market prices as a basis for transfer prices was moderated by the fact that the transfer price was fixed once and applied throughout the entire financial year: when market prices rose the transfer price was low, and when prices fell it was too high. Furthermore, the average market price did not take into account selling costs incurred by the sales department, which meant that transfer prices could theoretically always remain below market prices. For example, in 1889–90, Montluçon received 1,376 tons of 'gros 3e qualité'.[42] It was sold commercially for 13.12F/ton in 1889 and 12.32F/ton the following year. Montluçon recorded its price at 11.5F/ton, some 12 per cent and 7 per cent below market values.[43] For 'menu brut et lave',[44] the market price was 9.25F/ton in 1889 and 10.23F/ton the following year; it was accounted for in Montluçon at 8.77F/ton, 5 per cent to 14 per cent below market prices. Transfer prices were generally set a little above the previous year's market prices. The Mines Service took these differences into account when it fixed royalties by assuming that the price of coal consumed by the factories was undervalued by one sixth.[45]

Coke was also transferred at prices that were fixed by head office. In 1896–7, coke from the Decazeville mine was delivered to the factory for 14F/ton, despite its cost price of 14.67F/ton that was based on the cost of coal dust plus the cost of carbonization. The following year Commentry sold its coke to Montluçon for 16F/ton and commercially for 15.91F/ton. A year later, coke cost 17.12F/ton and was sold on the market for 17.99F/ton and to the Montluçon factory for 17F/ton.[46]

The policy of fixing transfer prices at market values was flawed as a transfer price could be above market price or well below cost price. For example, to help Fourchambault in 1886 the transfer price of Montluçon pig iron was fixed far below its cost price at 62F/ton, which was the price of pig iron from the blast furnaces in the east, and the price of second-grade pig iron was fixed at 82F/ton, resulting in a loss for Montluçon of around 7F/ton.[47] Montluçon was not always penalized by this policy, such as in 1888–9 when standard iron was transferred to Fourchambault at 72.5F/ton when it only cost 69.93F/ton to produce. However, the following year when the price of raw materials increased, the cost price rose to 78.67F/ton and the transfer price only increased to 75.88F/ton resulting in a loss for the Montluçon factory. Ten years later pig iron was transferred to Fourchambault at 67F/ton was sold commercially by Montluçon for 78.80F/ton.[48] Not surprisingly, Montluçon management complained about this loss.

The Decazeville factory also complained regularly. 'Special irons that cost us 74.69F have been transferred at 54F to Fourchambault'. Transport alone cost

11F/ton and the average cost price of all types of irons was 64.62F/ton.[49] The transfer price of coke was increased by 40 per cent in 1900, and a further increase was planned.

While transfer prices were adjusted to market prices to give a more accurate picture of the results of each site, we can assume that factories paid above-market prices for coal as they would have no doubt received price reductions for their large orders on the open market, and they would have also received poor quality coal that couldn't have been sold elsewhere. One explanation was that Henri Fayol favoured his mines which inflated their results and also the bonuses for their directors. This policy did not have any noticeable influence on overall corporate profits.

Trade Agreements

Henri Fayol felt that competition should be tempered by alliances between producers. He wrote in IGM that 'friendly relations [are] permitting of the settlement of most common interests by joint agreement'.[50] In practice, he supported selling through trading syndicates that grouped together several producers.

Members of a trading syndicate handed all of their production over to the syndicate that took charge of sales activities and then shared orders amongst the members. Members were paid the sales price less selling expenses. As Commentry-Fourchambault et Decazeville's sales director, Joseph Carlioz, explained 'the common sales syndicate is an agreement signed between producers of the same product by which the each engages to only sell through a unique seller, called a syndicate, that is no other but the collective of producers themselves'.[51] Most often these freely organized syndicates did not include all producers. The commercial risk of non-payment was shared amongst the members of the syndicate.[52]

These French trade syndicates were legally tolerated so long as they did not speculate or confiscate wealth. Members could freely join and leave according to established rules and any conflicts were arbitrated outside the legal system. French trade syndicates operated very differently to both German Wirtschaftskartellen[53] that were governed by specific legislation and American trusts that were prohibited by the Sherman Anti-Trust Act in 1890.

Agreements between iron and steel producers were commonplace when answering large tender offers. For example, when the Compagnie des Chemins de Fer d'Orléans ordered 12,000 tons of rails in 1841, Decazeville, Le Creusot, Alais and Fourchambault collectively won and shared the tender.[54] Thirty-five years later in 1876 these punctual agreements were systematized when the 'Longwy syndicate'[55] began selling metallurgical products from Lorraine, and other more or less stable arrangements between producers followed, and in 1919 the various French syndicates were grouped together into the 'Metallurgical Produce Syndicate'[56] that operated until the 1950s. At its apogee it had 750 employees and centralized all orders for the French metallurgical industry.

In 1888 Commentry-Fourchambault et Decazeville had already taken part in eleven trade syndicates.[57] Henri Fayol continued this policy with the most characteristic arrangement being the beam syndicate,[58] of which the company was a founding member. 'Founded in 1896, the steel beam syndicate with its common selling desk focused on sales of I and U sections in France and in the colonies. In 1909, there were twenty three member factories'.[59] This syndicate grouped together all steel beam manufacturers, including Schneider – it imposed a standardization of product dimensions and quality and promoted the use of beams in construction, notably through brochures.[60] The beam syndicate was initially presided by Jules Astruc (1862–1955), architect of the church, Notre Dame du travail, in Paris whose nave had been built using exposed steel beams.[61] The sales director of Commentry-Fourchambault et Decazeville, Joseph Carlioz (1860–1946), succeeded Astruc[62] as syndicate president. The syndicate was renewed every five years or so.

In 1896 Commentry-Fourchambault et Decazeville had a quantum of 2,500 tons with production at the Decazeville factory accounting for 700 tons[63] and when investment in the factory significantly increased its capacity, the company contentiously negotiated for an increase in the quantum to 10,000 tons in 1910 and 12,000 tons in 1911.[64] In 1911–12, 15,800 tons of steel beams were sold with an 8 per cent margin and the following year 18,500 tons were sold with a 14 per cent margin, representing 27 per cent of the factory's overall production. The factory's overall profit margins were a similar 7 per cent and 13 per cent those same years. The prices fixed by the beam syndicate reflected market trends and generated profits similar to those for other products.[65] The beam syndicate was a perfect example of a sales arrangement for metallurgical produce, and there were other syndicates for machine wire, pipes, springs, axles and rails.

The 'machine syndicate'[66] sold the iron wire rod used by wireworks. It was founded in 1887 by the Longwy steelworks and four other factories to reduce production levels with Sessevalle, the managing director of Commentry-Fourchambault et Decazeville, as its founding president. Sales prices first increased to 40F/ton[67] before quickly falling.

> The machine syndicate is rattled. At its last meeting there were a number of dissensions between partners and they were close to tabling its dissolution at the next meeting. We had to contest the figure of 1000 tons that were conceded to us as our share in 1889 sales; when added to our wire production this number would be far from guaranteeing operations for only one station; it must be deliberated once more.

In December 1888 'the machine syndicate is still standing. Commentry-Fourchambault has been allotted 1,500 tons instead of 1,000'.[68] This quantum was increased to 2,600 tons in 1892, the results were satisfactory in 1893, and the syndicate was still functioning in 1895, at which time the three-year arrangement was renegotiated: 'we had to accept an increase of 650t'.[69] These quantities of wire rod were produced at Fourchambault and, after the factory closed, by another company from 1901.

There were also punctual arrangements between producers. For example, in 1891 Commentry-Fourchambault concluded an agreement with five other companies for high resistance wire that was used to win a bid for 1,200 tons of telegraphic wire, of which 200 tons were produced by the company. The same year, an agreement was reached with Firminy for the railway markets in the west of France, with each partner bidding every second year. An agreement made in 1890 for bearings and railway ties allowed for sales of 900 tons and an arrangement concerning cast iron support bearings won all bids for a total of 20,000 tons. Commentry-Fourchambault's quantum was 7 per cent at a very favourable price that drew attention from competitors and threatened the agreement.[70]

The Montluçon factory specialized in iron pipes, producing 9,500 tons in 1890 and entering an agreement with other producers in 1890 that was broken in 1893, and then restored in 1894. Over this period, Montluçon produced between 3,000 tons and 7,000 tons of pipes. The agreement was again broken in 1902 and production fell by 500 tons in 1904, and rose to 1,400 tons in 1907.[71]

The Imphy factory manufactured leaf and spiral springs for the railway and automobile markets and belonged to the automobile spring syndicate that managed 2,000 tons in 1891, but was then abandoned in 1892 as its prices were too high and some of its members sold directly to market at lower prices. Another agreement for railway springs (leaf, spiral and Belleville springs) handled around 1,000 tons and Imphy produced 950 tons of springs in 1894 and 1,168 tons in 1895. In 1896 a syndicate for all spring types was restored between eight producers in which Commentry-Fourchambault had a 25.5 per cent quantum amounting to some 1,200 tons. Although prices increased, the syndicate took 60F/ton in costs for its first year of operations and the factory lost 31,000F. The following year the Denain et d'Anzin company broke the agreement, causing prices to fall. Spring production at Imphy rose to a high of 1,300 tons in 1898 for a profit of 70,000F, representing a 10 per cent profit margin[72] although spring production only represented 6 per cent of total production at the Imphy factory. The agreement between spring producers kept functioning informally and in 1903, when the Terrenoire factory (close to Saint Etienne, Loire) stopped producing springs the other former members of the syndicate bought its share, including Commentry-Fourchambault et Decazeville who paid 30,000 F as pro rata of its quota.[73] The company extended this informal agreement by partnering with three other producers (Allevard, Firminy et Saint Chamond) from 1907 until the War to supply springs for the Paris Lyon Méditerranée railway.[74]

A similar arrangement was sought for nickel sheet and in agreement with other producers, the Imphy factory obtained 50 per cent of a contract to supply sheet for artillery at 3.2F per kilogram, but when the Denain et d'Anzin company undercut prices at 2.5F, Commentry-Fourchambault et Decazeville tendered alone and won the following calls at 2.3F per kilogram for an annual production of 1,300 tons. This product became a profitable speciality of Imphy, making 105,000F in 1904–5 – some three quarters of the factory's profits.[75]

Commentry-Fourchambault was a founding member of an axle syndicate in 1892. While the partnership was profitable, the company withdrew from it before rejoining in 1905. It then definitively withdrew from the syndicate in 1910 when the company's quantum was not increased despite new capacity at the Decazeville factory[76] and the company stopped producing axles in 1912.

From 1904 the export syndicate for metallurgical products,[77] such as rails, beams and splice bars, was a member of the international rail cartel. It unofficially operated in France as a national arrangement for rails. While members shared contracts, there was no central organization such as that used by the beam syndicate and instead each company used its own sales network. Commentry-Fourchambault et Decazeville joined on 1 February 1910, and until then Decazeville had only produced 600 tons of rails and had sold them locally. The new Thomas steelworks and the reversible mill allowed the factory to produce competitive, quality rails in much larger quantities than before and after the first order was delivered late due to production difficulties, the company received a steady flow of regular orders.[78]During the 1911–2 financial year Decazeville produced 22,500 tons of rail and sold them at a 10 per cent profit margin, and while the following year's sales fell to 17,000 tons, prices were 14 per cent higher and despite a 6 per cent increase in cost prices, margins increased to 16 per cent.[79] The Thomas steel process also produced 250 kilograms of dephosphorization slags per ton of steel that could be used as fertilizer by farmers. In 1910, Decazeville signed an agreement with the Sociétés Réunies des Phosphates Thomas for exclusive sales rights in five departments close to Decazeville, in exchange for 2.5 per cent royalties on sales. This allowed the company to reduce the cost price of iron by 10 per cent.[80]

As competition for coal depended mainly on distances due to transportation costs, the mines neighbouring Decazeville, in the Aubin mines basin, could all sell to the same customers and so Henri Fayol promptly entered a sales agreement with the three largest local mines. Three reserved catchment areas were defined, but the demands of each company made the agreement difficult. The first agreement was based on the 1894 deal, at constant prices with the Compagnie des Chemins de Fer d'Orléans. The agreement 'functions passably even though it is not well defined'. Initially the associates only agreed on competing with English coal, but they progressively built an excellent relationship and by 1897 'the three collieries from the Aveyron more or less agree, from a commercial point of view with the collieries from the Tarn, Albi and Carmaux'. In 1913, the Decazeville mine left 33 per cent of the market to the Société des Aciéries de France (Aubin mines). 'We live on very good terms with our neighbours and we are all clear about the renewal of our contracts'.[81] Such cooperation between collieries from the same region could only work thanks to information shared between the sales departments, and telephones had been installed to facilitate communications.

Further afield the company encountered catchment area conflicts. It sought an agreement with other collieries in the south-west and negotiated with collieries in the south-east, imitating agreements between competing mines from the north.[82] In 1897 a project for a sales syndicate between collieries in the Nord and the Pas de Calais was abandoned when the potential partners could not reach a satisfactory agreement and it was replaced by a simple 'chamber' that was to treat agreements on a case by case basis. The collieries in the Centre region and Midi areas of France came to a similar arrangement under the auspices of Henri Fayol, and the first common action involved lobbying the government to increase duties on English coal by 1.2F/ton (around 5 per cent) from 3F to 4F, although there was, however, a lack of consensus between the mines[83] and no changes were made. In 1901 when the collieries from the Nord and Pas de Calais signed an agreement by the name of 'statistical office',[84] negotiations between the collieries from the Centre region and the south of France began anew. In 1902 negotiations covered 80 per cent of production capacity. Mines were to pay 1F per 1,000 tons of coal to cover the costs of this agreement. Clément de Curières de Castelnau (1849–1907), mine director at La Grand-Combe (Gard), was to preside in place of Henri Fayol, who withdrew to facilitate an agreement.[85] Schneider (Le Creusot), however, sabotaged the project as the company was both a coal producer and its metallurgical factories were also large coal consumers. 'In 1902, when the pressure from the Nord was strong, Epinac (Saône et Loire) and Commentry both turned to Schneider for support and local relief for poor sales'. Schneider however believed that it:

> had no interest in the agreement working; it could procure us some advantages as sellers, but our otherwise more important situation as buyers requires that competition be as active as possible; we add that, under these conditions we should withdraw, but remain in contact with the representatives of the collieries to remain informed.

In conclusion,

> Schneider little appreciated the attempts by Fayol, the director of Commentry-Fourchambault, to reach an agreement between the collieries of the Centre region and the Midi on the one hand and the collieries of the Nord and the Pas de Calais on the other, with a view to sharing the coal market[86]

and so it foiled them.

Commentry-Fourchambault et Decazeville participated in a number of syndicates, but only the beam and rail syndicates lasted. In 1911–2 the company's produce sold through these syndicates accounted for 50 per cent of total tonnage sold by the Decazeville factory and 57 per cent of its profits. Membership of the two syndicates was essential for the smooth operations of the factory. Henri Fayol was otherwise unsuccessful in his attempts to make arrangements with his competitors. The company was a member of the machine syndicate, but as production was limited to Fourchambault, he left his quantum to the factory's new owner in 1901. It was also part of the pipe syndicate, but it only lasted from 1894 to 1902. In 1896 Fayol played an important role in reaching an agreement for the sale of springs that were made at the company's Imphy plant, but the arrangement only lasted for that one year, and at the same time he unsuccessfully sought an agreement for the sale of nickel sheet. In 1910 the company also left the axles syndicate because it would not increase its quantum, and Fayol failed in his attempts to unite the collieries from the Centre and the Midi from 1894 to 1902. Henri Fayol's strong belief in syndicates[87] was not shared by his contemporaries.

Henri Fayol did not join any other existing syndicates, such as the sheet and plate steel syndicate founded in 1895 that controlled 90 per cent of the market in 1914, or the association of the iron ore producers from the Meurthe et Moselle department, founded in 1907, that the Joudreville mine could have joined, or the seamless steel tubes syndicate that was founded in 1910.[88]

One can ask why there were so many agreements for metallurgical products, however short-lived, and yet no agreement for coal sales. There are several possible reasons. Firstly, the French trade syndicates were inherently fragile because of the permanent risk that a member sells at a lower price. Companies had disparate equipment and diverging interests. Their costs were not at all similar. This created difficulties for building alliances.

Secondly, metallurgical syndicates that specialized in a type of product generally grouped together a small number of members, whereas any agreement between coal producers would have had to include all mines to deal with the issues at the borders of each catchment area. It was more difficult for so many companies to agree. The agreement between the collieries from the Nord and Pas de Calais essentially involved sharing sales information (statistics office) and lacked a central organization, akin to the beam syndicate.

Thirdly, market conditions were very different for the coal and metallurgical industries. Sales volumes were constantly increasing, growing by 2.3 per cent per year for coal, and almost 5 per cent per year for iron from 1888 to 1913. The average price of iron was stable due to technological progress in blast furnaces, and despite an increase in the price of raw materials including iron ore (1.5 per cent per year increase) and coal (0.7 per cent). Other strong fluctuations in external factors also influenced these industries, with instability strongest for metallurgical products thus reinforcing the need for regulatory mechanisms such as trading syndicates.

Market instability came both from prices and quantities, which when multiplied together give the total value of sales. Coal sales peaked in 1901, 1908 and 1913, and bottomed in 1896, 1905 and 1910, with peaks rising to between 7 per cent and 12 per cent per year above the troughs. Iron sales more strongly fluctuated, peaking in 1890, 1900 and 1907 and bottoming in 1895, 1901 and 1904, with peaks at 20 per cent to 40 per cent per year above troughs. Falls in coal prices were also moderated by the growth in coal sales, whereas iron sales dropped by 23 per cent in 1901, and 12 per cent in 1904.[89] The activity of metallurgical products, both in terms of price and quantity, was very unstable, whereas fluctuations in the coal market were less pronounced. Consequently, metallurgists sought regulatory mechanisms to deal with the instability in their industry. Producer agreements were a means of dampening price variations. Coal producers on the other hand did not need such tools. Agreements between French metallurgists did not significantly increase prices as imports were always freely priced. For the Decazeville factory, agreements on beam and rail sales were essential as they represented half of the factory's sales in 1912–13, with a margin similar to that on other products.

Conclusion

Even though the sales function is not considered an important part of Henri Fayol's theory, he did devote much effort to it, as he no doubt remembered how his father had sold fabrics and clothes.[90] He first built a global sales structure, dividing France up into regions with a salesman assigned to each region reporting either to headquarters or to one of the company's sites. When a salesman took an order he passed it on to the appropriate site according to the overpass principle. This allowed local sales to develop and it also loosened the constraint of vertical integration where outlets for coal had remained essentially internal.

Coal sales to large customers and local customers allowed the company to follow market prices closely. Internal sales to factories were recorded as close to the market price as possible at a transfer price that was fixed annually by the Paris head office. As this price could be below cost price, the company's transfer price policy favoured some sites and penalized others. It also influenced the board's view of a site's performance and the bonuses paid to local directors.

Henri Fayol sought out sales agreements with his competitors whenever possible, and successfully reached arrangements in markets for specialized iron and steel products, such as beams and springs. This strategy worked particularly well for steel beams and allowed the beam syndicate to impose a much-appreciated standardization of products across the industry. Beams became substitutable from one producer to another and customers could use standard tables to calculate their needs for specific beams. However, such agreements were fragile as it only took one member to withdraw from the syndicate for competition to start anew.

In 1912 the Decazeville factory sold half of its production via syndicates while the Imphy factory was more exposed to competition with quality being a key factor. Commentry and Brassac coal was also more exposed to competition than Decazeville coal that was protected by trade agreements with local mines. Distance was an important factor in determining the price of goods, and catchment areas were limited to the area surrounding sites until the railway lowered transport costs and allowed the company to service more distant customers. The Paris market remained elusive, however, for companies in the Centre region, as the factories and mines from the Nord and the east were more competitive and with lower cost prices. The railway also allowed English coal to be delivered in the hinterland behind the ports, resulting in a loss of local commercial dominance and an increase in competition.

8 THE TECHNICAL FUNCTION

All managers are involved at differing degrees in the technical function. According to Henri Fayol, 85 per cent of a workman's abilities, 30 per cent of an engineer's and 15 per cent of a manager's are technical.[1] For Fayol the engineer, this function had a dominant position although he did relativize its importance. In *IGM* he noted that 'all these contribute to make the technical function, and in consequence technical ability, stand out from and overshadow other abilities that are just as necessary for, and sometimes more conducive to, the progress and prosperity of businesses'.[2]

As an engineer Henri Fayol undertook studies to resolve practical issues with mine operations, conducted experiments and theorized his results. When he was faced with mine fires he studied the spontaneous combustion of coal by experimenting with piles of powdered coal of varying heights and measuring temperatures at regular intervals.[3] When land collapses required the company to compensate land owners, Henri Fayol studied ground movements following the excavation of underground deposits. He experimented with sand packed between two sheets of glass and withdrew part of the sand to simulate an underground gallery which allowed him to see that there remained non-collapsed land above landslide crowns.[4] He also developed a theory of coal formation in river deltas to explain the extent and localization of coal deposits by experimenting with flowing water laden with detritus in a coal wash plant. Although his publications date back to 1881,[5] his findings are attributed to the American geologist, Grove Karl Gilbert (1843–1918), and the phenomenon is known today as the 'Gilbert-delta'.[6]

As managing director he made sure the company used the latest technologies. The factories continually renewed their plant, Imphy researched and developed new products, the mines maximized their production by fighting mine fires, centralizing extraction in a well-equipped central shaft, using explosives, testing American cutting machines, using strip mining as soon as it was possible, and most of all, enhancing the value of coal by sorting, washing and agglomerating it in briquettes. Henri Fayol also introduced electricity at his different sites for lighting, electrical motors and the telephone, and he invested in typewriters and duplicators for office work, adopting new technologies as soon as they were stabilized.

Metallurgical Technology

Before Pierre Emile Martin (1824–1915) left the Fourchambault factory he had begun experimenting with regenerative furnaces (Siemens process). Around 1865 while he was working in his own company, Martin put the finishing touches to his furnace and patented it, allowing Commentry-Fourchambault et Decazeville to benefit from the Martin process without paying royalties, in compensation for its contribution to earlier research on the process.[7] After his departure, engineers no longer experimented internally with metallurgical processes and the company acquired the most up-to-date material and technology licences, notably for the Decazeville factory. Henri Fayol also funded a large applied research program into nickel steels at the Imphy factory, resulting in special steels that allowed for product innovations in armour-plating, springs and precision instruments.

New technologies allowed the Imphy factory to develop special steels that it could sell at high prices in a non-competitive market and the Decazeville factory to increase its capacity and lower the manufacturing costs of standard metallurgical products through scale economies.

The Reconstruction of the Decazeville Factory

In 1892 the Decazeville factory was completely rebuilt as no improvements had been made to the factory over the previous ten years. At the time, the factory's 1MF balance sheet value was equivalent to the scrap value of installations. The rebuild took ten years and cost 4.3MF.[8] In 1899, 24,000 tons of iron per year were produced in the factory's two blast furnaces, with the puddling furnace producing 7,000 tons of iron and the Martin furnaces 21,000 tons of steel. Their refractory linings allowed them to process phosphorus-bearing ores. Three different sized rolling mills produced commercial iron and structural steels allowing a total of 26,000 tons of finished goods to be produced by the factory including rails, steel beams and strips, sheets and axles.[9] After this large investment, Henri Fayol looked to triple capacity by installing a Thomas steelworks, the only plant capable of producing low-priced steel. Initially planned for 1908 at a cost of 7MF, it was not operational until 1909 and a number of early difficulties meant that it did not produce rails for the mill before the start of 1910. As the new steelworks increased the factory's capacity to more than 70,000 tons per year, all upstream and downstream plants had to be resized including blast furnaces, coke furnaces, rope-way conveyors to bring the iron ore, new iron mines (Batère, Muret to complete Mondalazac and Kaymar), a blowing machine, boilers, mixers, bridge cranes, roasting iron ores, reversing mills.

Henri Fayol oversaw the design and construction of two new factories on the Decazeville site, the first with a capacity of 20 kilotons and the second

70 kilotons. In 1912 he began building a third steel works at Pont-à-Vendin (Pas-de-Calais) in collaboration with the Lens collieries with an initial planned capacity of 300,000 tons at a cost of 36MF that was increased to over 400,000 tons at a cost of 50MF and then 65MF.[10] The factory was to begin operating in 1914 but was destroyed during World War I.

At Decazeville there were no metallurgical product innovations and only one small process innovation: a slag-crusher that was developed in 1911 and used to transform and recycle sterile wastes as sand. It would seem that this crusher was a commercial failure and only sold to the Guyana gold mines.[11] Alexandre Pourcel advised the Decazeville factory to acquire the best available equipment and license the best techniques of the time. He also consulted to a number of other companies from 1890 onwards, was a member of the American Institute of Mining and Metallurgical Engineers, and the Iron and Steel Institute in the United Kingdom – now the Institute of Materials, Minerals and Mining – and he was awarded its Bessemer medal in 1907. Pourcel was seconded by Pierre Girin (1866–1926), another Ecole des Mines de Saint Etienne graduate who managed the metallurgical department that oversaw all the factories.

The various investments in the Decazeville factory tripled its productivity from 15 tons per worker per year in 1893–4, to 50 tons in 1912–13, allowing salaries to increase 35 per cent over this same period. The new plant offered significant economies of scale that resulted in a 27 per cent increase in the cost price of iron over the period despite a 44 per cent increase in coal prices. The cost price of beams even fell by 23 per cent.[12]

Research into Special Steels

The Imphy factory was 15 kilometres to the south of the city of Nevers (Nièvre) and the Fourchambault factory was 10 kilometres to the north, which meant that both factories were faced with the same difficulties: distance from ores, coal and the Paris market. Nevertheless, Fourchambault was closed in 1901 whereas Imphy was very successful and still operates today as part of the Mittal Group. Henri Fayol identified early on a unique technical skill and in 1892 explained to the board of directors that 'some manufacturing successes at Imphy lead us to believe that this factory can prosper once more without major tooling costs'. In October of that same year he added that 'Imphy has demonstrated remarkable vitality: new and difficult productions have been successfully made. Serious profits are being made'.[13] As managing director, Henri Fayol continued to support the factory, specializing it in nickel steels with excellent results. He explained to the board of directors in December 1894 that

> for the past few months a nickel steel exhibiting remarkable qualities of resistance, elongation and a resistance to oxidation have caught the attention of the artillery and

> the navy. It should be said that none of this has so far been converted to profits and that trials could even lead to new investments, yet one must note that these poor factories in Nièvre, without hope for such a long time and so under-equipped have given proof of vitality over the past few years that should to be encouraged.

This specialization led to 60,000F of investment in research and new tooling.[14] Henri Fayol provided Imphy with a well-equipped laboratory and experimented with all possible combinations of iron and nickel, leading to three categories of alloy: low nickel content (less than 7 per cent) with high elasticity appropriate for cannons; average nickel content (8 per cent to 17 per cent) to which a little chrome, manganese and molybdenum were added, making them very hard and excellent for armour-plating; greater than 18 per cent nickel content that were very difficult to work with.[15] Such iron-nickel alloys interested the military who ordered armour-plating and canon parts in 1895 and 1897.[16] Profits for these alloys were high, although punctual as the flow of orders was very low, and so Imphy continued to produce traditional products such as shovels and spades for farmers, and castings and springs for automobiles and wagons.

The Imphy factory had extensive experience in nickel steel by the time it sold a sample containing 30 per cent nickel to Charles Edouard Guillaume (1861–1938), a Swiss born employee of the International Bureau of Weights and Measures in Sèvres near Paris, in 1896. Its thermal expansion coefficient was largely below that of platinum, the least expansive metal known at the time. Guillaume had identified a promising research project but lacked the financial resources to purchase other samples.

> I went straight to see Mr Henri Fayol, managing director of the Commentry-Fourchambault Company to explain my hopes and our misery. He simply said: "What do you need to continue your work? We are behind you." And so began a collaboration during which over six hundred alloys were supplied at no cost to the International Bureau. In autumn 1896 I had reached the minimum expandability possible for an alloy containing around 36 per cent nickel and whose value is equal to a tenth the expandability of iron. Marc Thury proposed that this alloy be called Invar. Follow-up studies sought to examine all of the causes of expandability in nickel steels; an immense number of measures allowed the identification of the influence of additives: manganese, carbon, chrome, brass; other research led us to describe the actions of thermal or mechanical treatments. And thus a rigorously nondilatable alloy became a reality.[17]

Royalties for this patent were shared, with Guillaume receiving 40 per cent. In 1897 Guillaume partnered with the Swiss watchmaker, Paul Perret, to develop a spiral spring of invariable elasticity with 28 per cent nickel content. Commentry-Fourchambault et Decazeville and Guillaume received 15 per cent and 10 per cent of the patent royalties respectively for this invention.[18] In 1919 Guillaume developed a harder alloy called Elinvar containing 36 per cent nickel, 12 per cent chrome and 1.2 per cent manganese. He was named head of the

International Bureau of Weights and Measures in 1915 and won the Nobel Prize in Physics in 1920. The partnership with Charles Edouard Guillaume worked well, and the factory continued its research activities into alloys.

Once the company could choose the coefficient of expansion, it developed a steel that behaved like glass and began manufacturing reinforced glass and metal pins for glass light bulbs. As previous pins had been made of platinum, this new 47 per cent nickel steel was called 'platinite' and the processes were jointly patented in 1882 and 1889 with Saint Gobain and two individual inventors, Léon Appert and André Larnaude. However, Thomas Edison's discoveries were instead used to produce electric light bulbs by the Larnaude company from 1898 in Issy les Moulineaux near Paris (100 workers in 1903), and Commentry-Fourchambault et Decazeville had difficulty selling platinite in Europe and in the USA.[19]

The company also collaborated with Léon Guillet (1873–1946), a future professor of metallurgy and director at the Ecole Centrale de Paris. In 1902 he worked for the De Dion-Bouton car manufacturer and asked the Commentry-Fourchambault et Decazeville Company to supply him with samples of nickel steel to continue his research into special steels. Henri Fayol enthusiastically agreed to work with him[20] and they were jointly awarded a patent.[21] This research allowed Guillet and Portevin to categorize different stainless steels in 1909, at the same time as Walter Giesen in Germany.

Imphy's research activity gave it a durable competitive advantage. The factory's competence was collective and not simply based on the knowledge of its engineers, but also came from its workers, its technicians and its foremen. It was collective and could not be moved as demonstrated by the lesser success of Imphy engineers when they were transferred to Decazeville.

Other opportunities for research collaborations were ruled out as they did not converge with existing programs. For example, in 1890 an inventor of a new railway splice bar by the name of Coulon unsuccessfully asked the company for project financing in return for exclusive use of his invention. In the same year, Berlier invented a system of siphons under the Seine river and unsuccessfully asked the company to provide the necessary iron pipes for 1MF.[22] In both projects the inventor expected the company to cover their industrial risks by financing the project. Such partnerships were risky and sometimes failed. For example, prior to Fayol's directorship, the company had acquired half the rights to a patent for a motor for 150,000F and the exclusive supplier rights for metal parts from the Bénier brothers. The Béniers sold their share of the patent to the 'Compagnie des moteurs à chaud'[23] that went bankrupt in 1892.[24]

Commentry-Fourchambault et Decazeville's metallurgical activity developed in two directions: an increase in production capacity to reduce cost prices, and the development of special steels for new usages. The technological orientations in the mines were very different.

Mining Technology

Mining operations involve first extracting upper layers of coal and then those that are deeper down and close to the limit of the deposit. As extraction advances, work productivity tends to fall and cost prices increase. Commentry-Fourchambault et Decazeville's main objective for investing in mining technology was to counter this effect. The annual coal output per miner (in the pit and on the surface) was around 250 tons when Henri Fayol was director of the Commentry mine, but it fell to 200 tons in 1901, and a lowly 130 tons in the years leading up to its exhaustion. Henri Fayol used mining technology to plan production over the long term and exhaust deposits rather than to increase productivity, and also to enhance the value of coal so as to sell it at a higher price. Technical engineering information was freely shared between all mines and so was not a competitive advantage.

The Sustainability of Mining Operations

Operating a mine is by nature a temporary pursuit as one day the deposit will be exhausted. Perpetuating operations involves extracting all possible coal with the least possible effort and leaving nothing to spontaneously perish through causes such as fire.

The Fires

Coal fires were the scourge of collieries in the nineteenth century as not only did they destroy mined coal but they also prevented extracting the surrounding coal. Henri Fayol was faced with this technical problem early in his career[25]and he successfully developed new techniques to overcome it and became a specialist in the extinction of mine fires. His approach involved first confining the fire so that no air was available to fuel it by building a barrier across galleries. He also invented a breathing apparatus that allowed crews to work in smoke-filled environments. Once the fire was confined, galleries were dug above it and a mix of water, clay and quick-dry cement was poured down on to the fire, sticking to the coal and isolating it from the air. These methods were invented by Henri Fayol prior to 1865 and they contributed to his nomination as director of the Commentry mine, yet some of his engineers failed to use his methods.

The last major Commentry mine fire broke out on the fifth and sixth levels of the St Charles pit and lasted for seven years. The pit was reputed as dangerous, as noted by an engineer from the Mines Service in 1874: 'The coal on this level is very inflammable and spontaneous fires often flare up that are very difficult to fight. Until now all fires have been mastered, and it is hoped that they will be completely taken care of in the coming year'.[26] On 31 August 1875 four miners died of smoke-inhalation after a fire started in the pit.[27] At the time, Henri Fayol was preparing for his wedding which was planned for 22 November 1875 in Moulins, 70 kilometres from Commentry and was replaced by the chief engineer, Georges de Goumoëns (1840–1903).[28]

The fire was reported in the 1875 annual report of the Mines Service as follows:

> All measures had been taken to extinguish the underground fire that started last August on the sixth level of the St Charles pit (east section) and that caused the accident of 31 August (four workers dead by asphyxiation). A large barrier going from the floor to the ceiling of the layer and rising up to the fifth level backfill inhibits air from reaching the fire; the sixth floor gallery is also barricaded by doors on the back-draft side. It is hoped that in a short time, the fire will have disappeared and work can begin there, which will however only be done with great precaution and measures to avoid any chance of gas explosions or irruption of smoke.[29]

Henri Fayol took over firefighting operations at the start of 1876 by which time the fire had spread. His first concern was to better confine it using a second barrier behind the fire in the same gallery. It took the company a year to dig around the fire to erect the barrier and the fire was circumscribed in December 1876.

> The fire ... is not out yet ... We have abundantly doused the coal mass neighbouring the fire by bringing water through the conduits in the level five gallery and in transversal galleries. At present, the wall is almost at ambient air temperature indicating that the fire is well diminished ... At present we are drilling through the vertical plane, a horizontal cut that is preceded by boreholes and involves taking necessary precautions to avoid accidents. As soon as the gallery on the sixth is barricaded behind the fire, the necessary preparations will be made. To avoid explosion we only use safety lamps (Museler system) for these works. We hope to finish with the fire sometime next year.[30]

In early 1877 the Mines Service wrote that the fire 'is now circumscribed in a very small space', but it continued to smolder and when the Mines Service engineer visited again in August 1877, two years after the fire had started, he noted that

> lately Mr Fayolle (sic) imagined, an ingenious method of mounting barriers which have obtained very good results and that apparently would have extinguished the fire in a few months if it had been used at the outset. This method involves opening large bore holes in the coal from above the fire by cuts made at the upper level and then pouring down these holes a concrete and clay mixture'.[31]

Several months later, at the start of 1878 the Mines Service engineer again noted that

> the fire that had first appeared in August 1875 at the 6th level of the St Charles pit is now circumscribed to a very small space. It is hoped to be rid of it in several weeks, mainly thanks to Me Fayolle's (sic) ingenious method of safely creating a barrier in the smoke filled galleries.

The fire was gradually extinguished beginning in 1878 'largely by the process of cementing', a method that 'gives excellent results' and in July 1879 'several fires that had been impossible to isolate with other means previously employed were able to be controlled'.[32] But it was not until June 1882 that

> the process used by the mine director, Mr Fayol that involved using pipes to bring water from the surface to underground works and resulting in very high water pressure allowed for the fires inside the Commentry mine to be completely eradicated.[33]

The fire in the St Charles pit burned for seven years, from 1875 to 1882 as it had not been dealt with quickly enough. It was left to spread for several months before Henri Fayol's methods were used to first confine it and then to cover it with cement and clay and drench it with water. The engineer in charge at the time, Goumoëns made mistakes and no-one dared disturb Fayol who was on holidays preparing his wedding. Goumoëns later left the Commentry mine to marry in Switzerland where his family owned a castle and he went on to manage a colliery close to Switzerland in Ronchamp (Haute Saône).

Another fire broke out in 1875 in the Forêt pit and it was extinguished in early 1876.[34] On 19 November 1878 a fire on the eighth floor of the Sainte Aline pit led to the sealing off of 900 metres of galleries using six successive barriers. 'On 25 November a door to one of the barriers was opened and men wearing breathing apparatus were able to build a new one in the gallery 50m in front of the fire, in the direction of the original air flow'.[35] Two other barriers were built on the other side of the fire by 30 November, thus reducing the length of the condemned galleries to 140 metres. The covering process was used and the fire was rapidly extinguished. It flared again in June 1882 and was quickly extinguished using the same methods.

While in early 1884 the company believed that 'we are today completely safe from fires that were once the cause of so much difficulty'[36] there were still fires in the cuttings and even underground. For example, on Sunday 5 July 1885 smoke was observed in a gallery leading to the Saint Aline pit. Workers equipped with breathing apparatuses set up four temporary canvas barriers at the ends of the gallery and a clay barrier was made in front of the burning wall. Air flow was restored to the gallery using an air intake sleeve, two miners equipped with breathing apparatus inspected the fire, the wall was doused using fire houses and burning coal was dug out. The next day a second gallery was dug above the fire and the burning area was covered with a cement-clay mixture. Ten days later the temperature had fallen to 24°C, compared with 20°C for the rest of the mine. Success of mine firefighting depended on the speed at which action was taken.

There were also mine fires at Decazeville. They had occurred naturally and sporadically before mining began in the area and continued to be fuelled by air entering through cracks in the ground. When mining galleries reached ancient fires, the new oxygen supply meant that fires flared anew. Underground fires could burn for months and some worksites close to ancient fires were even so hot that miners worked in their underwear.[37] Henri Fayol systematically supervised the Decazeville engineers in their fight against mine fires and they used the techniques developed at Commentry.[38] Iron pipes were installed to bring the cement-clay mix down from the surface to be injected under pressure into the gallery walls. Once the hot coal was treated, warm coal could be mined without it igniting.[39] From 1910 water and sand were piped into the hotter parts of the mine to be successfully used as backfill as the sand filled all the cracks where the air flow could fan any fires.[40]

Only security lamps were used in proximity to fires and rescue teams were equipped with breathing apparatus and oxygen tanks to treat smoke-inhalation victims.

The Flow of Materials

The extraction of coal was decentralized. In the underground galleries, the coal was shovelled into carts that were attached together in a small horse-drawn convoy and in Commentry they were pulled to the surface up an inclined plane or up a shaft in a steam engine-driven lift. In 1891 Henri Fayol requested funding to bore a new shaft at the Commentry mine and replace the six existing shafts that were deteriorating. The estimated cost of 0.8MF was justified by the cost of repairing the shaft and the intention to mine the untouched coal surrounding the existing shafts.[41] The central shaft was finished in 1895 for a cost in excess of 1MF. Double-deck lifts were used to raise six tubs, carrying up to 400 kilograms of coal each, up a 4.5 metre-diameter cylindrical shaft. The 300 horse power hoist motor allowed for one trip per minute. The capacity of the shaft was 385,000 tons per year for an eight-hour workday[42] which meant that all of the Commentry coal could be brought up the one shaft. A similar shaft was bored at Decazeville in 1904.[43]

In 1880 workers entered the Commentry mine through the cuttings and along an entrance slope, and in 1891 they also entered by a spiral staircase in the Juillet shaft. At the time, the horses were walked up the slope and out of the mine to spend the night in the stables on the surface.[44]

Iron ore arrived in Decazeville from a mine in Mondalazac 30 kilometres away. It was first transported by cart to the railway station and then by a company-owned railway to Decazeville. Henri Fayol decided to have a rope-way conveyor built in 1908 but the system was not operational until 1910 due to disagreements with landowners. A similar conveyor was installed in Imphy in 1911 between the factory and the canal.[45]

The Commentry carts could carry 400 kilograms of coal while the Decazeville carts were twice as big but less manoeuvrable. Henri Fayol decided to replace the bigger carts with smaller ones and in 1904 1,200 older carts were still to be converted at a cost of 150,000F.[46]

Improvements to the flow of materials directly impacted operating costs but Henri Fayol chose not to mechanize underground haulage as had been done in Blanzy from 1872[47] and waited until 1903 before installing hoists on the inclined planes at Decazeville.[48]

Mining Techniques

In order to keep operating costs to a minimum, Henri Fayol looked for ways to reduce global costs through savings on ancillary costs rather than by increasing production rhythms and productivity. For example, he reduced the costs of backfill and timbering. When coal is extracted from underground mines it leaves a void. In order to avoid a cave-in and subsidence of the above lying land, coal was replaced at the time with a backfill of sand or stones. In Commentry before 1882, this activity was performed at night by specialized miners. Henri Fayol experimented with miners themselves directly replacing the coal with backfill as it was being extracted. This task accounted for 10 per cent of work time, and wages were adjusted accordingly. Such an organization of work did not increase productivity but rather reduced overall costs as the carts carried the backfill into the mine when they arrived to cart the coal which meant that they no longer circulated empty or at night.[49] Timbering had also been performed at night until Henri Fayol did away with specialized timberers and had teams of hewers install timber supports during the day.[50] Progressive timbering improved mine safety although timberers still worked at night to repair and maintain the galleries.

Timber work was mainly in oak except in areas where there was a fire risk and old, slightly arched rails were used. Wood was one third the cost of iron but deteriorated much more rapidly and so Henri Fayol worked at increasing the life of oak timber work by treating them with a mixture of tar and iron sulphate to prevent wood rot. Soaking oak in this mixture for twenty-four hours increased its working life by seven years.[51] The way timbers were installed was also important and Henri Fayol insisted that timber work be as robust as possible and in some places used stronger 'English timbering' where beams mutually reinforced each other. This method also reduced costs by 0.12F/ton.[52] Engineers from the Mines Service noted after each inspection that timber work was well done and well maintained.

Henri Fayol also reduced costs between 1895 and 1900 at Decazeville by employing lower-paid manual workers. Average pay fell over this period although hewers' wages remained constant. The labourers assisted the hewers but were paid 0.75F/day less[53] with higher wages reserved for experienced workers. By 1899, labourers represented half of the pit's workforce. This change in the balance between qualified and non-qualified workers was limited to maintain the skills of the hewers. Average wages increased from 1898 onwards.[54]

Explosives

The pick was the main tool used to mine coal, and became a universal symbol of the trade. The main galleries were bored using explosives and the shaft with dynamite. A visitor to the Commentry mine in 1868 remarked that explosives were already being used at the time to bore a shaft.[55] The extraction of coal, however, was performed manually. In 1882 an engineer from the Mines Service wrote that in Commentry

> the extraction of coal is by pick. In rock galleries were the use of explosives is necessary, ordinary powder is generally used, although not dynamite which was necessary to sink a shaft; the workers found the latter repulsive as, they say, its gases fouled the atmosphere at the work-site'.[56]

Prior to 1888 explosives were considered a possible cause of firedamp explosions. In 1887 and 1888 in Sevran-Livry, François-Ernest Mallard(1833–94) and Henri Le Chatelier (1850–1936) tested the effect of explosives on mining environments and showed that explosives could be used if the temperature of the explosion was not too high.[57] Explosives were used to extract coal from 1888 onwards. A crowbar and then a hand drill were used to bore a hole, into which a charge was inserted. Productivity was higher but the coal was more fragmented with fewer large pieces of coal that could be sold at higher prices. Between 1885 and 1895 productivity of underground miners at Commentry and Montvicq increased by 15 per cent, whereas the amount of large, first-quality coal extracted fell by one third.[58]

After 1890, any mine considered subject to explosion or excessive coal dust had to use certified explosives. An explosive called 'Grisounite', produced by Favier in the Pyrénées Orientales Department at Paulilles, was successfully used at Commentry[59]to bore through the rock in the galleries, but proved more troublesome for coal extraction.[60]

The cost of explosives were deducted from a worker's pay to prevent their overuse. In 1891, the 900 miners at Montvicq used a total of 700 kilograms of explosives per month, representing the equivalent of one charge per day and per team.[61] The use of explosives involved specific risks that necessitated strict procedures as we will see in the following chapter. In 1912 it was decided that open pit miners should no longer pay for their use of explosives and following this decision, productivity increased by 20 per cent.[62]

American Mechanical Cutters

From the end of the nineteenth century English mines began using machinery to extract coal. In 1880 the Blanzy mine (in Saône et Loire) trialled the use of a coal cutter but the test failed because of rock present in the local coal deposits. In 1898, four collieries including Commentry-Fourchambault et Decazeville financed Adolphe André Dubois de Gennes' (1858–1916) mission to the USA to study the use of mining machinery.[63] Henri Fayol no doubt received the results of the study before the 1900 conference as he began by trialling a large 1,800 kilogram cutting machine[64] followed by a lighter 350 kilogram pick machine manufactured by the American company Sullivan. This compressed air cutter was first tested in the company's strip mines. The manufacturer even used a photo of this French trial in its international catalogue at the time.[65]

Management paid a great deal of attention to these trials and rapidly sought to ascertain how many workers could be replaced and what the impact would be on cost price.[66] Engineers were optimistic as a gallery had been bored at twice the usual speed[67] and Henri Fayol mentioned these tests to the board of directors in January 1901: 'We esteem that ten or so cutters will replace 120 workers. Unfortunately, we still do not have the amount of compressed air necessary. We must begin by installing air compressors'.[68] The board decided to inspect the machines at the Bourran mine when it next visited Decazeville in 1901.[69]

Much hope was placed in these new machines: 'We are very much counting on the use of cutting machines that our new compressed air plant should allow us to regularly operate from January 1903' at three sites[70] and in May 1903, Henri Fayol decided that the 'cutting tests at Decazeville were sufficiently satisfactory that we acquire several cutters more'.[71] At the end of 1903, the Decazeville director considered that

> the yield improved in little time through the use of cutters ... Over the last year the use of these machines in the few mines where it was possible increased the yield of hewers and miners by more than 20 per cent and resulted in an average decrease in cost price of 0.3F.[72]

The fall in production costs by 2 per cent from the previous year was attributed to the use of these machines.[73]

One team used the cutter during the day and another at night to maximize the use of the machine, but this disrupted operations as mining was mainly done during the day. The use of cutters was not simple: the worker sat on a 1.5 metre by 2 metre wooden platform, held the cutter by the handles with both hands and blocked a wheel with his foot to avoid recoil. An accident occurred in March 1903 when the machine's teeth hit a mass of clinker embedded in the coal causing the machine to shift and fall off the platform. The operator was unable to stop it falling and had two fingers crushed.'[74]

In 1903 the Decazeville mine was equipped with compressors installed close to the central power station so that it could run a larger number of cutters. The Mines Service was pessimistic concerning these trials: 'the results of using machine tools have not been positive; the irregular deposit, the inconstant hardness of the coal have until the present prevented their generalization to the Aubin basin. Several Sullivan cutters are only being tested'.[75] From 1907 the Decazeville mine lacked several hundred workers[76] and the cutters brought the productivity gains necessary to overcome this lack of labour. The cutters that had been purchased continued to be used.

The company's experience with cutters was recalled in 1920: 'In the past, there were trials of Sullivan mechanical cutters. But the control of these machines was rather sensitive and tiring, and they were abandoned', probably during the war.[77]

Use of the Sullivan cutter was not particularly advantageous. It replaced explosives for extraction but timbering remained manual and columns of coal had to be left to avoid cave-ins. Furthermore, it was still necessary to shovel coal into mine tubs, and as extraction was mainly manual these machines were not widely used. Around one hundred cutters were in use in France in 1901 and only 1 per cent of British coal was extracted using mechanical cutters.[78]

Henri Fayol experimented with various technologies to increase yields and reduce cost prices, continuing to evaluate them when they were in use and abandoning them when they were found to be of little benefit.

Strip Mines

The operating costs of a strip mine are much lower than those of an underground mine. Some coal deposits in Decazeville lay just below the surface, only covered by a layer of soil. Strip mining involved removing this upper layer of soil before extracting the coal. This mining technique was used whenever possible and between 1892 and 1897 the company spent 400,000F more than planned on this type of extraction.[79] The Combes and Lassalle strip mines allowed the Decazeville mine to lower its cost price, and in particular by employing lesser skilled and lesser paid miners.[80]

From 1910 Ruston-Proctor steam-powered excavating machines were used for earth-moving in the strip mines[81] but they could have been used earlier as they were already available in 1877. In 1900 the cost price of strip activities was one third lower than that of underground mines.

The Deposit

All mining is greatly facilitated when the scope, depth and wealth of a deposit are all precisely known, as it avoids boring shafts and galleries that lead nowhere. This was the purpose of Fayol formulating his theory of deltas about the formation of coal in lakes and applying it when he was managing director of Commentry-Fourchambault et Decazeville. In 1899, an engineer from the Mines Service noted that the company 'is guided by the theory of deltas' in its search for new layers of coal.[82] But did this brilliant theory allow them to lower exploration costs?

In 1871 Henri Fayol began boring a new shaft, the Juillet shaft. Engineers from the Mines Service accorded him little chance of success, yet one year later, at depth of 310 metres the company discovered a large coal deposit. The pit was equipped with a steam engine to hoist the extracted coa,l and 400 miners worked the shaft in 1874. In 1877 Henri Fayol sunk the shaft to 345 metres but found no more coal.[83]

In 1882 Henri Fayol decided to explore the depth of coal deposits and continued to bore the Saint Aline shaft, starting at a depth of 158 metres. By 1886, a depth of 610 metres had been reached, but no coal found. This unsuccessful exploration cost the company 150,000F.[84]

In 1888 the Raynauds shaft was bored to mine a small formation of anthracite but only a thin deposit of poor quality coal was found at 113 metres. The Mines Service engineer concluded that 'these results give little hope. Mr Fayol's theories had created expectations'. Around 200,000 tons of anthracite was nonetheless mined from 1892 to May 1894.[85]

Henri Fayol wanted to explore the possibility that the deposit in the north of Brassac continued into the Allier valley. In 1905 he paid 60,000F for a sounding at Breuil sur Couze but only mineral water was found at a depth of 180 metres, and he nonetheless laid a claim to its commercial exploitation.[86] A pharmacist, Louis Tixier had the source classed as a mineral water in 1932, and it is today sold as a slightly carbogaseous water in drug stores under the 'Hydroxydase' brand from the 'Marie-Christine' spring.

The surveying of deposits was more difficult along the perimeter of the leasehold as some blocks of coal could be mined by neighbouring collieries. The Commentry-Fourchambault concession at Montvicq neighboured that of the Châtillon-Commentry concession at Doyet and the two companies decided to cooperate. They exchanged the plans of their deposits in 1888 and agreed not to mine within 25 metres of the leasehold boundary. This cooperation was reinforced in 1898 when the two companies agreed to jointly mine the coal adjacent to the boundaries with each company compensated for the coal on his concession that was mined by his neighbor.[87]

We can see from these examples that Henri Fayol used his theory to understand the lie of deposits at his mines, but exploration risks remained nonetheless and he still bored a number of unproductive shafts.

The Enhancement of Coal

The Commentry mine built a private railway as early as 1846 to transport coal by rail to Montluçon and then by the Berry canal to its factories and this line was extended to Montvicq in 1878. By the transporting of cheaper coal, the company improved its profit margins. Henri Fayol understood this process of product enhancement that lies somewhere between engineering and sales. He built on it by preparing coal for delivery (sorting and washing), using coke furnaces and agglomerating coal dust into briquettes.

Centralized Sorting Washing Workshop

Coal was extracted both in large pieces and as dust, as one could not be produced without the other: they were joint products. To best enhance the value of production, these joint products had to be separated and sold at different prices. This was done for example in Commentry in 1893 where 'large first quality' sorted coal was sold at 22.3F/ton while the unwashed dust was sold at 13.09F/ton.[88] Coal was prepared in such a way as to separate these two grades of produce and sell them at different prices. Earlier in 1854 there were three coal qualities at Commentry: 'large and square' coal that accounted for half of production, and 'gaillette' and 'slack' grades that accounted for one quarter of production each.[89] Coal preparation for each pit was instituted by Henri Fayol and by 1885 there were fourteen qualities at Commentry and nine at Montvicq, of which two accounted for 77 per cent and 56 per cent of sales respectively.

The company decided to build a central washing, sorting and screening workshop in Commentry at the end of 1886 to better prepare coals and increase productivity. For an initial investment of 300,000F, the mine expected to save 35,000F per year and for 350,000F invested it expected to save 80,000F per year.[90] The ambitious second option was chosen and the workshop was finished in 1888 for a total cost of 400,000F. The technical operating of the workshop copied that of a Schneider workshop in Decize (Nièvre) with a number of improvements, including conveyor belts developed by Lemière in Montvicq that were later copied by Schneider in Decize.[91] The workshop began operating in 1887, allowing all the rocks and half the dust to be removed, and by 1894 there were 26 different qualities of coal with eightfold price differentials and four qualities that accounted for 70 per cent of total production.

The new coal preparation process worked as follows. The underground teams loaded coal into three tubs according to three different grades. The wagons for each quality were then tipped into three coal hoppers. The coal was then sorted by size as it passed through sieves made of perforated steel sheet and shaken by a 6 horse power steam engine. The first sheet with small holes screened the smallest pieces of coal and dust and the remaining coal passed onto a sieve made up of two sheets that sorted coal into three different categories. After screening, the coals all had the same granulometry and slack coal was then washed and what floated was coal and what sunk was sterile. For large lumps of coal, the remaining pieces of rock were removed by hand. The coal then moved along conveyor belts that the sorters could stop when there were too many rocks. It was a production line with the possibility of regulating its speed depending on the required work. The sorters worked in teams of eight at the same table and with rotating stations, they were paid 0.2F per hectolitre of removed rock and the sorters were women and children aged between 13 and 16.

When rocks were stuck to coal, two breakers separated the residual coal and sorters were docked for the quantity of recovered coal at 0.5F/hectolitre. 'The average age of sorters (young people) was 2.09F, and that of breakers 2.17F. There were 82 sorters and 14 breakers'.[92] The six Commentry screens could handle all coal production at the mine. The cost price was 0.34F/ton. The three qualities of large sized coal accounted for 14 per cent of the sorted volumes and 24 per cent of the weight and, with a smaller sterile proportion, this coal could be sold at higher prices. In 1885 untreated 'gaillette' was sold at 10.7F/ton and washed 'gaillette' for 43 per cent more at 15.29F/ton. Washing reduced weight but it was also very profitable.[93]

Preparation activities allowed for a range of coal qualities and price differentiation. The objective of this process was commercial, seeking the highest revenues from the mix of coal that was extracted as these calibrated and cleaned products were easier to identify and sell on the market at more profitable prices. Production and profits at the Commentry mine thus increased at the same time as sales to the factories fell.

Coke and Agglomerates

Washed and unwashed slack coal (small coal pieces and dust) represented 45 per cent of the coal extracted from the Commentry mine in 1893.[94] It was enhanced as coke for factories and briquettes for the railways and the commercial market. Coke was made by baking slack in an airless furnace, which makes it melt and fuse and it then solidifies as it cools. The resulting product is less brittle and exempt of volatile elements such as coal-gas and it is mainly used in blast furnaces.

In 1896 Henri Fayol improved the Coppée coke ovens in Decazeville by installing a tar and benzol recovery process. He visited a similar plant in northern France and sent his engineers to study the Otto-Hoffmann system in Silesia where coal had similar properties to that from Decazeville. After comparing the technical and economic qualities of Solvay, Coppée, Carvès and Otto technologies, the German-made oven was chosen. It was ordered in March 1897 and the ovens were operational in early 1899.[95] The new coke required modifications to the blast furnaces.

In June 1886 when coal sales fell due to a global recession, Henri Fayol visited a small briquette making operation in Saint Etienne. Upon his return, he proposed building one for a cost of 20,000F. He tested the process and showed the results to a few selected customers and the board of directors. By 1887 the company was producing 4,000tons,[96] the railways became customers and the price of coke remained more stable than that of coal.[97] Agglomeration plants were then built at the other mines. In 1895 coke was sold at 18.92F/ton and briquettes at 22.31F/ton, and both were made with washed slack coal worth 15.83F/ton.[98] These processes both greatly enhanced the product.

Electricity

At the end of the nineteenth century, companies used electricity for lighting to replace gas, for motors to replace steam engines and for the telephone to replace the telegraph. Typewriting and inexpensive document duplication technologies were also used by Commentry-Fourchambault et Decazeville for office work.

Lighting

Direct current electricity was first used to replace gas lighting. At the 1878 World Fair in Paris, the Opera was lit up by arc lamps and several shops and theatres then followed. At the 1881 International Exposition of Electricity in Paris, Edison presented his incandescent lamps and a generator capable of powering one thousand seventy watt lamps. Later, in 1888 the city of Toulouse used electric lighting and in 1893, Georges Westinghouse used discoveries made by Nicolas Tesla to win the bid to install electricity across the USA. Westinghouse used alternative current that could be transported across longer distances with smaller losses.

The use of electricity required a generator which was often steam-powered and Henri Fayol rapidly decided to invest in this new technology and built an electrical power station at Imphy in 1895.[99] Electrical lamps replaced gas lighting in 1901 in Decazeville and 1903 in Commentry[100] and a specialized department was created to manage these new installations.

Electric Motors

The company's second investment in electricity was the acquisition of electrical motors and the powerful generators that were required to run them. The replacement of steam engines by electrical motors reduced the quantity of coal consumed by the mine. A generator was first installed in Decazeville in 1903, and five were planned for 1910. In 1913 a small electrical distribution network was built in a co-production agreement with the Société Electrique de la Sorgue et du Tarn.[101] Generators had been installed earlier at the Imphy site and electrical furnaces for coal production were tested as early as 1909. Brassac planned to build its own generator in 1912.[102]

The Telephone

The Italian Antonio Meucci invented the telephone in 1871, and work by Alexander Bell in 1876 accelerated its diffusion. Paris had a telephone network for the 1878 World Fair that was operated commercially from 1879 by a private company, and a small number of interurban lines began operating in 1884 before the entire network was nationalized five years later in 1889. Henri Fayol no doubt used the telephone network in Paris at the time he was named managing director, but would not have used it as director of the Commentry mine.

In August 1891, the Nevers and Montluçon Chambers of Commerce decided to create a telephone network between their departments and Paris and Commentry-Fourchambault provided 13,000F in interest-free funding, representing 8 per cent of the total cost of the project.[103] The telephone line between Imphy and Fourchambault was operational in 1891[104] and the line to Paris was established in 1896. Telephone lines connected the different Decazeville installations prior to 1897, and by 1900 the site operated forty-five telephones that were connected through a private network, although the line to Paris was not operational before 1905. The company's electricity department installed and repaired the telephones.[105] The number of telephones in Decazeville was increased in 1911 for security reasons. The company continued communicating the number of striking workers to Paris by encoded telegram to ensure the confidentiality of transmissions.

Henri Fayol installed telephone technology as soon as possible at each of the company's sites and he anticipated the arrival of telephone lines by creating a private network in Decazeville.

Typewriters

During the twentieth century, documents were written using a metallic nib. These pens were made with a steel nib from 1820 in Great Britain (the 'J pen').

It was significant progress compared to the goose feather used for centuries previous. Metallic nibs were manufactured in France from 1856 ('Sergent-Major quill'), correct handwriting was taught at school, and specialized employees worked in every office to take dictation or recopy drafts.

Typewriters were invented and improved in the eighteenth and nineteenth centuries. They entered commercial use when Remington began manufacturing them in 1874 in the USA and they were first imported into France in 1883. Improvements to their design in 1892 introduced typed lower-case letters and allowed the typist to see what was being typed.

Decazeville's management began using a typewriter in 1892. A carbon copy on onionskin of all documents was kept, and can be found in the archives today. At the time, top management sent handwritten letters and did not regularly use typewriting until 1900. The Mines Service began using typewriters in 1894.

The Duplication of Documents

Ralph Wedgewood patented carbon paper in London in 1806, but it required writers to exert a certain amount of pressure, which was problematic with metal nib pens. Carbon paper was increasingly used to duplicate documents with the introduction of the typewriter.

The invention of the hectographical process allowed for inexpensive duplication of documents. Text was written by hand or typed onto paper using a violet-coloured methyl dye, and an image of the text was then transferred to an inked gelatine surface and copies of the original text were simply made by pressing sheets of paper against it. Machines developed by Edison and Gestetner mechanized this process.

In 1870 and 1880 Thomas Edison (1847–1931) patented his mimeograph machine that used an electrical quill to perforate a stencil made from waxed mulberry paper. It was sold under various brand names including 'Roneograph' and 'Roneo machine', a contraction of 'Rotary Neostyle Roneograph', and in 1900 stencils could be made in a typewriter by removing the ink ribbon.

In 1881 David Gestetner (1854–1939) invented the 'Cyclostyle', a machine that made small cuts in a stencil for ink to pass through. In 1855 the stencil was made from bamboo fibre called Takamatsu paper that was covered with paraffin and which punched very easily. A rotating machine using this process called an 'automatic cyclostyle' was patented in 1891, and starting with this machine Gerstetner developed the office duplication industry and employed several thousand people.

Handwritten documents in mauve-coloured ink were produced at the Commentry-Fourchambault head office and at the Decazeville site from 1892, although we do not know which technique was used.

Conclusion

The technical function was important for Henri Fayol and was strongly linked with other functions in the company. It played two roles in the operations of Commentry-Fourchambault et Decazeville under Henri Fayol: the first involved lowering production costs through the use of modern equipment, and the second involved inventing new products. Before investing in new machinery to lower costs Henri Fayol collected information, tested the machines, undertook study tours to evaluate the technology if necessary and then invested if the results were positive. This process was repeated several times in the mines for the Sullivan cutters, for the coal preparation plant and for the Otto coke furnaces. He used the same process to acquire technologies for the factories, including reversible mills, Martin-Siemens furnaces and Thomas converters. All of these technology investments sought to lower operating costs.

The annual reports for each mine and factory show a constant concern by engineers to improve production processes. They modified procedures, grilled iron ores, washed coals, agglomerated dusts, studied and tested new machines as they arrived on the market, such as electrified motors, and they imagined a new plant. These innovations were evaluated based on the necessary investment levels and reductions to production costs before being proposed to general management and the board of directors, who decided how best to finance them. The installation of a new plant and innovations followed an established timetable, but sometimes ran overtime when suppliers did not respect their engagements. The engineering chain of command worked constantly on improvements that could be seen in higher profit margins at constant sales prices.

Henri Fayol also invested in the Imphy research facilities with the objective to develop innovative products that possessed unique qualities and were targeted to niche markets. These products were developed in collaboration with external scientists, and royalties were shared on any patents. For example, the company developed nickel steel alloys such as Invar, Elinvar and platinite with Charles Edouard Guillaume. Henri Fayol also recruited engineers reknown for their research such as Jean Werth (1855–1928), who was recruited in 1891 and developed a theory on the tempering of steel in 1885, and Pierre Chevenard (1888–1960), recruited in 1911 and admitted to the Académie des Sciences in 1946.

Technical innovations were made to allow for new, commercially successful products such as those at Imphy, or to lower production costs. While productivity also increased significantly at the Decazeville factory, and to a lesser degree in the mines, Henri Fayol most probably did not consider it to be a measure of the performance of investments in new technologies. Fayol knew only too well how mining productivity depended on worksite conditions, and in particular the terrain, such as the solidity of the upper layer of coal, the regularity and depth of the seam and the brittleness of coal. For example, worker levels and production in each of the eight pits at the Commentry mine reported by the Mines Service in 1874 show wide differences in productivity. The reported average productivity of 900 kilograms per day and per miner meant little when some pits produced more than 1,200 tons, and others no more than 230.[106] Some pits produced 33 per cent above average and others 75 per cent below. Wages were similar, however, as they were adjusted for operational difficulties.

For Henri Fayol the technical function served the company through the various management functions. It affected planning by making increases in production capacity possible, by reducing production costs or by opening new markets with innovative products. A mastery of technical skills and technologies allowed for the correct execution of plans, while the skills of management were the best guarantee that the best forecasts become reality.

9 THE SECURITY FUNCTION

Henri Fayol described a security function whose object was

> to safeguard property and persons against theft, fire and flood, to ward off strikes and felonies and broadly all social disturbances liable to endanger the progress and even the life of the business. It is the master's eye, the watch-dog of the one-man business, the police or army in the case of the state. It is, generally speaking, all measures conferring security upon the undertaking and requisite peace of mind upon the personnel.[1]

Henri Fayol used guards to counter the first risk of theft. Thefts were reported in the annual reports, such as in 1908 when there were four thefts at the Decazeville factory, or in 1912–13 when logs and four bronze models were stolen from the foundry. The culprits for the theft of logs were caught and sentenced to a month in prison.[2]

The second risk was fire and the main fire risk was in the collieries. Fire destroyed the produce that the company intended to sell, it stopped operations by preventing miners from entering certain galleries and it heated the mine and made conditions difficult for miners. Fires were costly, and so Henri Fayol invented effective ways to prevent them, including surveillance outside of work hours, training of miners and foremen and breathing equipment for deleterious conditions (see chapter 8). Henri Fayol noted in 1908 that the company had paid 300,000F more in insurance premiums than it had received in compensation over the previous 30 years, and thus decided that the company would become its own insurer, and created a provision for this purpose.[3]

The third risk was flooding due to the constant infiltration of water, which was drained to the surface. In Brassac in 1896, 400m^3 were drained per day, which was equivalent in volume to a day's coal production.[4] Storms and the flooding of local rivers also increased the chance of a mine flooding and operations would have to stop until the water was drained. The Decazeville mine was flooded in 1897.[5]

The fourth risk was strikes, for even if during a strike a company no longer pays its workers, it also stops producing, selling and making profits. Henri Fayol sometimes justified wage increase and benefits as a means of avoiding a strike. In order to protect collieries from this risk, in 1906 the CCHF suggested creating an insurance fund where the insurance coverage involved the reimbursement of overhead costs. Henri Fayol was favourable but no agreement was signed, most probably because premiums were high since strikes were more frequent at the others collieries. In 1912 the board clearly considered that its financial reserves were insurance for any strike action.[6] In the field, guards and the local director kept Henri Fayol informed of union activities in Decazeville. The local director received a detailed account of union meetings and the workers suspected that management was spying on them.[7] The director used encrypted telegrams to inform Henri Fayol in Paris of any union activity and in particular of the number of striking workers.

The mining and metallurgical industries were considered by both the public and the state to be responsible for a large number of workplace deaths with around 200 deaths per year in the collieries alone. Public pressure was important, which leads us to suppose that the first goal of the security function was to avoid fatalities and accidents.

The Number of Accidents

The Decree of 3 January 1813 listed the risks in mines as cave-ins, floods, fire, asphyxiation, breakages to machines, motors, cables, chains, baskets and harmful emissions. It required fatal and serious accidents to be declared to the local mayor and to the engineer from the Mines Service who would then investigate and make the necessary recommendations to eliminate any dangers.

Accidents were part of industrial life at the time. For example, in 1885 0.17 per cent of French miners were killed, 3.5 per cent were injured and unable to work for more than twenty days and 17.5 per cent were incapacitated for at least four days. Over time, the number of fatalities fell, and in 1912 out of a total of 200,000 French miners 268 were killed (0.13 per cent), 639 were permanently incapacitated (0.32 per cent) and 44,000 were injured and unable to work for four days or more (22 per cent).[8] The number of minor accidents grew, most probably because there was a tendency to declare them following the 1898 law on compensation. A miner had one chance in five of being killed or incapacitated over his forty-year working life and had an average of nine minor accidents. It was almost certain that a miner would be injured during his career.

The accident rates and their consequences in the French metallurgical industry were similar to those in the collieries at the time. For example, in 1912 out of a total of 130,000 workers, 126 were killed (0.1 per cent), 383 were permanently incapacitated (0.3 per cent) and 46,000 workers had to cease work for at least four days (35 per cent).[9] The French mining and the metallurgical industries were equally dangerous.

For comparison, the risk of injury or death in French factories as a whole was half that in the metallurgical and mining industries. In 1912, out of the 5 million workers in the manufacturing sector 0.05 per cent were killed at work, 0.1 per cent were permanently incapacitated and a little over 10 per cent were obliged to stop work for more than four days following an accident. Mining and metallurgy were two of the most dangerous industries and the statistics indicate that they caused the most accidents.

French legislators were concerned with safety in the mining and metallurgical industries, but they considered accidents to be a fatality and noted that they were lower than in neighbouring countries. In 1890 there were 0.2 per cent of deaths amongst both British and Belgian miners and after comparing these industries to those with fewer workers but where fatalities were higher, Louis Lacombe, a member of parliament and chairman of the parliamentary commission into mine safety and working conditions, concluded that 'the mining industry has ceased being the most dangerous', remarking that death rates in the mining industry were half that in navigation and car road traffic accidents.[10]

Such a fatalistic attitude could also be seen in the reports from the Mines Service on the causes of accidents. They most often faulted the workers, and in particular those who were injured. For example in 1895 there were 31 accidents in the Allier department and 'of these 31 accidents, 23 were blamed on imprudence, inattention or clumsiness on the part of the victims, one was a case of clumsiness of a workmate and seven other cases were considered to be fortuitous'. Sometimes the organization of work was to blame in which case the mine's operators were reprimanded. 'Remarks were made to the operators of four mines concerning accidents that, while not implying legal responsibility revealed operational and surveillance shortcomings. In each case these operators deferred to these observations and agreed to comply'.[11]

The Mines Service was required to inspect any mine where a fatal accident had occurred and make recommendations. In 1884 at Commentry a workman was killed before dawn in a cave-in at an open pit quarry that was being mined for backfill and where the quarry face was more than five metres in height. The Mines Service recommended that the director no longer work the quarry before daybreak and that the quarry face remain at 45° when the terrain was unstable, and the director of the mine agreed in writing 'to respect these instructions'.[12]

There were few accidents at Fayol's mines compared with the national average and other mines in the area with similar deposits. In the thirty years before the war, national mortality rates varied between 0.13 per cent and 0.17 per cent, which was significantly above the mortality rates at Commentry-Fourchambault et Decazeville.

- This mortality rate was ten times lower (0.015 per cent) at Commentry with only two deaths between 1888 and 1895.[13]
- There were three deaths at the Montvicq mine over the same period, representing a rate of 0.04 per cent.

- There was only one death for these two mines between 1902 and 1904, representing a mortality rate of 0.02 per cent.[14]
- The mortality rate was 0.08 per cent at Decazeville where twenty-four miners were killed over the twelve-year period from 1902 to 1914.[15]

The low mortality at Henri Fayol's mines reflects the effectiveness of his security activities in the management of operations. There were more accidents at the metallurgical factories. For example, over the 1907–1908 period, of the 1,134 employed at the Decazeville factory, 489 workers were injured, some seriously, representing a proportion of 43 per cent; two workers were killed (0.17 per cent), two were partially disabled and three victims were unable to work for more than three months. Three quarters of injured workers were unable to work for between eleven days and three months and one sixth were incapacitated for up to ten days. Injuries accounted for a total of 10,501 sick days, at an average of twenty-one days per worker, and 476 days of hospitalization. The factory paid 22,000F in sick leave, 3,000F for hospital care and 10,000F in invalidity pensions representing 3 per cent of total payroll. Benefits were paid to the most injured workers, three pensions were paid to widows (280F/year) and the costs of three funerals were also paid for (100F per person). Some workers sued the company for greater indemnities and at the end of the year there were 12 such cases in progress, representing 2.5 per cent of total cases.[16]

Henri Fayol paid attention to these accidents and dedicated a chapter to them in the annual report. Between 1888 and 1914 he reported six accidents to the board of directors that had resulted in twelve fatalities (five in the factories and seven in the mines) and six serious injuries.

- In February 1893 the roof of the two mills collapsed at the Decazeville factory killing one worker and breaking the leg of another.[17]
- In December 1898 in the Commentry mine, a cave-in killed two miners and seriously injured another as they were timbering the intersection of two galleries.[18]
- An accident at the Decazeville mine on 7 September 1899 caused the death of three workers and a supervisor, and injured two other workers, including one seriously.[19]
- An explosion at the Fourchambault factory in November 1900 injured two workers.[20]
- In January 1901 two workers, including a blaster, were killed by an explosion of dynamite at the Brassac mine.[21]
- In April 1903 at the Montluçon factory, an explosion due to water infiltrations in the crucible of the blast furnace killed two workers.[22]

Henri Fayol was aware of all accidents and succeeded in limiting the number of deaths in his factories, deliberately applying all regulatory measures taken by the government to reduce the number of accidents.

Indemnities Provided for by the Law of 9 April 1898

Prior to 1898, employers could decide whether or not to compensate injured workers. The courts heard any litigation and the onus was on the worker to prove that the employer was at fault. The Law of 9 April 1898 reinforced the rights of workers in all industries by no longer requiring the worker to prove his employer's fault when claiming compensation. The law also set a wage-based compensation scale for more than four days' sick leave. Compensation did not cover the first four days of sick leave until the Law of 31 March 1905 included them in any compensation paid for more than ten days' sick leave. This later legislation appears to have increased the average number of days of sick leave taken. In the case of permanent incapacity, the Law of 9 April 1898 obliged an employer to pay a pension equivalent to two thirds of the worker's wages. If the worker was still able to work at a reduced wage, compensation was calculated as the equivalent of half the wage reduction. In the event of death, the spouse received a pension equivalent to 20 per cent of wages, plus 15 per cent for a single child, 25 per cent for two children, 35 per cent for three children, 40 per cent for larger families, and orphans were paid a pension of 20 per cent. The employer was also obliged to pay medical and funeral expenses (100F fixed sum).

Commentry-Fourchambault et Decazeville applied these compensation scales.[23] The mutual insurance society covered medical expenses after ninety days of sick leave and the company paid any necessary complement. Workers were free to contest the compensation awarded by the company in court, where they were represented by a state-appointed lawyer. Here are several cases of work accidents at the Decazeville factory and the compensation paid by the company. The first accident was fatal, the second was serious and the third was minor:

- '31 August 1907 accident. Lafragette, a machine operator at the maintenance department was killed by the explosion of a steam valve he was handling. His widow was left with three children including two orphaned of father and mother and one orphaned only of father. We offered a maximum of 60 per cent before the President of the Court, a rate not accepted by the widow who has sued us. On 11 March 1908 the Court read its judgement condemning [the company] to pay an annual pension to the widow of 240F for 20 per cent, 180F to the child orphaned of father for 15 per cent and 20 per cent to the each of the children orphaned of father and mother representing a pension of 480F until the age of sixteen. The pensions are due from the day of the accident' representing a total of 75 per cent of wages.[24]
- 'On 15 April 1909 Auguste Tabardel, a straightener at the small mill caught his left foot in a knot formed by a bar of metal strip as it exited the cylinders, which required his leg to be amputated. We offered a reduc-

tion [in aptitude to work] of 14 per cent'. On 3 March 1910 the court awarded a reduction of 65 per cent on a salary of 750F/year; Tabardel claimed 80 per cent on a wage of 1500F; he appealed; the Montpellier appeals court maintained the rate at 65 per cent but increased the reference wage to 1500F.[25]

- 'Jean Baptiste Laporte, a labourer fell victim to an accident on 30 April 1906 that resulted in a partial ankylosis of the right middle finger. An agreement could not be found when before the President of the Court, and this worker sued us on February 8 1907. Laporte did not show twice when summoned by the court designated expert. The court awarded Laporte a pension of 92.4F per year starting on 1 November 1906, corresponding to a depreciation of 14 per cent'.[26]

There are many records of such accidents as the government had enacted specific laws, and investigations were often made public in order to determine causes and responsibilities. Prior to the Law of 1898, security delegates gave a contradictory version of accidents from 1892 onwards.

Security Delegates

The English Law of 10 August 1872 that authorized miners to elect and remunerate security delegates was later copied by the French government in the Law of 8 July 1890. The idea was to entrust elected miners with the inspection of the mines. They conducted twice monthly inspections of all worksites and of any accident site where the incapacity due to the accident was more than twenty days. The election of security delegates was mandatory and they were paid by the state for all inspections but still continued to work as miners. Their reports, including the operator's annotations, if any, were sent to the prefect and to the Mines Service.

Delegate elections were the opportunity for unions to demonstrate their representativeness. In Decazeville in December 1892 two delegates were elected, including Victor Mazars, the secretary of the miners' union. In 1891 Henri Fayol informed the board that the mining delegates designated by the socialists had all been elected.[27]

Mazars published his reports in a local paper. For example, on 25 February 1893 during his regular visits, he was notified by the foremen of an accident at the mine. He went directly to the worksite, which he observed to be very narrow and where only one person could work at a time. At 1.30 a.m. the hewer at the mine face, Auguste Paul, was injured when he detonated an unexploded dynamite charge when he struck it with his pick. The charge could have been left in the coal earlier in the day but the miners working the day shift insisted that they had bored two holes and exploded two charges. The delegate could not make any definitive conclusions as to the cause of the accident that was not too serious, as the miner was only hit in the face by coal dust.[28] On 3 June that same year J. Pradel the security delegate for another part of the mine visited the site of an accident that had injured Louis Garouste two days earlier. Around 6 m^3 of burning coal had fallen during a meal break, and as Garouste was shovelling it into the tubs a second cave-in of burning coal trapped his legs. He was able to escape by himself and returned home without assistance.[29]

We can see from these two examples that security delegates had little power to reduce risks as they visited worksites several days after accidents had occurred. They could interrogate witnesses but when not working in teams, miners were often alone. Nevertheless the number of mining deaths in France fell from 1892 onwards as legislation gradually raised awareness in the collieries of the importance of security.

Security Rules and Regulations at Collieries

Another approach to security involved establishing rules and regulations for professional practices to limit risks. Henri Fayol had seventy-five pages of security rules written for the Commentry mine.[30] The role of the head miner is detailed in thirty articles. The first article states:

> 1. The head miner is in charge of monitoring all works undertaken in his area. He commands and directs all the workers that execute them. He is also in charge of policing his work-site for order, worker safety, the correct execution of work and the conservation of material and works.

He was a polyvalent manager in charge of everything taking place in his pit, including security. The head miner also intervened in the case of accidents that had resulted in physical injury:

> When a worker is slightly injured, the head miner alerts the office, if the injury is serious he alerts the office and the doctor and, for these different situations, he follows the instructions contained in the description of the health service. He then goes to the office or sends the deputy head miner, as soon as possible to give the explanations that the divisional engineer may need concerning the accident. He completes the information form sent to him by the office as soon as he receives it.[31]

The Mines Service considered the organization of the health service at Commentry to be excellent: 'The health service continues to be the well-organized, the Commentry mine is truly a model in this matter'.[32]

When a miner did not respect the security rules he could be fined, nonetheless despite this threat there were still a number accidents that were often caused by explosives. For example, in Commentry on 5 August 1891, for example, a grisounite charge failed to explode. When a worker tried to remove the charge it exploded in his face and damaged his eyes. An engineer from the Mines Service advised how to avoid such accidents in the future: when an explosive fails notify the deputy-head and accompany him back to the worksite, report to the head miner who will decide on a course of action, do not return for an hour, trigger the explosion using a second charge more than 20 centimetres from the first. He concluded that 'these instructions were well known to workers and regularly applied in Montvicq and Commentry'.[33] A similar accident however reoccurred in 1893 at the Decazeville mine.

The use of rules and regulations assumes that accidents are caused by deviation from 'best practices' and that avoiding accidents involves explaining the best practices and identifying the errors that exacerbate risks. The Mines Service was responsible for overseeing mining safety and it made localized recommendations that led to differences in preventive measures between mines. The Law of 25 July 1895 unified these rules[34] but was insufficient, and after the Courrières catastrophe of 1907 (1,100 dead), a more detailed set of regulations emerged from a wider consultative process and were enacted by decree on 13 August 1911, and applicable from 1913 onwards.

In 1909 Henri Fayol undertook an in-depth study of these regulations so that they could be applied in Decazeville.[35] He insisted that all laws be respected, whatever the state may decide, and he had anticipated most of these obligations. For example, when the Campagnac mine was acquired in 1908 it did not comply with the standards of the time, and so Henri Fayol fenced the above-ground installations, built a new lamp room, refectories for above-ground personnel, showers, toilets and ladders in the pit and had elevator buffers installed. The cost of these works was estimated at between 60,000F and 80,000F.

The regulations imposed a variety of measures pertaining both to the mine operator, such as fencing off the pit on all levels, and to working practices, such as the use of explosives and the repositioning of fallen carts back on rails.

In 1929 Commentry-Fourchambault et Decazeville published an extract of 225 articles in 23 pages from the official 1911 regulations for its workers.[36] It notably concerned the hygiene of the worker and the working environment following the Law of 12 June 1893 on factory hygiene that stipulated the installation and use of external showers and portable toilets in underground worksites and work time limits at worksites subject to water infiltrations and high temperatures.

We cannot say whether these rules efficiently reduced the number of accidents: the 1895 law did not lower the number of deaths, the 1911 law was not applied until 1912, and in 1913 a serious explosion in a mine neighbouring Decazeville killed twelve workers.[37] Regulations had to evolve with mining techniques and workers also had to be trained in them.

Security Measures

One effective way of improving security was to analyse the causes of each accident, determine how they could have been avoided and adopt either material or procedural measures to avoid the same risk in the future. Material measures were designed to be fail-safe by making dangerous handling impossible or by automatically intervening in the case of danger. Here are some examples adopted in Henri Fayol's mines and in other mines at the time.

- Shaft elevator 'parachutes': in the case where an elevator cables breaks and the cabin falls, parachutes could be used as breaks on the rails to slow the fall. At the Carmaux mines in 1877 Paul Fayol invented a reliable and lighter system than that, which was commonly used at the time.[38] The system was installed in Commentry in 1884 in the Juillet shaft that was used by the workers. 'If the cable breaks the cabin can only fall two metres'.[39] When such an incident occurred in the main shaft of the Decazeville mine in 1905, the only consequence was that operations were stopped for two days.[40]
- Guard rails on all extraction machines: each machine with moving parts had to be surrounded by a barrier that prevented anyone from approaching the machine.
- Guard rails at each landing to avoid anyone falling down the shaft:[41] barriers were sometimes missing, as was the case in 1903 when a student from the Ecole des Maîtres Mineurs de Douai[42] fell down the shaft and killed himself. A barrier was missing and the mine was found to be responsible.[43]
- Automatic gates at each landing: a gate automatically rises when the elevator cabin is in position and closes when it leaves. This system was used throughout the company in 1885.[44]
- Fire hoses, stretchers, oxygen bottles, first aid kits.
- Locks on explosives stores and padlocks on transport crates.
- Security lamps: Some coal contained methane that escaped during mining operations and this 'firedamp' could asphyxiate miners and become explosive when mixed with air. The challenge involved detecting firedamp, airing the zone and avoiding igniting it. In 1817 Humphry Davy invented a security lamp that used a metal grill to contain the flame, and although there was no firedamp risk at Commentry-Fourchambault et Decazeville's mines, security lamps were used on worksites that were made dangerous by coal dust. The Mines Service also undertook extensive research to develop an apparatus to detect levels of firedamp and forced aeration through ventilation was installed throughout the mines.

- Breathing apparatus to fight fires: breathing apparatus were used in Commentry from 1873 and at Decazeville after 1892. As an outside observers noted: 'Apparatuses were proposed for workers to be able to enter and move amongst unbreathable gases. One of the best was proposed by the director of the Commentry mine, Mr Fayol';[45] 'Fayol's apparatuses were of different types: an apparatus with nose clip, a dual valve mouthpiece and a fresh air breathing tube; an apparatus with a portable tank in the form of bellows providing the required air for breathing and for fuelling a lamp, said to be usable for twelve to fifteen minutes; apparatus with a portable tank also in the form of bellows, regularly fed with fresh air by a pump connected to it by a long hose. With the hope of creating easy to use apparatuses, Mr Fayol decided against using compressed air'.[46]

The list of measures is long, as security involved managing a number of details. Material measures were complemented by security procedures which sought to limit risks by regulating behaviours. Some of the procedures used at Commentry-Fourchambault et Decazeville's mines included:

- The guards regularly patrolled the perimeter of the mine during the day.
- Underground worksites were patrolled during the night and on non-worked days to check for fires.
- The lamps assigned to miners were numbered and noted so that the lamp room knew which miners were still underground.
- When a miner saw a fire he would attempt to extinguish it and notify his superiors.
- When they were first used there were 'no written regulations for the use of explosives; for dynamite oral instructions based on the manufacturers own recommendations were sufficient'.[47] Accidents led to stricter regulations, including a locked store, the storing of charges and detonators separately, transporting and firing by a specialized miner (known as a 'blaster'), detonation forbidden until all personnel are clear of the area and a specific procedure for misfires.[48]

The authorities were particularly concerned about charges being stolen, as workers could keep any allotted charges to use in the case of social unrest. In 1893 an explosion targeted a guard at the Commentry mine and the perpetrator was never found[49] and in 1894 the police found explosives at a miner's home.[50] Mine management ensured that only those charges necessary for operations were in circulation and foremen were charged with monitoring the use of explosives both to ensure the security of miners and that unused charges were not stolen: 'A reliable hewer is in charge of monitoring the insertion of charges and blasting at each work-site'.[51]

Explosives, fuses and detonators were supplied twice a week in exchange for a request order signed by both foremen and engineers. Timberers transported the explosives to the worksite in locked wooden crates, and charges were stored separately from the detonators in a locked above ground and dry store.[52] Explosives were under the responsibility of specialized miners called blasters, although this did not completely eliminate accidents, as in Decazeville in 1901 when a blaster and a miner were both killed as the former was distributing charges.[53] Before exploding a charge, miners watered heaps of dust, retreated and then blocked access to the site. A number of accidents were caused by unexploded charges and the procedure described in the regulations required workers to wait an hour, notify superiors, and drill a hole using electricity 20 centimetres from the first so as to explode a second charge. A non-exploded charge should never be left by the team that placed it.[54]

These procedures did not eliminate all accidents but they did reduce their frequency. In contrast, there were no procedures at the iron and steelworks, and accidents were more frequent.

Conclusion

The risks perceived by business owners during the nineteenth century were firstly those that could hinder operations, such as a mine catching fire, a boiler exploding or a mill breaking down. The risk of death or injury was minimized or hidden, and it was not until 1861 that the Mines Service began publishing statistics on accidental deaths even though they had been recorded since 1833.[55]

When an accident caused bodily harm, management first looked to avoid litigation by denying its responsibility. The following anecdote illustrates this mentality.

Émile Mâle (1862–1954) was born in Commentry, he became a specialist in medieval art and was elected to the Académie Française in 1927. He told a story from his childhood about his grandfather who was a foreman at the Commentry mine.

> Around 1855, an event occurred with serious consequences; one of his workers broke a leg. So as not to have to pay compensation to the injured worker, the Director Mr Mony demanded that my grandfather attest that the accident happened outside the work-site and was therefore not a workplace accident. My grandfather refused to make a false declaration and, when threatened with dismissal, he was remained resolute. Mr Mony who could not accept being opposed, ordered him to immediately leave the mine. That day, the Saint Simonian [Mony] did not play a proud role. Dismissed so unjustly from the Commentry mine, my grandfather went to find work at the Doyet mine. He joined as a simple worker and had his son join with him. My father also worked at the Commentry mine on my grandfather's work-site. They both left together.[56]

This happened six years before Henri Fayol began working as an engineer at the mine. We do not know whether Fayol would have accepted the use of such blackmail.

Legislation modified the balance of power between workers and management as accidents were more regularly declared and compensation obtained. A large number of other security measures could have been taken to lower the number of accidents and injuries, such as requiring workers to wear hard hats, safety glasses, work boots or gloves. At the time, the army also lacked the same equipment, and in 1914 soldiers were not issued with metal helmets, which led to a great number of head injuries at the start of the War. The French army did not issue Adrian helmets until September 1915, the English Brodie helmet was issued several months later, the German helmet was issued in 1916 and American soldiers were issued the English helmet in 1917.

Henri Fayol learnt the importance of security in his battles against the Commentry fires. He relied heavily on the mine's operational hierarchy to ensure its security with one of the objectives of regular visits, for example, being to identify dangerous situations and eliminate them. In his theory he considered security to be a separate function, which accounted for 5 per cent of a workman's abilities and 10 per cent for those at levels from the foremen through to the director.[57] These abilities no doubt covered what could be called the 'security culture', a collective effort that lowered the number of deaths in the mines under Fayol's management.

Penalties also reinforced an awareness of security amongst workers, as any breach of regulations was sanctioned by a fine, a suspension or the worker's dismissal. The intention was for other workers to learn not to reproduce the same dangerous acts. Penalties were suggested but never decided on by foremen: 'Recall that supervisors, master miners, foremen and other employees in direct contact with workers cannot determine a sanction without referring to their superior'.[58] Henri Fayol insisted that sanctions should never be a result of poor interpersonal relationships and required that a third party intervene, most often the foreman's superior, to objectively examine the facts.

Henri Fayol was lucky to avoid major accidents, such as those that occurred in other mines. For example, in foreign mines there were 290 fatalities in Wales on 23 June 1894, 236 fatalities on 18 June 1894 in Silésie, 180 fatalities in the Sarre on 17 March 1885, and in France there were 49 fatalities at Campagnac on November 1888, 45 fatalities in Graissessac in February 1877, 43 fatalities in La Machine on 18 February 1890 and 21 fatalities at Blanzy on 3 February 1895. Such 'luck' could also be the result of good management practices, although Henri Fayol rarely mentioned them no doubt because of the possibility of unforeseen events in matters of security. When questioned about accidents by members of parliament in Decazeville on 11 May 1895 he simply said that there were 'as many as the average for mine accidents'.[59]

Further evidence of Henri Fayol's resolve to reduce accidents can be found in the access he gave to researchers from Liévin to exhausted galleries in Commentry and Montvicq in 1912 and 1913[60] so that they could more closely study gallery explosions.

Mechanical problems were also a mining risk. For example, in 1886 pumping equipment at Commentry broke down and production was stopped for fifteen days. Henri Fayol installed another pumping machine in a second shaft to avoid this risk in the future,[61] applying his principle of duplicating any essential element. Commercial risks were also reported in the annual report including customer incidents, reclamations, poor quality and non-payments and he had the takings checked every month.

Henri Fayol's security function was an anticipation of what we today call 'risk management', a part of management that has been written about by scholars since the 1960s.[62] While it is by no means as exhaustive as current practice, it shows that over a century ago Fayol identified a problem that is still ignored by a number of management theories and remains poorly understood by many managers today.

10 CONCLUSION

Was Henri Fayol a Fayolian manager? He was clearly a good manager, as he brought his company back to profit and multiplied its sales by three and its share price by five between 1888 and 1913. He was a good manager both for shareholders and for the personnel as there were few industrial disputes and wages were slightly above those of other local businesses. Customers were satisfied in so far as they could purchase coal and metallurgical products at market prices even though they were located outside the main regions of French industrial growth at the time. He was respected by other mine and steelworks directors, even though they sometimes refused to enter into selling agreements with him. He knew how to negotiate the purchase of collieries in financial difficulty and invest in jointly operated iron mines and partnerships to launch major industrial projects at Joudreville and Pont-à-Vendin. He was also actively involved in professional associations including the Comité Central des Houillères de France and the Comité des Forges. Henri Fayol remained nonetheless a salaried manager of a medium-sized company that grew at an average rate compared to the sector as a whole. He lacked the stature of the Schneiders at Le Creusot, who were manager-owners and whose enterprise grew strongly and made healthy profits by building machinery such as cannons and locomotives.

Henri Fayol enjoyed great industrial success, firstly with the Commentry mine that was the cash cow that covered the losses of the other sites and financed investments, and secondly with the Decazeville site that became profitable once it was modernized. Some investments were not as profitable as expected, such those in the Joudreville mine and the Pont-à-Vendin factory because of World War I, and in the Brassac mine which reached profitability ten years later than expected. Henri Fayol had hoped that the Brassac deposits of 10 million tons of coal could be mined over 50 years at a rate of 200,000 tons per year for an annual profit of 600,000F. He planned to invest around 1MF that would be financed by profits over the first five years of operations, and production was to be increased to 400,000 tons after 15 years.[1] These plans were never realized, possibly because of a lack of personnel and the high costs of mining a small leasehold under the Allier river.

Henri Fayol the manager was also a theorist. His daily actions as a manager reflect his theories and give them greater depth. The emphasis he placed on the administrative function could lead us to believe that he neglected the technical, commercial, financial, accounting and security functions, and yet his company obviously needed all of these functions to survive. We often overlook Fayol's novel vision of these six corporate functions. The functions did not correspond to a dedicated part of the organizational structure but were instead transverse, each involving multiple actors across the company according to their abilities, in the same way as several organs contribute to the same function in biology. The understanding of the term 'function' was no doubt inhibited by its English translation as 'operation' and later as 'activity',[2] both preventing any association to be made with biological functions.

In biology the structure (the organs) are distinct from the functions: one is anatomical, the other is functional. The 'respiratory function' involves the lungs, the mouth and the nose, the heart, the blood and the oxygenation of cells. Several organs participate in the same function. The nutrition function, the reproductive function, the motor function, and so on, all also involve several organs working together towards the same goal. Some organs, such as the mouth and blood can be involved in several functions. Today's management vocabulary would no doubt replace the word 'function' with 'system'.

All of these functions were important for Commentry-Fourchambault et Decazeville's success, and here is what we have learned about them by studying Henri Fayol's actions as a manager.

The finance function was the simplest as it only concerned a small number of individuals, notably the shareholders, the board of directors and the managing director. This function ensured that capital was available for industrial projects and in return for capital the company distributed dividends. When dividends were high it was easier to raise capital.

Commentry-Fourchambault et Decazeville was on the verge of liquidation in 1888. When the company returned to profits it adopted a strategy of self-financing where the majority of gross profits were reinvested or provisioned as reserves. Such prudence was appreciated by shareholders, who had inherited their stock from their ancestors, and took a long term perspective to the management of their family's patrimony. They were emotionally attached to the company and Henri Fayol was able to perceive that and satisfy their desire for prudent corporate management and at the same time impose a vision of a perennial enterprise that grew with its market.

In his doctrine Henri Fayol did not talk about relations between general management and owners. He only alluded to them in his 1925 interview (appendix 2). He adhered to traditional, liberal ideas that the state should let companies freely organize themselves, and he participated in the collective lobbying activities of colliery employers to defend this right. He scrupulously conformed to legislation when it was passed, whether it pertained to working conditions in mines, accidents, retirement, injuries or the length of the working day. He also used political opportunities to advance his industrial strategy, but there was no place for such exceptional actions in his general theory of management.

Henri Fayol did not neglect the commercial function, but instead let his sales director Joseph Carlioz, a professor at the Paris-based French business school HEC, develop the subject. This function was concentrated in the sales department, although the delivery and production departments also contributed to ensure that orders were produced on time. Fayol himself was also a salesman, negotiating with the company's biggest customers. When negotiations were at a standstill he looked for solutions by taking a more global view of the company's offer, bringing in an outside expert or accepting a compromise. He built a network of salesmen to canvas smaller but potentially higher margin customers, and he expected his salesmen to be ethical in their dealings with customers and the company. Each salesman worked for a specific establishment and used the principle of the overpass to transmit an order to another site that was better placed to satisfy it. Even though Henri Fayol invested in a realistic sales organization, he believed that strong competition between salesmen could be unnecessarily costly and destabilize the industry. He preferred selling agreements between producers, although he often had difficulty arranging them, notably for the sale of coal.

The technical function was the realm of Henri Fayol's engineers. They combined their skills to develop new steel at Imphy and they installed new equipment in the factories to increase capacity and lower production costs. It was also a lack of such technical skill at Decazeville that delayed the inauguration of the Thomas steelworks and then weighed on profitability from 1908 to 1910. The technical function was essential to Commentry-Fourchambault et Decazeville: it was central to the training of the company's engineers and, no matter what Henri Fayol may have said, was central to the company's culture. Fayol's own research was based on this technical and scientific culture.

The security function was performed both by workers and by the entire operational hierarchy. It was similar to the immune system of a living being, which distinguishes what it is from what it is not so as to defend against any intrusions of germs and viruses, maintains its integrity through homeostasis, and reacts to situations it considers uncomfortable or dangerous. In the same manner, the company faced a number of threats and required mechanisms to eliminate any perturbations. It was the equivalent of today's 'risk management', and this contemporary concept no doubt found inspiration in Henri Fayol's experience with fighting mine fires earlier in his career. Henri Fayol was able to theorize this function by explaining that there were no specialists, such as firemen for fires, and guards to protect against theft. He believed that all of the hierarchy should be involved in security and in particular during rounds. He established rules in the mines that prohibited dangerous behaviour, security measures that physically prevented some accidents and supported research into explosions in underground galleries. There were fewer accidents at the Commentry-Fourchambault et Decazeville Company than elsewhere, but he was lucky during his tenure as managing director not to have had a major catastrophe with a number of fatalities, as was common in the industry at the time and still occasional today. He also had difficulty transferring this security culture to the Decazeville site and to the factories in particular. His efforts in terms of security would today be considered insufficient, yet at the time they opened the way for future improvements.

The accounting function would at first view appear to be the sole domain of the accounting department, both at headquarters and at the sites. This was most definitely not the case as accountants relied on all levels of the hierarchy and on all departments to provide them with data and verify the accuracy, or at least the plausibility, of any accounting output. The accounting function was the equivalent of today's 'information system'. The accounting department collected and compiled data on the daily operations of the entire company that it communicated on a regularly basis or published in reports of varying periodicity. Daily output was required to determine wages, supply request forms were used to monitor the use of parts in the workshops and delivery notes were used to establish invoices. While the local accountants reported to the site director, he had no authority to verify their work, but instead the head of accounting regularly visited the sites to verify the work performed.

Henri Fayol added a management function[3] to these five distributed sub-functions[4] that is also distributed amongst different members of the organization. The higher an agent is in the hierarchy, the more he or she is involved in the administrative function. This function is more abstract and therefore less apparent than the other five. Fayol distinguished five 'elements'[5] that are sub-functions of the administrative function: planning, organizing, command, coordination and verifying. As is the case for the other functions, these elements do not reflect any particular division of work as there was no planning department, nor a verification department. Instead, the entire hierarchy was involved in each of these five sub-functions.

Each of these management sub-functions is at a varying temporal distance from operations: planning is a long-term activity, organizing is medium-term, commanding is short-term, coordinating is very short-term, just prior to action, and verifying is undertaken after the action has occurred. By encircling action with a succession of increasingly narrower temporal perspectives, Henri Fayol theorized a way of compelling events to follow human guidance. While working for Commentry-Fourchambault et Decazeville he planned between five and ten years ahead, he organized by creating a hierarchical structure that remained stable for several months and he commanded each month by meeting with his directors and encouraging them to give orders on-site in weekly meetings. He built several horizontal information systems around the overpass principle to harmonize the coordination of operations. Annual reports and the accounting department reported on operations, and in particular on sales, profit and production costs.

Activities at different temporal distances from operations can also be found in other domains. For example, in the aerospace industry there are four levels of anticipation. The design of a launch pad involves planning for a number of launches per year. The launch calendar is then set with provisional dates, which represents a second level of launch planning. Before each launch, the preparatory operations are sequenced and planned in great detail. The fourth level involves a countdown that triggers a succession of immediate actions and checks. If a check is negative or if a previous action is not completed, such as a fuel tank not being completely full, then the countdown is stopped. Corrective actions are engaged and if they are successful then the countdown continues, otherwise the launch is cancelled. Task execution is anticipated through a sequence of temporally closer operations. There are also several levels of anticipation in a theatrical production. The author's text is a timeless plan of what is to be played, organizing is the decision to play the piece in a given theatre, at a specific date with certain actors, a director and the financing of a specific producer, and commanding can be seen in the rehearsals where the director instructs the cast. When the piece is played, actors coordinate their work and adapt to the audience's reactions. In the case of a concert, the musical score is the also the plan, organizing involves the choice of each musician and the conductor, who commands during practice and coordinates execution on the day of the performance. There is also some horizontal coordination between the musicians themselves. In operations management, a difference is made between scheduling, that is, a detailed planning of operations, and launch, which takes into account the immediate state of the system, breakdowns and completed actions.

Henri Fayol's five sub-functions of management can be seen in his professional activities and by examining his actions we can also better comprehend their meaning.

The first sub-function is planning. How did Fayol plan? Henri Fayol presented a number of plans to the board of directors but none were ever considered to be final. Instead, they were used to justify industrial projects and multi-year investments. They replaced requests for credit that were made every year but that often lacked coherence from one year to the next, which resulted in over-investment in some factories and under-investment in others. Five- or ten-year planning was not a constraint, for if new ideas emerged, Henri Fayol proposed a new plan. Every year site directors were required to include a commercial forecast for the coming year with their annual report. Interestingly, no profitability ratios were calculated for any of Henri Fayol's plans and only the expected level of investment and profits were noted. Any profitability analysis was imprecise and plans were even sometimes approved by the board, even though some members considered the level of profitability to be too weak. Operations did not always unfold as planned as Fayol's forecasts for sales volumes, sales prices and production costs were often too optimistic and some projects suffered from a lack of labour, problems with suppliers or engineering difficulties in managing new technologies.

The second management sub-function is organizing which involves arranging productive resources, which were mainly human resources at the time. The management of human resources involved defining the roles of managers, their position in the organizational chart, their recruitment, their evaluation and their careers, recruiting workers and fixing wages at levels that both compensated worker contribution and avoided industrial disputes. Henri Fayol was strongly attached to principles of justice, rewarding some managers and sanctioning others that had underperformed. When faced with strikes, Fayol confronted unions both at local and national levels, all the while remaining informed of demands and sometimes anticipating them. He tried to react quickly to avoid conflict, learning from experience that any prolonged conflict was a defeat both for the employer and for workers.

The three final elements of management are commanding, coordinating and verifying. Commanding was essentially a face-to-face activity and mainly took place during department-head meetings. These meetings were also used for coordinating and verification, as all of the head's collaborators could collectively adjust their actions and report on work performed. Regular inspections by department heads were another opportunity for face-to-face contact, and on-site rounds were essential for commanding and verifying and also to resolve any coordination difficulties. Postal mail, coded telegrams and the telephone were also used for these activities.

Until the 1970s, European companies set up their operational information systems in the same way as Henri Fayol did at Commentry-Fourchambault et Decazeville. Without realizing, their approach was Fayolian, making natural, gradual improvements over time in the same way Fayol did. Commentry-Fourchambault et Decazeville appears quite modern, operating in the same way around the early twentieth century as companies of an equivalent size did some years later. Prior to computerization, these information systems required a large number of clerical staff, and especially for detailed reporting. In the 1960s employees, products, machines, customers and a number of other quantitative data were coded using punched cards. They prepared the way for management information systems and the computerization of data entry and processing towards the end of the twentieth century, where data is centralized in shared databases, orders are transmitted to lower levels and specialized reports or aggregate overviews are generated automatically or on demand for the various levels of management.

The working of Henri Fayol's company supports his theory and clarifies certain aspects that his doctrinal discourse did not. We will conclude our study of Henri Fayol's practice as a manager with two general remarks concerning the evolution of his thought and the non-publication of the third part to *Industrial and General Management*.

Henri Fayol's thought developed progressively, following both an intellectual process that is common to all research and a process of reaction to events that he encountered during his career. He worked as an engineer and a manager for more than fifty years and he matured his thought by selecting elements amongst his experiences that appeared most important, by identifying abstract concepts, choosing specific words to describe them and by articulating the intertwining of concepts. His successive notes and publications show how his thought evolved.[6]

Events themselves also influenced Henri Fayol's thought. He presented strikes differently after 1902, most likely because of the numerous strikes he had had to deal with and the heavy losses he had incurred. He had previously ignored workers' demands and used delaying tactics to avoid answering them. When he later understood how discontent could spread uncontrollably he began carefully monitoring wage levels at neighbouring sites, paid attention to workers' demands and instructed engineers to respond rapidly to them. Information and decision speed were the tools he used to avoid strikes spreading. His beliefs about unions and the relationship between government and industry also changed over time and these evolutions show that Fayol's management doctrine was not static, but instead was and should continue to be adapted to changing circumstances.

Our final remark concerns his non-publication of the third part of *Industrial and General Management*. In 1916 Henri Fayol announced four parts to his work, but only ever published two of them. The fourth part entitled 'Lessons from the War' was dangerous at the time as battles were raging on French soil and he most probably did not want to attract unwanted attention from army censors. It is more difficult to understand why he never published the third chapter, 'Personal Observations and Experiments'.

Some sections of the third chapter were never written: the fines and penalties system (§67), the strike statistics (§§288 to 304), Fayol's comments on the strikes at the Decazeville factory (§349) and his most recent views on trade agreements (§249). It would not have required much work for him to finish writing these parts.

Henri Fayol was careful when referring to people or events in his work, especially with regard to members of the board of directors or their descendants who were still active in the management of the company and may have taken offence to his writings. His opinion on the role of public authorities could have been counterproductive for his company at a time when the state essentially controlled economic activity. For example, he suggested in the third part of *IGM* that industrials seek to influence the government (§281), but that lobbying is efficient only if it is discreet. He also criticized legislation on unionising, suggesting that unions should have certain responsibilities (§357) but he no doubt knew that unions would never have accepted such legal constraints on their actions.

Incomplete and incoherent details may also have made Henri Fayol reticent to publish this text. In order to reduce production at Commentry from 1877 he progressively deployed a number of actions (§§106 to 109), which he later said were insufficient (§307). He dismissed a large number of workers which triggered the strike of June 1881 and then hid the truth about this conflict (see chapter 5). He also justified the closure of the Fourchambault factory in 1901 (§402) by citing competition from the north-east region of France. This is a logical explanation, and even though it was hidden by the favourable economic conditions of 1898–1900 the 1898 plan did not include either a reduction in activity or a reorientation of production. Instead, the activity at the factory was hurriedly wound down and the factory was closed within three months.

All of these reasons probably combined to make Fayol reluctant to publish the third part of *IGM*. He was probably also affected by the criticism he received when he presented an outline for this third part in 1908.[7] The text of this speech was never published, unlike many of his other communications and only a short summary was published in the congress proceedings. At the time, not everyone agreed on the need to openly discuss the daily management of organizations. These reasons remain simply hypotheses, and the non-publication of the third part of *IGM* remains a mystery.

A number of other misinterpretations of Fayol's work have emerged over time, caused by the abstract nature of his writing, the imprecision of translations and sometimes an inattentive reading of his writings. An examination of Henri Fayol's actions as a manager highlights these misunderstandings and helps better understand his thought. We will review several preconceived ideas about Henri Fayol's doctrine that this confrontation with facts have shown to be fallacious.

(1) Managers only plan, organize, command, coordinate and verify. In fact, when Fayol spoke of managers he only referred to the concept of ability. The abilities of a managing director are only 50 per cent managerial and the other half are spread equally between the technical, commercial, financial, accounting and security functions.[8] This allocation resembles a share of time spent. Henri Fayol was very active in the sales, financial, technical and accounting functions. Concrete management activities can be seen in the use of 'management tools' but which the manager never uses alone, such as department meetings where all subordinates participate.

(2) Managers have qualities that Henri Fayol resumed in a list. In reality, he knew that managers lacked certain qualities and looked to compensate by the

use of management tools, external consultants and staff. Far from being an ideal, his theory of management took into account realities, just as the security function remedied operational failures

(3) In 1916 Henri Fayol opposed the functional foremanship, as recommended by Frederick Taylor.[9]He criticized the concept as contradictory to the idea of unity of command,[10] but in 1925 he abandoned his antagonistic stance when he agreed to join Taylor's French followers to form the CNOF (Comité National d'Organisation Française). He justified his change of stance by saying that each functional head was in charge of a specific area of competence. He had already considered this when he annotated Taylor's *Shop Management* in 1913[11] and prior to 1888 he indicated a dual dependency for some workers on the Commentry organizational chart (see chapter 4). Unity of command was never meant to be an unwavering principle so long as multiple heads could not contradict each other.

(4) Henri Fayol never organized the work of his labourers. It is true that his 1916 work never mentions this point, yet we know that he reorganized the extraction in the Commentry mine (chapter 8) by removing the distinction between extraction and backfill teams that had previously succeeded one another day and night. Under Fayol's new organization, all workers performed the same tasks. The gains were not in terms of work rhythms but rather improved production costs which were determined by the flow of materials. The selection criterion was not the impact on individual productivity but rather on costs, including those of secondary tasks.

(5) The chain of command appears to be the only, if not the preferred communication channel. Information at Commentry-Fourchambault et Decazeville also flowed horizontally and in particular between the number of support departments and operational production teams. The rhythm of daily operations was given horizontally by the overpass and by the formal information systems rather than vertically by the hierarchy. Direct communication between departments was essential for the harmonious coordination of actions.

(6) Henri Fayol's world was one without conflict. In reality he fought many battles. One trace in his theory is the 'retirement of incompetent managers', as such an eviction would obviously be the result of some tension with a subordinate and we have described a number of such cases (see chapter 4). During his professional life he was involved in a number of confrontations including with the director of the Commentry mine who, at the start of his career gave orders over Fayol's head, with Mony who believed the Commentry mine to be inexhaustible, with a member of the board of directors who also wanted to be managing director (chapter 2), with Schneider who opposed a trade agreement between collieries (chapter 7), and with unions that he opposed at times of industrial disputes (chapter 5). He also confronted his peers who resisted the creation of a science of management. He was successful on many occasions, but never without a fight.

Henri Fayol's vocabulary created incomprehension. The word 'administration' has been translated relatively unopposed as 'management' since 1949. The French word 'contrôler' however is a false friend. Its meaning in French is 'to verify', 'to see the results', but translations have not always reflected this sense. Other expressions are insightful, such as 'outillage administratif' that perfectly corresponds to 'management tools' that did not exist elsewhere at that time. The word 'function' must be understood in its biological sense, as opposed to the 'organs' that make up the structure. The 'management elements' are sub-functions of the 'management function'.

It is unfair to simplify Fayol's work with an acronym such as POCCC (Prévoyance, Organisation, Commandement, Coordination, Contrôle)[12] in French, or POSDCORB (Planning, Organizing, Staffing, Directing, Co-Ordinating, Reporting and Budgeting) in English, as suggested by Luther Gulick[13] twenty years after the publication of *Industrial and General Management*.

Henri Fayol communicated his theory of management using the words of his time. Without modifying his thought, we can express it using a more contemporary vocabulary. Three points were essential for him:

1 The existence of systems that all parts of the company contribute to.
2 A specific management system that has six sub-systems.
3 The principles that should guide managers and external advisors, and management tools they can use whenever they lack the requisite skills.

For Fayol the daily operating of the company was based on six systems: the technical system that produced goods, the commercial system that sold them, the financial system that ensured access to and remuneration of financing, the security system to protect the company from various hazards, the accounting system that recorded the material and monetary flows and the management system that he deliberately distinguished from the five others.

All members of the organization are expected to contribute in varying degrees to each of these systems. The members of the board of directors expend 85 per cent of their effort on the financial system, while workers spend 85 per cent on the technical system. Sales department employees spend half of their time on the commercial system and the head of technical services also expends 15 per cent of his time. The managing director uses 50 per cent of his or her time on the management system. In fact, everybody contributes to this system in varying degrees according to their level in the hierarchy, including workers who devote 5 per cent of their time.

The management system was made up of five sub-systems: planning, organizing, commanding, coordinating and verifying. As noted earlier, these sub-systems differ by their temporal distance from productive operations: planning describes operations for the coming five or ten years; organizing installs productive resources for the coming year and, in particular, the human resources that are structured as a hierarchy; commanding launches operations in the short term; and coordinating ensures that operational adjustments are made in the immediate term by using horizontal information systems. This increasingly precise anticipation in an increasingly short time frame affords greater control over productive operations. Ex post verification then involves checking what actually happened and highlights variances to forecasts.

Fayol painted a systemic conceptual framework of organizations, where feedback allowed managers to attain their objectives. He also showed how a situation should be studied at different levels of magnification: macroscopic for long-term planning, more detailed to install productive resources, precise for short-term commanding and extremely detailed for coordination. Reports also vary in precision, from listings of individual, elementary activities to global summaries of business operations.

Fayol proposed the use of management tools to help the members of the organization use the management system. He also listed fourteen principles of management that could be associated with the various sub-systems.

Verifying is the the fifth management sub-system and 'consists in verifying whether everything occurs in conformity with the plan adopted'.[14] It is part of the management system and not the accounting system. As part of the management system the verifying sub-system is wider in scope than the accounting system. It involves producing more or less detailed reports, and for a range of time frames, on all aspects of the business. Accounting of course stills plays a central role by verifying inventories and expenditures, calculating profits, cost prices and margins. The accounting department devotes half of its time, and managers expend 20 per cent of their energy, on the verifying sub-system. Verification is the cornerstone of management feedback. The principles that can be associated with this sub-system are a stability of personnel to ensure the continuity of operations and continuous learning. If results are poor, verifying prepares for the retirement of incompetent managers that is part of the commanding sub-system.

Coordinating, the fourth management sub-system, involves ensuring 'harmony' in productive operations. The tools for coordination include meetings between a head and his or her subordinates, information systems and direct access to operational employees even if they are within another chain of command. Three principles can be associated with this sub-system: discipline, orderliness and mutual support.

Commanding is the third sub-system and it involves getting 'the optimum return from all employees'[15] that are under a head's command. The principles to respect here are hierarchy, centralization, equity and the subordination of individual interests to the common interest. The tools that help the head are the powers that are delegated to each agent and the use of mail to inform each employee of what needs to be done. The head must know each of his or her subordinates, inspect all productive services under his responsibility and retire incapable employees. Meetings with subordinates can also be used to give orders and receive accounts of work performed.

Organizing, the second sub-system of management, involves providing a business 'with everything useful to its functioning'.[16] This first involves organizing the personnel by structuring them in the form of a hierarchy, the result of which can be seen in an organizational chart. Human resource management involves recruiting, continuous training and remuneration. The principles that guide organization are unity of command, division of labour[17] and equity of remuneration.

Planning is the first sub-system of management and means to 'assess the future and make a provision for it'.[18] It takes the form of a business plan or a five to ten-year plan. Plans are prepared based on the company's history, internal documents and an analysis of the technical and commercial environment. The principles concerned are unity of direction of all agents and respect for their personal initiatives.

Fayol's vision of management combines a precise understanding of daily business activities through the use of management tools, a structuring of action based on the temporal distance between reflexion and the corresponding productive operations, and principles to guide managers that may appear to be based on common sense, but in reality are necessary for the coherence of their actions. This theory is both descriptive and prescriptive. It corresponds to the daily reality of Henri Fayol's company and it still remains a guide for managers today.

APPENDIX 1: THE THIRD PART OF *INDUSTRIAL AND GENERAL MANAGEMENT*

Industrial and General Management 3rd Part: Personal Observations and Experiments

Henri Fayol[1]

1 These *studies* are based on observations and experiments made throughout a long industrial career. Begun from the sole purpose of my personal instruction, subsequently pursued without interruption during a half-century under the pressure of ceaselessly growing managerial burdens, constantly enlightened, guided, verified by experiments, they helped me act quickly in my successive roles of engineer, of colliery director and of managing director of a large mining and metallurgical company, a line of conduct also as beneficial to matters that were entrusted to me as to myself.

2 How much effort, trials and errors I would have been saved if I myself had received the advice that I have tried to resume in *Industrial and General Management* in time. And while I was laboriously and dearly acquiring an education in management, thousands of my contemporaries, wrestling with the same difficulties, were undertaking the same research, just as my predecessors had done. Managerial operations generally leave few traces and new managers rarely adopt the methods of their predecessors. It is a perpetual recommencement.

3 It seemed to me that some principles, rules, procedures sanctioned by experiments, given prominence through public debate, would be of great service if revealed even to omnipotent managers and by offering youth a collection of knowledge that is presently difficult to acquire. And from here the attempt at a doctrine that I exposed under the title *Industrial and General Management.*

I: My Beginnings in Management

4 My entire career was spent in the service of the same company that was successively called:

5 Boigues, Rambourg et Cie limited partnership

6 Commentry-Fourchambault limited liability company

7 Commentry-Fourchambault et Decazeville limited liability company

8 I began as an area engineer at the Commentry collieries in 1860.

9 Graduating from the École des Mines de Saint-Étienne, I possessed largely sufficient technical skills. After several weeks, I was well enough aware of the operations to begin to be of a little service.

10 The school had given me no management methods.

11 My chief was the technical director of the collieries: 40 years old, strong, energetic, an iron will, tireless activity, completely honest, great experience, respected authority.

12 Seven direct subordinates: three head miners, senior miners, including one who was completely illiterate; two accounting supervisors, two night watchmen. Around four hundred workers.

13 The personnel included three other engineers and half a dozen department heads.

14 What exactly were my attributions? What attitude was deemed appropriate with the chief, with colleagues, direct subordinates, workers? What were the means of stimulating assiduity, activity, worker's zeal, intelligent and devoted collaboration from direct subordinates? ... All these questions that were at first obscure would become clearer with time as I carried out my duties.

15 Dating from my first years of service,[2] I have notes on the hiring and training of workers, on discipline and initiative, on the political and religious freedoms of employees, on their social relationships and on many other subjects that have never ceased to preoccupy me since.

16 I will confine myself to citing some that show how everyday operations are connected to questions of management.

17 '*May 1861*. The horse on the sixth floor of the St Edmond pit broke its leg this morning. I wrote a voucher to have it replaced. The stable master

refused the voucher as it was not signed by the director. The director was absent. No-one had been named to replace him. Despite my position, the stable master refused outright; his instructions he said, were clear. The injured horse was not replaced and the work on the sixth floor was lost.

18 'It appears to me that when the director is "absent" there should be someone tasked with replacing him.'

19 After similar incidents, I wrote some months later:

20 'A replacement should always be named in advance to replace the absent or delayed director.'

21 'Authority must always be represented.'

* *

22 '*June 1861*. Yesterday morning while I was at the St Edmonds pit, the director was visiting the St Etienne pit. He instructed the head miner to stop the worksite that I had opened several days previously.

23 'At tonight's debriefing, the director explained why he made this decision. His explanations contained neither criticism nor urgency. Nothing obliged him to deviate from the chain of command. Why did he not follow it? I am told it is in his habits and that he proceeds thus in the other divisions. It is not a good way to give prestige and initiative to young engineers.'

24 It should be noted that I was going on 20 years old.

* *

25 'April 1862. The direct instructions from the director to my subordinates are few and far between. Is it because he trusts me or because I have always defended – very respectfully yet firmly – the instructions I had given? Nevertheless, my initiative is now rather encouraged.

26 'June 1862. I had some difficulty in the beginning to have my authority accepted by two or three senior employees; this has been achieved. But one must admit that the discipline that reigns here greatly helped.

27 'By devotion, or by simple obedience, or by fear, everyone is under the influence of the director who is as hard on himself as he is on others and who is always the first to deal with laborious or dangerous chores.

* *

28 'January 1863. The director is very upset with the organization of the workshops. While they are mostly used by the mine, the workshops remained under the personal direction of the previous head of above-ground services,

currently director of the Montluçon factory and the railway that connects the mine to the canal. The workshop head received orders from the director of the mine and the director of Montluçon; he also receives others from time to time from the managing director who was previously the director of the mine. Among these three authorities the workshop head has found a degree of independence. This lack of unity of direction is a perpetual source of conflict.

29 'Business suffers from it.

30 'Same situation in the procurement division.'

II: Management Functions as Director of the Commentry Collieries

31 And so, little by little, my management education came from observing what happened around me.

32 I would not wait long to benefit from my short experience: in 1866, the director was dying, carried off in a short lapse of time by an eruptive disease. I was called on to replace him. I so became the technical director of one of the biggest French collieries at the time.

33 Above all, this unexpected distinction came from the services I had rendered in fighting mine fires.

34 This scourge that is now hardly heard of was back then a formidable obstacle to mining rich layers of flaming coal. The Commentry collieries were already well known at the time for their subterranean fires. The fires were quite extensive, especially in my division. The security of the worksites was at the mercy of an ever-possible surprise: one had to be vigilant and defend. The fight was extremely arduous. It will give an indication if I mention that I spent my first two nights at a fire and over one year a week did not go by without being called out to a fire at night. It was the main preoccupation of engineers: it wore down the director's robust health. Such was the situation, as fires were concerned, in 1860.

35 Five years later the situation had quite happily changed: new means made the fight less arduous and safer; we contained the fire's progression better than before. As changes in mining methods reduced the causes of overheating and blazes, we retook possession of areas that had for a long time been ravaged by fire. Yet there were still terrible attacks to bear.[3]

36 The managing director later told me that it was the role I played in one of these attacks that determined my nomination.

37 I had just left on vacation when a new fire started, rapidly developing into a major blaze. The director and three engineers succeeding each other day and night, could not stop it progressing. There was great concern; the managing director moved to Commentry to follow the events more closely. The director showed his disappointment with my absence and sent me letters and dispatches to recall me. Due to erroneous addressing I received these calls belatedly. I hurried back. I had been gone for ten days when I arrived at six o'clock in the morning. I went immediately down to the mine where I found the director consulting with the engineer that had spent the night, and the one that was going to replace him. Together we examined the situation; I exposed how I saw things and the procedure to follow and, feeling capable of correctly conducting operations by myself, I asked the director to send the other engineers back to their areas, which was done.

38 After he left, the director went to see the managing director (I know of what follows from the latter). The director, who had been quite preoccupied the day before, appeared completely reassured; so long as I was there, he had no longer any concerns. And the extraordinary thing that greatly struck the managing director was this model of devotion, who placed his mine clearly above all personal convenience, asked to make the most of my return to immediately go take medical treatment, something that he had needed for quite some time.

39 Several hours later, the managing director questioned me, trying to understand the turnaround in the director's state of mind; the director was absent for the following days, I was called on until all concern due to the fire had completely disappeared.

40 The memory that he kept of this incident convinced him to name me director when the director was carried away by smallpox six months later

41 To remarks his managing committee colleagues made to him about my youth he pleasantly replied: 'I am sixty-five, Fayol is twenty-five, that makes for an excellent average'.

42 From a technical point of view, I felt up to the situation; my concerns were much greater from a management point of view.

43 I had to first have my authority accepted by my previous day's colleagues, all older than me and some much more senior. Amongst the previous day's colleagues were the heads of workshops, stores, mechanical preparation and various external services that had remained up until then independent of the mine's technical management.

44 I employed all of my faculties to do so, and I succeeded, without too much difficulty, to promptly obtain a disciplined collaboration that became, with time, devoted.

45 Making the most of my managerial studies, I took the following decisions or resolutions from the start:

46 1 – Establish a business plan based on annual forecasts and decennial forecasts;

47 2 – Weekly department-heads meetings presided by the director;

48 3 – Organization charts showing all the services and all the functions with their incumbents;

49 4 – Clear determination of the attributions of each agent;

50 5 – Weekly reports (a) from the director to the managing director; (b) from the department-heads to the director; (c) copy of the latter sent by the director to the managing director.

51 6 – Profit and loss account, established for each month on the 20th of the following month;

52 7 – Detailed annual study of the organization of each establishment from the six following points of view: management, technical, commercial, finances, accounting and security;

53 8 – Careful observation of the principles and in particular the *unity of command*: 'for any action whatsoever, an employee should receive orders from one superior only'

1 Deputies

54 A head's deputy was designated in advance not only for management, but for all departments, so that in case of absence or impediment the position was never without a representative.

2 Weekly Meetings of Department Heads

55 All the department-heads (area engineers; heads of workshops, of procurement, of mechanical preparation, of sundry works, of the railway, etc.) met once a week under the director's presidency, with the following agenda:

56 a) Study the operations of each department over the past week.

57 b) Operating plan for the following week.

58 c) Procurement, maintenance, commercial claims issues.

59 d) Various projects ...

60 Thanks to these meetings, the different heads that had ignored one another, often leading to isolation, soon became interested in the whole business and cordially gave their opinion in all situations. The difficulty was not to stimulate their interest, but rather to avoid any friction during the discussion.

61 I cannot express the extent to which these meetings facilitated my task. Thus after extensive practice, I have not stopped recommending them and imposing them when it was in my power to do so.

3 Long Term Plan

62 I naturally felt the need to render an account of the general situation of the mine, all the sorts of resources that it disposed of and the means deemed appropriate to produce as much as possible and as cheaply as possible, a goal that had been given to me. I immediately began to make a long-term plan based on the participation of all the department-heads.

63 This operation at the start of my new functions has been the foundation of one of the most important articles of my management code. We saw in the chapter on *Planning* the utility and the necessity of a business plan, what it consists of and by what means it can be executed.

4 Annual Reports and Monthly Reports

64 These two sorts of reports sufficed for as long as I remained at Commentry.

65 Daily statistics, individual meetings with each department, the weekly meetings of department-heads and my own observations kept me sufficiently abreast of business operations.

66 The monthly report was above all a study of production and of cost prices. Its conclusions could only be used two or three months after the month that produced them.

67 Later, when my managing directorship kept me far from the mines and the factories and no longer allowed me to personally follow the operations of each establishment, I felt the need to receive *weekly reports* which I will talk about further on.

5 Transformation of the Fines and Penalties System

6 Measures Taken to Recruit and to Train the Personnel

68 The engineers were generally recruited from alumni of tertiary civil engineering schools.

69 The head miners were former labourers.

70 The supervisors, the accountants came from outside for the most part.

71 Under the firm management and under the influence of the example given by the previous director, the personnel had adopted excellent disciplinary habits. What was missing most was: the education of head miners and more intelligence, with better preparation of the supervisors and the accountants.

72 These shortcomings resulted:

73 1° – From the general lack of education in the area some years previously. The most intelligent workers had been made team leaders and head miners; but they did not always know how to read. The situation was improving thanks to the new schools.

74 2° – As for supervisors and accountants, they were recruited without method as and when necessary, and often upon recommendations that were motivated more by other interests than those of the mine.

75 I often asked myself, during my time as an engineer, how we could raise the worth of secondary personnel. I had remarked that young employees were well disposed to learn and I was convinced that among the children finishing primary school each year there were three or four intelligent enough and educated enough to reach, with time and an appropriate initiation, the highest secondary posts.

76 The time had come to use these two observations. The means, it seemed, was first to recruit the supervisors and accountants exclusively from among the young employees that were studying in our schools (it was the elimination of favoritism in recruitment), and then to develop the training of young employees and that given in our schools as much as possible.

77 On the first point I had to obtain the approbation of the manager – who was a member of parliament – I obtained it.

78 On the second point, I had a long series of efforts to make, of which I will say a few words.

1 Education of Employees

79 I offered young employees – and to seniors that so wanted – to take evening classes that I would run once a week, whose main goals were drawing, some basic physics, chemistry and mechanics, and a slightly more extensive study of mining and geology. Around twenty came.

80 The success exceeded my expectations. After five or six lessons, young men that had never drawn tackled sketches of machine parts. After ten months all my auditors discussed our operating methods, sought to understand the origins of the coal fields and could associate a drawing to the expression of an idea. The need for education had come; most of my students requested books to continue their studies. I suspended my evening classes; but the personnel's momentum for learning continued.

2 Education of Children

81 The primary school, entirely supported by the mine, was maintained by the Brothers of the Christian Schools. The good students who graduated at around 14 or 15 years old, knew spelling and arithmetic fairly well; their writing left a lot to be desired and they didn't know how to sketch. However they were made to write and draw a lot. Those most skilled in drawing spent several hours a day from the start to the end of the school year making copies of major paintings intended to be admired by parents on Awards Day.

82 The result that I had obtained teaching drawing in my evening classes gave me the idea to use the same method at school. One will forgive me for entering into some detail on this subject.

83 My first lesson dealt with drawing a brick. The plan, front view, side view, cross-section that I drew by hand on the blackboard, were also reproduced by hand on paper by the employees seated around a large table. The sketch was then dimensioned. Then we moved to drawing with a ruler and set square. Definition of parallels, perpendiculars, right angles ... Finally, two or three students went to the blackboard to sketch bricks and other shapes.

84 In the second class I sat my auditors in front of a simple machine part. Same process. Concerning a cylindrical part: definition of a circle, links between the diameter and the circumference; cylinders, cones, spheres, use of sections ...

85 I said that by the fifth or sixth lesson these young men took on sketching

machine parts. We could use drawings to explain a mining method or a geological cross-section to them.

86 It is this method that I was trying to introduce into primary school. The first attempt was unsuccessful. The drawing teacher did not know how to sketch; he didn't know how to teach it. A second teacher had a promising start; a third succeeded admirably. From then on, the end of year exhibition only exposed real-life drawings to admiring parents.

* *

87 (We should note in passing that this method of teaching graphic design that was introduced half a century ago in a Commentry primary school and that is widely taught in all upper primary schools, has still not entered secondary education in Paris's main colleges. Young graduates do not know how to sketch a simple device or a real-life machine part.)

* *

88 The question of teaching drawing found itself settled. That of writing remained. Together with the teachers I looked for the type of writing that was desirable in our industry and, thereafter the children were trained, from the start, to write this way. We had to wait some time for results: but they were entirely satisfactory. All that was left to do was to maintain it or perfect it through careful attention in the department – which was done. Ten or fifteen years later the employees of Commentry were renowned for their fine writing. Since then, the typewriter has greatly reduced the importance of this skill.

* *

89 I will finish with the question of primary school by adding that an advanced class was instituted to widen the knowledge of the more educated and the more intelligent students. These students no longer left school before the age of 15 or 16.

90 Every year the top ten school leavers were employed by the company and allocated, according to their abilities, to the studies and accounting offices, the forging or carpentry workshops and various other departments.

91 Carefully observed later by their direct supervisors, watched from afar by the director, these young people were constantly directed towards positions that they appeared able to fill.

92 Applied with care and consistency, this method produced remarkable results. The selection, the stimulus to progress, the part theoretical and part practical teachings according to goals, allowed a nursery of choice workers,

that the company has employed not only at its collieries but at all of its establishments, to emerge from an essentially farming population.

93 Here I speak not of the recruitment of engineers that I dealt with previously.

**

94 It is in these managerial conditions that I took the first step forward in my new functions.

95 Little by little the technical difficulties diminished; the underground fires, that were in the past a continuous threat to the security of the mine and the lives of workers, became rarer. Without doubt one still had to be ready to launch an attack, but we were much better armed. We had time to breathe and think about other things. Mine production that was only 300,000 tons in 1860 reached 500,000 tons in 1869; cost prices were satisfactory; wages were improving. Better prospects lay before us and it seemed that we only needed to see to developing production when the following belief seized my mind: 'The Commentry coal deposit that we were happy to consider, hitherto as inexhaustible, was in reality quite limited'.

96 In 1875, after long and serious consideration, I officially communicated the studies that had led me to believe that the mine's wealth would probably not be sufficient to allow 500,000 tons to be extracted annually for a further twenty years to the director.

97 When one knows that the Commentry coalmines were already, at the time, the main source of profit for the company, one can easily image how painful and troubling this communication was. As I expected, it was greeted unkindly: 'My opinion was a simple personal opinion. Did I have the necessary authority to comment on such a serious subject? Did there not remain, as I myself had admitted, vast stretches of the concession as yet unexplored and capable of containing layers of coal? ... '

98 To confront these objections, and to some others that were levelled at me, I had alas a profound conviction based on years of study and good documentation. I was sorry to have to defend conclusions that deeply saddened me and that I had drawn against my will.

99 They were only accepted some time later, after verifications made by an eminent engineer in whom both my director and I had full confidence, and once a large number of studies had been undertaken at different points of the concession. They had to resign themselves to accept my point of view, that is to consider as extremely probable, or even certain, the complete exhaustion of the deposit in twenty or so years, if we continued to extract 500,000 tons per year.

100 For the company it was an enormous reduction in the wealth and the annual revenue it believed it could count on, insecurity about the future for the personnel, a decrease in property values for the area.

101 It was a question of finding and using the best means to reduce these untoward consequences while making the most of what coal was left in the Commentry mine.

102 A business plan for the whole company should have been drawn up by mutual agreement between the mines and the factories under the guidance of general management. But we were not used to conferring or making plans encompassing the distant future. There was no contact between the personnel at the mines and at the factories; systematically or not, the watertight bulkhead prevailed between the two groups.

103 I believe that the company paid dearly for the lack of management meetings.

104 Be that as it may, I made my plan for Commentry and I entirely dedicated myself to its execution.

* *

105 It was agreed that production would gradually and voluntarily be reduced, so as to prolong the liquidation period. This prolongation should allow us:

106 1° – to find a more favorable outlet for coal in the marketplace than that offered by the factories.

107 2° – to give factories the time to find other sources of supply.

108 3° – to reduce the number of workers little by little by slowing down or halting recruitment.

109 4° – to temper the trend in housing construction that was steadily increasing amongst by the working class and across the area in the belief of a brilliant and unlimited future.

110 It was a difficult and delicate task. I was aided by staff whose memory stirs feelings of esteem, of affection, of acknowledgment, of strength, of devotion, of pride, of self-confidence ... I found no obstacle insurmountable with the colleagues I had surrounded myself with. How enjoyable it was to work on the development of the mine that we were all so fond of, as if it was our own! We would have liked to have made a greater place for it in the industrial world!

111 And so the central problem of the concession's wealth was studied with ar-

dour. All the personnel got involved; each brought their document or their idea. Several employees acquired advanced geological knowledge from this research. Thanks to these studies,[4] the life of the mine was increased by several years; but the perspectives for the future were not greatly changed and the veil of sadness that the thought of an inevitable and near end draped over all our operations was not lifted.

112 For want of the stimulant of grandness, our activity turned towards perfecting methods, the security and hygiene of workers, improving material, increasing individual productivity ... etc.

113 Numerous articles in the *Bulletin de la Société de l'Industrie Minérale* bear witness to the intellectual activity of the personnel at Commentry.

* *

114 Needless to say that *Management* at no point ceased to be one of my main preoccupations: the study of mineral resources, the view of the future, the business plan, the training of personnel, the coordination of effort, an active supervision and general control, made my life busy and useful; and in spite of the painful feeling that comes from the task of liquidating a grand industry going inescapably towards its end, I felt profoundly attached to the enterprise where I had begun my career and where I planned to finish it.

III Management Functions as Managing Director of the Commentry-Fourchambault et Decazeville Company

115 Such was the situation when I was asked, in February 1888, to take charge of the *Managing Directorship* of the Company.

116 I refused at first, backing away from the metallurgical task that I was not in the least prepared for, and also, I should instead say 'and especially', faced with the moral anguish that was going to befall the managing director with the closure of the Fourchambault forges that had just been decided by the board of directors. In the mind of the board and according to probabilities, the closure of this factory should shortly be followed by that of the Montluçon and Imphy factories. For the past few years, this group of factories represented a heavy burden that the exhaustion of the Houillères de Commentry meant could no longer be borne.

117 For I knew what it is to struggle with the sorry consequences of the end of a great industry, even when we have some time before us, and here it was a question of immediate liquidation that had grown urgent by the rapid progression of annual losses. I turned down the honour ... and the bitter cup.

118 They appealed to my devotion and I gave in on the condition that I would not proceed in closing the factories until I was assured, through personal investigation, that the closure was absolutely necessary for the common good.

119 The two letters, of which I provide a copy here, and the ensuing extracts from the minutes of the board of directors, show how I was admitted to my new functions.

120 Letter from Mr de La Rochette, President of the Board of Directors of the Commentry-Fourchambault limited company

121 'Paris, 3 March 1888

122 'Sir,

123 'As the health of Mr de Sessevalle obliges him to relinquish his duties, the Board, that knows and appreciates your devotion to our company, wishes to appoint you managing director.

124 'Regardless of your intentions in this respect, I greatly need to talk to you as soon as possible about the situation that M de Sessevalle's retirement puts us in. I write to ask you to come to Paris and meet me next Tuesday, March 6 at two o'clock, Place Vendôme.

125 'Accept, Sir, the assurance of my most distinguished sentiments.

126 'Signed: de La Rochette'

127 Letter from Mr de Sessevalle, managing director of the Commentry-Fourchambault limited company

128 'Paris, 3 March 1888

129 Dear Sir,

130 'The contents of the letter from Mr le Baron de La Rochette that you will receive by the same messenger as this one will not be of great surprise, and if you recall our private conversations, you will not be mistaken as to the true motives of my retirement.

131 'I do not need to tell you how strong my desire is for you to be my successor; the esteem I have for your character, and the confidence that your experience and your judgment inspires, have been known for some time.

132 'Until Tuesday then. Mr de La Rochette has arranged to meet you at two o'clock, but if you would like to talk with me you will find me at home all morning.

133 'Receive, dear Sir, the expression of my devoted sentiments.

134 'Signed: A. de Sessevalle"

135 I accepted and was named managing director on 8 March 1888.

136 Four months later, I had acquired the conviction that the closure of the Fourchambault forges was not immediately necessary; that it was, to the contrary, not only possible but useful for the company to keep them operating provisionally. I so proposed to the board of directors to adjourn the stoppage and to attempt a new trial run; here are the words that concluded my proposal:

137 'But, as I could have made a mistake in my calculations, as indeed we are not safe from changes in the sales price and the cost price of our competitors, nor from diverse events that could thwart our forecasts, and as the company must obviously protect itself from new ruinous mistakes, I add the following reserve to my proposition:

138 'Book-keeping, as accurate as possible and as rapid as possible will inform us, month by month on the operations of the factory and in the event that expected results are not attained the factory will be immediately closed.'

139 The following lines are the President's summary of the debate following my proposition at the board of directors' meeting on 7 July 1888.

...

140 'The President says that the Managing Director is not an interested witness with regard to the Fourchambault forge, and it is certainly not without good reason that after a conscientious study of the situation, he had to recognize ... the possibility of maintaining in activity, at least for the present, the Fourchambault forge in more preferable conditions for the company than those that would result from the closure of the factory.

...

141 'The board's mistrust, inspired by the sad disappointments of the forge, must not go so far as rejecting conclusions based on such precise data ... all that remains is to accept that these forecasts are as close as possible to the truth and then decide how to proceed.

...

142 Our duty is all laid out then; we can but adopt the conclusions of the managing director. But the board will not forget that these conclusions are based entirely on the assumption that the losses of Fourchambault will not exceed the direct benefits resulting from its operation; it is the sine qua non

condition for it remaining in activity. It will thus be necessary to attentively oversee factory operations and to set up bookkeeping so as to be able to report on the results achieved each month, and promptly decide the measures to take in the case where the hopes that we share with the managing director would be thwarted.'

143 The proposition, put to the vote, was unanimously accepted by the board of directors, less one abstention.

* *

144 I was thus placed by the circumstances, before an experiment of the greatest interest. Before describing it and to best help grasp its conclusions from a *managerial* point of view, I believed it useful to give a general idea of the constitution of the company, of its previous functioning and the conditions it found itself in in 1888.

IV Historical Overview of the Commentry-Fourchambault et Decazeville Company

145 The Commentry-Fourchambault et Decazeville Company was born in the middle of last century, in 1854.

146 Founded to bring together two great firms operating at the time: the Fourchambault metallurgical factory and the Commentry coal mines, it first took the form of a partnership limited by shares under the company name *Boigues, Rambourg et Cie* that it kept until 1874, the date of its transformation into a limited company.

147 Grouped around this core from the beginning were other establishments situated in the same regions and also operating in the coal and iron industries.

148 With Commentry, the Montluçon metallurgical factory and the Montvicq mine made up the Allier group.

149 The factories at Imphy and at La Pique, the foundries of Torteron, La Guerche and Feularde, made up, together with the Fourchambault forge and foundry, the Nièvre group. Lastly, a large iron ore and limestone mine in Berry guaranteed supplies for the blast furnace.

150 The fusion of these diverse establishments formed a very complete industrial group.

151 For twenty-five years, sustained prosperity, even brilliant sometimes, justified the creation of this association.

152 Then the growth of metallurgy in the east and the north of France became more and more threatening for the prosperity and even for the existence of the factories in the Centre. At the same time we realized that the coal discovered each year in Commentry was far from compensating that extracted; the end of the coal mine looked rather imminent. No longer having low-priced coal in abundance, competing with products from the north and the east, the factories in Nièvre and Allier ceased to be remunerative. Finally, the company's profits diminished to the point of preventing any distribution of dividends from 1885 onwards.

153 In 1888, the company was on the point of accepting its demise by immediately abandoning metallurgy and by unhurriedly finishing the exhaustion of the coal mine, when a managerial change occurred.

154 With the same mines and the same factories, with the same financial resources, the same commercial outlets, the same board of directors and the same personnel, the company that for the past few years was in jeopardy, recovered in an upward movement comparable to that of its fall.

155 The dividends chart hereafter makes this change quite noticeable.

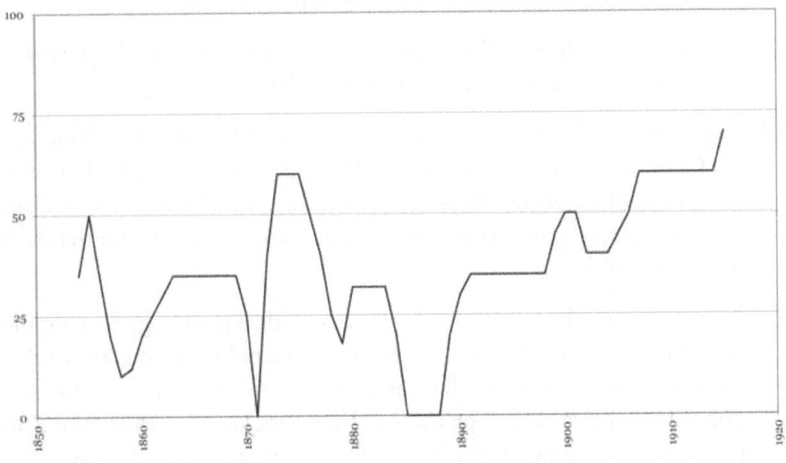

156 **Figure A.1: Dividends of the Commentry Fourchambault et Decazeville Company.**

157 I will come back to this change in bearing whose causes were purely managerial.

158 A few successful efforts having restored a relative prosperity, the closure of the factories was adjourned. Courageous resolutions prevailed; in a few years the acquisition of Brassac and Decazeville put new coal and

metallurgical domains, likely to replace those that were destined to disappear, in the hands of the company. The enterprise was audacious as these domains had only brought disappointment to their former owners; it was justified.

* *

159 Today (in 1916) little is left of the original elements of the company.

160 The two principal establishments: the Commentry and Montvicq coal mines and the Fourchambault forges have disappeared; the Berry placers are abandoned.

161 On the other hand:

162 The Brassac mines supply 120,000 tons per year; the Aveyron coal mines, with their production of 600,000 tons form one of the powerful masses of coal in the French Midi; the Decazeville forges have brought their annual production to 80,000 tons.

163 Of the original secondary elements, only one, Imphy, whose reason to be came neither from its proximity to combustibles nor ores, took on a new vitality.

164 The Montluçon blast furnaces are still seeking their way.

165 (Let us note, by the way, that these three factories have, since the start of the war, rendered great services to the national defence.)

166 Lastly, to complete the enumeration of the actual constituent elements of the Commentry-Fourchambault and Decazeville Company, I will mention the Joudreville iron mines of which it owns two thirds, the metallurgical factories of Pont-à-Vendin of which it owns two fifths, and the Batère mines, four fifths.

167 As it had in the beginning, the company made a grouping of coal mines, iron mines and metallurgical factories, considered to be in good working condition, but it no longer has the same centres of activity, nor the same populations of workers, nor the same markets, nor the same fabrication processes; everything singularly transformed itself in half a century.

* *

168 In 1854, the Centre region found itself particularly favoured. It had the Berry ores close by, pure in phosphorous and easy to reduce in the small furnaces of old. The Nièvre forests supplied charcoal in abundance and the cast iron that was forged was perfectly suited either to castings, or the forging of iron, primitively obtained from the bloomer, then from the puddling furnace. Thus furnaces were many in the Berry and in the Nièvre.

169 The substitution of coke for charcoal slightly displaced the axis of metallurgy; the furnaces drew nearer the mines and the little wood furnaces, scattered throughout the countryside, died out successively.

170 The Montluçon factory, connected to the placers by the Canal du Berry and to the Commentry coal mines by a special railway, developed rather strongly. The refined iron it produced found an easy outlet in the surrounding forges and in particular at Fourchambault.

171 From 1860 onwards the rise of the industry, resulting from the creation of the railways and the use of iron in constructions, gave importance to the factories that were the best placed to take in a supply of either ores or combustibles.

172 At that time, the Montluçon blast furnaces, the Fourchambault forges, the factories in the Nord and the Loire were fully operational. Despite its thick iron ore deposits, the Est was developing slowly on account of the mediocre quality of its products; for the same reason Decazeville was not taking full advantage of its natural riches.

173 However the forging of iron in the puddling furnace improved and the laminated products in the east and in the north had already greatly improved in quality when, around 1880, the Martin and Thomas forging processes made their appearance.

174 Thanks to these new processes, phosphorous was no longer an obstacle to the production of good metal; large factories were created on the marvellous deposits in the Est, where the ore only requires 10 francs expenditure per ton of cast iron; we succeed in producing an ingot of steel at 70 francs per ton. The iron is more and more replaced by super-mild steel or melted iron – less expensive and of much higher quality. All the forges that in the past exclusively made iron, reduced more and more their production or stopped it. After a long battle the Fourchambault forges had to accept their demise.

175 By a singular and grave coincidence, the Commentry collieries were being worked out and approached their end at the same time that the Fourchambault forges were succumbing to competition from the Est.

* *

176 Today the Allier collieries and the Fourchambault forges have gone and have been replaced by the Aveyron collieries and the Decazeville forges.

177 The factories at Imphy and Montluçon subsist.

178 The company possesses a colliery in the Puy de Dôme; it built up great

interests in the iron ore basin of Briey and, in association with the Lens mines, it completed the construction of the Pont-à-Vendin factory when war broke out.

* *

179 Such are the diverse enterprises whose management I took a more or less important part in from 1860 until today. It was my principal field of management observations and experiments. Moreover, thanks to the importance of the company that I represented, I was called on to participate in a number of committees, cooperatives, such as the Comité Consultatif des Chemins de Fer, le Comité des Houillères, le Comité des Forges, le Comptoir des Poutrelles, le Comptoir des Ressorts, the Advisory Board of the École Nationale des Mines de Saint-Étienne, the Advisory Board of the Conservatoire National des Arts et Métiers, etc. They were further fields of observation that I greatly took advantage of.

180 Yet, for an attentive observer there is no need for exceptional conditions to make managerial studies: the family home is an abundant source of observations and experiments, parliamentary debates agitate for the most part around management questions and there is perhaps not one issue of a major political journal where the administration of the state does not take a fair-sized place.

181 It is under these conditions that I made the following experiments and observations.

V Experiment of 1888

182 One of the most interesting *management* experiments that I was given to do took place at my debut in the managing directorship of the Commentry-Fourchambault Company. By the sole effect of circumstance, and without my intentions having anything to do with it, the experiment was ready to be as conclusive as possible.

183 The company had just decided to close the Fourchambault forges that, for a rather long time, were making losses, and it was preparing to terminate its corporate life by finishing the exhaustion of the Commentry mines. It was at this moment, in March 1888 that I was asked to take over the managing directorship of the company.

184 I mentioned above that after a few months study I proposed to the board of directors that the Fourchambault forge be provisionally kept operating and that my proposition was accepted.

185 At the time, without any change in the board of directors, nor in the financial resources of the company, nor in its commercial outlets, nor in its constituent elements, nor in its machinery, nor even in a noticeable way in its personnel, I saw the situation change, dividends reappeared and soon profits were sufficient to be able to contemplate reconstituting the parts of the mining and metallurgical domain that were destined to disappear. Discouragement made room for hope and a desire to live, and the Commentry-Fourchambault Company did not cease to occupy an honourable place amongst the major French industrial enterprises.

186 I believe I am able to affirm that this change in bearing of the Commentry-Fourchambault Company resulted entirely from the *managerial* processes employed, from the extension to the whole of the company of the processes previously applied in Commentry.

187 We know what these processes involve: *business plan* drawn up by means of annual previsions and decennial previsions; *department-heads meetings* in each establishment; *directors meetings* under the presidency of the managing director; *organization charts*; attentive *recruitment*; *training* of the personnel; active *control*; observation of general *principles*; rapid and clear *bookkeeping*, etc.

188 Such is my opinion, the unique cause of the change that occurred in the conduct of the Commentry-Fourchambault Company from 1888 onwards.

189 We can attribute it neither to an improvement in commercial conditions, as the competition from the north and the east was becoming increasingly redoubtable, nor to the situation at the Commentry mine that was growing poorer each day.

190 Nor can we attribute it to the *metallurgical ability* of the new managing director, which was non-existent. This incompetency brings to the foreground, in the circumstances, the importance of *managerial ability*.

191 I was told that an anxious and malcontent shareholder said at the time, not without reason: 'A metallurgist was needed, it was a miner that was chosen!' For the public who does not distinctly perceive managerial action, technical ability is only to be taken into account; from this point of view a managing director skilled both in mines, metallurgy and mechanical construction was necessary as the company was operating at the same time in these three industries. It's doubtful whether this man existed, and if he had existed and we could find him, one must ask oneself if an enterprise, whose future was not assured, would have succeeded in engaging him.

192 So posed, the problem would be more or less insoluble. Fortunately, it is posed otherwise: special technical ability must largely exist in each establishment; all the personnel – directors, engineers, foremen – must be endowed as completely as possible. As for the managing director, if he is sufficiently acquainted to understand the running of operations and take, with the aid of his staff, the decisions that the circumstances require, his *technical* skill is sufficient. In reality his role is essentially *managerial.*

193 I felt no less acutely my metallurgical lacuna. I was pressed to fill it, inasmuch as strictly necessary for my functions, by first making a six-month stay in the factories, then fairly frequent visits. I had immediately ruled out any pretence to equal in technical ability any one of the very many and very diverse specialists that formed the personnel of our factories. But I was responsible for the recruitment of such personnel. It was one of the great difficulties that I had to overcome; men of value do not readily enlist to serve a suffering company whose future is not assured. One of my first concerns was to constitute a staff: technical secretaries and consultants.

194 The same measures had been necessary in mechanical construction. But when it was necessary to demonstrate that the company could create for itself a new mining and metallurgical future and that these two industries were more than sufficient to absorb all the strength of the managerial personnel and all the financial resources of the enterprise, the managing director and the board of directors decided to first demise, then to sell the establishments known by the names of Fourchambault foundries and the La Pique foundries.

* *

195 There remained two groups of industries that brought into play a large number of *technical* and *commercial* specialties. Each of these specialties required agents that have for the most part devoted much intelligence and much time to acquire the necessary knowledge.

196 It is the occasion to note that one, always the same is *managerial ability*; that it applies to all sorts of enterprises; that its employ is of general usefulness, and that the notions that constitute it are neither more numerous nor more difficult to learn than those required by any technical specialty. The pains one would need to take to spread managerial notions is one hundred times less than those one takes to spread technical notions, and the result will perhaps be no lesser. All pupils of a class in management will not be outstanding managers – no more so than pupils of technical schools are not all first order technicians and pupils of military schools all eminent strategists; but the general level of management will rise and well-gifted men will rise quicker and higher.

197 If I had not felt supported by a certain amount of *managerial* experience, I would assuredly not have ceded to the instances that influenced me in 1888 to accept the burden of the managing directorship of the Commentry-Fourchambault Company.

* *

198 The liquidation of the *Commentry and Montvicq collieries*; the maintaining in activity of the *Fourchambault forges* for fourteen years after their condemnation; the transformation of production at the *Montluçon* and *Imphy* factories; the revival of the long-abandoned *Brassac mines*; the restoration and the development of the *Aveyron forges and foundries*; the [transformation] of the *Decazeville and Campagnac collieries*; a large part in the creation of the *Joudreville iron mines* and in the *Société métallurgique de Pont-à-Vendin* ...; all these companies, and some others of lesser scale, placed me before the various kinds of problems that big industry presents: technical problems, sales problems, financial problems, social problems ... There are none where the management function did not play a more or less important role. Through the difficulties encountered, the errors and mistakes committed, the company lived; it prospered and, since the beginning of the war, gave appreciated concourse to National Defence. One must conclude that the *management* function has been fulfilled in a satisfactory fashion.

199 I speak simply of these things, without pretension and without false modesty, with the sole desire of attracting attention to the importance of *managerial ability* and to the necessity of *management education.*

* *

200 I have had many other *management* experiments just as interesting as that of 1888; I have had none so conclusive because, in most cases, the change in *managerial* methods coincided with new technical and financial means. From a general point of view, I will confine myself then to say that my managerial *directives* have always been the same.

* *

201 It would be extremely interesting to know of the *management* processes employed by the great leaders of industry, numerous enough, who have found themselves in analogous situations, either with businesses in suffering that had to be revived, or with companies to create, or with companies to liquidate. I hope that my example will encourage imitators.

202 I will now confine myself to relate, at the whim of my memories, observations and experiments that have contributed to make up my management baggage.

203 Everybody can do as much in his milieu and draw the conclusions that, whether they confirm mine, or contradict them, can contribute to the formation of the doctrine.

204 If I touch here on technical, commercial or financial questions, it will uniquely be from a management point of view, in other words from the point of view of the relation of the management function with the other functions.

I Sales Management

1 Present Sales Organization of the Commentry-Fourchambault Company

205 The adopted organization seeks to conciliate the initiative, the control and the responsibility of the managing directorship, with the greatest decentralization possible. It confers extensive powers to each local directorate.

206 Under the authority of the local director, the sales servicing of each establishment is performed by one or two department heads depending on whether the purchases or the sales are combined or separate, and by salesmen.

207 Representation is provided:

208 1° – by one or several travelers residing in the establishment and visiting the clientele within a determined radius.

209 2° – by representatives domiciled at distant points and tasked with visiting a zone defined around their point of attachment.

210 3° – by agents attached to the other establishments of the company.

211 4° – by the office in Paris.

212 The national territory is divided into ... regions. A map fixes the composition of each region.

213 A salesman is assigned to each region that exclusively visits it on behalf of all the establishments of the Company.

214 With this organization, it was necessary to reconcile the principle of the *unity of command* and the obligation to move quickly, to *give satisfaction to customers as quickly as possible.*

215 Here is the method employed:

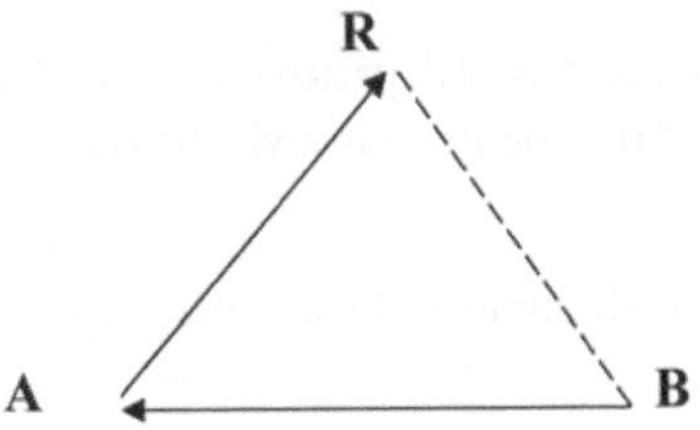

The salesman R pertains to factory A, he also does business for factory B. Factory B must address his instructions to R by passing them through A; that's the rule.

Figure A.2: Unity of command and sales at the Commentry-Fourchambault Company.

216 Nevertheless, a too rigorous application of the principle should not prejudice the correct running of affairs by slowing them or complicating them unnecessarily.

217 To go quickly, all the while ensuring observance of the principle of unity of command, we admitted the following simplifications:

218 1° – For an important, long-term affair, requiring regular correspondence (factories A and B agreed beforehand on this derogation; in every special case B and R will send A a duplicate of the exchanged correspondence, unless having been formally dispensed by A).

219 2° – For an urgent affair that must immediately be replied to. (In this case as in the previous one, the correspondence is sent in duplicate to the home factory A at the same time as to agent R).

220 3° – Generally speaking, after an agreement between A and B approved by general management.

221 Apart from of the duplicates specified above, there are others sent by the factories and the salesmen to the office in Paris who, in these circumstances, exert the necessary control over the functioning of all the services. General management is thus aware of incidents that arise and can intervene.

222 Thus comes into being a unity of method, a unity of management and a unity of command.

223 Here the *overpass* finds its application.

**

224 I've always recommended that agents of the sales department draw inspiration from the following precepts:

225 a) Loyalty in business is one of the best ways to succeed (loyalty is not synonymous with naivety).

226 b) Serving clients honestly and rapidly is one of the best means to keep them loyal.

227 c) The agent of the sales department is the technical department's defender vis-à-vis the clientele, and the defender of the clientele vis-à-vis the technical department.

228 d) One must avoid depending on a too small number of customers or suppliers.

Transfer Pricing

229 Among the trade questions that require the intervention of the *management* function, one of the most delicate and the most important is that of *transfer prices.* To give an idea, I can do no better than expose the role that these prices have played at the Commentry-Fourchambault et Decazeville Company.

* *

230 One of the reasons for the founding of the company in 1853 was the factories' need for coal and the need for an outlet for the collieries. In fact, the largest part of the production of the collieries was delivered to the factories.

231 A conventional price, called a *transfer price,* was established for an unlimited duration, probably taking account of market prices at the time. After several years this price was notably inferior to the commercial price, and the factories benefitted from a difference that sometimes exceeded their apparent benefits. In 1875 I saw the director of the Montluçon blast furnaces very disappointed when learning that the profit of his factory, of which he was proud, was notably inferior to that which the collieries would have realized, on the transfer price, by selling their coal to the public. He believed his factory prosperous although they were really at a loss.

232 Such illusions are deplorable. They distort ideas and can entertain a false sense of security. They were disastrous in the Montluçon and Fourchambault factories, big consumers of coal. A day came where they had to pay the combustible at everybody's price; not at all prepared, it near killed them.

* *

233 The question of *transfer prices* arises every time that, in the same company, one of the establishments is a consumer of materials of which the other is a producer.

234 The solution that comes naturally to mind is that the first only buys at con-

ditions when he deems it in his own interest to do so and the second only sells in similar conditions.

235 But cases arise where the two establishments have obliged relations and where nothing in the commercial situation allows them to discuss the sales price and the purchase price amongst themselves. Such is the case, for example, where colliery and factory are situated in the same locality, especially if this locality is somewhat isolated from any mining or industrial centre such that it is not easy for the mine to sell and for the factory to buy outside.

236 In that case, the superior authority is obliged to intervene.

237 The danger to avoid is that poorly established *transfer prices* distort cost prices, give illusions as to the progress of the business, benumb the vigilance of agents and divert them from seeking necessary improvements.

238 After having been confronted with the question of *transfer pricing* in an acute state in the old establishments of the company, I found it at Decazeville. It exists in most big companies.

239 The rule I adopted was the following:

240 a) Bring closer, as far as possible, the *transfer price* to that which would be the *commercial* price if the two establishments were foreign to each other.

241 b) Establish the *transfer price* in a way that simplifies the commercial relationships of the two establishments and their bookkeeping as much as possible.

242 This rule is not always easy to apply.

***

Trade Agreements

243 As soon as I had to occupy myself with the sale of Commentry coals, I sought to live intelligently with our two main competitors in the Centre. The memory of old and numerous poor mutual dealings was an obstacle; we overcame them through much goodwill and perseverance. Several small agreements were first established, and then more and more extensive ones and, with time, the agreement became close to general.

244 When the company took charge of Decazeville, I found the fuel market to be bitterly contested by the main producers of the region. The same efforts ended in the same result a few years later; a trade agreement reigned between old adversaries.

245 Convinced of the utility and the importance of trade agreements, I extolled and facilitated them every time that I was able.

246 What I think of them today is resumed in the following lines: ...

Consumer Cooperatives

247 I often had to reflect on the following problem:

248 The agents of a large company need lodgings and consumer goods of all sorts. If the houses and commerce exist, the company does not need to intervene. If the houses and commerce do not exist, it is obliged to create them. Yet all these cases arise from the industrial locality largely purveyed with lodgings and supplies to the one where all is missing. To what extent can and must the enterprise, the industrial company, intervene?

249 The right of workers to constitute consumer cooperatives is beyond discussion. In the case of an inhabited area where one wishes to establish an industry, the right of the employer is not debatable either. I know not for that matter where the exercise of these rights has caused conflicts.

250 It was not the same case for the intervention of a large company in the creation of consumer cooperatives when the cities were already provided for, more or less handsomely, with livelihoods.

251 This intervention had diverse modalities:

252 a) subvention to the workers' cooperative.

253 b) subvention and collaboration in the conduct of the cooperative.

254 c) participation in the constitution of capital and in the profits.

255 d) employer's shop, etc.

256 Employer intervention generally provided very great service to the management of the cooperative, above all at its beginnings. It became less useful as the founders of the workers' cooperative gained experience. No difficulty arose thus between employers and workers.

257 The conflicts came from somewhere else:

258 The workers' districts had grown; commerce and houses belonged to the inhabitants, for the most part former agents or children of former company agents, having many relatives, among the workers and employees, intelligent and influential.

259 The creation of a consumer cooperative compromised a heritage acquired through the relentless effort of one or of several generations. It is not necessary to understand greatly human nature to imagine the distress and anger that swept over those concerned.

260 If it is a purely workers' cooperative, one only has to defend oneself through standard commercial struggle; besides, the rivalry is generally not immediately overwhelming. But if it is an employer creation, more formidable, the blow is more marked, the ruin more threatening ... then all means are admissible to defend oneself – hostile and incessant critique – denigrating employers; excitation to strike. We note a rather large number of strikes including some very serious ones that had no other cause than a more or less employer cooperative.

261 When creating cooperatives the employers have not always sufficiently taken account of the interests of shopkeepers and of owners who, on the basis of established customs, had built a business by rendering services to the company through an independent and voluntary collaboration. This oversight sometimes cost the company, the workers and the area dearly.

262 No one contests that cooperation is a good means to reduce the cost price of consumer items. It is in the interests of the workers and the employers to have recourse. As always, moderation is to be observed.

263 Such are the principles observed for a long time by the Commentry-Fourchambault et Decazeville Company. They have done her well to date.

* * *

Industrial Management in its Dealings with Politics

264 In the first years of my career, I saw the managing director of the Commentry-Fourchambault company, Mr Mony, carry out his functions as mayor of Commentry and deputy for the Allier to great profit for the company, for the town and for the state. The colliery and the town both profited from the good relations that reigned between them; the parliament disposed of the experience of a great industrialist; the company benefitted from the benevolence of the government.

265 Mr Mony's notoriety and the government's support rendered any electoral pressure useless; by massively voting for the *boss*, the mining population only followed its own sentiment.

266 Approaching 1870, several clouds formed in this pure sky: the republican opposition was growing; the elections revealed defections amongst the

miners themselves; distrust insinuated itself between the elected representative and the electors ... the golden age had gone.

267 The War, the defeat and the change in government that followed had a deep repercussion on the spirit of the mining population; even the religious habits were modified; the miners that regularly attended the Sunday service stopped going to church and generally did not return.

268 From a political point of view, the national humiliation, the suffering, the misery for which the government was held responsible, was a responsibility that redounded upon the former official candidate. Despite enormous electoral efforts that were prolonged as far as 1878, the managing director of the company was not elected.

269 The second period was the obverse of the first: a hostile municipality; malevolent state public servants at all levels; violent electoral battles ... rendered the management of the colliery very difficult. To get at the political adversary, they attacked the industrial interests that he was in charge of.

270 We know how much the colliery industry was exposed to the interference of public authorities; it also had a large number of contacts with the municipalities; the streets, the roads, the sewers, the water, the electricity, the lighting, the police, the schools, etc., constantly brings together these two important interests. Here, as everywhere, amicable arrangements are worth more than hostility.

271 After the death of Mr Mony that occurred in 1883, the Commentry-Fourchambault company, convinced that in the current circumstances the candidacy of industry leaders and even that of secondary managers to elected positions were of a nature to sow division amongst the personnel, to provoke the malevolence of public authorities, in a word, to harm gravely the interests of the company, decided that until further notice the agents of the company should abstain from being candidates. It was otherwise understood that the freedom to vote of employees and workers would be rigorously observed.

272 Such is the line of conduct followed by the Commentry-Fourchambault et Decazeville company for some thirty years. I believe that it largely contributed to the relative tranquility that all the long-standing establishments of the company enjoyed during this third period.

273 In Decazeville, the participation of leaders in electoral battles lasted until the coming of the Commentry-Fourchambault company in 1892. A few years previously, we witnessed two members of the board of directors

of the Société des Mines et Usines de l'Aveyron compete for the worker's votes. And so the discord in the region was profound. It was not long before the electoral abstention practiced by the Commentry-Fourchambault company produced beneficial effects. Good relations were soon established between the company and the municipality that have not abated since, and that greatly facilitated the development of the industry and the town.

274 Electoral abstention, is it the final word of wisdom in the management of a large mining and metallurgical enterprise? I think not.

275 Without doubt we poorly imagine an industry leader in charge of serious industrial interests attending numerous parliamentary sessions. We don't like to imagine this industry leader soliciting the workers' votes either. But is it good that the government be systematically deprived of the counsel that experience with major affairs makes particularly interesting for the state? Is it good that industry endures, without defending itself, the assaults that socialism and unions launch on it without a truce?

276 Electoral abstention was suited to the thirty-year period that just passed. It allowed us to traverse without mishap the reign of the member of parliament wearing a blouse in Commentry; it allowed us to restore the social peace and the industrial discipline in Decazeville that the former electoral battles had deeply troubled. It had its reason for being and its utility.

277 But the political union and social situation has been considerably modified over the past thirty years: the form of government is no longer the objective of electoral battles; the strength of workers' unions has greatly increased; socialism is more menacing ...

278 A new situation required new means; they are in the process of being formed. The private action of industry leaders makes room, little by little, for more powerful, more enlightened and more poised collective action of the Comité des Forges and the Comité des Houillères; the experience and the competency of industrialists are condensed in these committees that are more and more listened to by public authorities. Thus each company is no longer isolated before the state or the unions; the personal action of the leader is not suppressed, but transformed. It remains to be settled. It is the beginning of a new period, none less difficult or less important than those previous.

279 Powerful workers unions – political action – employers unions – modification of electoral laws.

* * *

Industrial Management and its Relationship with Religions and Schools

280 The three cities that were meant to be the main centres of activity of the Commentry-Fourchambault et Decazeville Company blossomed around the middle of last century in analogous circumstances: rural populations, more or less exclusively Catholic, had come to settle around the blast furnaces, the rolling mills and the mine shafts, in a region until then barely inhabited. The Rambourg, Boigues and Decazes families, owners of the mines and factories were at the time represented by men that remain well known in their respective localities: S. Mony in Commentry – Duffaut in Fourchambault – Cabrol in Decazeville.

281 The means employed to satisfy the needs for religion and for teaching in the young cities were the same without there being an understanding between the founders, and despite the distance that isolated the new industries from one another, at this time with no railway.

282 The churches, the schools, the hospices, of which the state left the burden to the industrialists, were built by the latter. The boys' schools were confided to the Brothers of the Christian schools, the girls' schools and the hospices to Sisters.

283 Churches, schools, hospices, fulfilled their mission well and rendered great service to industry and to its personnel.

284 The entirely natural benevolence of the founders for these institutions was handed down to their successors; it has persisted through changes in owners; it has survived the laws for the secularization of teaching congregations and for the separation of the Church and the state; it is a rule for the Commentry-Fourchambault et Decazeville Company.

285 This rule reconciles with the absolute respect of the liberty of the personnel, as much from the point of worship as from that of school.

* * *

Strikes

286 Under my local or general direction, the following strikes took place at the Commentry-Fourchambault et Decazeville Company.

287 In Commentry:

288 from 1860 to 1916, in fifty-six years, one strike in 1881 – duration three days.

289 In Montvicq:

290 from 1878 to 1916, in thirty-eight years,

291 in Fourchambault

292 from 1888 to 1902, in fourteen years,

293 in Montluçon:

294 from 1888 to 1916

295 in Imphy :

296 from 1888 to 1916

297 in Brassac:

298 from 1890 to 1916 ...

299 at Decazeville Mine:

300 at Decazeville Forge

301 in Joudreville:

302 on the whole, from a total of ... years of work ... years of strike.

303 The people that imagine that mining and metallurgical workers are very often on strike will be surprised by this statistic. But, even if the strikes are not frequent, it should not be concluded that they are harmless. All are grave, some are disastrous.

304 I will give some details about the Commentry strike, the one in Montluçon and about the strike at the Decazeville forge in 19.. that present some interesting particularities.

Commentry Strike, June 1881

305 For some years the exhaustion of the mine and the restriction of work sites made a reduction in personnel necessary. The diverse measures taken to achieve this reduction with the least damage – such as, for example, the cessation of engaging workers above 20 years old – had not produced sufficient results, and it was becoming impossible to occupy the 1650 workers that remained at the start of the year 1881. At this time the company would offer work in its foundry in Montluçon and at its mine in Montvicq, both in the neighbourhood of Commentry.

306 It is in these circumstances that the dismissal of around two hundred work-

ers was decided. To a half, the most senior, we offered a pension (paid by the company); the others were offered work in Montluçon and in Montvicq. The dismissed workers had to cease work in Commentry on Saturday 4 June.

307 That day, I received an anonymous letter saying that if we did not go back on our determination nobody would come to work on 7 June after the Pentecost celebrations. The letter added that all the workers had decided not to work one day per week to avoid the dismissal of their *brothers*.

308 The Monday I learned that, during the day of Sunday and during the following night, the strike had been preached and prepared in several inns and I was brought several copies of handwritten posters that had been affixed in the streets of the town and at the mine.

309 On Tuesday, at one o'clock in the morning, three teams of four workers armed with axes and picks, posted along the main roads, tried to stop the miners coming to work. They didn't succeed. I had gone to one of the roadblocks and I had sent engineers to the others. The miners passed in our presence and the stations were more or less filled that day.

310 But on Wednesday morning, along all the roads that led from the neighbouring villages to the mine, men and women, amongst whom we recognized the most reputed families (we learnt later that they were there despite themselves), prevented the workers from passing; only 500 could go down. Some fights broke out. During the night death threats were levelled at those who had worked.

311 It was not possible for us to protect workers acting in good faith.

312 Upon order of the authorities, several gendarmerie brigades and four army companies came to Commentry and maintained order in the streets of the town and around the shafts; but the roads leading to the mine were ceaselessly intercepted by strikers that constantly pushed back the labourers heading to work. Nobody worked on Thursday, Friday and Saturday.

313 The managing director Mr. Mony had come to support and cover local management.

314 On Sunday 12 June, the following notice was posted on the mine:

315 'The mine workers of Commentry, that deserted work unexpectedly and without giving their fortnight, will be settled this eighteenth *and in full payment for all work done by them*.

316 'The workers desirous of resuming work can present themselves to the mine office, as from tomorrow *to contract new engagements*.'

317 On Monday morning, all the workers arrived to resume work.

318 Thus ended the strike without any reclamation other than the anonymous letter of 4 June that had been addressed to us. There was no question of wages, or hours of work, or workshop regulations. It is in the name of fraternity and solidarity that a few workers imposed the strike on the majority.

319 It was the first strike by the Commentry miners; it was also the last. Work did not stop for an instant during the *general strike of 1902* that had albeit been decided by a general congress of miners held in Commentry itself.

* * *

320 The 1881 strike was not the work of a union. There was no established union in Commentry at the time. A union would have sent delegates. It is said it was inspired by a socialist that already had at the time a beginning of celebrity and who had recruited several members amongst the mine workers of the Allier. He operated in the way of old secret societies of which several vestiges remained in the region. We were not a little surprised to find that the small number of ringleaders were almost all excellent workers, much appreciated in every respect. But what ignorance of management necessities. They naively believed that the organization of the personnel could be resolved, regardless of the economic situation of the company, by the will of management alone. The even forgot the daily necessities of the worker's household. A few hours conference with these good strays may have avoided the strike. But we did not suspect there was a need for this conference. Would a secret police have informed us? If that was a shortcoming, it found compensation in the company's managerial methods that can be resumed as benevolence and firmness. The salary of the Commentry miners was always at least equal, if not superior, to that of surrounding industrial populations; union, political and religious freedoms were always respected.

321 Thus when the instigators of the general strikeof 1902 pronounced their usual declamations against work in the mines, the Commentry miner simply expressed his regret to see this work disappear with the exhaustion of the colliery. His regret does not only concern the site he is used to; it embraces the land, the affections and often too the field and the house that he laboriously acquired and that he will have to leave ...

322 These diverse considerations help understand how the entire industrial life of the Commentry mining collectivity passed by with *only three days of strike.*

Montluçon Strike

323 Here are the terms the board of directors used to give an account of the Montluçon strike to the annual general meeting in 1901.

324 'The Montluçon strike originated in the pretension of a group of our casting workers to no longer work *per piece*, but only per day. We could not accede to this pretension without compromising the existence of the factory itself. We had clearly stated this to our workers on the first day, while enlightening them as much as possible about the general situation of metallurgy and about the inevitable consequences of a strike that would immobilize two thirds of the factory personnel.

325 'Our counsel was not heeded and it was only after five months of unemployment that the group of striking casters renounced all of their pretensions and asked to return to work.

326 'Unfortunately, as it had been too easy to foresee, the orders had taken other directions for the past five months. Our workers can only return to the factory as and when there are new orders, which we are actively seeking.'

327 This strike, begun 23 July 1901, ended 23 December of the same year.

328 On August 8 in Paris I received a visit from the Secretary of the Syndicat Général des Mouleurs de France, member of the Commission Supérieure du Travail, accompanied by the deputy secretary, counsellor to the industrial tribunal.

329 In the course of a long and very courteous conversation, M. S. made some remarks to me that cast a certain light on this strikeand on the ideas that prevailed at the time with the leaders of the casters' union. I resume them here:

330 'Your casters in Montluçon, M.S. told me, were perhaps wrong to strike at the moment; we would not have advised them to, at least not without taking the time to talk with you. I should even say that I heard several workers on site, and some of the most serious, speak highly of the company and recognize that, in a great many circumstances, it looked after them *very well.*

331 'But your casters are on strike. They do not want to do *piece work.* We have a firm mandate from the union to pursue the suppression of piece work and replace it with day labour, in all factories. For us it is an absolute principle. We will thus support the Montluçon casters with all our force.

332 '*Piece work* depreciates French industry by delivering inferior products to customers; piece work is not careful, is not *finished*. It removes skillful

workers and replaces them with task-workers.

333 'Employers are attached to it because it increases worker output, which has a doubly untoward result. It reduces wages, it reduces the number of occupied hands. It is a third of workers cast out whereas day work would occupy everybody.'

334 On my observation that the Montluçon factory, in the process of evolving, still insufficiently tooled, poorly prepared to battle competition, could not withstand a reduction in worker output, M. S. responded:

335 'If the Montluçon factory is closed, the work that will not be done there will be done in another foundry. We place ourselves at a higher and general viewpoint; we represent all casting workers of France and we must pursue abolition of *piece work*.'

336 Next to the Commentry miners' strike by *solidarity*, I thought it would be interesting to place the strike by *principle* of the Montluçon casters.

337 The words *solidarity* and *principle* shelter many good intentions and a strong dose of economic ignorance.

338 It is probable that amicable conversations between workers and employers, as it had been possible to have given the nature of existing relations, would have prevented these two strikes. But there was no preliminary conference. Facilitating these conferences, enlightening the workers, are means of fighting strikes. Well organized unions contribute to the use of these means.

* * *

339 We note: in *Commentry*: (1881)

340 the best workers' complete lack of knowledge of the economic conditions of the company and of managerial necessities;

341 the employer's lack of information about what is happening within an important group – not by number but by influence – of workers;

342 lack of means of conversation and discussion between management and the workers.

343 in *Montluçon* (1901)

344 same ignorance by workers of the economic conditions of the company;

345 the strong will, dictated by outside leaders from the casters' union, to relentlessly combat piece work;

346 no preliminary conversation.

347 at Decazeville-Forge ...

* *

348 While the responsibility for the future weighs on the employer, that this responsibility is strict towards customers, suppliers, creditors of all sorts, the responsibility of ringleaders is non-existent.

349 Little by little this responsibility is becoming effective from a moral point of view, in well-organized unions. It is up to legislators for it to become so legally.

350 Conclusion: enlighten workers as much as possible as to the *managerial* necessities of business;

351 Also enlighten the legislators so that in these matters that are of such high interest to the state, they do not forget to place responsibilities opposite rights.

Trade Unions

352 Even though they generally presented themselves, from the start, as adversaries of employers, the unions have not been fought by the Commentry-Fourchambault et Decazeville Company. In spite of this, perhaps even because of this, they did not develop much; most rallied only a negligible part, rarely half of the personnel. The isolation of our different establishments has, no doubt, contributed to this result.

353 I thus did not deal with well-established unions, veritable representatives of the workers. At an embryonic stage, the unions do not have the necessary authority to speak and to negotiate in the name of the collectivity. Like any minority wanting to dominate, they are rather violent and subversive. I believe that, in the interest of employers, as for that of workers, a union grouping the majority and legally constituted is by far preferable.

354 I do not intend to deal with the question of unions. I will confine myself to some thoughts.

355 In creating the right to unions the legislator forgot the essential principle of corresponding responsibility. It is a shortcoming to address.

356 One should not rely much more on the wisdom and the moderation of communities that on that of individuals. It was noted during the strikes in private industry and those in public services, in France and elsewhere.

357 We saw the very existence of the English nation threatened by a miners'

strike. The guilds do not hesitate in passing their interests before that of the state. And the state has not known, until now, to defend itself. Yet the social body must not let itself be destroyed by one of its members. It is a grave problem to resolve.

358 Henceforth, nothing can prevent this association, source of strength and of power; but one must regulate its functioning. I am convinced that the expansion of good principles of *management* will contribute to stopping this instrument of peace and well-being from remaining a cause for war and destruction.

359 Whatever the role reserved for workers' unions be in the government of business, the principles of management will lose none of their utility.

* * *

Appendix[5]

APPENDIX 2: HENRI FAYOL'S FINAL INTERVIEW

Source: 'An interview with Mr Fayol by Louis Marie du Crouzet', Social Chronicle of France, *The French Social Week*, January 1925, pp. 10–26[1]

Business Management and Management Tools

LMC – The management doctrine originated from a methodical and scientific study of industrial firms. Mr Fayol first applied it to the reorganization of a large mining and metallurgical company. It was in this milieu that it received the most sympathetic welcome and found the most disciples [...].[2]

We first ask Mr. Fayol which method, according to him, best allows one to evaluate the organization of a company and to identify the necessary reforms.

HF – 'I believe,' answered Mr Fayol, 'that the best approach is the study of what I called "management tools". If they are satisfactory, we will clearly see the state and workings of the company, and we can also immediately affirm that "planning, installing productive resources, command, coordination, verifying" are performed correctly, in other words the business is well managed. If they present shortcomings, they will most often reveal poor organization or errors committed in running the business.

'Management tools are actually of broad use. Not only is their study valuable for those who have to manage or control an industrial firm, but in my opinion their absence is a fundamental fault of our major public services and I hardly see another greater service to a country than to have them adopted by the state. It would be a starting point of essential reforms.

'What are these "management tools"? They are a vast collection of documents that cover the present, the past and the future, that involve contributions from elite personnel and that, when added to those coming from their other information sources, allow management to take, in the best conditions possible, decisions of which they can envisage the consequences and the repercussions.

'It essentially includes:

1 A general study

2 The business plan
3 The reports and accounts
4 The minutes of meetings of department heads
5 The organizational chart

'The "general study" concerns each of the parts and the entire company at the same time. It targets the present situation, its past and its probable future.

'The "history" recalls the reasons that determined the creation of the firm, the transformations it underwent and the results it provided.

'The "present situation" is the current state of each of the individual parts and the whole of the firm's resources and needs to be contemplated from all points of view.

'The "probable future" is that which can be foreseen by taking into account the past, the present and the economic, political and social events that may arise ...

'This study presupposes an experienced leader, a skillful handler of men, capable of obtaining from his subordinates a loyal and active collaboration, and largely taking his part of the responsibilities that the study requires of him.

'This study results in the general ideas, the directives of the "business plan".

'The "business plan" is the collection, the synthesis of diverse forecasts, annual, long-term, short-term, special, etc.

'It is a kind of table of the future where upcoming events figure with some clarity, according to our interpretation of them, and where far off events appear increasingly vague. It is the planned running of the company that is prepared for some time.

'The need for a business plan is acknowledged by all, but we are far from its widespread use. Many private companies leave much to be desired in this domain; its use by the state is exceptional.

'It's that the confection of the business plan demands a great effort from senior staff, and a competent and stable leader supported by a good staff at the head of the company.

'We can resume as follows the considerations that support the need for a long-term business plan and the advantages that result from its use:

'It is necessary in a slightly complex company to have carefully thought out directives in advance, which show the direction to follow for a relatively long period of time.

'These directives must be based on a deep understanding of the company, its current situation and the reasons for this situation and on external circumstances. As the justifying considerations are identified, if events render some incorrect, the consequences that were deduced from them can be modified.

'The business plan must result from the collaboration of all employees that enjoy authority and bear a responsibility.

'The practice of planning not only automatically allows the head to benefit from the reflections of the company's employees but forces the latter to study the improvements needed by their department. It is the best process to ensure a company automatically adapts to new circumstances.

'Collaboration between employees at various echelons of the hierarchy to establish these previsions allows them to come to a unity of views; it makes them understand the reasons for this or that decision and broadens their horizon.

'It increases the value of these employees and, furthermore, it allows them to judge, to clarify their responsibility and facilitates the head's control.

'For the head it is a precious guarantee of stability and good relations with those he controls. It is the corporate charter; once accepted by mutual agreement, it establishes a unified guiding volition and a mutual trust.

'The "reports and accounts", concerning the actual operations, are the complement to the business plan.

'Subordinates' reports to their superiors are made at each echelon of the hierarchy; they are daily, weekly, monthly and annual. They are a powerful means of control.

'The "minutes of meetings of department heads" are written up following the meeting that each week assembles the department heads of each site around the local director. Each department head expounds, in turn, the functioning of his department, the results obtained, the difficulties encountered. After discussion, the director concludes. They leave knowing what has to be done and also knowing that they will have to render an account. In one hour the director reviewed the past week's main events and the plans concerning the following week. For him it is a powerful means of coordination and control.

'The minutes of this meeting, where the entire life of the site unfolds, expounded by its principal actors, would be of great interest to the managing director. No report or correspondence could give him the personnel's view to the same degree.

'"Organizational charts" using braces, taking on the form of genealogical charts, allows an understanding at a glance, better than would be possible with a long description, of the entire corporation, the departments and their bounds, the chain of command, the organization of deputies, the position occupied by each employee, the head he reports to and the subordinates he commands.

'The chart draws attention to the overlaps or the encroachments, to the dualities of command, to the unoccupied positions ... It is a kind of template that denounces the corporation's imperfections and that can be effectively used each time one forms or completely or even partially modifies the organism.

'Accompanied by a clear definition of everyone's attributions, it specifies responsibilities and helps rapidly ascertain the employee that should be contacted to deal with a particular subject.

'Such are the management tools that I believe are useful to particularly draw attention to. Furthermore, we can widen the notion without difficulty. To know exactly what situation the company is in, it is essential that the cost price be correctly calculated. In this regard, the statistical documents extracted from accounting records to provide information to heads could be part of these tools.'

The Management Doctrine and the Social Question

LMC – The business world followed these ideas with interest. Your principles, your conception of the role of a modern head – essentially a facilitator and educator – carry a latent philosophy of authority [...].

Could the management doctrine shine some light on the study of labour and social issues?

The head must put his personnel in the most favorable conditions for production. He must also, according to you, try to develop individual initiative and use it as best as possible. When elaborating the business plan everyone must collaborate from the head of production to the managing director, and all ideas, all desires for improvement should be expressed, even though when sent through the hierarchy they may be modified or transformed so as to bring them into line with global views.

However, a strong hierarchy and very wide powers conceded to the head appear to you to be absolute necessities for the sound organization of work. Your disciples cannot then be sympathetic to the idea of joint management by workers, so dear to the demagogues in all the parties, in so far as it involves discussing technical and sales management measures by the delegates of different categories of personnel. The Russians who tried it out on a large scale found themselves in trouble, as did the various production cooperatives that did not give very wide powers to their director.

You reckon, however, that the head must be monitored to save him from the temptation of megalomania, and so that his actions remain subordinated to the interests of the firm.

But doesn't this mean supporting the current order of things [...]. It is conceivable that company directors do not necessarily yield to the representatives of money. Couldn't we imagine monitoring of the head that better represents workers interests on the one hand, and consumers on the other?

HF – 'I do', responds Mr Fayol to this second question, 'like to compare the social body of a company to two opposing pyramids. The upper pyramid in a limited liability company consists of shareholders and the board of directors; the lower pyramid, the different echelons of employees down to the shop-floor workers; the common summit represents the managing director. For the state, the upper pyramid consists of the electors, the parliament and the president of the Republic; the lower pyramid, the ministers and public servants; the common summit, the head of government.

'Until recently, I worked exclusively on the organization of work, in other words the lower pyramid. It is an essential task that can be considered as being self-sufficient. I temporarily left aside the organization of the upper pyramid whose main role is to choose and then control the head. This organization concerns the delicate question of distribution. What I can say is that it would greatly benefit from being studied scientifically, without fear of exposing abuses, but also without demagogic intent. This study could be guided by the broad principle of the subordination of vested interests to the general interest. In the current circumstances, I believe it should be a necessary complement to the management doctrine.'

The Reform of Public Administrations

LMC – It appears that your personal activity has been above all devoted these last years to the study of necessary public service reforms [...]. May I take the liberty of asking you to elaborate on your views and hopes?

HF – 'I believe it is in the organization of public services and of government that the management doctrine can be of greatest service. This is easy to comprehend: the respect of a sound doctrine is all the more indispensable when the enterprise is larger and more complex, when it requires a larger management team and more managers, when it is called on to have a longer duration and when its management requires more continuity. In a business where the head can follow all the details, smooth operations can be ensured by his worth alone, despite the violation of some management rules and the abandon of some otherwise excellent processes. It is completely different in vast organizations where it is less a question of having a virtuoso than orienting, coordinating, harmonizing the efforts of key managers.

'Public opinion that is above all familiar with the running of small companies, attaches exaggerated importance to the role of individuals.

'In a big company, a public service or a modern state, the volume and the complexity of business require completely different practices to those in a small company or a feudal state.

'The head of the company, boss, managing director or chairman of the board cannot personally take care of all operations. Consequently he delegates a part of his powers to his subordinates – high-level department heads in industry, ministers and directors in the state – and keeps senior management for himself. But this creates such a variety of problems that he sometimes has neither the leisure nor the necessary skill to deal with them appropriately. He often sees himself using preparatory studies for his decisions, as well as the extensive documentation required by the company.

'The problem of the administrative organization in a large company, a public service or even a government can be presented in these terms, as a question that is essential for smooth operations, and first of all the organization of senior management with its three essential elements: a head – a staff – management tools.

'These simple notions are sometimes forgotten even in industry; in our large public services they seem to be completely ignored. I had the opportunity – thanks to an initiative of M. Louis Deschamps[3]– to study the organization and the functioning of the postal administration; more recently I examined the tobacco monopoly. My conclusions were similar. You are familiar with those of my study of the postal administration

1 An unstable and incompetent leader at the head of the company
2 No long term planning
3 No balance sheet
4 Abusive and excessive intervention by parliamentarians
5 No stimulus for zeal, no reward for services rendered
6 No responsibility

'No real reform of public services is possible without that of its ultimate authority– the government. This does not for that matter require a change in regime or constitution, but deep modifications in ministerial and parliamentary morals. What is the logical conception of the ministerial organization of the government? No doubt the following:

'The head of government, positioned at the summit of the administrative hierarchy by the confidence accorded by the head of state, is in charge of the all the country's interests. He assumes the management of the entire government enterprise, and leads it towards its goal by making the most of available resources. Invested with the widest authority, he ensures the functioning of all the essential functions of the state. Head of the ministers, he selects them, recommends them to the head of state and to parliament for approval, and for important questions, gives them directives or dictates the solutions to them. The general powers that are vested in him allow him to plan, install productive resources, command, coordinate and verify all of the public services. This mission and its heavy demands absorb all of this man's activity. It is exclusive of any other activity: the head of government will be discharged of any portfolio.

'The ministers, direct subordinates to the head of government, few in number so as to be in direct contact with him, are in charge of the running of a group of major public services. Heads of the directors of their ministry, they exercise their authority over the branch of the government enterprise that is entrusted to them. They receive directives from the head of government, interpret them and devolve them to their subordinates.

'Under the minister's authority, the directors ensure the running of their service. Head of the employees in the service, they exercise wide powers over them concerning nominations, promotion, remuneration, retirement etc.

'The head of government, ministers, directors must possess a high level of management ability, namely the ability to plan, install productive resources, coordinate and verify. It is desirable that they also have a large as possible professional skill and general knowledge about the other functions of the governmental enterprise. This professional skill and such general knowledge result habitually from the stability of the man in his employment. Furthermore, the head of government and the ministers must possess a parliamentary eloquence.

'Yet the possession of these abilities and powers by the directors, the ministers and the head of government would not be enough to ensure the sound senior management of the state. Whatever their skills and their working capacity, the heads alone cannot suffice to all their obligations of correspondence, receptions, conferences, diverse procedures; they must attend to preparatory studies, have the business plan drawn up, stimulate and make improvements, ensure command and verification. It is under these conditions that the staff must resort to management tools.

'The staff of the head of government, of each ministry and of each administration, includes a secretariat of specialist counsel and controllers. Furthermore, the head of government commands an advisory board.

'I pointed out earlier what I meant by management tools, I again insist on the results of using long-term plans. Let's suppose that in each ministerial department, a business plan is drawn up by functionaries, approved by the minister and submitted by him first to cabinet and then to parliament. The unity of views exists. Everyone knows what his superior requires of him, what his subordinates should accomplish. Parliament, head of government, ministers, directors ignore nothing of their respective goals; "regular reports" addressed by the directors to their minister, by the ministers to the head of government, by the head of government to parliament, show that the plan is faithfully executed. Instead of being compelled to do so by way of question or interpellation, the cabinet spontaneously communicates all useful information to the house. And so confidence replaces the mistrust that reigns at present between the managing powers of the state.

'Is it really useful to recall the current state of affairs?

'For several decades in France, the head of government is surrounded by twelve or fifteen ministers together with several secretaries of state. Besides all of the public services, the head of government is in charge of managing a major ministerial department.

'He has neither a corps of controllers, nor specialist-counsel, nor an advisory board. He does not have any management tools either.

'He would have no refuge if he did not enjoy the hospitality offered to him by a ministerial department that he is in charge of managing.

'He has none of the recognized necessary means of action to perform his tasks as head. He has too many ministers to be able to manage them. He holds both the role of head of government that he is already unable to perform, with that of head of a ministerial department.

'The same abuses can be found in the constitution of ministries. As he takes possession of his post each minister finds himself immediately confronted with a large number of affairs that are foreign to him. He has no management tools that can enlighten him, he rarely has a staff of specialists, he lacks the advice of the head of government. He generally finds himself in direct relations with some twenty subordinates. We don't know what one should fear the most: his active intervention or his inaction. Daily operations are carried out for better or worse by directors acting independently of one another, without control, without coordination, in the same way the ministers do. It is the regime of watertight bulkheads.

'Parliament's activity, bereft of appropriate means of information or verification, also has oft-questionable effects. Finance bills are voted without their details having been studied and matured by those who must implement them, and thereafter without having evaluated the possibility or the cost of their execution, having been evaluated. The suppression or the restoring of monopolies are recommended without the services that run them being called upon to draw up a real plan allowing the study of their possible future and the clarification of those conditions in which their cession or their maintenance would be advantageous for the general interest.

'Savings committees are created; some have done a considerable amount of work of which the application would be fertile both in savings and in improved services rendered. Yet these committees, outside the services they were investigating, without a direct link to the ministers in charge, could not create either in the administration, or the government, the frame of mind necessary to accomplish the proposed reforms. It is, incidentally, impossible to know what practical objections they could face, the concerned services not having been called on to give their opinion.

'In the functioning of the public service, vested interests easily interfere with the development of services, so long as no overall long-term plan has been adopted.

'Modifications to teaching programs are decided without regular consultation of the faculty concerned, and in such a way that all continuity and coordination of studies may disappear.'

LMC – The gravity, just as the reality of this disorder, are hardly debatable, but can't we fear that it is the serious consequence of our regime, or its mores, the reform of which appear quite difficult? A gulf has formed between the administration and the executive authority. Ministers, houses of parliament and the nation itself seem convinced that a government must only be inspired by feelings and seek to translate popular directives into laws and decrees: acts of execution, pure administration is secondary.

During their campaign, parliamentarians, whatever their party be, do not seek to explain the need for certain methods of study and control, but almost exclusively to create some movements of enthusiasm for the points of their programme that differ from that of their rivals, to excite and build passions. Many accept to be almost exclusively the servants of the vested interests of their voters or of their circumscription, and the danger is even more serious the more local is the vote. Is it excessive to say that a reform, like the decentralization that all wish for, that doesn't interest one party as such but runs counter to some vested interests, has no chance of being accomplished?

The ministers have generally stood out by their ability to assimilate knowledge while working in commissions, and by their expository talents. Often by profession, almost always by temperament, ministers and parliamentarians alike are essentially orators. They excel at pleading their chosen cause, at seeking out the arguments in its favour, at imagining them against their adversaries. They hardly have a feeling for what is a real task of management.

Can we reform these mores?

HF – 'I believe', responds Mr Fayol, 'that one should never despair of the success of a just idea. First of all it is an essential condition for action. Over my last sixty years of observations, I have seen ideas triumph that we could have thought condemned, and I have learnt to be patient. As far as I'm concerned, when I published, seven years ago, as a modest article of a technical review my notes on "Industrial and General Management" I never dreamed they would have the effect I observe outside the industrial field.

'Measure the distance covered by these ideas in public opinion and services in various countries: translations, conferences or original studies made in most European countries [...] I was called on to study the organization of the postal administration, that of tobacco. Even though my thought was sometimes distorted, my "authority" was evoked in parliamentary circles, union meetings, etc. I never expected such a rapid diffusion.

'I believe we should try and accustom the public to the scientific analysis of facts, to the observation of social realities to allow it to free itself from the trickery of words and hollow phrases

'It would be very interesting to evaluate recent legislation and to look for all the major and applicable laws that could have been voted essentially following sentimental directives, and compare them to the importance of administrative measures: budget vote, customs laws, laws concerning various public services, etc. whose study is dictated by the necessity of things.

'One should also make a nomenclature of problems that arise in each ministry and the number of which can be resolved by the a priori application of principles, and one with questions that essentially require a methodical examination of the situation and the possibilities. In such a study we would probably find the explanation for governmental failings and the impotence of ministers to undertake efficient action.

'Other studies can contribute to enlightening the public. It's the evaluation of the enormous pecuniary interest attached to the quality of the directorate of public services, and more so of government. It is not only a question of the few savings that can be obtained by reducing the number of functionaries, but above all the considerable advantages that would result from the correct use of taxes, from accurate tax collection, from the smooth operating of post and telephone services, from the satisfactory productivity of monopolies, from the high speed of court decisions, from public education programs better thought-out and set-up with more continuity, etc. ...

'We could never overestimate these advantages.'

The Management Doctrine and the League of Nations

LMC – During the last session of the League of Nations[4] in Geneva, you agreed to give a conference under the auspices of the International University Federation. What place do you consider possible for management studies amongst the preoccupations of leaders or permanent bodies of the League of Nations?

HF – 'Several important considerations appear to be able to make the League of Nations take, directly or indirectly, the initiative of undertaking a general study of the organization of work, or even production, encompassing the wide-ranging management problems as I have done. First of all, the imperfect organization of work in a large number of public and private companies, through their constantly repeated effects, in the end cause material damage of the same order as the wars that continue to threaten us at more or less distant intervals; secondly there is no doubt that the nations cannot continue a strong association unless they are capable of taking and keeping serious commitments, just as trading syndicates and producer associations, so useful for the rational exploitation of a country's riches, are only viable between well-managed industrial companies. There is hope that this study will result in a notably improved government of nations and their economic situation.

'It is in a similar spirit that the Brussels International Conference was held in 1920. "What can and must be done", points out the president Ador,[5] "is a conscientious study of the economic and financial situation of every state and a search for the best ways to encourage work and remedy the ills that, if they persist, will drive the world to ruin." It is in the same spirit that productivity inquiries were organized by the International Labour Organization.[6]

'Can we try to evaluate the management of states, their major public services and their major private companies?

'The difficulty would be considerable if the management doctrine, while indicating the goal to achieve, did not specify the study's framework, and did not provide scientific methods of observation. It would allow an appreciation of the manner in which the finances are managed in the different states that make up the League of Nations; it would above all enable the drawing up of a programme of necessary reforms and provide public opinion with the satisfaction that it has the right to claim.'

WORKS CITED

Abadie, I., 'Etude sur les feux des mines de houille, d'après les exemples tirés du bassin houiller de Decazeville' (Study of Coal Mine Fires, According to Examples Taken from the Decazeville Coal Basin), *Annales des mines* (July 1902) and *Génie civil* (4, 11, 18, 25 October 1902).

—, 'Lutte contre les feux de mines, résultats obtenus aux mines de Decazeville' (Fighting Mine Fires, Results Obtained in the Decazeville Mines), *Revue de l'industrie Minérale*, 148, pp. 65–74; 149. pp. 89–103 (1927).

Anonyme, *La Poutrelle métallique dans ses principales applications* (The Steel Beam and its Main Uses) (Paris: Comptoir des Poutrelles, 1910).

—, 'Enquête sur les moyens techniques susceptibles d'augmenter la production des houillères françaises (commission de Decazeville)' (Study into the Technical Means to Increase the Production of French Collieries (Decazeville Commission)), *Comptes rendu mensuels de la Statistiques de l'Industrie Minérale*, 17:1 (January–February 1920), pp. 83–104.

Auclair, A., *La grande industrie dans l' Allier: XIXe-XXe siècles* (Heavy Industry in the Allier: XIX-XX centuries) (Clermont-Ferrand: CRDP d'Auvergne, 1995).

—, *Stéphane Mony: 1800–1884: l'un des fondateurs de la grande industrie dans le Bourbonnais* (Stéphane Mony: 1800–1884: One of the Founders of Bourbonnais Heavy Industry) (Montmarault: Association du pays de Montmarault, 1996).

—, *Histoire des Houillères du Bourbonnais* (History of the Bourbonnais Collieries) (Clermont-Ferrand: Éd. Racines, 1999).

—, *Les ingénieurs et l'équipement de la France: Eugène Flachat, 1802–1873* (Engineers and Equipment in France: Eugène Flachat, 1802–1873) (Le Creusot: Écomusée de la communauté urbaine Le Creusot-Montceau-les-Mines, 1999).

Auclair, A. and P. Couderc, *La sidérurgie en Bourbonnais: essor industriel et croissance urbaine de 1840 à 1990* (The Bourbonnais Steel Industry: Industrial Development and Urban Growth from 1840 to 1990) (Aurillac: Gerbert, 2000).

Auclair, A., P. Couderc and J.-M. Molinès, *La sidérurgie en Bourbonnais: Cie Commentry Fourchambault Decazeville: l'usine des hauts fourneaux de Montluçon dite Usine Forey, 1840–1967* (The Bourbonnais Steel Industry: Commentry Fourchambault Decazeville Co.: The Montluçon Blast Furnace and Factory, Known as the Forey Factory, 1840–1967) (Montluçon: Cercle d'archéologie de Montluçon et de la région, 2009).

Benoist, C., *L'organisation du travail* (The Organization of Labour) (Paris: Plon, 1905).

Boscus, A., *Économie et société dans le bassin industriel nord-aveyronnais: 1900–1950* (Economy and Society in the Industrial Basin of North Aveyron: 1900–1950) (Montreuil: Institut CGT d'histoire sociale, 1997).

Bouillet, J-B., '1900! la fermeture des forges de Fourchambault en 1901, le rôle d'Henri Fayol'

(1900! The Closure of the Fourchambault Forges in 1901, Henri Fayol's Role), La situation du nivernais en 1900: 13 et 14 octobre 2000, *Cinquièmes rencontres d'histoire de la métallurgie* (Guérigny: Les amis du vieux Guérigny / Centre d'études de la métallurgie nivernaise, 2001), pp. 221–40.

Bouvier, J., 'L'histoire de l'usine de Allevard (1871–1914): un exemple significatif' (History of the Allevard Factory (1871–1914): A Major Example), *Annales. Économies, Sociétés, Civilisations,* 19:6 (1964), pp. 1236–41.

Breeze, J. D., 'Discussion of the Translation of Some of Fayol's Important Concepts', in D. A. Wren and T. Sasaki (eds), *Henri Fayol and Process School* (London: Pickering & Chatto Publishers, 2004), pp. 221–48.

Buisson, C., 'Note sur la préparation des charbons' (Note on the Preparation of Coal), Congrès des mines et de la métallurgie 1900, *Bulletin de la société de l'industrie minérale,* third series, tome 15 (1901), pp. 390–426.

Carlioz, J., *Comptoirs de vente en commun* (Trade Syndicates) (Nevers: Imprimerie Mazeron frères, 1905).

CCHF, *Rapports des ingénieurs des mines aux conseils généraux sur la situation des mines et usines en 1899* (Reports from Mines Service Engineers to General Councils on the Situation of Mines and Factories in 1899) (Paris: CCHF, 1900).

Chevallier, E., *Les salaires au XIXe siècle* (Salaries in the Nineteenth Century) (1887; Paris: Hachette, 1971).

Cohen, Y., 'Fayol, un instituteur de l'ordre industriel' (Fayol, a Teacher of Industrial Order), *Entreprise et Histoire,* 34 (December 2003), pp. 29–67.

Conus, M-F., 'Une entreprise face à la gestion des "risques majeurs": la compagnie des mines de Courrières (1852–1944)' (A Business Faced With 'Major Risks': The Courrières Mining Company (1852–1944)), *Histoire économie et société,* 25:4 (2006), pp. 61–78.

Conus, M-F. and J.-L. Escudier, 'Sécurité et transformation du système productif, application à l'industrie française du charbon (1817–1988)' (Security and Transformation of the Production System, Application to the French Coal Idustry (1817–1988)), *Entreprise et Histoire,* 17 (1997), pp. 49–71.

Corporative des mouleurs en métaux de France, *Compte rendu officiel du quatrième congrès tenu les 14, 15 et 16 juillet 1899 à Montluçon* (Official Minutes of the Fourth Congress held on July 14, 15 and 16 1899 in Montluçon) (Paris: imprimerie Jean Allemane, 1900).

Crouzet, F., 'Le charbon anglais en France au XIXe siècle' (English Coal in France in the Nineteenth Century), in L. Trenard (ed.), *Charbon et Sciences Humaines. Actes du colloque organisé par la Faculté des Lettres de l'Université de Lille en mai 1963* (1963; Paris et La Haye, 1966), pp. 173–206.

Dredge, J., *Les établissements de MM. Schneider et Cie, historique des mines & usines, leurs développements successifs* (The Establishments of Messrs Schneider and Co, History of the Mines and Factories, their Successive Development) (Nevers: impr. de Mazeron frères, 1903).

Dredge, J., *The Works of Messrs. Schneider and Co.* (London: Bedford Press, 1900).

Dron, G., *Rapport de la commission des mines* (Report of the Mining Commission) (Paris: Imprimerie de la Chambre des députés, 1903), Chambre des députés, session de 1903, annexe au procès verbal de la séance du 2 avril 1903, no. 878.

Fayol, H., 'Note sur le boisage aux houillères de Commentry (emploi du fer et des bois préparés)' (Note on the Timbering of Commentry Collieries (Use of Iron and Prepared Timber)), *Bulletin de la Société de l'Industrie Minérale,* série 2, tome 3 (1874), pp. 569–76.

—, 'Études sur l'altération et la combustion spontanée de la houille exposée à l'air' (Study of the Alteration and the Spontaneous Combustion of Coal Exposed to Air), *Bulletin de la Société de l'Industrie Minérale*, Congrès de Paris, 1878, médaille d'or, série 2, tome 8 (1878), pp. 487–746.

—, 'Note sur le boisage, le déboisage et le remblayage dans les houillères de Commentry' (Note on Timbering, Drawing of Timbers and Backfill in the Commentry Collieries), *Comptes rendus mensuels de la Société de l'Industrie Minérale* (June 1878).

—, 'Étude sur le terrain houiller de Commentry' (Study of the Commentry Coal Fields), *Comptes rendus des séances de l'Académie des Sciences* (16 May 1881).

—, 'Sur le terrain houiller de Commentry, Expériences faites pour expliquer la formation' (In the Commentry Coal Fields: Experiments Undertaken to Explain its Formation), *Comptes rendus des séances de l'Académie des Sciences* (30 May, 1881).

—, 'Étude sur le terrain houiller de Commentry, sa formation attribuée à un charriage dans un lac profond' (Study of the Commentry Coal Field, its Formation due to Bedload in a Deep Lake), *Comptes rendus des séances de l'Académie des Sciences* (20 June 1881).

—, 'Note sur la suppression du poste de nuit dans le remblayage des grandes couches' (Note on the Suppression of Night Work to Backfill Large Layers), *Comptes rendus mensuels de la Société de l'Industrie Minérale* (October 1882).

—, 'Note sur les mouvements de terrain provoqués par l'exploitation des mines' (Note on Terrain Movement Caused by Mining Operations), *Bulletin de la Société de l'Industrie Minérale*, série 2, tome 14 (1885), p. 805.

—, 'Résumé de la théorie des deltas et histoire de la formation du bassin de Commentry' (Resume of the Theory of Deltas and the History of the Formation of the Commentry Basin), *Bulletin de la Société Géologique de France* (August 1888).

—, 'Exposé des principes généraux d'administration' (Exposé of the General Principles of Management), Congrès du cinquantenaire de la Société de l'Industrie Minérale, Congrès de Saint Étienne, *Comptes rendus mensuels des réunions de la Société de l'Industrie Minérale* (16 juin 1908), pp. 240–2.

—, 'Administration Industrielle et Générale', *Bulletin de la Société de l'Industrie Minérale*, (Paris: Dunod, 1916), trans. J. A. Cobrough (1930), *Industrial and general administration*, and by C. Storrs (1949), *General and Industrial Management*, in D. A. Wren and T. Sasaki (eds), *Henri Fayol and Process School* (London: Pickering & Chatto Publishers, 2004), pp. 429–508 and 511–644.

—, *Notice sur les travaux scientifiques et techniques de Henri Fayol* (Notice on the Scientific and Technical Works of Henri Fayol) (Paris; Gauthier Villars, 1918).

Fayol, P., 'Essais de havage mécanique en France' (Trials of Mechanical Cutters in France), *Bulletin de la société de l'industrie minérale,* Congrès des mines et de la métallurgie 1900, third series, tome 15 (1901), pp. 311–15.

Fells, M. J., 'Fayol Stands the Test of Time', *Journal of Management History*, 6:6 (2000), pp. 345–60.

Flachat I., *Société anonyme de Commentry-Fourchambault. Réponses au questionnaire de la commission de l'Exposition universelle de 1878* (The Anonymous Society of Commentry-Fourchambault. Responses to the Questionnaire of the 1878 World Fair commission) (Paris: impr. de P. Dupont, 1878).

Fontaine, A., 'L'Échelle mobile dans les mines de la Grande-Bretagne' (Mobile Scales in Great Britain's Mines), *Annales des mines* (September, 1895), pp. 5–31.

Fontvieille L. and A. Prigent, 'La technique et le travail dans les fluctuations de longue période: l'évolution des transports dans le fond des mines' (Technique and Work During Long Period Fluctuations: The Evolution of Transportation on the Mine Floor),

Technologies, idéologies, pratiques, 9:2 (1990), pp. 169–83.

Fraboulet, D., *Quand les patrons s'organisent: stratégies et pratiques de l'Union des industries métallurgiques et minières 1901–1950* (When Employers Get Organized: Strategies and Practices of the Union des Industries Métallurgiques et Minières 1901–1950) (Villeneuve d'Ascq: Presses universitaires du Septentrion, 2007).

Freedeman, C. E., 'Cartels and the Law in France before 1914', *French Historical Studies*, 15:3 (Spring, 1988), pp. 462–78.

Friedel G., 'Note sur les les systèmes de fermeture des recettes en usage dans la région de Commentry' (Note on the Systems of Receiving Gates in Use in the Commentry Area), *Annales des Mines*, 3 (1893), pp. 199–202.

Gennes (de) A., 'Déhouilleuses employées aux Etats-Unis' (Mining Machines in Use in the United States), *Bulletin de la Société de l'Industrie Minérale*, Congrès des mines et de la métallurgie 1900, third series, tome 15 (1901), pp. 332–44.

Gilbert G. K., 'The Topographic Features of the Lake Shores', *US Geological Survey, 5th annual report 1883–84* (Washington, 1885), pp. 75–123.

Grand, 'Bobine folle, parachute, roue de wagonnet, appareils dus à Paul Fayol' (Loose Reel, Parachute, Cart Wheel, Devices Attributable to Paul Fayol), *Bulletin de la Société de l'Industrie Minérale* (1879), pp. 927–36.

Grüner E., H. Darcy and C. Ledoux, 'Loi sur les caisses de retraite des ouvriers mineurs' (Law on Retirement Funds for Mining Workers), Société d'économie sociale; Réunion mensuelle du groupe de Paris; séance du 17 décembre 1894. *La réforme sociale*, tome 29 (1895), pp. 410–31.

Guillaume, C.-E., 'Esquisse de ma vie' (Outline of My Life), *Université de Paris* (1921), reprint *Le Marteau pilon*, Tome 4 (1992), pp. 138–42.

Guillet, L., 'Notice biographique de Pierre Girin' (Biographical Note for Pierre Girin), *Revue de la métallurgie*, 11, (November, 1926), p. 685.

Guitton, H., *Fête du travail à la mine de Commentry 28 septembre 1873* (Labour Day at the Commentry Mine 28 September 1873) (Montluçon: Impr. de Crepin-Leblond, 1873).

Gulick, L. H., 'Notes on the Theory of Organization' in L. Gulick and L. Urwick (eds), *Papers on the Science of Administration* (New York, NY: Institute of Public Administration, 1936), pp. 3–35.

Hardy-Hémery, O., *De la croissance à la désindustrialisation. Un siècle dans le Valenciennois* (From Growth to Disindustrialization. A Century in Valencienne Area) (Paris: Presses de la Fondation des Sciences Politiques, 1984).

Haton de la Goupillière, J., 'Rapport de la commission d'études de l'emploi des explosifs dans les mines à grisou' (Report by the Investigating Commission into the Use of Explosives in Firedamp Mines), *Annales des mines*, 18 (1888), p. 699.

Kotter, J. P., *The General Managers* (New York, NY: The Free Press, 1982).

Lacombe, L., 'Rapport' (Report), *Documents parlementaires chambre 6e législature 1893–1898*, séance du 2 juillet 1896 annexe no. 1982 (1896), pp. 1280–307.

Lambert-Dansette J., *Genèse du patronat 1780–1880* (Genesis of Employer Groups 1780–1880) (Paris: Hachette, 1991).

Le Chatelier, H., *Le grisou* (Firedamp) (Paris: Gauthier-Villars, 1892).

Lemonnier, P. and F. Valton, *1854 rapport de stage* (1854 Internship Report), Bibliothèque Ecole des Mines de Paris cote, M1854/558 (Commentry, 15 novembre 1854).

Levasseur, É., *Salariat et salaires* (Wage Earners and Wages) (Paris: O. Doin et fils, 1909).

Lévêque, L., 'Historique des forges de Decazeville, 1826–1914' (History of the Decazeville Forges, 1826–1914), *Bulletin de la Société de l'industrie minérale*, 19 (1916), pp. 5–97.

Longevialle (de), M., *La Société Commentry-Fourchambault et Decazeville, 1854–1954, Introduction du baron Pierre Hély d'Oissel, conclusions de Louis de Mijolla*, (The Commentry-Fourchambault et Decazeville Company, 1854–1954, Introduction by Baron Pierre Hély d'Oissel, Conclusions by Louis de Mijolla) (Paris: Office de propagande générale, 1954).

McKay, J. P., *Pioneers for Profit; Foreign Entrepreneurship and Russian Industrialization 1885–1913* (Chicago, IL: Chicago University Press, 1970).

Mâle, E., *Souvenirs et correspondances de jeunesse* (Memories and Correspondence from Youth) (Nonette: Créer, 2001).

Mallard, E., 'Rapport supplémentaire sur l'étude des questions relatives à l'emploi des explosifs en présence du grisou' (Additional Report on the Study of Questions Concerning the Use of Explosives in the Presence of Firedamp), *Annales des Mines*, 8e série tome 14 (1888), pp. 319–76.

—, 'Rapport sur l'étude des questions relatives à l'emploi des explosifs en présence du grisou' (Report on the Study of Questions Concerning the Use of Explosives in the Presence of Firedamp), *Annales des Mines*, 8e série tome 14 (1888), pp. 197–283.

—, 'Commission d'étude de l'emploi des explosifs dans les mines à grisou; essais pratiques faits dans quelques exploitations de mines' (Study Commission into the Use of Explosives in Firedamp Mines; Practical Trials Undertaken at Several Mining Operations), *Annales des Mines*, 8e série tome 16 (1889), pp. 15–123.

Mazars, L., *Terre de mine, bassin d'Aubin et Decazeville* (Land of Mines, Aubin and Decazeville Basin) (Rodez: édition Fil d'ariane, 1999).

Mehr R. I. and B. A. Hedges, *Risk Management In The Business Enterprise* (Homewood, IL: Richard Irwin, 1963).

Mintzberg, H., *The Structuring of Organizations: A Synthesis of the Research* (Englewood Cliffs, NJ: Prentice-Hall, 1979).

Mitchell, B., *International Historical Statistics, Europe, 1750–2005 and the Americas, 1750–2005*, 6th edn (Basingstoke: Macmillan, 2007).

Montusès, E., *Le député en blouse* (The Deputy in Overalls) (Moulins: Les Cahiers du Centre, 1913).

Office du travail, *Salaires et durée du travail dans l'industrie française* (Wages and Working Hours in French Industry), tome 2 (Paris: Imprimerie nationale, 1894).

—, *Salaires et durée du travail dans l'industrie française* (Wages and Working Hours in French Industry), tome IV (Paris: Imprimerie nationale, 1897).

Passaqui, J-P., *La stratégie des Schneider: du marché à la firme intégrée, 1836–1914* (The Strategy of the Schneiders: From Market to Integrated Firm) (Rennes: Presses universitaires de Rennes, 2006).

Peaucelle, J-L., 'Henri Fayol et la guerre de 1914' (Henri Fayol and the War of 1914), *Revue Française de Gestion*, 136 (2001), pp. 121–34.

Peaucelle J-L, J. A. Ariza Montès, B. Beaudoin, T. Boyns, A. C. Morales Gutierrez, J. N. Retière, T. Sasaki and I. Smith, *Henri Fayol, inventeur des outils de gestion* (Henri Fayol, Inventor of Management Tools) (Paris: Économica, 2003).

Peaucelle, J-L. and C. Guthrie, 'The Private Life of Henri Fayol and his Motivation to Build a Management Science', *Journal of Management History*, 18:4 (2012), pp. 469–87.

—, 'Henri Fayol' in M. Witzel and M. Warner (eds), *The Oxford Handbook of Management Theorists* (Oxford: Oxford University Press, 2013), pp. 49–73.

Pezet, E., *Chrétiens au service de la cité, de Léon XIII au Sillon et au M.R.P., 1891–1965* (Chistians in the Service of the City, from Leo XIII to Sillon and M.R.P., 1891–1965) (Paris: Nouvelles Editions Latines, 1965).

Place (de), H., 'Rapport sur les appareils respiratoires de H Fayol' (Report on H Fayol's Breathing Apparatus), *Bulletin de l'Industrie Minérale (*1873), pp. 34–5.

Rae, J., *Eight Hours for Work* (1894: Freeman Press, 2009).

Reid, D., 'The Role of Mine Safety in the Development of Working-Class Consciousness and Organization: The Case of the Aubin Coal Basin, 1867–1914', *French Historical Studies* 11 (1981), pp. 98–119.

—, 'Fayol: From Experience to Theory', *Journal of Management History* (Archive), 1:3 (1995), pp. 21–36.

—, 'Reading Fayol with 3D glasses', *Journal of Management History* (Archive), 1:3 (1995), pp. 63–71.

—, *The Miners of Decazeville: A Genealogy of Deindustrialization* (Cambridge, MA: Harvard University Press, 1985).

Reybaud, L., *Commentry & Fourchambault, Rapport sur la condition morale, intellectuelle et matérielle des ouvriers qui vivent de l'industrie du fer* (Commentry & Fourchambault, Report on the Moral, Intellectual and Material Situation of Workers Living from the Iron Industry) (Paris: Académie des sciences morales et politiques, 1868).

Rougeron, G., *Histoire de Commentry et des Commentryens* (History of Commentry and the Commentryens) (Charroux-d'Allier: Cahiers bourbonnais, 1987).

Rousiers (de), P., *La question ouvrière en Angleterre* (The Worker Issue in Engand), (Paris: Firmin-Didot, 1895).

Sasaki T., *Henri Fayol: Sono Hito to Keiei Senryaku, soshite Keiei no Riron* (Henri Fayol: His Life and His Work, and Strategic Management) (Tokyo: Bunshin-do, 1984).

—, 'Henri Fayol's Family Relationships', *Journal of Management History*, 1:3 (1995), pp.13–20.

—, 'The Comambault Company Revisited', *Keizai Shu-shi* (Journal of Economics), Faculty of Economics, Nihon University, 68:4 (January 1999), pp. 113–28.

—, 'Fayol et la Comambault' (Fayol and Comambault), *Entreprises et Histoire*, 34 (2003), pp. 8–28.

Say, J.-B., *Traité d'économie politique* (A Treatise on Political Economy), 1st edn (Paris: Déterville, 1803).

Simiand, F., *Le salaire des ouvriers des mines de charbon en France, Contribution à la théorie économique du salaire* (Wages of Coal Mine Workers in France, Contribution to the Economic Theory of Wages) (Paris: Edouard Cornély, 1907).

Sullivan Machinery Company, *Modern Methods of Producing Coal*, 48 (1902).

Taylor, F. W., *The Principles of Scientific Management* (New York and London: Harper & Brothers, 1911).

Threlfall, R., 'The Spontaneous Heating of Coal, Particularly During Shipment', *Journal of the Society of Chemical Industry*, 28:14 (1909), pp. 759–73.

Thuillier G., *George Dufaud et les débuts du grand capitalisme dans la métallurgie, en Nivernais au XIXe siècle* (George Dufaud and the Beginnings of Big Business in the Steel Industry, in Nivernais in the Nineteenth Century) (Paris: SEVPEN, 1959).

Tingaud H., 'La vie quotidienne à Imphy entre 1884 et 1914' (Daily Life in Imphy between 1884 and 1914),La situation de la Nièvre en 1900. Cinquièmes rencontres d'histoire de la métallurgie (Guérigny: Les amis du vieux Guérigny, 2001), pp. 103–16.

Vaslin J.-M., 'Henri Fayol, théoricien du management' (Henri Fayol, Management Theoretician), *Le Monde* (27 January 2004), p. v.

Williams, A. amd M. H. Heins, *Risk Management and Insurance* (New York, NY: McGraw Hill, 1964).

Wren D. A., 'Henri Fayol: Learning from Experience', *Journal of Management History*, 1:3 (1995), pp. 5–12.

—, 'Henri Fayol as a Strategist: A Nineteenth Century Corporate Turnaround', *Management Decision*, 39:5–6 (2001), pp. 475–87.

Wren D. A., A. G. Bedeian and J. D. Breeze, 'The Foundations of Henri Fayol's Administrative Theory', *Management Decision*, 40:9 (2002), pp. 906–18.

Wren D. A. and T. Sasaki, *Henri Fayol and Process School* (London: Pickering & Chatto Publishers, 2004).

Archives

Archives Départementales de l'Allier, Parc de Bellevue, 03400 Yzeure, France (ADAl)

Archives Départementales de l'Aveyron, 25 avenue Victor Hugo, 12000 Rodez, France (ADAv)

Archives Départementales de Haute Loire, 31 avenue de Tonbridge, 43000 Le Puy-en-Velay, France (ADHL)

Archives Départementales de la Nièvre, 1 bis rue Charles Roy, 58000 Nevers, France (ADN)

Archives Nationales, 59 rue Guynemer, 90001, 93383 Pierrefitte-sur-Seine Cedex, France (AN)

Archives Nationales du Monde du Travail, 78 Boulevard du Général Leclerc, 59100 Roubaix, France (ANMT)

Centre d'Histoire de Sciences Politiques, 56 rue Jacob, 75006 Paris, France (CHSP)

Institut Marc Sangnier, 38 Boulevard Raspail, 75007 Paris, France

Periodicals

Annales des Mines
Annales. Économies, Sociétés, Civilisations
Annuaire du Comité Central des Houillères de France
Bulletin de l'Office du Travail
Bulletin de la Société de l'Industrie Minérale
Bulletin de la Société Géologique de France
Bulletin du Ministère du Travail et de la Prévoyance Sociale
Chronique Sociale de France
Comptes Rendus des Séances de l'Académie des Sciences
Comptes Rendus Mensuels de la Société de l'Industrie Minérale
Dépêche (La)
Écho des Mines et de la Métallurgie
Entreprise et Histoire
Fonderie (La)
French Historical Studies
Génie Civil
Histoire économie et société
Journal of Management History
Journal of the Society of Chemical Industry
Keizai Shu-shi (Journal of Economics)
Management Decision
Marteau pilon (Le)
Monde (Le)
Petit journal (Le)

Réforme sociale (La)
Revue de l'Industrie Minérale
Revue de la métallurgie
Revue Française de Gestion
Statistiques de l'Industrie Minérale (SIM)
Technologies, idéologies, pratiques
Voix des travailleurs (La)

NOTES

Introduction

1. D. A. Wren and T. Sasaki (eds), *Henri Fayol and Process School* (London: Pickering & Chatto Publishers, 2004).
2. 'Outillage administratif'.
3. T. Sasaki, *Henri Fayol: Sono Hito to Keiei Senryaku, soshite Keiei no Riron* (Henri Fayol: His Life and His Work, and Strategic Management) (Tokyo: Bunshin-do, 1984); T. Sasaki,'Henri Fayol's Family Relationships', *Journal of Management History*, 1:3 (1995), pp.13–20; T. Sasaki., 'The Comambault Company Revisited', *Keizai Shu-shi* (Journal of Economics), Faculty of Economics, Nihon University, 68:4 (January 1999), pp. 113–28; T. Sasaki, 'Fayol et la Comambault' (Fayol and Comambault), *Entreprises et Histoire*, 34 (2003), pp 8–28.
4. D. Reid, 'The Role of Mine Safety in the Development of Working-Class Consciousness and Organization: The Case of the Aubin Coal Basin, 1867–1914', *French Historical Studies*, 11 (1981), pp. 98–119; D. Reid, *The Miners of Decazeville: A Genealogy of Deindustrialization* (Cambridge, MA: Harvard University Press, 1985); D. Reid, 'Fayol: From Experience to Theory', *Journal of Management History* (Archive), 1:3 (1995), pp. 21–36; D. Reid, 'Reading Fayol with 3D glasses', *Journal of Management History* (Archive), 1:3 (1995), pp. 63–71.
5. A. Boscus, *Économie et société dans le bassin industriel nord-aveyronnais: 1900–1950* (Economy and Society in the Industrial Basin of North Aveyron: 1900–1950) (Montreuil: Institut CGT d'histoire sociale, 1997).
6. A. Auclair, *La grande industrie dans l'Allier: XIXe-XXe siècles* (Heavy industry in the Allier: XIX-XX centuries) (Clermont-Ferrand: CRDP d'Auvergne, 1995); A. Auclair, *Stéphane Mony: 1800–1884: l'un des fondateurs de la grande industrie dans le Bourbonnais* (Stéphane Mony: 1800–1884: One of the Founders of Bourbonnais Heavy Industry) (Montmarault: Association du pays de Montmarault, 1996); A. Auclair, *Histoire des Houillères du Bourbonnais* (History of the Bourbonnais Collieries) (Clermont-Ferrand: Éd. Racines, 1999); A. Auclair, *Les ingénieurs et l'équipement de la France: Eugène Flachat, 1802–1873* (Engineers and Equipment in France: Eugène Flachat, 1802–1873) (Le Creusot: Écomusée de la communauté urbaine Le Creusot-Montceau-les-Mines, 1999); A. Auclair and P. Couderc, *La sidérurgie en Bourbonnais: essor industriel et croissance urbaine de 1840 à 1990* (The Bourbonnais Steel Industry: Industrial Development and Urban Growth from 1840 to 1990) (Aurillac: Gerbert, 2000); A. Auclair and P. Couderc, J.-M. Molinès, *La sidérurgie en Bourbonnais: Cie*

Commentry Fourchambault Decazeville: l'usine des hauts fourneaux de Montluçon dite Usine Forey, 1840–1967 (The Bourbonnais Steel Industry: Commentry Fourchambault Decazeville Co.: The Montluçon Blast Furnace and Factory, Known as the Forey Factory, 1840–1967) (Montluçon: Cercle d'archéologie de Montluçon et de la région, 2009).

7. Fayol used the word 'expériences' which has two different meanings in French: 'experiences' and 'experiments'. Fayol sought to show that his observations were scientific, so we have chosen to translate 'expériences' as 'experiments'. The use of the plural supports this translation.
8. H. Fayol, 'Administration Industrielle et Générale', *Bulletin de la Société de l'Industrie Minérale* (Paris: Dunod, 1916), trans. J. A. Cobrough, *Industrial and General Administration* (1930), and C. Storrs, *General and Industrial Management* (1949), in D. A. Wren and T. Sasaki (eds), *Henri Fayol and Process School* (London: Pickering & Chatto Publishers, 2004), pp. 429–508 and 511–644, on pp. 531 and 644.
9. H. Fayol, 'Exposé des principes généraux d'administration' (Exposé of the General Principles of Management), Congrès du cinquantenaire de la Société de l'Industrie Minérale, Congrès du Sainte Etienne, *Comptes rendus mensuels des réunions de la Société de l'Industrie Minérale* (16 juin 1908), pp. 240–2; D. A. Wren, A.G Bedeian and J.D. Breeze, 'The foundations of Henri Fayol's administrative theory', *Management Decision*, 40:9 (2002), pp. 906–18.
10. D. A. Wren, 'Henri Fayol: Learning from Experience', *Journal of Management History*, 1:3 (1995), pp. 5–12.
11. H. Fayol, *The Third Part of Industrial and General Management* (1916), Henri Fayol collection, Centre d'Histoire de Sciences Politiques, 56 rue Jacob, 75006 Paris, France, HF 5bis DR3. (see Appendix 1)
12. Reid, *The Miners of Decazeville: A Genealogy of Deindustrialization*, chapter 6, note 5.

1 The Industrial Context: The Coal and Steel Industries in Nineteenth-Century France

1. B. Mitchell, *International Historical Statistics, Europe, 1750–2005 and the Americas, 1750–2005*, 6th edn (Basingstoke: Macmillan, 2007).
2. F. Crouzet, 'Le charbon anglais en France au XIXe siècle' (English Coal in France in the Nineteenth Century), in L. Trenard (ed.), *Charbon et Sciences Humaines. Actes du colloque organisé par la Faculté des Lettres de l'Université de Lille en mai 1963* (1963; Paris et La Haye, 1966), pp. 173–206, on pp. 184, 186, 190 and 202.
3. 'Service des mines'.
4. Law of 18 May 1874.
5. Law of 22 March 1841.
6. E. Chevallier, *Les salaires au XIXe siècle* (Salaries in the Nineteenth Century) (1887; Paris: Hachette, 1971), pp. 38 and 133.
7. Hereafter, a sum in francs per day will be written F/day.
8. E. Levasseur, *Salariat et salaires* (Wage Earners and Wages) (Paris: O. Doin et fils, 1909), p. 132.
9. D. Reid, *The Miners of Decazeville: A Genealogy of Deindustrialization* (Cambridge, MA: Harvard University Press, 1985), p. 26.
10. Office du travail, *Salaires et durée du travail dans l'industrie française* (Wages and Work-

ing Hours in French Industry) (Paris: Imprimerie nationale, 1894), tome 2; Office du travail, *Salaires et durée du travail dans l'industrie française* (Wages and Working Hours in French Industry) (Paris: Imprimerie nationale, 1897), tome 4, p. 548.

11. Office du travail, *Salaires et durée du travail dans l'industrie française* (1897), p. 267.
12. Office du travail, *Salaires et durée du travail dans l'industrie française* (1897), p. 562.
13. Office du travail, *Salaires et durée du travail dans l'industrie française* (1897), p. 562; Office du travail, *Salaires et durée du travail dans l'industrie française* (1894).
14. F. Simiand, *Le salaire des ouvriers des mines de charbon en France, Contribution à la théorie économique du salaire* (Wages of Coal Mine Workers in France, Contribution to the Economic Theory of Wages) (Paris: Edouard Cornély, 1907), p. 5.
15. Simiand, *Le salaire des ouvriers des mines de charbon en France, Contribution à la théorie économique du salaire*, p. 246.
16. Simiand, *Le salaire des ouvriers des mines de charbon en France, Contribution à la théorie économique du salaire*, pp. 291–3.
17. J.-B. Say, *Traité d'économie politique* (A Treatise on Political Economy), 1st edn (Paris: Déterville, 1803), p. 322.
18. Simiand, *Le salaire des ouvriers des mines de charbon en France, Contribution à la théorie économique du salaire*, p. 337.
19. Simiand, *Le salaire des ouvriers des mines de charbon en France, Contribution à la théorie économique du salaire*, p. 345.
20. *Statistiques de l'Industrie Minérale*, 1913, pp. 10 and 44.
21. H. Fayol, *The Third Part of Industrial and General Management* (1916), Henri Fayol collection, Centre d'Histoire de Sciences Politiques, 56 rue Jacob, 75006 Paris, France (hereafter CHSP), HF 5bis DR3, §§145–75. See Appendix 1.
22. Hereafter million francs written MF.
23. Hereafter million tons to be written Mt.
24. Archives Nationales du Monde du Travail, 78 Boulevard du Général Leclerc, 59100 Roubaix, France (hereafter ANMT), 59AQ10, p. 146; 59AQ17 AG, du 25 mars 1899.
25. ANMT, 59AQ820, pp. 98–164, rapports de la commission des comptes.
26. ANMT, 59AQ17, Assemblée Générale de mars 1899.
27. ANMT, 59AQ820, p. 152.
28. M-F. Conus and J.-L. Escudier, 'Sécurité et transformation du système productif, application à l'industrie française du charbon (1817–1988)' (Security and Transformation of the Production System, Application to the French Coal Industry (1817–1988)), *Entreprise et Histoire*, 17 (1997), p. 60.
29. Archives Nationales, 59 rue Guynemer, 90001, 93383 Pierrefitte-sur-Seine Cedex, France (hereafter AN), F14/8359, Redevance Commentry 1892.
30. ANMT, 110AQ102, p. 62; 110AQ94, rapport 1904–5.
31. ANMT, 110AQ95, Rapport 1907–1908, tables, p. 28.
32. Fayol, *The Third Part of Industrial and General Management*, §156. See Appendix 1.
33. A. Auclair and P. Couderc, *La sidérurgie en Bourbonnais: essor industriel et croissance urbaine de 1840 à 1990* (The Bourbonnais Steel Industry: Industrial Development and Urban Growth from 1840 to 1990) (Aurillac: Gerbert, 2000), p. 130.
34. ANMT 59AQ7 to 59AQ13.
35. H. Fayol, *The Third Part of Industrial and General Management* (1916), Henri Fayol collection, Centre d'Histoire de Sciences Politiques, 56 rue Jacob, 75006 Paris, France, HF 5bis DR3, §154. See Appendix 1.

2 The Financial Function and Corporate Governance

1. H. Fayol, *General and Industrial Management*, trans. C. Storrs (1949), in D. A. Wren and T. Sasaki (eds), *Henri Fayol and Process School* (London: Pickering & Chatto Publishers, 2004), p. 536.
2. Fayol, *General and Industrial Management*, Table V, p. 545.
3. Fayol, *General and Industrial Management*, p. 595.
4. 'Tableau d'organisation'.
5. H. Fayol, *The Third Part of Industrial and General Management* (1916), Henri Fayol collection, Centre d'Histoire de Sciences Politiques, 56 rue Jacob, 75006 Paris, France, HF 5bis DR3, §§115–43 and 323–36. See Appendix 1.
6. Hereafter 1,000,000F to be written 1MF.
7. T. Sasaki, 'Fayol et la Comambault' (Fayol and Comambault), *Enterprises et Histoire*, 34 (2003), p. 12.
8. Henri Fayol possibly felt that he belonged to these families of industrial owners. Amongst his 'advice to future engineers', he argued that 'you have the legitimate desire to win an honorable place by giving your service'. One possible way was through a good marriage: 'do not lose sight of the fact that marriage is the most important act of civic life and that on that act hangs much of life's happiness and success in a career, and that you should make every effort to be worthy of a good helpmate and make a choice worthy of yourself' (H. Fayol, *General and Industrial Management*, trans. C. Storrs (1949), in D. A. Wren and T. Sasaki (eds), *Henri Fayol and Process School* (London: Pickering & Chatto Publishers, 2004), pp. 623 and 627). In 1870 his younger brother, Paul Fayol married the daughter of the mine director in Carmaux where he was employed. His position in the company was assured until the death of his father-in-law, at which time he resigned. As for Henri Fayol, he could have married the daughter of one of his directors, Glachant, but she was twenty-five years his junior and he had little contact with her. Furthermore, Glachant was in charge of the factories and never came to the Commentry mine. On the other hand, Anatole Le Brun de Sessevalle spent summers at Montassiégé, the family château in Néris les Bains that was 7 kilometres from Commentry. He was married to Aline Félicité Rambourg (1826–97), the granddaughter of Nicolas Rambourg (1751–1827) one of the founders of the mine and also a member of the board of directors. He had three daughters born in 1851, 1861 and 1865. Henri Fayol no doubt visited the De Sessevalle family. The firstborn, Pauline Charlotte, married a nobleman and soldier by the name of Bernard de Froissard (1841–1917) on 6 July 1875. She had four children and died in 1884 in childbirth. It is possible that Henri Fayol unsuccessfully courted Pauline Charlotte before marrying Adélaïde Céleste Marie Saulé, the daughter of a storekeeper from Moulins, 70 kilometres distant from Commentry, on 22 November 1875, remaining in the same middle class that he had grown up in (J-L. Peaucelle and C. Guthrie, 'The Private Life of Henri Fayol and his Motivation to Build a Management Science', *Journal of Management History*, 18:4 (2012), pp. 469–87.). His family situation did not permit him to become a member of the board of directors.
9. Archives Nationales du Monde du Travail, 78 Boulevard du Général Leclerc, 59100 Roubaix, France (hereafter ANMT), 59AQ9, p. 192, article 21 des statuts.
10. ANMT, 59AQ12, p. 304.
11. ANMT, 59AQ10, p. 59.
12. ANMT, 59AQ9, p. 194.

13. ANMT, 59AQ8, p. 148; 59AQ9, p. 46.
14. Fayol, *General and Industrial Management*, p. 595.
15. Archives National du Monde du Travail, 78 Boulevard du Général Leclerc, 59100 Roubaix, France (hereafter ANMT), 59AQ8, pp. 169, 171.
16. H. Fayol, *The Third Part of Industrial and General Management* (1916), Henri Fayol collection, Centre d'Histoire de Sciences Politiques, 56 rue Jacob, 75006 Paris, France (hereafter CHSP), HF 5bis DR3, §191. See Appendix 1.
17. Paris Mining School.
18. Adolphe Mony was particularly interested in literature and the arts and created several plays and sculptures.
19. Ivan Flachat was in reality a distant nephew of his half-brother Eugène Flachat (1802–73), with whom he was quite close.
20. Central School for Arts and Manufacturing.
21. The Solferino bridge was demolished a century later in 1960.
22. I. Flachat, *Société anonyme de Commentry-Fourchambault. Réponses au questionnaire de la commission de l'Exposition universelle de 1878* (The Anonymous Society of Commentry-Fourchambault. Responses to the Questionnaire of the 1878 World Fair commission) (Paris: impr. de P. Dupont, 1878).
23. A. Auclair, *Les ingénieurs et l'équipement de la France: Eugène Flachat, 1802–1873* (Engineers and Equipment in France: Eugène Flachat, 1802–1973) (Le Creusot: Écomusee de la communauté urbaine Le Creusot-Montceau-les-Mines, 1999), p.38.
24. A. Auclair, *Stéphane Mony: 1800–1884: l'un des fondateurs de la grande industrie dans le Bourbonnais* (Stéphane Mony: 1800–1884: One of the Founders of Bourbonnais Heavy Industry) (Montmarault: Association du Pays de Montmarault, 1996), p. 65.
25. ANMT, 59AQ8, pp. 56 and 80.
26. ANMT, 59AQ8, p. 101.
27. ANMT, 59AQ8, pp. 127–8.
28. ANMT, 59AQ8, pp. 130 and 140.
29. ANMT, 59AQ8, p. 142.
30. Fayol, *The Third Part of Industrial and General Management*, §143. See Appendix 1.
31. ANMT, 59AQ12, pp. 18, 146 and 288.
32. Fayol, *The Third Part of Industrial and General Management*, §§95–9. See Appendix 1.
33. ANMT, 59AQ8, p. 150.
34. ANMT, 59AQ10, p. 376.
35. ANMT, 59AQ10, pp. 376–9, reports by Girin, Dumas, Bresson, Pourcel.
36. ANMT, 59AQ8, pp. 357 and 362.
37. CHSP, HF4DR1.
38. ANMT, 59AQ9, p. 128.
39. Archives Nationales du Monde du Travail, 78 Boulevard du Général Leclerc, 59100 Roubaix, France (hereafter ANMT), 59AQ10, pp. 218–19.
40. ANMT, 59AQ8, pp. 248–58.
41. ANMT, 59AQ10, pp. 109–16.
42. J. P. McKay, *Pioneers for Profit; Foreign Entrepreneurship and Russian Industrialization 1885–1913* (Chicago, IL: Chicago University Press, 1970), p. 327.
43. ANMT, 59AQ11, p. 47.
44. H. Fayol, *The Third Part of Industrial and General Management* (1916), Henri Fayol collection, Centre d'Histoire de Sciences Politiques, 56 rue Jacob, 75006 Paris, France (hereafter CHSP), HF 5bis DR3, §§271–6. See Appendix 1.

45. Central Council of the French Collieries.
46. Archives Départmentales de la Nièvre, 1 bis rue Charles Roy, 58000 Nevers, France (hereafter ADN), 106J-9, document 16.
47. Fayol, *The Third Part of Industrial and General Management*, §§271–6. See Appendix 1.
48. Archives Nationales du Monde du Travail, 78 Boulevard du Général Leclerc, 59100 Roubaix, France (hereafter ANMT), 110 AQ 1, dossier 7, 1892.
49. ADN, 106J-9, document 16.
50. ANMT, 110AQ1, dossier 7.
51. ANMT, 59AQ10, p. 240.
52. ANMT, 59AQ10, pp. 76, 132 and 275.
53. ANMT, 59AQ10, p. 295; 59AQ11, p. 254.
54. ANMT, 59AQ11, pp. 115–18, 131–6.
55. Archives Départmentales de Haute Loire, 31 avenue de Tonbridge, 43000 Le Puy-en-Velay, France (hereafter ADHL), S 632.
56. ANMT, 59AQ11, pp. 136, 144, 155, 156, 159, 284, 309 and 328.
57. ADHL, S 632.
58. ANMT, 59AQ11, pp. 18, 32 and 42.
59. ANMT, 59AQ11, p. 103.
60. ANMT, 59AQ11, pp. 108–9.
61. CHSP, HF4DR6.
62. ANMT, 59AQ9, pp. 132 and 172.
63. D. Fraboulet, *Quand les patrons s'organisent: stratégies et pratiques de l'Union des industries métallurgiques et minières 1901–1950* (When Employers Get Organized: Strategies and Practices of the Union des Industries Métallurgiques et Minières 1901–1950) (Villeneuve d'Ascq: Presses universitaires du Septentrion, 2007).
64. ANMT, 59AQ9, pp. 38, 80; 59AQ13, p. 114.
65. ANMT, 59AQ9, pp. 277–8.
66. ANMT, 59AQ9, pp. 24, 118 and 144.
67. ANMT, 59AQ12, pp. 7 and 50.
68. ANMT, 59AQ9, p. 281.
69. ANMT, 59AQ11, pp. 157, 168 and 286.
70. ANMT,110AQ95, rapport 1907–8 contentieux, pp. 22–3.
71. ANMT, 59AQ11, pp. 186, 216, 286, 304, 336, 358 and 384; 59AQ12, pp. 34, 56, 62, 118, 122, 164, 184, 192 and 316; 59AQ13, pp. 62 and 68.
72. ANMT, 59AQ9, pp. 188 and 386
73. ANMT, 59AQ11, pp. 24, 36 and 82.
74. ANMT, 59AQ11, pp. 24
75. ANMT, 59AQ12, p. 12.
76. CHSP, HF5bis DR1; HF4DR4, 29 juillet 1898.
77. Archives Nationales, 59 rue Guynemer, 90001, 93383 Pierrefitte-sur-Seine Cedex, France (hereafter AN), F14–4089.
78. ANMT, 59AQ8, pp. 184 and 227.
79. ANMT, 59AQ9, pp. 118 and 130.
80. ANMT, 59AQ10, p. 370; ANMT, 59AQ11, pp. 326 and 386.
81. *Écho des mines et de la métallurgie*, 1883–1904; *Annuaire du Comité Central des Houillères de France*, 1908, 1912.
82. Archives Nationales du Monde du Travail, 78 Boulevard du Général Leclerc, 59100 Roubaix, France (hereafter ANMT), 59AQ8, p. 279.

83. ANMT, 59AQ8, pp. 26, 114, 174, 252, 260, 262, 268, 280, 284, 289 and 302.
84. ANMT, 59AQ10, p. 89.
85. ANMT, 59AQ17, exercice 1903–4, p. 10.
86. ANMT, 59AQ8, pp. 306 and 310.
87. ANMT, 59AQ17, AG du 21 janvier 1892.
88. ANMT, 110AQ821, rapport Mines de Decazeville 1900–1, p. 46.
89. ANMT, 59AQ14bis, p. 96.
90. ANMT, 59AQ8, pp. 349 and 370.
91. ANMT, 59AQ11, p. 220.
92. ANMT, 59AQ17, AG du 28 mars 1905.
93. ANMT, 59AQ, p. 277.
94. ANMT, 59AQ17, AG du 6 avril 1906.
95. ANMT, 59AQ17, AG du 28 mars 1911.
96. ANMT, 59AQ12, p. 282, conseil d'administration du 18 janvier 1911.
97. ANMT, 59AQ13, p. 14.
98. ANMT, 59AQ12, pp. 106–118, 129, 137, 139, 190, 268 and 367–9; 59AQ13, pp. 18–21, 50, 75, 81, 108 and 134.
99. ANMT, 59AQ8, p. 228.
100. Archives Nationales du Monde du Travail, 78 Boulevard du Général Leclerc, 59100 Roubaix, France (hereafter ANMT), 59AQ818 to 821.
101. ANMT, 59AQ9, p. 26; 59AQ10, p. 160; 59AQ12, pp. 170, 174, 332 and 369; 59AQ13, p. 53.
102. ANMT, 59AQ10, p. 286.

3 Planning

1. H. Fayol, *General and Industrial Management*, trans. C. Storrs (1949), in D. A. Wren and T. Sasaki (eds), *Henri Fayol and Process School* (London: Pickering & Chatto Publishers, 2004), p. 582.
2. Archives Nationales du Monde du Travail, 78 Boulevard du Général Leclerc, 59100 Roubaix, France, 59AQ14bis, p. 1; 59AQ10, p. 75.
3. T. Sasaki, 'Fayol et la Comambault' (Fayol and Comambault), *Enterprises et Histoire*, 34 (2003), pp. 8–28.
4. A. Auclair, P. Couderc and J.-M. Molinès, *La sidérurgie en Bourbonnais: Cie Commentry Fourchambault Decazeville: l'usine des hauts fourneaux de Montluçon dite Usine Forey, 1840–1967* (The Bourbonnais Steel Industry: Commentry Fourchambault Decazeville Co.: The Montluçon Blast Furnace and Factory, Known as the Forey Factory, 1840–1967) (Montluçon: Cercle d'archéologie de Montluçon et de la région, 2009), p. 74.
5. Archives Nationales du Monde du Travail, 78 Boulevard du Général Leclerc, 59100 Roubaix, France (hereafter ANMT), 59AQ8, p. 8.
6. ANMT, 59AQ8, p. 55.
7. ANMT, 59AQ8, p. 176.
8. ANMT, 59AQ8, pp. 221 and 330.
9. ANMT, 59AQ8, p. 211, 24 janvier 1889.
10. ANMT, 59AQ8, p. 261, 10 octobre 1889.
11. ANMT, 59AQ8, pp. 308 and 332.
12. ANMT, 59AQ8, p. 89.
13. ANMT, 59AQ9, p. 337.

14. ANMT, 59AQ8, pp. 343–6; 59AQ9, pp. 34, 56, 89 and 113.
15. ANMT, 59AQ9, pp. 226, 244, 268 and 307.
16. ANMT, 59AQ9, pp. 356 and 390; 59AQ10, p. 10.
17. ANMT, 59AQ10, pp. 44, 54, 85, and 137 to 142; Archives Départmentales de l'Aveyron, 25 avenue Victor Hugo, 12000 Rodez, France (hereafter ADN), N 106J1, note du 15 février 1898, pp. 17 and 59.
18. J-B. Bouillet, '1900! la fermeture des forges de Fourchambault en 1901, le rôle d'Henri Fayol' (1900! The Closure of the Fourchambault Forges in 1901, Henri Fayol's Role), La situation du nivernais en 1900: 13 et 14 octobre 2000, *Cinquièmes rencontres d'histoire de la métallurgie* (Guérigny: Les amis du vieux Guérigny/Centre d'études de la métallurgie nivernaise, 2001), pp. 221–40.
19. ANMT, 59AQ10, pp. 307, 332 and 377; 59AQ11, p. 8, ADN, 106J1, document 7.
20. ANMT, 59AQ8, p. 387; 59AQ9, p. 8.
21. ANMT, 59AQ9, pp. 25, 59–76.
22. ANMT, 59AQ9, p. 93.
23. ANMT, 59AQ9, pp. 81, 148, 236 and 310.
24. ANMT, 59AQ10, pp. 89, 91, 126–7; ADN, 106J1, note du 15 février 1898, p. 27.
25. ADN, 106J1, note du 15 février 1898 p. 4.
26. ANMT, 59AQ10, p. 205.
27. ANMT, 59AQ10, p. 255.
28. ADN, 106J1, programme du 1er janvier 1900.
29. ANMT, 59AQ11, pp. 14, 37, 172 and 275.
30. ANMT, 59AQ11, pp. 276–9, 290–301 314, 349, 353 and 372–4.
31. D. A. Wren, 'Henri Fayol as a Strategist: A Nineteenth Century Corporate Turnaround', *Management Decision*, 39:5–6 (2001), pp. 475–87.
32. H. Fayol, *The Third Part of Industrial and General Management* (1916), Henri Fayol collection, Centre d'Histoire de Sciences Politiques, 56 rue Jacob, 75006 Paris, France (hereafter CHSP), HF 5bis DR3, §§145–78. See Appendix 1.
33. Archives Nationales du Monde du Travail, 78 Boulevard du Général Leclerc, 59100 Roubaix, France (hereafter ANMT), 59AQ14bis, p. 91.
34. ANMT, 59AQ14bis, pp. 48–9.
35. ANMT, 59AQ14bis, pp. 53 and 56–7.
36. ANMT, 59AQ14bis, p. 48.
37. ANMT, 59AQ14bis, p. 132.
38. ANMT, 59AQ14bis, p. 126.
39. Archives Départmentales de la Nièvre, 1 bis rue Charles Roy, 58000, Nevers, France, N 106J1, document 22.
40. H. Fayol, *General and Industrial Management*, trans. C Storrs (1949), in D. A. Wren and T. Sasaki (eds), *Henri Fayol and Process School* (London: Pickering & Chatto Publishers, 2004), p. 581.
41. Archives Nationales du Monde du Travail, 78 Boulevard du Général Leclerc, 59100 Roubaix, France (hereafter ANMT), 110AQ1.
42. ANMT, 59AQ11, p. 292.
43. ANMT, 59AQ14bis, p. 49.
44. Archives Départmentales de la Nièvre, 1 bis rue Charles Roy, 58000 Nevers, France, 106J1, document 22 p. 22.
45. ANMT, 59AQ11, p. 304.
46. ANMT, 59AQ9, p. 93.

47. H. Fayol, *General and Industrial Management*, trans. C. Storrs (1949), in D. A. Wren and T. Sasaki (eds), *Henri Fayol and Process School* (London: Pickering & Chatto, 2004), p. 583.
48. ANMT, 59AQ9, pp. 326–9.
49. ANMT, 59AQ10, p. 6.
50. ANMT, 59AQ12, pp. 156, 216, 270, 296 and 216; 59AQ14bis, p. 86.
51. ANMT, 59AQ14bis, p. 2.
52. Fayol, *General and Industrial Management*, p. 579. Text underlined in the French edition.
53. ANMT, 59AQ14bis, p. 96.
54. ANMT, 59AQ9, pp. 40, 76 and 84.
55. L. Lévêque, 'Historique des forges de Decazeville, 1826–1914' (History of the Decazeville forges, 1826–1914), *Bulletin de la Société de l'industrie minérale*, 19 (1916), pp. 5–97, pp. 19–21.
56. J.-L. Peaucelle, 'Henri Fayol et la guerre de 1914' (Henri Fayol and the War of 1914), *Revue Française de Gestion*, 136 (2001), pp. 121–34.
57. H. Fayol, *General and Industrial Management*, trans. C. Storrs (1949), in D. A. Wren and T. Sasaki (eds), *Henri Fayol and Process School* (London: Pickering & Chatto, 2004), pp. 582–3.

4 Organizing: The Management of Managers

1. H. Fayol, *General and Industrial Management*, trans. C. Storrs (1949), in D. A. Wren and T. Sasaki (eds), *Henri Fayol and Process School* (London: Pickering & Chatto, 2004), p. 587.
2. Archives Nationales du Monde du Travail, 78 Boulevard du Général Leclerc, 59100 Roubaix, France (hereafter ANMT), 59AQ13, p. 67.
3. Fayol, *General and Industrial Management*, p. 589.
4. Fayol, *General and Industrial Management*, p. 607.
5. H. Fayol, *General and Industrial Management*, trans. C. Storrs (1949), in D. A. Wren and T. Sasaki (eds), *Henri Fayol and Process School* (London: Pickering & Chatto, 2004), p. 568.
6. 'Corps social'.
7. Fayol, *General and Industrial Management*, p. 588.
8. Fayol, *General and Industrial Management*, p. 612.
9. Fayol, *General and Industrial Management*, p. 612; H. Fayol, *The Third Part of Industrial and General Management* (1916), Henri Fayol collection, Centre d'Histoire de Sciences Politiques, 56 rue Jacob, 75006 Paris, France, §§49 and 54. See Appendix 1.
10. Archives Nationales du Monde du Travail, 78 Boulevard du Général Leclerc, 59100 Roubaix, France (hereafter ANMT), 59AQ8, p. 148.
11. AMNT, 59AQ9, pp. 30–1.
12. Fayol, *General and Industrial Management*, p. 590.
13. F. W. Taylor, *The Principles of Scientific Management* (New York and London, Harper & Brothers, 1911).
14. ANMT, 59AQ9, p. 28.
15. Fayol, *General and Industrial Management*, p. 596.
16. ANMT, 59AQ12, p. 249.
17. ANMT, 59AQ12, p. 249; 59AQ11, pp. 232 and 244; 59AQ790, p. 28; Archives

Départmentales de la Nièvre, 1 bis rue Charles Roy, 58000 Nevers, France, 106J-10.
18. ANMT, 59AQ8, pp. 190, 212, 346, 363 and 366; 59AQ903.
19. ANMT, 110 AQ 57, rapport mine Decazeville 1900–1901, XI personnel.
20. Saint Etienne Mining School.
21. ANMT, 59AQ9, p. 361; 59AQ10, pp. 227 and 358; 59AQ11, p. 146.
22. Henri Fayol collection, Centre d'Histoire de Sciences Politiques, 56 rue Jacob, 75006 Paris, France (hereafter CHSP), HF4DR2.
23. H. Mintzberg, *The Structuring of Organizations: A Synthesis of the Research* (Englewood Cliffs, NJ: Prentice-Hall, 1979).
24. Workers estimated based on Archives Nationales, 59 rue Guynemer, 90001, 93383 Pierrefitte-sur-Seine Cedex, France (hereafter AN), F/14/3879; AN, F/14/8282 and AN, F/14/8359.
25. Chart based on 'Organisation du service technique des houillères de Commentry-Montvicq' (1888), CHSP, HF4DR2.
26. H. Fayol, *The Third Part of Industrial and General Management* (1916), CSHP, HF 5bis DR3, §§12–13. See Appendix 1.
27. H. Fayol, *General and Industrial Management*, trans. C. Storrs (1949), in D. A. Wren and T. Sasaki (eds), *Henri Fayol and Process School* (London: Pickering & Chatto Publishers, 2004), p. 589.
28. Chart based on 'Organisation du service technique des houillères de Commentry-Montvicq' (1888), CHSP, HF4DR2; employee numbers estimated from AN, F/14/8359, AN, F/14/8282, AN, F/14/3879 and C. Buisson, 'Note sur la préparation des charbons' (Note on the Preparation of Coal), *Bulletin de la société de l'industrie minérale*, Congrès des mines et de la métallurgie 1900, third series, tome 15 (1901), pp 390–426; A. Auclair, *Stéphane Mony: 1800–1884: l'un des fondateurs de la grande industrie dans le Bourbonnais* (Stéphane Mony: 1800–1884: One of the Founders of Bourbonnais Heavy Industry) (Montmarault: Association du pays de Montmarault, 1996), p. 98; A. Auclair, *Histoire des Houillères du Bourbonnais* (History of the Bourbonnais Collieries) (Clermont Ferand: Éd. Racines, 1999), p. 172.
29. CHSP, HF4DR2, pp. 13, 16–17.
30. CHSP, HF4DR2, pp. 13, 16–17.
31. Fayol, *General and Industrial Management*, p. 594.
32. We use the word 'overpass' to translate the word 'passerelle' instead of 'underpass' as suggested by J. D. Breeze in 'A Discussion of the Translation of Some of Fayol's Important Concepts', in D. A. Wren and T. Sasaki (eds), *Henri Fayol and Process School* (London: Pickering & Chatto Publishers, 2004), pp. 221–48. In French, 'passerelle' is commonly used to refer to a narrow, sometimes temporary footbridge. This word also has a figurative meaning: to join two parallel paths, such as two career paths. The word 'overpass' appears to best capture this meaning.
33. Fayol, *General and Industrial Management*, p. 569.
34. Fayol, *General and Industrial Management*, p. 569.
35. Fayol, *The Third Part of Industrial and General Management*, §§214–23. See Appendix 1.
36. Archives Nationales du Monde du Travail, 78 Boulevard du Général Leclerc, 59100 Roubaix, France (hereafter ANMT), 59AQ9, pp. 31–2.
37. ANMT, 59AQ17, Assemblée Générale extraordinaire 5 juillet 1892, p. 23 article 20 des statuts.
38. H. Fayol, *General and Industrial Management*, trans. C. Storrs (1949), in D. A. Wren

and T. Sasaki (eds), *Henri Fayol and Process School* (London: Pickering & Chatto Publishers, 2004), p. 565.

39. Fayol, *General and Industrial Management*, p. 565.
40. ANMT, 58AQ8, p. 24
41. ANMT, 59AQ8, pp. 24, 94 and 286.
42. ANMT, 59AQ11, pp. 280 and 375; 59AQ12, p. 69.
43. J. Lambert-Dansette, *Genèse du patronat 1780–1880* (Genesis of Employer Groups 1780–1880) (Paris: Hachette, 1991), p. 265.
44. M-F. Conus, 'Une entreprise face à la gestion des "risques majeurs": la compagnie des mines de Courrières (1852–1944)' (A Business Faced With 'Major Risks': The Courrières Mining Company (1852–1944)), *Histoire économie et société*, 25:4 (2006), pp. 61–78.
45. In 1906 the mine employed 7,000 liners and produced more than 2Mt of coal.
46. ANMT, 59AQ10, pp. 152 and 238; 59AQ11, p. 284.
47. ANMT, 59AQ8, p. 366.
48. Fayol, *General and Industrial Management*, p. 613.
49. ANMT, 59AQ11, p. 273.
50. ANMT, 59AQ11, p. 268.
51. ANMT, 59AQ12, p. 154.
52. ANMT, 59AQ10, p. 374.
53. ANMT, 59AQ12, p. 81.
54. ANMT, 59AQ11, p. 214.
55. ANMT, 59AQ12, p. 248.
56. Nancy Mining School.
57. ANMT, 59AQ12, pp. 248 and 264.
58. ANMT, 59AQ9, p. 222.
59. ANMT, 59AQ11, p. 146.
60. ANMT, 59AQ9, p. 222.
61. School of Arts and Trades.
62. Fayol, *General and Industrial Management*, p. 573.
63. ANMT, 59AQ9, p. 360; 59AQ10, pp. 226 and 358; 59AQ11, p. 206.
64. L. Guillet, 'Notice biographique de Pierre Girin' (Biographical Note for Pierre Girin), *Revue de la métallurgie*, 11 (November 1926), p. 685.
65. ANMT, 59AQ12, p. 154.
66. ANMT, 59AQ11, p. 288.
67. ANMT, 59AQ9, pp. 98, 348 and 364; 59AQ11, p. 244.
68. Henry Fayol collection, Centre d'Histoire de Sciences Politiques, 56 rue Jacob, 75006 Paris, France (hereafter CHSP), HF4DR6 8 novembre 1910, 'Recherche d'un directeur pour Decazeville'.
69. ANMT, 59AQ12, p. 264.
70. Y. Cohen, 'Fayol, un instituteur de l'ordre industriel' (Fayol, A Teacher of Industrial Order), *Entreprise et Histoire*, 34 (December 2003), pp. 29–67.
71. ANMT, 59AQ10, p. 76; 59AQ11, p. 12.
72. ANMT, 59AQ12, p. 232.
73. Fayol, *General and Industrial Management*, p. 573.
74. ANMT, 59AQ11, pp. 14 and 118; 59AQ9, p. 222; 59AQ10, p. 327.
75. ANMT, 59AQ11, p. 274.
76. ANMT, 59AQ10, p. 226.

77. ANMT, 59AQ9, p. 162; 59AQ11, p. 286; 59AQ12, pp. 70 and 262.
78. ANMT, 59AQ9, pp. 126 and 144.
79. Fayol, *General and Industrial Management*, p. 632.
80. Fayol, 'Elimination des incapables', *General and Industrial Management*, pp. 571–2.
81. ANMT, 59AQ8, p. 162.
82. ANMT, 59AQ8, pp. 190 and 194.
83. ANMT, 59AQ8, p. 190.
84. ANMT, 59AQ9, pp. 24 and 158.
85. ANMT, 59AQ10, pp. 39 and 145.
86. ANMT, 59AQ10, pp. 36, 68 and 64.
87. ANMT, 59AQ9, p. 240.
88. ANMT, 59AQ8, pp. 189, 213 and 355; 59AQ9, pp. 90 and 191.
89. ANMT, 59AQ9, p. 90.
90. ANMT, 59AQ9, p. 360; 9AQ10, p. 358; 59AQ11, p. 82.
91. ANMT, 59AQ8, pp. 354 and 380; 59AQ9, p. 64.
92. ANMT, 59AQ9, p. 124.
93. ANMT, 59AQ11, p. 374.
94. ANMT, 59AQ9, p. 222.
95. ANMT, 59AQ700, p. 185.
96. ANMT, 110AQ7, dossier 6.
97. ANMT, 59AQ10, p. 294.
98. ANMT, 59AQ647, Rapport annuel Imphy 1896–1897, pp. 3 and 23.
99. ANMT, 59AQ11, p. 281.
100. Fayol, *General and Industrial Management*, p. 598.
101. H. Fayol, *General and Industrial Management*, trans. C. Storrs (1949), in D. A. Wren and T. Sasaki (eds), *Henri Fayol and Process School* (London: Pickering & Chatto Publishers, 2004), p. 539.
102. Archives Nationales du Monde du Travail, 78 Boulevard du Général Leclerc, 59100 Roubaix, France, 59AQ14bis, p. 130. The text is underlined in the original document.
103. Fayol, *General and Industrial Management*, p. 555.
104. Fayol, *General and Industrial Management*, p. 557.

5 Organizing: The Management of Workers

1. H. Fayol, *General and Industrial Management*, trans. C. Storrs (1949), in D. A. Wren and T. Sasaki (eds), *Henri Fayol and Process School* (London: Pickering & Chatto Publishers, 2004), pp. 556, 572, 575.
2. D. Reid, *The Miners of Decazeville: A Genealogy of Deindustrialization*, (Cambridge, MA: Harvard University Press, 1985), pp. 49–50.
3. H. Fayol, *The Third Part of Industrial and General Management* (1916), Henri Fayol collection, Centre d'Histoire de Sciences Politiques, 56 rue Jacob, 75006 Paris, France, HF 5bis DR3, §303. See Appendix 1.
4. Archives Nationales du Monde du Travail, 78 Boulevard du Général Leclerc, 59100 Roubaix, France, 59AQ14bis, p. 130.
5. Reid, D., *The Miners of Decazeville: A Genealogy of Deindustrialization*, (Cambridge, MA: Harvard University Press, 1985), p. 50.
6. G. Dron, *Rapport de la commission des mines* (Report of the mining commission) (Paris: imprimerie de la Chambre des députés, 1903), Chambre des députés, session de 1903,

annexe au procès verbal de la séance du 2 avril 1903, no. 878, tome 3, p. 278.
7. A. Auclair, *La grande industrie dans l'Allier : XIXe-XXe siècles* (Heavy Industry in the Allier) (Clermont-Ferrand: CRDP dAuvergne, 1995), pp. 93–4.
8. Archives Nationales du Monde du Travail, 78 Boulevard du Général Leclerc, 59100 Roubaix, France (hereafter ANMT), 59AQ9, p. 136.
9. ANMT, 59AQ10, p. 216.
10. ANMT, 59AQ12, p. 255.
11. ANMT, 59AQ12, p. 392; 59AQ13, p. 12.
12. ANMT, 59AQ11, p. 186.
13. ANMT, 59AQ12, p. 181.
14. ANMT, 59AQ10, p. 329.
15. ANMT, 59AQ11, p. 58.
16. ANMT, 59AQ10, pp. 47 and 329; 59AQ12, pp. 212 and 214.
17. ANMT, 59AQ13, pp. 26 and 112.
18. ANMT, 59AQ12, pp. 6 and 262.
19. Reid, *The Miners of Decazeville: A Genealogy of Deindustrialization*, p. 292, note 69; Archives Nationales, 59 rue Guynemer, 90001, 93383 Pierrefitte-sur-Seine Cedex, France (hereafter AN), F7-12772.
20. ANMT, 59AQ10, p. 224.
21. ANMT, 59AQ10, p. 237.
22. ANMT, 59AQ12, pp. 52 and 186.
23. ANMT, 59AQ13, p. 10.
24. ANMT, 59AQ9, p. 36.
25. Reid, *The Miners of Decazeville: A Genealogy of Deindustrialization*, p. 119.
26. Reid, *The Miners of Decazeville: A Genealogy of Deindustrialization*, p. 118.
27. ANMT, 110 AQ 95, rapport annuel, usine de Decazeville 1907–8.
28. ANMT, 110AQ61, Rapport 1912–13, fascicule 1, p. 14, 13 personnel.
29. ANMT, 59AQ12, p. 48.
30. ANMT, 59AQ12, pp. 84, 178, 192 and 204; 59AQ13, p. 7.
31. A. Boscus, *Économie et société dans le bassin industriel nord-aveyronnais: 1900–1950* (Economy and Society in the Industrial Basin of North Aveyron: 1900–1950) (Montreuil: Institut CGT d'histoire sociale, 1997), pp. 257, 258, 699.
32. Reid, *The Miners of Decazeville: A Genealogy of Deindustrialization*, p. 120.
33. ANMT, 110AQ96, rapport 1912–13, p. 26.
34. *La Dépêche*, vendredi 6 mars 1914.
35. ANMT, 110AQ61, rapport mines 1911–12.
36. Boscus, *Économie et société dans le bassin industriel nord-aveyronnais: 1900–1950* (Economy and Society in the Industrial Basin of North Aveyron: 1900–1950), p. 699.
37. ANMT, 59AQ12, pp. 162, 166, 172, 188, 208, 212, 232, 238 and 250.
38. AN, F/14/8282, rapport sur Commentry 1886, 1889; ANMT, 59AQ8, p. 38.
39. ANMT, 59AQ10 to 59AQ12.
40. *Bulletin de l'Office du Travail*, 1906, pp. 82, 198, 297, 396, 527, 758, 1172; 1907, pp. 82, 191, 295, 407, 633, 742, 861, 1235; 1908, pp. 100, 197, 305, 406, 697.
41. *Bulletin de l'Office du Travail*,1894, pp. 372, 438; 1895, pp. 273, 336, 621.
42. AN, F12–12764, Allier, commissariat spécial aux chemins de fer, gare de Commentry.
43. *Bulletin de l'Office du Travail*, 1901, pp. 590, 664, 745, 804; 1902, pp. 421, 813; 1903, pp. 141, 766, 854.
44. AN, F/14/8282, Commentry 26 novembre 1888.

45. ANMT, 59AQ9, p. 164.
46. ANMT, 59AQ10, pp. 320, 324 and 370.
47. ANMT, 59AQ9, pp. 123–4.
48. ANMT, 59AQ9, p. 10.
49. ANMT, 59AQ820, p. 58; *Rapports des ingénieurs des mines aux conseils généraux sur la situation des mines et usines en 1899* (Reports from Mines Service Engineers to General Councils on the Situation of Mines and Factories in 1899), (Paris: Comité Central des Houillères de France, 1900), p. 118.
50. ANMT, 59AQ820, p. 58; *Rapports des ingénieurs des mines aux conseils généraux sur la situation des mines et usines en 1899* (Reports from Mines Service Engineers to General Councils on the Situation of Mines and Factories in 1899), (Paris: Comité Central des Houillères de France, 1900, p. 118.
51. ANMT, 59AQ12, pp. 24, 88, 117, 265 and 354.
52. ANMT, 59AQ12, pp. 332 and 348.
53. L. Mazars, *Terre de mine, bassin d'Aubin et Decazeville* (Land of mines, Aubin and Decazeville basin) (Rodez: édition Fil d'ariane, 1999), p. 76.
54. ANMT, 59AQ13, p. 74.
55. I. Flachat, *Société anonyme de Commentry-Fourchambault. Réponses au questionnaire de la commission de l'Exposition universelle de 1878* (The Anonymous Society of Commentry-Fourchambault. Responses to the Questionnaire of the 1878 World Fair Commission) (Paris: impr. de P. Dupont, 1878), p. 42.
56. *La Dépêche*, lundi 8 septembre 1902.
57. ANMT, 110AQ59, Rapport 1907–8 Mine de Decazeville.
58. H. Fayol, *General and Industrial Management*, trans. C. Storrs (1949), in D. A. Wren and T. Sasaki (eds), *Henri Fayol and Process School* (London: Pickering & Chatto Publishers, 2004), p. 561.
59. Fayol, *General and Industrial Management*, p. 562.
60. Fonds Henri Fayol, Centre d'Histoire de Sciences Politiques, 56 rue Jacob, 75006 Paris, France (hereafter CHSP), HF4DR5. See Appendix 1.
61. L. Reybaud, *Commentry & Fourchambault, Rapport sur la condition morale, intellectuelle et matérielle des ouvriers qui vivent de l'industrie du fer* (Commentry & Fourchambault, Report on the Moral, Intellectual and Material Situation of Workers Living from the Iron Industry) (Paris: Académie des sciences morales et politiques, 1868), p. 33.
62. D. Reid, *The Miners of Decazeville: A Genealogy of Deindustrialization* (Cambridge, MA: Harvard University Press, 1985), p. 29.
63. Reid, *The Miners of Decazeville: A Genealogy of Deindustrialization*, p. 29.
64. Fayol, *General and Industrial Management*, p. 562.
65. Archives Nationales du Monde du Travail, 78 Boulevard du Général Leclerc, 59100 Roubaix, France (hereafter ANMT), 59AQ647, exercice 1897–8.
66. Fonds Henri Fayol, CHSP, HF 5bis.
67. Fayol, *General and Industrial Management*, p. 560.
68. Archives Nationales, 59 rue Guynemar, 90001, 93383 Pierrefitte-sur-Seine Cedex, France (hereafter AN), F/14/8282, Commentry 22 mars 1894 visite au puits St Charles, Allier rapport annuel 1894.
69. ANMT, 110AQ48.
70. ANMT, 110AQ48.
71. AN, F12–12764, 19 juin 1908.
72. ANMT, 110AQ102, pp. 63–5.

73. Drivers were in charge of the steam engines that powered the mills. Steam engines were replaced by electrical engines from 1903 to 1910.
74. A. Boscus, *Économie et société dans le bassin industriel nord-aveyronnais: 1900–1950* (Economy and Society in the Industrial Basin of North Aveyron: 1900–1950) (Montreuil: Institut CGT d'histoire sociale, 1997), annexes.
75. ANMT, 110AQ48.
76. A. Fontaine, 'L'Échelle mobile dans les mines de la Grande-Bretagne' (Mobile Scales in Great Britain's Mines), *Annales des mines* (September, 1895), pp. 5–31.
77. *Petit journal*, 8 November 1902.
78. H. Fayol, *General and Industrial Management*, trans. C. Storrs (1949), in D. A. Wren and T. Sasaki (eds), *Henri Fayol and Process School* (London: Pickering & Chatto Publishers), p. 563.
79. Fayol, *General and Industrial Management*, p. 564.
80. Hereafter francs per ton written F/ton.
81. *Statistiques de l'Industrie Minérale*, 1888, p. 45.
82. Archives Nationales du Monde du Travail (hereafter ANMT), 59AQ8, p. 277.
83. ANMT, 59AQ668, rapport 1890–1891.
84. Archives Nationales, 59 rue Guynemer, 90001, 93383 Pierrefitte-sur-Seine Cedes, France, F/14/8282, Allier rapport annuel 1890.
85. 'Réunion de travail sur les grèves' (Meeting on Strikes), *La Réforme Sociale*, 1890, p 29 ; 'Les grèves leurs causes et leurs résultats' (Strikes, Their Causes and Their Results) *La Réforme Sociale*, 1890, p 324.
86. ANMT, 59AQ12, p. 265.
87. ANMT, 59AQ11, p. 367.
88. ANMT, 59AQ10, p. 202.
89. ANMT. 59AQ10, p. 245.
90. ANMT, 59AQ10, p. 300.
91. ANMT, 59AQ10, pp. 311, 314 and 318.
92. ANMT, 59AQ12, pp. 22, 88.
93. ANMT, 110AQ47, DG à Seigle 8 juillet 1908, cited by D. Reid, The Miners of Decazeville: A Genealogy of Deindustrialization (Cambridge, MA: Harvard University Press, 1985), p. 295, note 127.
94. ANMT, 59AQ10, p. 316.
95. ANMT, 59AQ12, p. 394; 59AQ13, p. 5.
96. ANMT, 110AQ71, p. 62.
97. ANMT, 110AQ102, p. 67.
98. ANMT, 59AQ12, p. 258.
99. H. Fayol, *The Third Part of Industrial and General Management*, Henri Fayol collection, Centre d'Histoire de Sciences Politiques, 56 rue Jacob, 75006 Paris, France, HF 5bis DR3, §§305–19. See Appendix 1.
100. Archives Nationales du Monde du Travail, 78 Boulevard du Général Leclerc, 59100 Roubaix, France, (hereafter ANMT), 59AQ7, pp. 236–41.
101. Archives Nationales, 59 rue Guynemer, 90001, 93383 Pierrefitte-sur-Seine Cedex (hereafter AN), F12–4656.
102. G. Rougeron, *Histoire de Commentry et des Commentryens* (History of Commentry and the Commentryens) (Charroux-d'Allier: Cahiers bourbonnais, 1987), p. 184.
103. AN, F12–4656, rapports de gendarmerie du 9 juin 1881.
104. E. Montusès, *Le député en blouse* (The Deputy in Overalls) (Moulins: Les Cahiers du Centre, 1913), p. 22.

105. Montusès, *Le député en blouse,* pp. 23 and 26.
106. Fayol, *The Third Part of Industrial and General Management*, §§272–74. See Appendix 1.
107. Fayol, *The Third Part of Industrial and General Management*, §§325–40. See Appendix 1.
108. ANMT, 59AQ 668, Rapport annuel Montluçon exercice 1889–1890.
109. ANMT, 59AQ11, p. 9.
110. Bulletin de l'Office du Travail, janvier 1902, p. 8.
111. *La fonderie*, no. 20, 26 août 1901 to no. 28, 27 avril 1902; 'Corporative des mouleurs en métaux de France', *Compte rendu officiel du quatrième congrès tenu les 14, 15 et 16 juillet 1899 à Montluçon* (Official Minutes of the Fourth Congress held on July 14, 15 and 16 1899 in Montluçon) (Paris: imprimerie Jean Allemane, 1900).
112. ANMT, 59AQ821, Montluçon exercice 1900–1, p. 31.
113. H.Fayol, *General and Industrial Management*, trans. C. Storrs (1949), in D. A. Wren and T. Sasaki (eds), Henri Fayol and Process School (London: Pickering & Chatto Publishers, 2004), p. 562.
114. ANMT, 59AQ11, pp. 73–5.
115. ANMT, 59AQ821, exercice 1902–3, p. 140.
116. ANMT, 110AQ58, rapport 1905–1906 fascicule 1, XX situation ouvrière.
117. ANMT, 59AQ668, rapport annuel au service des mines 1890–1.
118. ANMT, 110AQ51, lettre du 20 avril 1904.
119. ANMT, 110AQ61, Rapport annuel 1912–13, fascicule 1, p. 70.
120. ANMT, 110AQ49, 25 février 1914.
121. ANMT, 59AQ10, p. 13.
122. D. Reid, *The Miners of Decazeville: A Genealogy of Deindustrialization* (Cambridge, MA: Harvard University Press, 1985), p. 129.
123. Fayol, General and Industrial Management, p. 557.
124. ANMT, 110AQ50 dossier 5, rapport du garde général des usines.
125. Archives Nationales du Monde du Travail, 78 Boulevard du Général Leclerc, 59100 Roubaix, France (hereafter ANMT), 59AQ10, p. 234; H. Fayol, *The Third Part of Industrial and General Management,* Centre d'Histoire de Sciences Politiques, 56 rue Jacob, 75006 Paris, France (hereafter CHSP), Henri Fayol Collection, HF 5bis DR3, §§232–45. See Appendix 1.
126. ANMT, 59AQ8, pp. 109–10.
127. ANMT, 59AQ9, pp. 124, 175, 172 and 190.
128. E. Grüner, H. Darcy and C. Ledoux, 'Loi sur les caisses de retraite des ouvriers mineurs' (Law on Retirement Funds for Mining Workers), Société d'économie sociale; Réunion mensuelle du groupe de Paris; séance du 17 décembre 1894. *La réforme sociale*, tome 29 (1895), pp. 410–431, 415.
129. ANMT, 59AQ9, p. 232.
130. ANMT, 59AQ9, p. 232.
131. ANMT, 59AQ10, pp. 377–8.
132. ANMT, 59AQ, p. 336.
133. ANMT, 110AQ54, dossier 1, lettre de DD à DG 1911, cited by D. Reid, *The Miners of Decazeville: A Genealogy of Deindustrialization* (Cambridge, MA: Harvard University Press, 1985), p. 293.
134. ANMT, 111AQ297, cited by Reid, *The Miners of Decazeville: A Genealogy of Deindustrialization*, p. 293; note 90.
135. Archives Nationales, 59 rue Guynemer, 90001, 93383 Pierrefitte-sur-Seine Cedex, France (hereafter AN), F/14/8282, Allier rapport annuel 1888 à 1894.

136. ANMT, 59AQ8, pp. 297–8.
137. AN, F/14/8282, Commentry et Montvicq, 1897 sociétés de secours.
138. ANMT, 59AQ820, p. 58 exercice 1896–7.
139. AN, F14/8289, Aveyron rapport de l'ingénieur général 1893.
140. ANMT, 110AQ61 rapport 1912–1913, fascicule 1, p. 43.
141. Reid, *The Miners of Decazeville: A Genealogy of Deindustrialization*, p. 127.
142. ANMT, 59AQ9, p. 97.
143. AN, F/14/8282, Commentry visite du 19 avril 1894.
144. The official time was set based on the culmination of the sun in Paris. Today this corresponds to 6 o'clock in winter and 7 o'clock in summer.
145. ANMT, 59AQ8, p. 358.
146. C. Benoist, *L'organisation du travail* (The Organization of Labour) (Paris: Plon, 1905), p. 190.
147. ANMT, 59AQ8, p. 292; 59AQ10, p. 319.
148. ANMT, 59AQ8, p. 359.
149. ANMT, 110AQ42.
150. ANMT, 59AQ12, pp. 116 and 209.
151. ANMT, 110AQ42, lettre au CCHF le 10 février 1908, note du 7 mai 1910.
152. P. de Rousiers, *La question ouvrière en Angleterre* (The Worker Issue in Engand) (Paris: Firmin-Didot, 1895), p. 320.
153. A. Auclair, P. Couderc and J.-M. Molinès, *La sidérurgie en Bourbonnais: Cie Commentry Fourchambault Decazeville: l'usine des hauts fourneaux de Montluçon dite Usine Forey, 1840–1967* (The Bourbonnais Steel Industry: Commentry Fourchambault Decazeville Co.: The Montluçon Blast Furnace and Factory, Known as the Forey Factory, 1840–1967) (Montluçon: Cercle d'archéologie de Montluçon et de la région, 2009) p. 134.
154. ANMT, 110AQ71, p. 4.
155. H. Guitton, *Fête du travail à la mine de Commentry 28 septembre 1873* (Labour Day at the Commentry Mine 28 September 1873) (Montluçon: Impr. de Crepin-Leblond, 1873).
156. ANMT, 59AQ9, p. 128.
157. ANMT, 59AQ820, p. 111.
158. ANMT, 59AQ13, p. 6.
159. AN, F/14/8282, visite à Commentry du 10 juillet 1891.
160. AN, F/14/8282, visite à Commentry le 21 mai 1894.
161. ANMT, 59AQ820, exercice 1895–6, p. 22.
162. ANMT, 59AQ12, p. 70.
163. ANMT, 59AQ10, p. 368.
164. Archives Nationales du Monde du Travail, 78 Boulevard du Général Leclerc, 59100 Roubaix, France, 110AQ48.
165. O. Hardy-Hémery, *De la croissance à la désindustrialisation. Un siècle dans le Valenciennois* (From Growth to Disindustrialization. A Century in Valencienne Area) (Paris: Presses de la Fondation des Sciences Politiques, 1984), p. 61.
166. D. Reid, *The Miners of Decazeville: A Genealogy of Deindustrialization* (Cambridge, MA: Harvard University Press, 1985), p. 121.
167. G. Dron, *Rapport de la commission des mines* (Report of the Mining Commission) (Paris: Imprimerie de la Chambre des députés, 1903), Chambre des députés, session de 1903, annexe au procès verbal de la séance du 2 avril 1903, no. 878, p. 196.

6 Coordinating, Commanding, Verifying: Information Systems and the Accounting Function

1. The French verb 'contrôler' that was used by Fayol means 'to verify', 'to monitor', 'to check' or 'to inspect' after operations had taken place. Accordingly, we have translated this verb as 'to verify'.
2. H. Fayol, *General and Industrial Management*, trans. C. Storrs (1949), in D. A. Wren and T. Sasaki (eds), *Henri Fayol and Process School* (London: Pickering & Chatto Publishers, 2004), pp. 631, 637 and 641.
3. J. P. Kotter, *The General Managers* (New York, NY: The Free Press, 1982) cited in M. J. Fells, 'Fayol Stands the Test of Time', *Journal of Management History*, 6:6 (2000), pp. 345–60, p. 402, figure 1.
4. Fayol, *General and Industrial Management*, p. 631.
5. Fayol, *General and Industrial Management*, p. 637.
6. Fayol, *General and Industrial Management*, p. 631.
7. Fayol, *General and Industrial Management*, p. 640.
8. Fayol, *General and Industrial Management*, p. 636.
9. Fayol, *General and Industrial Management*, p. 637.
10. Fayol, *General and Industrial Management*, p. 641.
11. Fayol, *General and Industrial Management*, p. 638.
12. Henri Fayol collection, Centre d'Histoire de Sciences Politiques, 56 rue Jacob, 75006 Paris, France, HF5bis DR1; J.-L.Peaucelle and C. Guthrie, 'Henri Fayol' in M. Witzel and M. Warner (eds), *The Oxford Handbook of Management Theorists* (Oxford: Oxford University Press, 2013), pp. 49–73, on pp. 56–8.
13. Fayol, *General and Industrial Management*, p. 635.
14. 'Transmission des documents'.
15. Centre d'Histoire de Sciences Politiques, 56 rue Jacob, 75006 Paris, France (hereafter CHSP), HF4 DR2.
16. Archives Nationales du Monde du Travail, 78 Boulevard du Général Leclerc, 59100 Roubaix, France (hereafter ANMT), 110AQ244, conférences D.
17. CHSP, HF4DR2, 'Organisation du service technique des houillères de Commentry-Montvicq' 1888.
18. ANMT, 59AQ790, p. 183.
19. ANMT, 110AQ96, rapport annuel 1913–14.
20. H. Fayol, *General and Industrial Management*, trans. C. Storrs (1949), in D. A. Wren and T. Sasaki (eds), *Henri Fayol and Process School* (London: Pickering & Chatto Publishers, 2004), p. 642.
21. ANMT, 59AQ790, p. 183.
22. ANMT, 59AQ10, p. 236.
23. ANMT, 110AQ152.
24. Fayol, *General and Industrial Management*, p. 574.
25. Archives Nationales, 59 rue Guynemer, 90001, 93383 Pierrefitte-sur-Seine Cedex, Paris (hereafter AN), F14–3866.
26. J-L. Peaucelle, J.A. Ariza Montès, B. Beaudoin, T. Boyns, A.C. Morales Gutierrez, J-N. Retière, T. Sasaki and I Smith, *Henri Fayol, inventeur des outils de gestion* (Henri Fayol, Inventor of Management Tools) (Paris: Économica, 2003).
27. Henri Fayol collection, Centre d'Histoire de Sciences Politiques, 56 rue Jacob, 75006 Paris, France (hereafter CHSP), HF4DR2.

28. AN, F14–8282, Commentry visite du 22 mars 1894.
29. 'Registre matricule'; Archives Départmentales de la Nièvre, 1 bis rue Charles Roy, 58000 Nevers, France (hereafter ADN), N 106J-9, Règlement pour l'admission des ouvriers.
30. 'Livret de voyage'.
31. 'Bulletin d'admissibilité'.
32. ANMT, 110AQ61, rapport 1912–13, fascicule 1, p. 14 XIII personnel.
33. CHSP, HF4DR2, p. 86.
34. G. Dron, *Rapport de la commission des mines* (Report of the Mining Commission) (Paris: imprimerie de la Chambre des députés, 1903), Chambre des députés, session de 1903, annexe au procès verbal de la séance du 2 avril 1903, no. 878, tome 3, pp. 191 and 248.
35. Dron, *Rapport de la commission des mines*, tome 3, p. 146.
36. AN, F12/12764, 21 fév 1909.
37. ANMT, 110 AQ38, sécurité dossier 1, pp. 19–20.
38. ADN, 106J-1, document 7.
39. In 1912 the profits and losses were exceptionally sent on the nineteenth of the month (Archives Nationales du Monde du Travail, 78 Boulevard du Général Leclerc, 59100 Roubaix, France (hereafter ANMT), 110AQ61, rapport 1912–13 fascicule 3).
40. H. Fayol, *General and Industrial Management*, trans. C. Storrs (1949), in D. A. Wren and T. Sasaki (eds), *Henri Fayol and Process School* (London: Pickering & Chatto Publishers, 2004), p. 535.
41. Fayol, *General and Industrial Management*, pp. 593, 594, 596.
42. Fayol, *General and Industrial Management*, p. 642, 635.
43. Fayol, *General and Industrial Management*, p. 537.
44. 'Bureau'.
45. Archives Nationales, 59 rue Guynemer, 90001, 93383 Pierrefitte-sur-Seine Cedex, France (hereafter AN), F/14/3879, visite Commentry du 18 juillet 1884.
46. ANMT, 59AQ111 to 165; 59AQ67 to 89; 59AQ95 to 108; 59AQ773 to 800.
47. ANMT, 59AQ784.
48. Archives Départmentales de la Nièvre, 1 bus rue Charles Roy, 58000 Nevers, France (hereafter ADN), N 106J-7, document 12.
49. ANMT, 59AQ14bis, p. 91.
50. ANMT, 110AQ102; 110AQ96, rapport annuel 1912–1913 (incorrectly entitled 1913–14), tables pp. 1–3.
51. ANMT, 110AQ96, rapport annuel 1912–13, tables, p. 9.
52. ANMT, 110AQ96, rapport annuel 1912–13, tables, p. 21ff., text pp. 2, 30.
53. ANMT, 110AQ96, rapport annuel des ventes 1912–13.
54. ANMT, 59AQ8 p. 194; 59AQ9, p. 145.
55. ANMT, 110AQ96.
56. ANMT, 110AQ1.
57. D. Reid, *The Miners of Decazeville: A Genealogy of Deindustrialization* (Cambridge, MA: Harvard University Press, 1985), p. 122.
58. Archives Départmentales de Haute Loire, 31 avenue de Tonbridge, 43000 Le Puy-en-Valay, France, S632, Rapport de la Ligue pour la défense des Droits de l'Homme et du Citoyen, 17 septembre 1905.
59. ADN, 106J-1; ADN, 106J-7; ANMT, 110 AQ 23, Dossier 2; 59AQ903; 110AQ9, Dossier 1; 110AQ21.
60. ANMT, 110AQ71; 110AQ102.

61. H. Fayol, *General and Industrial Management*, trans. C. Storrs (1949), in D. A. Wren and T. Sasaki (eds), *Henri Fayol and Process School* (London: Pickering & Chatto Publishers, 2004), p. 638.
62. Fayol, *General and Industrial Management*, p. 641.

7 The Commercial Function: Sales and Pricing

1. H. Fayol, *General and Industrial Management*, trans. C. Storrs (1949), in D. A. Wren and T. Sasaki (eds), *Henri Fayol and Process School* (London: Pickering & Chatto, 2004), p. 536.
2. Archives Nationales, 59 rue Guynemer, 90001, 93383 Pierrefitte-sur-Seine Cedex, France (hereafter AN), F14–4089; F14/8359.
3. Archives Nationales du Monde du Travail, 78 Boulevard du Général Leclerc, 59100 Roubaix, France (hereafter ANMT), 59AQ8, pp. 196, 198 and 211.
4. ANMT, 59AQ8, p. 287.
5. ANMT, 59AQ11, p. 15.
6. ANMT, 59AQ11, p. 9.
7. ANMT, 59AQ8, p. 286.
8. ANMT, 59AQ9, p. 125.
9. ANMT, 59AQ9, p. 125.
10. ANMT, 59AQ647, Rapport annuel Imphy 1895–6 p. 25.
11. A. Auclair, P. Couderc and J.-M. Molinès, *La sidérurgie en Bourbonnais: Cie Commentry Fourchambault Decazeville: l'usine des hauts fourneaux de Montluçon dite Usine Forey, 1840–1967* (The Bourbonnais Steel Industry: Commentry Fourchambault Decazeville Co.: The Montluçon Blast Furnace and Factory, Known as the Forey Factory, 1840–1967) (Montluçon: Cercle d'archéologie de Montluçon et de la région, 2009), p. 125.
12. ANMT, 59AQ9, p. 62.
13. ANMT, 59AQ9, p. 145.
14. H. Fayol, *The Third Part of Industrial and General Management* (1916), Henri Fayol collection, Centre d'Histoire de Sciences Politiques, 56 rue Jacob, 75006 Paris, France, §§218–26. See Appendix 1.
15. ANMT, 59AQ668, service central rapport 1890–1, p. 11; 110AQ96, rapport 1912–13 ventes.
16. AN, F7-12764.
17. Fayol, *The Third Part of Industrial and General Management*, §§227–31. See Appendix 1.
18. ANMT, 110AQ95, rapport annuel 1907–8 ventes.
19. ANMT, 59AQ8, pp. 47, 118 and 265; 59AQ9, p. 66.
20. ANMT, 59AQ9, pp. 102, 104 150, 224, 312 and 264.
21. ANMT, 59AQ9, p. 382; 59AQ10, p. 1, 150; 59AQ12, pp. 42 and 194; 59AQ13, p. 122.
22. *Statistiques de l'Industrie Minérale*, 1913, p. 20.
23. ANMT, 59AQ9, pp. 99 and 105.
24. ANMT, 59AQ8, p. 354.
25. ANMT, 59AQ10, p. 22.
26. ANMT, 59AQ11, pp. 236 and 374.
27. Archives Départmentales de la Nièvre. 1 bis rue Charles Roy, 58000 Nevers, France (hereafter ADN), 106J-6.
28. ANMT, 59AQ10, p. 2; 59AQ11, p. 236; 110AQ7; 59AQ13, p. 75.

29. ANMT, 59AQ8, p. 123; 59AQ9, p. 249; 59AQ10, pp. 2, 18.
30. ADN, 106J-15; ANMT, 110AQ7; ANMT, 59AQ909.
31. ANMT, 59AQ11, p. 113.
32. J. Dredge, *The Works of Messrs. Schneider and Co.* (London: Bedford Press, 1900); J. Dredge, *Les établissements de MM. Schneider et Cie, historique des mines & usines, leurs développements successifs* (The Establishments of Messrs Schneider and Co, History of the Mines and Factories, their Successive Development) (Nevers: impr. de Mazeron frères, 1903)
33. ANMT, 59AQ10, pp. 27 and 204; 59AQ11, pp. 45 and 187; 110AQ7.
34. ANMT, 59AQ668, rapport annuel au service des mines 1890–1.
35. ANMT, 59AQ9, p. 99; 59AQ820, p. 131.
36. AN, F/14/8282, Allier remarques sur le rapport annuel 1894.
37. Annuaire du Comité central des houillères de France, 1907, 1913.
38. ANMT, 110AQ96, exercice 1912–13, rapport sur les ventes.
39. ANMT, 59AQ8, p. 122; 59AQ 668, rapport annuel Montluçon 1889–90.
40. ANMT, 59AQ9, p. 316.
41. Archives Nationales du Monde du Travail, 78 Boulevard du Général Leclerc, 59100 Roubaix, France (hereafter ANMT), 59AQ8, pp. 109–11; 59AQ10, p. 234; H. Fayol, *The Third Part of Industrial and General Management*, Henri Fayol collection, Centre d'Histoire de Sciences Politiques, 56 rue Jacob, 75006 Paris, France (hereafter CHSP), HF 5bis DR3, §§232–45. See Appendix 1.
42. 'Thick third quality'.
43. Archives Nationales, 59 rue Guynemer, 90001, 93383 Pierrefitte-sur-Seine Cedex, France (hereafter AN), F14/8359, redevances Commentry 1889 et 1890; ANMT, 59AQ668, Rapport annuel Montluçon 1889–1890.
44. 'Dust and washed'.
45. AN, F14–4089, redevance 1884.
46. ANMT, 59AQ820, pp 78, 129–30 and 235.
47. ANMT 58AQ8, pp. 30 and 36.
48. ANMT, 59AQ668, Rapport annuel Montluçon, 1889–1890; 59AQ820, p. 204.
49. ANMT, 59AQ820, p. 288; 110AQ102, p. 7.
50. H. Fayol, *General and Industrial Management*, trans. C. Storrs (1949), in D. A. Wren and T. Sasaki (eds), *Henri Fayol and Process School* (London: Pickering & Chatto Publishers, 2004), p. 575.
51. J. Carlioz, *Comptoirs de vente en commun* (Trade Syndicates) (Nevers: Imprimerie Mazeron frères, 1905), p. 25.
52. Archives Nationales du Monde du Travail, 78 Boulevard du Général Leclerc, 59100 Roubaix, France (hereafter ANMT), 59AQ10, p. 157.
53. 'Economic cartels'.
54. L. Lévêque, 'Historique des forges de Decazeville, 1826–1914' (History of the Decazeville forges, 1826–1914), *Bulletin de la Société de l'industrie minérale*, 19 (1916), p. 58.
55. *Le comptoir de Longwy.*
56. *Le comptoir des produits sidérurgiques.*
57. G. Thuillier, *George Dufaud et les débuts du grand capitalisme dans la métallurgie, en Nivernais au XIXe siècle* (George Dufaud and the Beginnings of Big Business in the Steel Industry, in Nivernais in the Nineteenth Century) (Paris: SEVPEN, 1959), p. 110.
58. 'Le comptoir des poutrelles'.
59. J. Lambert-Dansette, *Genèse du patronat 1780–1880* (Genesis of Employer Groups

1780–1880) (Paris: Hachette, 1991), vol. 5, p. 35.
60. Anonyme, *La Poutrelle métallique dans ses principales applications* (The Steel Beam and its Main Uses) (Paris: Comptoir des Poutrelles, 1910).
61. ANMT, 59AQ10, p. 109.
62. ANMT, 59AQ9, p. 320.
63. ANMT, 59AQ605 (1), p. 58; 110AQ102, p. 5.
64. ANMT, 59AQ12, pp. 196 and 322.
65. ANMT, 110AQ96, rapport 1912–13 Forge Decazeville, p. 12.
66. 'Le comptoir de la machine'.
67. ANMT, 59AQ8, pp. 113 and 170.
68. ANMT, 59AQ8, pp. 196, 202 and 210.
69. ANMT, 59AQ668, service central rapport 1890–1, p. 20; 59AQ9, pp. 96, 97, 280 and 284.
70. ANMT, 59AQ668, service central rapport annuel 1890–1, pp. 20–8.
71. ANMT 59AQ9, pp. 96 and 194; 59AQ668; 59AQ11, p. 54; 59AQ821, pp. 112 and 251.
72. ANMT, 59AQ668, service central rapport 1890–1, p. 22; 59AQ9, pp. 28 and 311; 59AQ820, p. 96; 59AQ647, rapports Imphy 1894–5, p. 35; 1895–6, pp. 22 and 54; 1896–1897, p. 7; 1897–8, pp. 9 and 16.
73. ANMT, 59AQ11, p. 163.
74. Compagnie des Chemins de fer de Paris à Lyon et à la Méditerranée; J. Bouvier, 'L'histoire de l'usine de Allevard (1871–1914): un exemple significatif' (History of the Allevard Factory (1871–1914): A Major Example), *Annales. Économies, Sociétés, Civilisations*, 19:6 (1964), pp. 1236–41, on p. 1241.
75. ANMT, 59AQ647, Rapport Imphy 1896–7, pp. 2 and 3; Rapport Imphy 1904–5; 59AQ648, rapport annuel, p. 1.
76. ANMT, 59AQ9, p. 96; 110AQ58, Rapport mine Decazeville 1904–5, p. 3; 59AQ12, p. 218.
77. 'Le comptoir d'exportation des produits sidérurgiques'.
78. ANMT, 59AQ12, pp. 217, 218, 250, 260, 308, 314, 322 and 392; 59AQ13, pp. 68, 74 and 80: 110AQ95, rapport 1907–8, p. 17.
79. ANMT, 110AQ96, rapport 1912–13.
80. ANMT, 59AQ12, pp. 210–12; 110AQ96, rapport 1913–14 cahier statistique no. 2, p. 8.
81. ANMT, 59AQ9, pp. 134, 142, 144, 146, 151 and 200; 59AQ10, p. 38; 110AQ61, rapport 1912–13, fascicule 5, rapport 1912–13, fascicule 5.
82. ANMT 59AQ9, pp. 194, 239, 248 and 291.
83. ANMT, 59AQ10, pp. 38–9.
84. 'Office statistique'.
85. ANMT 59AQ11, pp. 72 and 77.
86. J.-P. Passaqui, *La stratégie des Schneider: du marché à la firme intégrée, 1836–1914* (The Strategy of the Schneiders: From Market to Integrated Firm) (Rennes: Presses universitaires de Rennes, 2006), pp. 258–9.
87. H. Fayol, *The Third Part of Industrial and General Management* (1916), Henri Fayol collection, Centre d'Histoire de Sciences Politiques, 56 rue Jacob, 75006 Paris, France, HF 5bis DR3, §§246–8. See Appendix 1.
88. C. E. Freedeman, 'Cartels and the Law in France before 1914', *French Historical Studies*, 15:3 (Spring, 1988), pp. 462–78.
89. *Statistiques de l'Industrie Minérale*, from 1888 to 1913.

90. J.-L. Peaucelle and C. Guthrie, 'The Private Life of Henri Fayol and his Motivation to Build a Management Science', *Journal of Management History*, 18:4 (2012), pp. 469–87.

8 The Technical Function

1. H. Fayol, *General and Industrial Management*, trans. C. Storrs (1949), in D. A. Wren and T. Sasaki (eds), *Henri Fayol and Process School* (London: Pickering & Chatto Publishers, 2004), p. 540.
2. Fayol, *General and Industrial Management*, p. 535.
3. H. Fayol, 'Études sur l'altération et la combustion spontanée de la houille exposée à l'air' (Study of the Alteration and the Spontaneous Combustion of Coal Exposed to Air), *Bulletin de la Société de l'Industrie Minérale*, Congrès de Paris, 1878, médaille d'or, série 2, tome 8 (1878), pp. 487–746.
4. H. Fayol, 'Note sur les mouvements de terrain provoqués par l'exploitation des mines' (Note on Terrain Movement Caused by Mining Operations), *Bulletin de la Société de l'Industrie Minérale*, série 2, tome 14 (1885), p. 805.
5. H. Fayol, 'Étude sur le terrain houiller de Commentry' (Study of the Commentry Coal Fields), *Comptes rendus des séances de l'Académie des Sciences* (16 May 1881); H. Fayol, 'Sur le terrain houiller de Commentry, Expériences faites pour expliquer la formation' (In the Commentry Coal Fields: Experiments Undertaken to Explain its Formation), *Comptes rendus des séances de l'Académie des Sciences* (30 May 1881); H. Fayol, 'Étude sur le terrain houiller de Commentry, sa formation attribuée à un charriage dans un lac profond' (Study of the Commentry Coal Field, its Formation due to Bedload in a Deep Lake), *Comptes rendus des séances de l'Académie des Sciences* (20 June 1881); H. Fayol, 'Résumé de la théorie des deltas et histoire de la formation du bassin de Commentry' (Resumé of the Theory of Deltas and the History of the Formation of the Commentry Basin), *Bulletin de la Société Géologique de France* (August 1888).
6. G. K. Gilbert, 'The Topographic Features of the Lake Shores', *US Geological Survey*, 5th *annual report 1883–1884* (Washington, 1885), pp. 75–123.
7. Archives Nationales du Monde du Travail, 78 Boulevard du Général Leclerc, 59100 Roubaix, France (hereafter ANMT), 58AQ8, p. 11.
8. ANMT, 110AQ821, rapport Mines de Decazeville 1900–1, p. 46.
9. ANMT, 59AQ10, p. 231.
10. ANMT, 59AQ13, pp. 13 and 83.
11. AMNT, 110AQ14, dossier 7.
12. ANMT, 59AQ102, p. 7.
13. ANMT, 59AQ9, pp. 40 and 77.
14. ANMT, 59AQ9, pp. 246, 247, 254 and 260.
15. ANMT, 59AQ647, Rapport Imphy 1895–6, p. 4.
16. ANMT, 59AQ9, p. 316; 59AQ10, pp. 40 and 292; 59AQ11, p. 380.
17. C.-E., Guillaume, 'Esquisse de ma vie' (Outline of My Life) (1921), (Le Marteau pilon, 1992) tome 4, pp 138–42, on p. 139.
18. ANMT, 59AQ10, p. 4.
19. ANMT, 59AQ10, p. 280; 59AQ11, pp. 88, 138 and 166.
20. L. H. Guillet, 'Notice biographique de Pierre Girin' (Biographical Note for Pierre Girin), *Revue de la métallurgie*, 11 (November, 1926), p. 685.
21. ANMT, 59AQ790, p. 35.

22. ANMT, 59AQ8, pp. 285, 294, 295, 302 and 307.
23. 'Engine Company'.
24. ANMT, 59AQ9, p. 41.
25. H. Fayol, *The Third Part of Industrial and General Management*, Henri Fayol collection, Centre d'Histoire de Sciences Politiques, 56 rue Jacob, 75006 Paris, France, §§33–9. See Appendix 1.
26. Archives Nationales, 59 rue Guynemer, 90001, 93383 Pierrefitte-sur-Seine Cedex, France (hereafter AN), F/14/3879, visite de Commentry, 12 octobre 1874.
27. Archives Nationales du Monde du Travail, 87 Boulevard du Général Leclerc, 59100 Roubaix, France (hereafter ANMT), 59AQ7, p. 44.
28. ANMT, 59AQ7, p. 44.
29. AN, F/14/3879.
30. AN, F/14/3879.
31. AN, F/14/3879.
32. AN, F/14/3879.
33. AN, F/14/3879.
34. AN, F/14/3879.
35. AN, F14–3879, rapport Allier 1878.
36. AN, F14–3879, rapport Allier 1883.
37. ANMT, 110AQ2, le 9 septembre 1892.
38. I. Abadie, 'Etude sur les feux des mines de houille, d'après les exemples tirés du bassin houiller de Decazeville' (Study of Coal Mine Fires, According to Examples Taken from the Decazeville Coal Basin), *Annales des mines* (July 1902) and *Génie civil* (4, 11, 18, 25 October 1902).
39. I. Abadie, 'Lutte contre les feux de mines, résultats obtenus aux mines de Decazeville' (Fighting Mine Fires, Results Obtained in the Decazeville Mines), *Revue de l'industrie Minérale*, 148 (1927), pp. 65–74 and *Revue de l'industrie Minérale*, 149 (1927), pp. 89–103.
40. ANMT, 59AQ12, p. 186; 59AQ13, p. 8.
41. ANMT, 59AQ8, pp. 349–50.
42. AN, F/14/8282, rapports annuels, 1892, 1893, 1894.
43. ANMT, 59AQ11, p. 210.
44. AN, F/14/3879, Commentry 19 juillet 1880; F/14/8282, visite Commentry 10 juillet 1891.
45. ANMT, 110AQ30, dossier 4; 59AQ12, pp. 184, 254 and 296.
46. ANMT, 59AQ11, pp. 280–1.
47. L. Fontvieille and A. Prigent, 'La technique et le travail dans les fluctuations de longue période: l'évolution des transports dans le fond des mines' (Technique and Work During Long Period Fluctuations: The Evolution of Transportation on the Mine Floor), *Technologies, idéologies, pratiques*, 9:2 (1990), pp. 169–83, p 179.
48. AMNT, 110AQ57, rapport 1903–4.
49. H. Fayol, 'Note sur la suppression du poste de nuit dans le remblayage des grandes couches' (Note on the Suppression of Night Work to Backfill Large Layers), *Comptes rendus mensuels de la Société de l'Industrie Minérale* (October 1882).
50. H. Fayol, 'Note sur le boisage, le déboisage et le remblayage dans les houillères de Commentry' (Note on Timbering, Drawing of Timbers and Backfill in the Commentry Collieries), *Comptes rendus mensuels de la Société de l'Industrie Minérale* (June 1878).
51. H. Fayol, 'Note sur le boisage aux houillères de Commentry (emploi du fer et des bois

préparés)' (Note on the Timbering of Commentry Collieries (Use of Iron and Prepared Timber)), *Bulletin de la Société de l'Industrie Minérale*, série 2, tome 3 (1874), pp. 569–76, p. 569.

52. AN, F14/8282, visite Montvicq 27 août 1887, visite Commentry 13 juin and 10 décembre 1889.
53. D.Reid, *The Miners of Decazeville: A Genealogy of Deindustrialization* (Cambridge, MA: Harvard University Press, 1985), p. 127.
54. ANMT, 110AQ48, salaires ouvriers de 1893 à 1899; 110AQ102, p. 67.
55. L. Reybaud, *Commentry & Fourchambault, Rapport sur la condition morale, intellectuelle et matérielle des ouvriers qui vivent de l'industrie du fer* (Commentry & Fourchambault, Report on the Moral, Intellectual and Material Situation of Workers Living From the Iron Industry) (Paris: Académie des sciences morales et politiques, 1868), p. 23.
56. AN, F/14/3879, visite à Commentry le 6 juillet 1882.
57. E. Mallard, 'Rapport sur l'étude des questions relatives à l'emploi des explosifs en présence du grisou' (Report on the Study of Questions Concerning the Use of Explosives in the Presence of Firedamp), *Annales des Mines*, eighth series, tome 14 (1888), pp. 197–283; E. Mallard, 'Rapport supplémentaire sur l'étude des questions relatives à l'emploi des explosifs en présence du grisou' (Additional Report on the Study of Questions Concerning the Use of Explosives in the Presence of Firedamp), *Annales des Mines*, eighth series, tome 14 (1888), pp. 319–76; E. Mallard, 'Commission d'étude de l'emploi des explosifs dans les mines à grisou; essais pratiques faits dans quelques exploitations de mines' (Study Commission into the Use of Explosives in Firedamp Mines; Practical Trials Undertaken at Several Mining Operations), *Annales des Mines*, eighth series, tome 16 (1889), pp. 15–123; H. Le Chatelier, *Le grisou* (Firedamp) (Paris: Gauthier-Villars, 1892); J. Haton de la Goupillière, 'Rapport de la commission d'études de l'emploi des explosifs dans les mines à grisou' (Report by the Investigating Commission into the Use of Explosives in Firedamp Mines), *Annales des mines*, 18 (1888), p 699.
58. AN, F14–8359; F14–8360.
59. AN, F/14/8282, Allier rapport 1890.
60. AN, F/14/8282, visite à Commentry 10 juillet 1891.
61. AN, F/14/8282, rapport Allier 1891.
62. ANMT, 110AQ61, rapport 1912–13, fascicule 3.
63. A. (de) Gennes, 'Déhouilleuses employées aux Etats-Unis' (Mining Machines in Use in the United States), *Bulletin de la Société de l'Industrie Minérale*, Congrès des mines et de la métallurgie 1900, third series, tome 15 (1901), pp. 332–44.
64. P. Fayol, 'Essais de havage mécanique en France' (Trials of Mechanical Cutters in France), *Bulletin de la société de l'industrie minérale*, Congrès des mines et de la métallurgie 1900, third series, tome 15 (1901), pp. 311–15.
65. Sullivan Machinery Company, *Modern Methods of Producing Coal*, 48 (1902), p. 26.
66. ANMT, 110AQ1, lettre de Courtindu 7 décembre 1900.
67. AN, F/14/8291, visite Lassalle Bourran 24 décembre 1900.
68. ANMT, 59AQ10, p. 331.
69. ANMT, 59AQ10, p. 362.
70. ANMT, 110 AQ 57, exercice 1901–2, dossier 1, p. 2, Combes, Bourran and Miramont pits.
71. ANMT, 59AQ11, p. 143.
72. ANMT, 110 AQ 57, exercice 1902–3, dossier 1, p. 2.
73. ANMT, 59AQ821, p. 176, commission des comptes 1902–3.

74. AN, F/14/8415, accident 16 mars 1903.
75. G. Dron, *Rapport de la commission des mines* (Report of the Mining Commission) (Paris: Imprimerie de la Chambre des députés, 1903), Chambre des députés, session de 1903, annexe au procès verbal de la séance du 2 avril 1903, no. 878, tome 4, p. 374.
76. ANMT, 59AQ12, p. 42.
77. Anonyme, 'Enquête sur les moyens techniques susceptibles d'augmenter la production des houillères françaises (commission de Decazeville)' (Study into the Technical Means to Increase the Production of French Collieries (Decazeville Commission)), *Comptes rendu mensuels de la Statistiques de l'Industrie Minérale*, 17:1 (January-February 1920), pp. 83–104, p. 98.
78. P. de Rousiers, 'Les mines et les huit heures', *La Revue de Paris*, 1 février 1902, (Paris: Chaix), pp. 6–7.
79. ANMT, 59AQ10, p. 6.
80. D. Reid, *The Miners of Decazeville: A Genealogy of Deindustrialization*, p. 151.
81. ANMT, 59AQ818, exercice 1908–9, p. 183; 59AQ13, p. 8; L. Lévêque, 'Historique des forges de Decazeville, 1826–1914' (History of the Decazeville Forges, 1826–1914), *Bulletin de la Société de l'industrie minérale*, 19 (1916), pp. 168, 176 and 179.
82. AN, F/14/8282, Montvicq 14 décembre 1889.
83. AN, F14/3879, visite à Commentry le 17 octobre 1871; F14/3879, Rapport annuel 1872, visite Commentry le 9 octobre 1873; F/14/3879, rapport annuel Allier 1877, 1879, 1884.
84. AN, F/14/8282, Allier rapport annuel 1886 et 1888.
85. AN, F/14/8282, Allier, rapport annuel annexe 1888; F/14/8282, visite Commentry10 juillet 1891; F/14/8282, Allier rapport annuel 1892 et 1894.
86. ANMT, 59AQ11, p. 242, 308 and 312.
87. AN, F/14/8282, Allier rapport annuel annexe 1888; ANMT, 59AQ820, exercice 1898–9 p. 237.
88. AN, F14/8359.
89. P. Lemonnier and F. Valton, *1854 rapport de stage* (1854 Internship Report), Bibliothèque Ecole des Mines de Paris cote, M1854/558 (Commentry, 15 novembre 1854), p. 384.
90. ANMT, 59AQ8, pp. 39–43.
91. AN, F/14/8282, Allier rapport annuel annexe 1888, visite à Montvicq 27 août 1887.
92. C. Buisson, 'Note sur la préparation des charbons' (Note on the Preparation of Coal), *Bulletin de la société de l'industrie minérale*, Congrès des mines et de la métallurgie 1900, third series, tome 15 (1901), p. 419.
93. AN, F14 8282, rapport Allier 1895.
94. AN, F14/8359.
95. ANMT, 59AQ9, pp. 359 and 360; 59AQ10 pp. 11, 15 and 101.
96. ANMT, 59AQ8, pp. 22, 38 and 118.
97. ANMT, 59AQ9, pp. 254, 264 and 316.
98. AN, F14 8282, rapport Allier 1895.
99. H. Tingaud, 'La vie quotidienne à Imphy entre 1884 et 1914' (Daily Life in Imphy between 1884 and 1914), La situation de la Nièvre en 1900. Cinquièmes rencontres d'histoire de la métallurgie (Guérigny: Les amis du vieux Guérigny, 2001), pp. 103–16, p. 115.
100. Archives Nationales du Monde du Travail, 78 Boulevard du Général Leclerc, 59100 Roubaix, France (hereafter ANMT), 110 AQ 341; 59AQ821, p. 190.

101. ANMT, 110AQ58, rapport 1904–1905; 110AQ60, rapport 1909–1910; 59AQ13, p. 76; 110 AQ 36.
102. ANMT, 59AQ12, pp. 181 and 382.
103. ANMT, 59AQ8, p. 372 and 273.
104. Tingaud, 'La vie quotidienne à Imphy entre 1884 et 1914', p. 115.
105. ANMT, 110AQ38, lettre du 19 septembre 1911; 110AQ244, 18 novembre 1914.
106. Archives Nationales, 59 rue Guynemer, 90001, 93383 Pierrefitte-sur-Seine Cedex, France, F/14/3879, Commentry 12 octobre 1874.

9 The Security Function

1. H. Fayol, *General and Industrial Management*, trans. C. Storrs (1949), in D. A. Wren and T. Sasaki (eds), *Henri Fayol and Process School* (London: Pickering & Chatto, 2004), p. 536.
2. Archives Nationales du Monde du Travail, 78 Boulevard du Général Leclerc, 59100 Roubaix, France (hereafter ANMT), 110AQ61, Rapport 1912–13 fascicule 1, 19 Police.
3. ANMT, 59AQ12, p. 91.
4. ANMT, 59AQ820, p. 62.
5. ANMT, 59AQ819, p. 30.
6. ANMT, 59AQ12, pp. 11, 73 and 82; 59AQ13, p. 15; Archives Départmentales de la Nièvre, 1 bis rue Charles Roy, 58000 Nevers, France, 106J-2.
7. ANMT, 110AQ49; 110AQ50.
8. *Statistiques de l'Industrie Minérale* 1912, pp. 138–9.
9. *Bulletin du ministère du travail et de la prévoyance sociale* 1914; no. 4, p. 262; no. 5, p. 340.
10. L. Lacombe, 'Rapport' (Report) (1896), *Documents parlementaires chambre 6e législature 1893–1898*, séance du 2 juillet 1896, annexe no. 1982, pp. 1280–307, on p. 1284.
11. Archives Nationales, 59 rue Guynemer, 90001, 93383 Pierrefitte-sur-Seine Cedex, France (hereafter AN), F/14/8282, Allier rapport 1895.
12. AN, F/14/8282, Allier rapport 1894.
13. AN, F/14/8282.
14. AN, F/14/8414.
15. ANMT, 110AQ71, fascicule 13 p. 11.
16. ANMT, 110AQ95, rapport 1907–8, contentieux, p. 10.
17. ANMT, 59AQ9, p. 105.
18. ANMT, 59AQ10, p. 157.
19. ANMT, 59AQ10, p. 232.
20. ANMT, 59AQ10, p. 321.
21. ANMT, 59AQ10, p. 326.
22. ANMT, 59AQ11, p. 140.
23. Archives Nationales du Monde du Travail, 78 Boulevard du Général Leclerc, 59100 Roubaix, France (hereafter ANMT), 59AQ10, p. 232.
24. ANMT, 110AQ95, rapport annuel 1907–8, contentieux, p. 16.
25. ANMT, 110AQ95, rapport annuel 1909–10, contentieux, p. 13.
26. ANMT, 110AQ95, rapport annuel 1907–8, contentieux, p. 16.
27. Archives Nationales du Monde du Travail, 78 Boulevard du Général Leclerc, 59100 Roubaix, France, 59AQ8, p. 352.

28. *La voix des travailleurs* du 2 mars 1893, p. 3.
29. *La voix des travailleurs* du 15 juin 1893, p. 3.
30. Archives Nationales du Monde du Travail, 78 Boulevard du Général Leclerc, 59100 Roubaix, France (hereafter ANMT), 110 AQ 38, dossier 1.
31. Henri Fayol collection, Centre d'Histoire de Sciences Politiques, 56 rue Jacob, 75006 Paris, France, HF4DR2.
32. Archives Nationales, 59 rue Guynemer, 90001, 93383 Pierrefitte-sur-Seine Cedex, France (hereafter AN), F/14/3866, visite à Commentry le 10 juillet 1861.
33. AN, F/14/8282, rapport Allier 1891.
34. ANMT, 110AQ38, dossier 2.
35. ANMT, 110AQ38, dossier 3.
36. ANMT, 110AQ38, dossier 2.
37. ANMT, 59AQ13, p. 56.
38. Grand, 'Bobine folle, parachute, roue de wagonnet, appareils dus à Paul Fayol' (Loose Reel, Parachute, Cart Wheel, Devices Attributable to Paul Fayol), *Bulletin de la Société de l'Industrie Minérale* (1879), pp 927–36.
39. Archives Nationales, 59 rue Guynemer, 90001, 93383 Pierrefitte-sur-Seine Cedex, France (hereafter AN), F/14/3879, visite à Commentry le 18 juillet 1884.
40. Archives Nationales du Monde du Travail, 78 Boulevard du Général Leclerc, 59100 Roubaix, France (hereafter ANMT), 110AQ58, rapport annuel 1905–6 fascicule 1, 13 accidents.
41. AN, F/14/3879, rapport annuel Allier 1885.
42. Douai School for Master Miners.
43. AN, F14–8415, 21 mars 1903.
44. AN, F/14/3879, visite Montvicq du 20 octobre 1885; G. Friedel, 'Note sur les les systèmes de fermeture des recettes en usage dans la région de Commentry' (Note on the Systems of Receiving Gates in Use in the Commentry Area), *Annales des Mines*, 3 (1893), pp. 199–202.
45. AN, F/14/3879, Allier rapport de l'ingénieur en chef 1874.
46. H. de Place, 'Rapport sur les appareils respiratoires de H Fayol' (Report on H Fayol's Breathing Apparatus), *Bulletin de l'Industrie Minérale* (1873), pp. 34–5, p. 148.
47. AN, F/14/3879, visite à Montvicq le 9 août 1881.
48. ANMT, 110AQ38, dossier 2, article 167 and onwards.
49. ANMT, 59AQ9, p. 98.
50. AN, F/14/8282, visite à Commentry le 22 mars 1894.
51. AN, F/14/8282, visite à Montvicq le 15 décembre 1894.
52. AN, F/14/8282, visite de Commentry le 16 mars 1900, 110AQ38, dossier 2, règlement pour les ouvriers à Commentry, articles 31–46.
53. ANMT, 59AQ10, p. 326.
54. ANMT, 110AQ38, dossier 2, articles 171–82.
55. M.-F. Conus and J.-L. Escudier, 'Sécurité et transformation du système productif, application à l'industrie française du charbon (1817–1988)' (Security and Transformation of the Production System, Application to the French Coal Industry (1817–1988)), *Enterprise et Histoire*, 17 (1997), pp. 43–4.
56. E. Mâle, *Souvenirs et correspondences de jeunesse* (Memories and Correspondence from Youth) (Nonette: Créer, 2001), p. 60; Saint Simon's followers generally supported industrial action. The Doyet mine was 10 kilometres from Commentry.
57. H. Fayol, *General and Industrial Management*, trans. C. Storrs (1949), in D. A. Wren

and T. Sasaki (eds), *Henri Fayol and Process School* (London: Pickering & Chatto Publishers, 2004), p. 540.

58. Archives Nationales du Monde du Travail, 78 Boulevard du Général Leclerc, 59100 Roubaix, France (hereafter ANMT), 110AQ43, 1893 note de la direction de Decazeville.
59. L. Lacombe, 'Rapport' (Report) (1896), *Documents parlementaires chambre 6e législature 1893–1898*, séance du 2 juillet 1896 annexe no. 1982, p. 1306.
60. ANMT, 59AQ13, pp. 12 and 74.
61. Archives Nationales, 59 rue Guynemer, 90001, 93383 Pierrefitte-sur-Seine Cedex, France, F/14/8282, visite à Commentry les 20 août et 4 novembre 1887.
62. See R. I. Mehr and B. A. Hedges, *Risk Management In The Business Enterprise* (Homewood, IL: Richard Irwin, 1963) and A. Williams and M. H. Heins, *Risk Management and Insurance* (New York, NY: McGraw Hill, 1964).

10 Conclusion

1. Archives Nationales du Monde du Travail, 78 Boulevard du Général Leclerc, 59100 Roubaix, France, 59AQ8, pp. 311–12.
2. H. Fayol, *General and Industrial Management*, trans. C. Storrs (1949) in D. A. Wren and T. Sasaki (eds), *Henri Fayol and Process School* (London: Pickering & Chatto Publishers, 2004), pp. 434 and 535.
3. 'Fonction administrative': the French word 'administration' is used by Fayol to mean 'management'.
4. 'Elements d'administration'.
5. Fayol, *General and Industrial Management*, p. 577.
6. J-L. Peaucelle, J.A. Ariza Montès, B. Beaudoin, T. Boyns, A.C. Morales Gutierrez, J-N. Retière, T. Sasaki and I Smith, *Henri Fayol, inventeur des outils de gestion* (Henri Fayol, Inventor of Management Tools) (Paris: Économica, 2003).
7. D. A. Wren, A. G. Bedeian and J. D. Breeze, 'The Foundations of Henri Fayol's Administrative Theory', *Management Decision*, 40:9 (2002), pp. 906–18.
8. Fayol, *General and Industrial Management*, p. 540.
9. F. W. Taylor, *The Principles of Scientific Management* (New York and London: Harper & Brothers, 1911).
10. Fayol, *General and Industrial Management*, p. 600.
11. Peaucelle, Ariza Montès, Beaudoin, Boyns, Morales Gutierrez, Retière, Sasaki and Smith, *Henri Fayol, inventeur des outils de gestion*, p. 41.
12. J.-M. Vaslin, 'Henri Fayol, théoricien du management' (Henri Fayol, Management Theoretician), *Le Monde* (27 January 2004), p v.
13. L. H. Gulick, 'Notes on the Theory of Organization' in L. Gulick and L. Urwick (eds), *Papers on the Science of Administration* (New York, NY: Institute of Public Administration, 1936), pp. 3–35.
14. Fayol, *General and Industrial Management*, p. 641.
15. Fayol, *General and Industrial Management*, p. 631.
16. Fayol, *General and Industrial Management*, p. 587.
17. Fayol does not refer to Adam Smith's theory on productivity gains through the division of labour.
18. Fayol, *General and Industrial Management*, p. 577.

Appendix 1: The Third Part of *Industrial and General Management*

1. Translator's note: This text is archived at the Centre d'Histoire de Sciences Politiques (56 rue Jacob, 75006 Paris, France) in the Henri Fayol collection under the reference number HF 5bis DR3. It consists of 106 pages of typed double-spaced text on mauve-colored paper. The text is dated 1916. Some words are underlined and italicized. Henri Fayol corrected the text by hand using a pencil. These corrections are reproduced here. In the original document, missing text is replaced by ellipses or by half-blank pages that are not reproduced here.
2. Translator's note: These notes were written daily from the 1860s onwards, and they were re-read and corrected in 1916.
3. I recounted the story of the Commentry mine fires in the *Bulletin de la Société de l'Industrie Minérale* under the title 'Études sur l'altération et la combustion spontanée de la houille exposée à l'air', in 1878. This work was awarded the gold medal of the *Société de l'Industrie Minérale.* Here is the review made in 1909 by Richard Threlfall in the *Journal of the Society of Chemical Industry* of 31 July 1909: 'The literature on the subject of the *spontaneous combustion of coal* is very voluminous ... an index to that specifically concerning combustion on ships appears as an appendix to the report of the N.S.W. Royal Commission (1896). What I have to say on the subject has already been more or less published in the reports of two Royal Commissions which sat at Sydney (N.S.W.) from 1896 to 1900, both of which I was connected and in a Board of Trade (Marine department) Paper No. 110 in the matter of the damage by fire sustained by the ship "Walter H. Wilson." the technical part of which was written by me. The first important work on this subject is attributable to Director E. Richters, a chemist in the Mining School of Waldenberg. It was published in *Dingler's Polytechnisches Journal* of December 19, 1868' 'The second classic work on the subject of the spontaneous combustion of coal is entitled "Etudes sur l'altération et la combustion spontanée de la houille exposée a l'air," by Henri Fayol, engineer, Directeur des Houilleres de Commentry et de Montvicq. This was published in the *Bulletin de la Société de l'Industrie Minérale* (2nd series, vol. 8, 3rd part, 1879). It forms a volume of 260 pages, and *is certainly the finest example of a technical investigation I have ever seen or I have ever heard of. This work should be read by every student in order that he may learn how worthy technical research can be when it is undertaken in a critical and scientific spirit*'. What follows are five or six pages of textual citations from my studies on the alteration and the spontaneous combustion of coal. I wish for *management studies* to receive similar compliments thirty years after their publication. Translator's note: Richard Threlfall was an English chemist and engineer, elected fellow to the Royal Society in 1899. He worked at the University of Sydney, Australia from 1886 to 1899, during which time he chaired the Royal Commission on the Spontaneous Heating of Coal Cargoes. Henri Fayol had no doubt heard of Threlfall in this capacity. In 1899 Fayol sent Threlfall his 1879 publication and cites at length Threllfall's summary of his work (from R. Threlfall, 'The Spontaneous Heating of Coal, Particularly During Shipment', *Journal of the Society of Chemical Industry*, 28:14 (1909), pp. 759–73) in his candidacy to the *Académie des Sciences* (H. Fayol, *Notice sur les travaux scientifiques et techniques de Henri Fayol* (Notice on the Scientific and Technical Works of Henri Fayol) (Paris: Gauthier Villars, 1918), pp. 21–33). The latter part of Threlfall's career was spent in consulting where he applied his scientific knowledge to solving industrial problems (source: H.W.B, 'Sir Richard Threlfall. 1861–1932'. Obituary Notices of Fellows of the Royal Society, (1932), vol. 1, no. 1, pp. 45–53).

4. It was the starting point for the 'Study of the Commentry coal field' undertaken conjointly by Messrs. Henri Fayol, Charles Brongniart, René Zeiller, Bernard Renault ... Sauvage ... *Bulletin de la Société de l'Industrie Minérale*, 1886 – 'Lithology and stratigraphy' par Mr. H. Fayol, Institute award).
5. Translator's note: For the following twenty-five pages Henri Fayol describes the industrial history of each establishment. He provides charts for the production of coal and steel products. These pages are not reproduced here. He finishes his text by listing the names of all managing directors since the founding of the company and provides a copy of the official decision in 1884 to name his predecessor as the unique managing director.

Appendix 2: Henri Fayol's Final Interview

1. Translator's note: The journal *Chronique sociale de France* was created to promote Catholic social thought and contribute to social debate. The text cites sixteen publications written by Fayol and his followers. Only the following nine texts have been found: V. Carlhian, 'l'administration expérimentale' (Experimental Management), *La Chronique sociale de France,* (1924), pp. 277–92 and 330–8; J. Carlioz, *Le gouvernement des entreprises commerciales et industrielles. Leçons professées à l'école des Hautes Études Commerciales* (The Governance of Commercial and Industrial Concerns. Lessons Taught at the School of Hautes Études Commerciales) (Paris: Dunod, 1921); P. Doncoeur, *Une école des chefs, le fayolisme* (A School for Leaders, Fayolism) (Paris: Action populaire, 1921); H. Fayol, 'Conférence sur L'Administration industrielle et générale' (Conference on Industrial and General Management), *École supérieure de guerre et Centre des Hautes Études Militaires*, 5 and 14 May 1923 (1923); R. Mazerat, 'La doctrine administrative – L'administration expérimentale – le Fayolisme' (The Management Doctrine – Experimental Management – Fayolism), *Communications faites à l'académie de Marine*, 9 February 1923 and 8 February 1924 (1924); J.-P. Palewski, *Le Rôle du Chef d'Entreprise dans la Grande Industrie* (The Role of Business Leaders in Heavy Industry) (Paris: Presses universitaires de France, 1924); L. Pouydraguin, *La Fonction administrative dans le domaine militaire* (The Management Function in the Military Domain) (Paris: Dunod, 1921); A. Schatz, *L'Entreprise gouvernementale et son administration* (The Government Enterprise and its Management) (Paris: Grasset, 1922); J. Wilbois and P. Vanuxem, *Essai sur la conduite des affaires et la Direction des hommes* (Essay on the Running of Business and the Management of Men) (Paris: Payot, 1920). We have removed all references to these and replaced them by a bracketed ellipse [...] to improve the clarity of the translation. This text is Henri Fayol's last publication. It was published in the form of an interview with Louis Marie du Crouzet. This name is a pseudonym of Louis Marie de Mijolla (Source: E. Pezet, *Chrétiens au service de la cité, de Léon XIII au Sillon et au M.R.P., 1891–1965* (Christians in the Service of the City, from Leo XIII to Sillon and M.R.P., 1891–1965) (Paris: Nouvelles Editions Latines, 1965)). Louis de Mijolla (1891–1974), first in his class at the Ecole des Mines de Saint Etienne in 1913, enrolled to fight on the front in 1914, and later joined the French air force in 1916. He wounded his leg on 4 August 1916. In 1917 he was recruited by Henri Fayol and became director of the Imphy plant in 1933. He was named managing director of the Commentry-Fourchambault and Decazeville Company on 1 September 1942 and remained at the head of the company for sixteen years (Source: M. de Longevialle, *La Société Commentry-Fourchambault et Decazeville, 1854–1954, Introduction du baron Pierre Hély d'Oissel, conclusions de Louis de Mijolla* (The Commentry-Fourchambault

et Decazeville Company, 1854–1954, Introduction by Baron Pierre Hély d'Oissel, Conclusions by Louis de Mijolla) (Paris: Office de propagande générale, 1954)). In 1910 Louis de Mijolla belonged to Marc Sangnier's 'Sillon', a leftist Catholic group. De Mijolla stressed on his managers the importance of contacts with the personnel and their representatives. In August 1943, he toured Germany to provide moral support to his 300 workers that had been made prisoners-of-war or sent as part of the Compulsory Work Service (STO). He called them 'deported workers' and was fined 20,000F by a German tribunal. He was the first employer to establish a works council as required by an ordinance of 22 February 1945. He maintained excellent contacts with worker unions. In 1945, he founded a group of Christian business leaders (Association des Cadres et Dirigeants de l'Industrie pour le progrès social et économique, ACADI). He was friends with Paul Ramadier, an atheist and socialist who was mayor of Decazeville from 1919 to 1960. When he retired in 1958 he brought together all of the company's unionists that he had worked with to bid them farewell. While Louis de Mijolla's actions are those of a left-leaning Catholic, they are also that of a Fayolist that legitimizes unions as the representatives of the the workers (Source: Mijolla collection, Institut Marc Sangnier, 38 boulevard Raspail 75007 Paris). Was Fayolism implacably anti-union? The answer is mostly 'no'. While Henri Fayol did actively fight the unions, his stance was not at all an original one. All employers at the time did the same, and even today many still behave in the same way. Henri Fayol was also fundamentally legalistic, strictly applying and respecting the laws on safety representatives, relief funds, retirement and working hours.

2. Translator's note: References to works authored by Fayol's disciples have been omitted and replaced by [...].
3. Translator's note: Louis Deschamps, (1878–1925) French minister for postal administration from 28 November 1919 to 16 January 1921.
4. Translator's note: The League of Nations was founded in 1919 with the same aims as the UN.
5. Translator's note: Gustave Ador (1845–1928) was a Swiss politician who arranged for the implantation of the League of Nations in Geneva.
6. Translator's note: The International Labour Organization (ILO) was founded in 1919.

INDEX

For Product Safety Concerns and Information please contact our EU representative GPSR@taylorandfrancis.com Taylor & Francis Verlag GmbH, Kaufingerstraße 24, 80331 München, Germany